An American Half-century

An American Half-century

Postwar Culture and Politics in the USA

Edited by *Michael Klein*

Pluto  Press

LONDON & BOULDER, COLORADO

First published 1994 by Pluto Press
345 Archway Road, London N6 5AA
and Westview Press
5500 Central Avenue, Boulder
Colorado 80301, USA

Copyright © individual authors, 1994

British Library Cataloguing in Publication Data
A catalogue record for this book is available from the British Library

ISBN 0 7453 0500 8 hbk

Library of Congress Cataloging in Publication Data
An American half-century : postwar culture and politics in the USA /
edited by Michael Klein.
290 p. 23 cm.
Includes bibliographical references and index.
ISBN 0-7453-0500-8 (hbk).
1. United States – Civilization – 1945– 2. United States – Politics
and government – 1945–1989. I. Klein, Michael, 1939–92.
E169.12.054 1992
973.92–dc20 92-8801
CIP

Designed, typeset and produced for Pluto Press
by Chase Production Services, Chipping Norton, OX7 5QR

Contents

Contributors

Introduction: The Roads Not Taken   1
  Michael Klein

1. The Cold War and the Culture of Resistance   10
   Norman Markowitz

2. So that the Dead may not be Killed Again:
   Mailer, Doctorow and the Poetics of a Persecuting Society   30
   Richard Godden

3. 1968: The Two Cultures   59
   Todd Gitlin

4. The World Turned Upside Down:
   The Alternative Press and Visionary Politics in the US
   in the 1960s   69
   Jackie DiSalvo

5. The Meaning of the 1960s   82
   Abbie Hoffman

6. Students, Capital and the Multiversity:
   Radical Challenges to the Dominant Pattern of American Higher
   Education from Berkeley to Livingston   86
   Michael Klein

7. 'The Deep Immortal Wish': Radicalism and Modern
   American Poetry   117
   Jeffrey Walsh

8. Side Saddle on the Golden Calf: Moments of Utopia in
   American Pop Music and Pop Music Culture   141
   John Storey

9. What Feminism has said about Motherhood   157
   Ann Snitow

10. Black Women: Constructing the Revolutionary Subject   172
    bell hooks

11. Malcolm X and the Crisis in Black America   192
    Manning Marable

12. Beyond the American Dream: Film and the
    Experience of Defeat   206
    Michael Klein

13. The Making of a Consensual Majority:
    Political Discourse and Electoral Politics in the 1980s   232
    Michael X. Delli Carpini

14. US Television and the Gulf Conflict   274
    Gene Michaud

15. The 1990s and Beyond: After the Gulf   285
    Noam Chomsky interviewed by Michael Klein

Index   291

Contributors

Michael Klein (1939–1992) Publications include: *The Apocalyptic Discourse* and *The Vietnam Era*.

Jeffrey Walsh teaches at Manchester Metropolitan University. Publications include *Tell Me Lies about Vietnam*.

Norman Markowitz teaches at Rutgers University. He is author of *The Rise and Fall of the People's Century*.

Richard Godden teaches at the University of Keele, UK. He is the author of *Fiction and Capital*.

Jackie diSalvo teaches at the City University of New York (CUNY) and is the author of *War of Titans*.

Abbie Hoffman, author, activist, played a prominent part in the protest movements of the 1960s and 1970s in the United States.

Todd Gitlin is professor of sociology and director of the mass communications programme at the University of California at Berkeley. His books are *The Whole World is Watching*, *Inside Prime Time*, and *The Sixties: Years of Hope, Days of Rage*.

John Storey is lecturer in Cultural Studies at Sunderland Polytechnic, UK. He has published work on cultural theory and popular culture.

Ann Snitow teaches at the New School in New York. She is editor of *The Politics of Sexuality*.

bell hooks teaches at Oberlin College. She is author of *Ain't I a Woman*.

Manning Marable is Professor of Political Science and History, at the Center for Studies of Ethnicity and Race in America, University of Colorado, Boulder.

Michael Delli Carpini teaches at Barnard College, Columbia University. He is author of *Stability and Change in American Politics*.

Gene Michaud teaches at the William Joiner Center for the Study of

War and Social Consequences, University of Massachusetts, Boston. He is co-editor of *From Hanoi to Hollywood*.

Noam Chomsky is Professor of Linguistics at the Massachusetts Institute of Technology, and author of numerous books including *The Fateful Triangle* (1983), *Turning the Tide* (1985), *The Culture of Terrorism* (1988) and *Necessary Illusions* (1989), all published by Pluto Press in the UK.

This book is dedicated to my step-mother, Marguerite Perrin-Klein, and to my wife, Gillian Parker-Klein, in love and gratitude.
The lif so short, the craft so long to lerne ...
     Michael Klein 1939–92

The people are on the march all over the world and ... we can, if we are sympathetic, channel these revolutionary forces for the constructive welfare of the whole world ... Some have spoken of the 'American Century'. I say that the century on which we are entering – the century which will come out of this war – can and must be the century of the common man.

Henry Wallace

And the multi-story mausoleums of Wall Street
blocked out the spires of the New Jerusalem
across Hart Crane's bridge to the Future
    and Whitman's ferry to Eternity
for at least another millennium.
So why bother even making the motions?
I sat with an old comrade whose father had just died
in the village apartment where we had erstwhile
    plotted the revolution
speaking of paradises lost and the experience of defeat.
here & there friends began quietly gathering in small groups ...

Jackie DiSalvo, 'Passing Over, Easter' 1991 (poem)

There is neither a first nor a last word and there are no limits to the dialogic context (it extends into the boundless past and the boundless future). Even *past* meanings, that is those born in the dialogue of past centuries, can never be stable (finalized, ended once and for all) – they will always change (be renewed) in the process of subsequent, future development ... At any moment there are immense, boundless masses of forgotten ... meanings, but at certain moments ... they are recalled and invigorated in renewed form (in a new context). Nothing is absolutely dead: Every meaning will have it's homecoming festival ...

Mikhail Bakhtin

Introduction: The Roads Not Taken

Michael Klein

All books have their intended audiences. This collection of essays is aimed at students of modern American culture and society in humanities, cultural studies, media and film, literature, history, African-American and women's studies, and sociology of education courses. The contributions are written from a variety of disciplinary perspectives as the world that we seek to understand better cannot be fully comprehended by a single academic mode of discourse. Contributors include Manning Marable, bell hooks, Ann Snitow and Noam Chomsky in the US, and Richard Godden and Jeffrey Walsh in England.

In a larger sense this book is intended for students and scholars of all ages and occupations who are interested in tracing the course of radical dissent and oppositional cultural production in the US in modern times, and setting it in context of the history of the period. Most of the essays are concerned with assessing the ways that radicalism in the US has intersected with the dominant culture, evaluating moments when it has flourished as well as periods of repression and defeat.

It offers challenging perspectives for a new generation of students and scholars who may not be able to understand fully (or shape) the world they live in unless they have a sense of the problems, achievements and structures of feeling and thought of the immediate past. Thus although the latter chapters are concerned with the 1980s and the 1990s it is a work of re-collection as well as of analysis, aiming at recovery of historical memory as well as its interpretation. In this respect it is a companion volume to *The Vietnam Era: Media and Popular Culture*[1] which focused upon a period of ferment, of exploration of alternatives, and of opposition to war, to spiritual and economic poverty, and to institutionalized racism. *The Vietnam Era* was concerned with media and popular culture in the US and in Vietnam in the 1960s. This collection of essays has a wider brief: radical and establishment culture and society in the period from US entry into the Second World War to the present. Many of the essays are concerned with media, literature, film and other aspects of culture. Let me briefly sketch the larger context.

In February 1941, as the US entered the Second World War, Henry Luce proclaimed the birth of 'the American Century'.[2] An historian has commented that 'Luce propagated a program for a postwar peace based consciously on opposition to any social change inconsistent with American free enterprise, and on the expansion of the American enterprise system throughout the world.'[3] There was also a certain cultural component to Luce's manifesto as he was publisher of *Life* and *Time* magazines. In a sense Luce's dream of an American Century was an updated mixture of Adam Smith, the White Man's Burden, Manifest Destiny and Rudyard Kipling. It was subsequently given coherent political, economic, ideological and military form by the Truman doctrine, was appropriated by Johnson in Vietnam, and further realized by Reagan and by the post-containment foreign policy of George Bush. Half a century has passed since Luce set out his vision of *pax Americana*. Times have changed. Or have they?

> In the modern world ... has any country ever enjoyed the kind of pre-eminent power which the United States has now? ... Neither Louis XVI's France nor Philip II's Spain stood so high above their rivals, as America now stands above the rest of the world.[4]

If there is irony in the above quote from an editorial in a May 1991 issue of the *Independent* it is unintentional: in unleashing an awesome and genocidal display of military power in the Gulf War; in dispatching diplomatic emissaries to broker political settlements in Ethiopia and other areas in the Third World; and in writing plans for transition from socialism to capitalist market economies in the former Soviet Union and Eastern Europe, the US stands above the rest of the world as the first half of Luce's American Century draws to a close. However, as Paul Kennedy has pointed out in *The Rise and Fall of the Great Powers*,[5] the military and imperial power of *ancien régimes* may mask their economic and ultimate political decline. The American economy is at present plagued by de-industrialization, by rising foreign debt and by the penetration of foreign powers; there has also been a decline in the general quality of social life as well as in the purchasable standard of living of the individual wage earner. Export of capital and internationalization of the economy, which are conditions of empire, are also major causes and symptoms of its decline.

Pre-eminent power? This was initially achieved at Hiroshima in 1945, where the US flaunted its monopoly of nuclear power and capacity to rain destruction upon its enemies, after which hopes for the continuation and further development of the US–Soviet alliance that was established during the Second World War (and which US

Vice-President Henry Wallace viewed as the basis for the ushering in of 'a century of the common man', in conscious contrast to Henry Luce's vision of the American Century) were dashed.[6] After the end of the Second World War and the destruction of the broad democratic political and cultural alliance against fascism the Cold War began outside the US and was soon followed by domestic repression (the House Un-American Activities Committee, McCarthyism, etc.) at home.

However in the 1960s and early 1970s US monopoly of global power was dramatically limited: by a series of national liberation struggles abroad, especially in Vietnam, Cuba and Chile; by Soviet nuclear capacity; by the economic and technological achievements of socialist and certain non-aligned nations; by radical dissent and protest at home on issues that ranged from struggles for civil rights and equality for Afro-Americans and other minorities to opposition to the war in Vietnam; by protest in Europe against the continuation of the US war in Vietnam; by ideas and images generated by these oppositional movements in France, Portugal, Ireland and England, as well as by Cuba, and in China during the cultural revolution. It was also a period marked by the emergence of new ideas about freedom, about happiness, about what life should be, about work and about gender, which were expressed at all levels of the culture.

In a sense it has been a process of one step forward and two steps back. On one level the 'new world order' of the late 1980s and 1990s stands in dramatic contrast to the world of the Vietnam era. This is demonstrated by the awesome display of Old Testament genocidal retribution seen in the Gulf War; and the development of US authored plans for deconstructing the economies of Eastern Europe and remnants of socialism in the Soviet Union, and replacing them with market economies that guarantee an open door to foreign capital and investment.[7] While some critics have contended that we have arrived at 'an end to history', and live in a 'postmodern' world where the 'old grand narratives' no longer apply, it may be that the impersonal and disordered dynamics and power relations of imperialism continue to structure our experience of life. Indeed the past half-century may be best understood as an age of late capitalism and imperialism:

> Imperialism is capitalism at that stage of development in which the dominance of monopolies and finance capital has established itself; in which the export of capital has acquired pronounced importance; in which the division of the world among the international trusts has begun; in which the division of all the territories of the globe among the biggest capitalist powers has been completed ...

> The fact that the world is already divided obliges those contemplating a redivision to reach out for every kind of territory ... The rivalry ... in the striving for hegemony ... (is often) not so much directly for themselves as to weaken the adversary and undermine his hegemony ...
>
> Far from representing a post industrial society, late capitalism ... constitutes generalized universal industrialization for the first time in history. Mechanization, standardization, overspecialization and parcellization of labour, which in the past determined only the realm of commodity production in actual industry, now penetrate into all sectors of social and cultural life. It is characteristic of late capitalism that agriculture is step by step becoming just as industrialized as industry, the sphere of circulation (credit cards and the like) just as much as the sphere of production, and recreation just as much as the organization of work.[8]

Media, culture and art (realms of experience and ideology) may be a window on history as history may be a window on culture. Writing the conclusion of the *U.S.A.* trilogy John Dos Passos argued that America was divided into 'two nations', and that this was not only an economic and political division but also represented a set of cultural contradictions.[9] This conflict remains. The divisions were heightened in the 1960s, not only as a response to the Vietnam War and the civil rights movement, but also as the process of mechanization of the superstructure resulted in heightened penetration of education by the imperatives of capital (for example at the University of California, Berkeley), as the dominant culture was perceived as increasingly commodified, fragmented and 'unreal', and as work was perceived as requiring an irrational and life-denying amount of 'surplus repression'.

By the 1990s the power relations were somewhat reversed. Within the US exploitation had intensified: people were working 30 per cent more in an effort to maintain a 1960s standard of living. Abroad there was intensified economic, military and cultural penetration of areas not fully colonized. For example, in 1991 the US government launched a major military intervention in the Middle East in which perhaps 150,000 Iraqis died, primarily as a result of aerial bombardment of Hiroshima or Vietnam-like ferocity. During the Gulf War the Harvard University Chapel republished a book entitled *Prayers for Private Devotions in War-Time*, and incorporated the text in its regular prayer services. The book had been used by congregations during the Second World War and the Korean War, but had fallen into disuse and went out of print in the Vietnam era, in response to changes that had taken place in popular culture, ideology and belief. I quote several extracts from the 1991 edition:

> Most High God, who ridest upon the wings of the wind and makest the clouds thy chariots: We commit to thine especial care the airmen of our flying force. Give them a clear eye and a cool mind ...
>
> Almighty God, we make our earnest prayer that thou will keep the United States in thy holy protection; that thou wilt incline the hearts of the citizens to cultivate a spirit of subordination and obedience to government ...[10]

The first extract is an affirmation of Manifest Destiny; it cloaks genocide with divine sanction. The second extract implies that radical opposition to government policies (the spectre of the 1960s) is simultaneously unGodly and un-American; it counsels loyalty, obedience and subordination to the status quo. It is a blast from the early 1950s. It may have expressed the perspective of a large number of Americans once the war in the Gulf was in high gear. However there were also counter statements. In the same period many churches voiced their opposition to the war. Protests took place to chants of: 'We can stop the war/We've done it before/We can do it again', which consciously echoed and thus reaffirmed the vision of the anti-Vietnam War protest movement of the 1960s. It is also of interest that films produced and distributed in this period included: *Dances with Wolves* (a western not just sympathetic to Native Americans but which features scenes in which they are rendered as subjects, not objects, and speak in their own language); *Guilty by Suspicion* (an indictment of the blacklist in Hollywood during the period of the early Cold War and of the House Committee on Un-American Activities); *The Long Walk Home* (a dramatization of the civil rights movement in Alabama in the 1960s); documentary films about the student and anti-war movements in Berkeley in the early 1960s, and civil rights and black liberation movements in the 1960s and 1970s. While in certain respects these films may be problematic, they are a further illustration that even in bad times radical dissent has survived, that oppositional cultural production, however marginalized, has attempted to challenge the ideology of the power elite or has intervened to establish a dialogue with the dominant forces in society in the heartland of America.

There is another example of the (temporary?) survival of ideological alternatives in the midst of an experience of defeat. The first issues of the Marxist journal *Monthly Review* appeared in 1949, during the onset of the Cold War. They contained articles by the eminent literary critic F.O. Matthiessen, by Henry Wallace, the former vice-president of the United States, and by Albert Einstein, the most prestigious scientist of the twentieth century. Einstein commented on the process of education in capitalist society in words that prefigure the Berkeley student rebellion of 1964:

> Production is carried on for profit not for use ... The crippling of individuals I consider the worst evil of capitalism. Our whole educational system suffers from this evil. An exaggerated competitive attitude is inculcated into the student, who is trained to worship acquisitive success (and the glorification of power) as a prequisite for a future career.[11]

Matthiessen died shortly after, a suicide. Wallace lost heart after the defeats of the Progressive Party, and of his counter-vision of a People's Century. A later generation, however, learned from what they attempted to achieve, as well as from their mistakes. In the 1960s their visions were re-proclaimed in the SDS Port Huron Statement, and on the steps of Sproul Hall in Berkeley by Mario Savio and Bradford Cleaveland.

During the Gulf War George Bush made a number of speeches proclaiming that 'we have kicked the Vietnam syndrome'. He was not simply talking about the history of a past military conflict, but about radical opposition to a whole set of political, economic and cultural policies that coalesced around opposition to the Vietnam War. Although the radical movement of the 1960s was defeated by a combination of factors, including its own disunity, cultural sectarianism, a fragmented agenda and certain illusions about the American dream, the spectre of its heritage has haunted presidents from Nixon to Bush, even as they have been able to construct electoral majorities against social liberalism and radical dissent. Equally important, Bush was affirming the policies and values of Luce's American Century: Manifest Destiny; expansionism; glorification of power; worship of acquisitive success; production for profit; capitalism; imperialism, etc. Counter to this is the radical ideal of a People's Century where human beings can set their own houses in order and build kind and caring cooperative commonwealths. The contradiction between these two cultures in the period 1941–91 is the focus of this book.

The roots of modern North American radical culture run as deep as capitalism, as do the dynamics of expansion and plunder, whether free soil, Manifest Destiny or imperialist. The seeds were brought by the utopian settlers and revolutionary kingkillers on the run who came to the colonies from England, Ireland and Scotland in the seventeenth century; by African slaves who through the Bible connected their situation with histories of the oppression of peoples, and later in the nineteenth century by immigrants from countries with socialist traditions and working-class organizations. It has also often been a radicalism in contradiction not only with organized power but within itself, a series of groups and movements with many agendas inspired by and betrayed by a belief in the democratic American Dream of linear progress. It is a movement that has often known the experience of defeat resulting from global factors – perhaps to a greater extent now than at any other time in its history.

Given the North American gospel of success it is often difficult for us to envision the experience of defeat as an aspect of history, of life. People of the Third World (in Vietnam, Ireland, Latin American and the Middle East, for example) often have a different understanding of history and generation: shared traditions of oppression and defeat, as well as the historical memory of victories (and shared visions of the goals of liberation) sustain them in dark times, contribute to the development of a sense of unity, community and resistance. The future emerges out of a dialogue of past and present, given certain material conditions. As the US becomes ever more what Noam Chomsky has defined as the 'enforcer state' of the post-Gulf 'new world order' (a nation beset by economic declines at home that is the result of an accumulation crisis; the export of capital; an intensified penetration by multinational capital), certain areas and regions of national life may take on some of the characteristics of Third World societies. It is unlikely that Luce's vision of 'the American Century' will prevail in the twenty-first century. However, the life-denying problematics of late capitalism and imperialism remain.

Moreover a certain process of decline has begun. This can be measured in material terms at home (domestic production, debt, people's standard of living and situation at work), in the nation's economic position relative to other regions in the world, as well as in a decline in the general quality of life and of the environment. In addition, from the late 1970s the dominant culture has re-sanctioned America's undertaking the role of world policeman (being an enforcer nation) as well as the de-evolution of essential social, economic and political reforms that were achieved in the 1930s and 1960s/early 1970s. Certain areas of American life have taken on an Alphaville-like Third World quality: wastelands occupied by a commuting workforce by day and the homeless by night. There is a real sense in which America now consists of Dos Passos' 'two nations', which are becoming further decentred into regions and peoples while the economic integrity of the state-as-a-whole becomes more precarious – though affirmed by the dominant culture – as it is abandoned by domestic capital. A process of stagnation, regression and decline is in progress. These are the boundaries of a radical strategy for the twenty-first century. As the American half-century draws to a close the republic is at a crossroads.

Leo Marx has commented that at the apex/moment of decline of empires there is often a flowering of oppositional culture. As dominant empires are swept by a process of rapid change and contradiction, develop military-economic castes, begin to stagnate economically and politically and take on some of the characteristics of an *ancien régime*, a certain clarity is achieved: 'we think of Alexandria in the time of Theocritus and of Virgil's Rome, of Shakespeare's or Wordsworth's London, Rousseau's Paris and Tolstoy's Moscow ...'[12] Marx denotes the 1960s in the United States as the beginning of an analogous period, of 'pastoralist' criticism of 'the system', 'of struggle with organized power'. Marx further places the radicalism of the New Left, the civil rights movements, and of Mario Savio in Berkeley in an American tradition of dissent that dates back to Thoreau, Jefferson and Paine:

> Hence Savio's restatement of Thoreau's stern recommendation in 'Civil Disobedience': 'Let your life be a counter-friction to stop the machine.'[13]

It is as apt a description of the ethos of American radicalism as any. It allows for periods of resistance and for periods of Walden-like retreat. New problems will require new solutions.

Many of the essays in this book were written initially in a period of detente and subsequently revised and re-revised in the aftermath of the Gulf War, and of continuing changes in the east of Europe, including the collapse of the Soviet Union. Thus there is a certain mixture of pessimism and optimism, an internal dialogue within articles as well as a dialogue amongst articles. To highlight this process I have included the final version of an article on American culture and public opinion by Michael X. Delli Carpini. In the text completed during the Gulf War he concludes: 'We have met the enemy and he is us.' It is a chilling indictment. Later he continues to search for a path forward. What else.

Notes

1. Michael Klein (ed.), *The Vietnam Era: Media and Popular Culture in the US and Vietnam* (London and Winchester, Massachusetts: Pluto Press, 1990).

2. Henry Luce, 'The American Century', *Life Magazine*, X (17 February, 1941), pp. 61–3.

3. Norman Markowitz, *The Rise and Fall of the People's Century: Henry Wallace and American Liberalism 1941–1948* (New York and London: Macmillan, 1973).

4. Editorial, the *Independent* (UK) 26 March 1991, p. 24.

5. Paul Kennedy, *The Rise and Fall of the Great Powers* (New York: Random House, 1987).

INTRODUCTION 9

6. Markowitz, *The Rise and Fall of the People's Century*, esp. pp. 50–7.

7. According to a report on the front page of the *Guardian* (UK) on 1 June 1991 proposed conditions for US aid to the Soviet Union included 'allowing wholly owned foreign businesses to operate in the Soviet Union and repatriate their profits', 'sweeping reforms leading to a market economy', and 'an end to Soviet support for the Castro regime in Cuba'. The *Financial Times* in a front page article on 3 June 1991 noted that the proposed economic programme for restructuring the Soviet economy had been drawn up in consultation with US economists at Harvard! This sort of interference in the internal affairs of a major sovereign nation is reminiscent of Western colonialist powers' treatment of China in the late nineteenth century. Thus the 'new world order' takes on characteristics of Luce's 'American Century'. In using the term 'American Century' in this essay I am calling attention to a policy that is a goal not a fact; the US today of course faces significant economic competition from Japan and Germany (and perhaps by extension from the EC in the future).

8. V.I. Lenin, 'Imperialism the Highest Stage of Capitalism' (1916), reprinted in *Lenin: Selected Works* (Vol. 2, Part 2) (Moscow: Foreign Languages Publishing House, 1950), pp. 524, 527; Ernest Mandel, *Late Capitalism*, quoted in Fredric Jameson, 'Periodizing the 60s', in Jameson et al., *The 60's Without Apology* (Minneapolis: University of Minnesota Press, 1984), p. 207.

9. John Dos Passos, 'The Big Money' in *U.S.A.* (New York: Random House, 1937), p. 462.

10. *Prayers for Private Devotion in War-Time* (Cambridge, Massachusetts: The Memorial Church of Harvard University, 1991), pp. 25, 29.

11. Albert Einstein, 'Why Socialism', *Monthly Review* Vol. 1, No. 1 (May 1949), p. 14. In the following issue of *Monthly Review* Henry Wallace – former US vice-president and later leader of the Progressive Party – argued that US progressives should define themselves as neither 'right-wing' nor 'left-wing', but as a movement of decent people who wanted peace, prosperity and social progress. His programme for a people's century/century of the common man included coexistence with socialism abroad, and an American adaptation of the mixed economy approach of the Scandinavian countries at home.

12. Leo Marx, 'Pastoralism in America', in Sacvan Bercovitch and Myra Jehlen (eds), *Ideology and Classic American Literature* (New York: Cambridge University Press, 1986), p. 62.

13. Marx, 'Pastoralism in America', p. 64. For his analyses of the 'ideological continuity' of dissent in America, see pp. 38, 62–4.

1. The Cold War and the Culture of Resistance

Norman Markowitz

'If we fight, perhaps we will die', Paul Henreid says to Humphrey Bogart in *Casablanca*, a quintessential film of the second popular front, the 'everything for victory' campaign of the centre-left coalition during the Second World War, 'If we don't fight the world will die.' Two years after the war, Bogart was starring the *Key Largo*, a film that can be interpreted as an attempt to revive democratic commitments in an atmosphere of corruption and reaction: at the same time, he joined other Hollywood liberals and progressives in a national campaign in support of the Hollywood Ten, targets of the House Un-American Activities Committee's 'investigation' of 'Communism' in Hollywood.¹

Humphrey Bogart would become in death a symbol to New Left radicals of the 1960s of a culture of resistance, even though Bogart in real life charted a much safer course than the figures he played in the movies: he supported Harry Truman over Henry Wallace in the 1948 presidential elections, as did the majority of Hollywood people who joined in the 1947 defence of the Hollywood Ten under the banner of the Hollywood Committee to Defend the First Amendment. Subsequently, Bogart, as was true of so many liberals who avoided the blacklist dragnets, became with his wife Lauren Bacall an Adlai Stevenson Democrat as Stevenson came to serve as a subdued surrogate Roosevelt for marginalized liberals in the 1950s.²

Artists, workers in the mass communications industry, could not by their work or their celebrity defeat the forces of cultural repression and reaction in postwar America. Only effective labour and political action could have accomplished that. Thus, Bogart and his colleagues in the Hollywood Committee to Defend the First Amendment were not able to do much to protect the civil liberties of their colleagues from the studio bosses, who in 1947 inaugurated an anti-Communist blacklist that would spread to radio, television and the press, affecting many thousands of cultural workers who had participated in political and trade union activities or sung songs, written books, made movies, that the blacklist organizers came to regard as 'Communist action, Communist front, or Communist influenced', in the language of the 'anti-subversive' laws passed by Congress in the period.

The battles for control of the Hollywood unions, which provided the only possible effective opposition to an employer's blacklist, were already being lost, as were the struggles to sustain united front and centre-left coalition politics in the larger labour movement.[3]

Nevertheless, political and cultural opposition to the domestic repressions and major initiatives of the Cold War continued to take place, producing intense and complex struggles in the labour movement, in civil rights organizations, in mass media and popular culture. Many figures associated with that opposition, from the sociologist C. Wright Mills to the folk singer Pete Seeger, would be influential in informing the consciousness of the anti-Cold War mass movements that developed out of the struggle against the Vietnam War in the United States. Also, the 'rebels without causes' of the 1950s, the beat poets, rock singers and alienated working-class youth of the anti-suburban counterculture, would serve as role models for the mass countercultural protests of the 1960s.[4]

While much of this opposition was either ignored or treated with redbaiting ridicule by mass media in the high Cold War period (1947-55), the resistance of Paul Robeson and those who stood with him at Peekskill, of those who collected millions of signatures in the US for the Stockholm Peace Petitions against the background of the Korean War, of those who wore the anti-McCarthy Green Feather at Joe Must Go campaigns on college campuses in the early 1950s, and who finally organized and demonstrated against the execution of Julius and Ethel Rosenberg, needs to be recovered if one is to understand the reviving protest movements of the 1960s.[5]

Furthermore, the development of the civil rights movement in the 1950s, and its huge political and cultural influence on everything that was to follow, can be seen ultimately as a victory of mass democratic culture, a culture of activism, inclusion and broad united fronts, against the political culture of the Cold War.[6] In that struggle the experiences of the mass protest left of the 1930s and 1940s were to be reasserted, and many left activists, condemned to a semi-underground existence by Cold War political repression, were to provide assistance to and solidarity with the civil rights movement.

All of this, both the continued resistance of a fragmented and marginalized popular front left, and the development of new radical critiques, acted as the negation, more ignored than polemicized against, of the dominant Cold War culture of the 1950s. In the world of censorship and self-censorship that pervaded the early postwar era, the domestic expressions of the dominant ideology was both self-consciously de-radicalized and smugly self-limited in its celebration of the consumerist present, except for a radical and limitless anti-Communism, which guarded the status quo. In an odd turn from the old debates within Marxist circles, those whom C. Wright Mills called the 'NATO intellectuals' proclaimed anti-Communist ideology pluralist and beyond ideology ('scientific') while it labelled critics of the Cold War 'revisionists'.[7]

Furthermore there was harsh political segregation, through the Smith Act of 1940, the McCarran Internal Security Act of 1950, and other federal and state legislative and administrative proscriptions of the Communist Party, USA, which had been an organizing and unifying centre for the popular front left, even for those radicals in its orbit who habitually distrusted it.

Mass organizations, labelled as front groups both by governmental and congressional 'regulatory' boards and committees,[8] would continue to hold concerts and other events to stimulate protest. Many of their activities, however, were centred around protecting their right to exist free of the encirclement carried out against them by both the state apparatus and the purged labour, civil liberties, and social action organizations, all of which purchased credibility with ruling circles by practising a politics of moderation and developing their own internal blacklists and restrictions on those within their ranks suspected of being pro-Communist.

As an expression of that political segregation, dominant media portrayed workers and intellectuals as natural antagonists, to be unified only in a mass consumer culture and in service to the Cold War, since the alliance of labour and the intellectuals in politics and culture had been the conscious policy of the popular front left.[9]

If one is to understand the political and cultural forms of resistance to the Cold War, the effects of the Second World War on US politics and society must be understood, along with the larger international context in which the Cold War developed.[10]

The War to Make the World Safe for Different Brands of Democracy

The Second World War was the culmination of both the United Front against Fascism and anti-fascist collective security campaigns initiated by the Communist-led left and the Soviet Union to avoid war by isolating fascism and reaction internally and internationally in the 1930s – in effect by containing the expansionist fascist dictatorships and compelling them to collapse of their own internal contradictions.

At the same time, national popular front movements in the 1930s sought to advance the economic and social rights of labour and the middle classes so as to weaken the power of monopoly capital, fascism's principal client, and remove the conditions for the rise of fascist mass movements. A politics of inclusion, uniting the centre and the left, and a labour-centred popular culture characterized the popular front movements of the 1930s. In the United States a culture of commitment – in which both the 'common man' and the alienated rugged individualists of the Bogart type overcame their cynicism to struggle against the business barons, gangsters, and native and foreign fascists who used established power to dominate the masses of people – was the leading expression of these principles.

The German attack on the Soviets and the Japanese attack on the US at Pearl Harbor in effect created the wartime collective security alliance in opposition to the fascist Axis that popular front activists had striven for as a means to prevent the war.[11]

In a context in which both Democratic and Republican politicians were routinely saying things like 'Stalingrad is the first line of defence of Chicago' and US military leaders and businessmen offered toasts to 'our heroic Soviet allies', official anti-Communism was at low ebb. While this era of Soviet-American 'good feelings' is often exaggerated,[12] pro-Soviet themes entered into popular culture through newspaper accounts of Soviet heroism, tours of Soviet military heroes and heroines, Soviet war relief and second front pageants spearheaded by Communist Party activists, including prominent cultural figures.

Also, a handful of war movies – most prominently *Mission to Moscow*, the film based on US ambassador Joseph E. Davies's bestselling memoir, which challenged mass-media stereotypes of the nature of Soviet society and Soviet culpability in the events leading to the outbreak of war – provided sympathetic portrayals of the Soviet people.

Since the negative concept of 'Stalinism' had served as the basis for political consensus among anti-Communist conservatives and the 'anti-Communist left', it was discarded for the duration of the war and temporarily replaced with the image of Stalin as Uncle Joe, the shrewd, strong, patient leader smoking his pipe and doing his bit to win the war.[13]

Prominent anti-Communists associated with the left, most importantly Sidney Hook, staged protests against *Mission to Moscow* and kept up attacks on defenders of long-term Soviet-American cooperation as 'fellow travellers' and 'totalitarian liberals', warning about Soviet intentions in postwar Europe in ways similar to that of Asia First conservatives during the war. Furthermore, discrimination against Communists in the military, in public service, and certainly in intellectual life hardly dissipated even during the 'honeymoon' years of the Soviet–American alliance.

It was not until the middle of the war that military restrictions channelling Communists in units of political and personal undesirables and barring troops listed as Communists from officers' candidate school were lifted. While an individual like Howard Fast, identified with the Party, might have his work published by bourgeois publishers, a review of Herbert Aptheker's *American Negro Slave Revolts* was lifted from the *New York Times*, in all likelihood because of the author's Communist Party affiliations.[14]

Also, when looked at carefully, the myriad of mass media accolades to the Soviet Union and the few 'pro-Soviet' films did not extol the Soviet revolution or Soviet socialism in order to explain the depth of Soviet resistance.

Rather, the partisan films, Lillian Hellman's *North Star*, *Counterattack* and *Song of Russia*, either used conventional stereotypes of Russians to portray the Soviets as a brave, happy peasant people rallying against their Nazi oppressors, mixed conventional Hollywood love stories with invasion themes, or focused on disciplined resistance fighters outmanoeuvring the Germans. Nor were the films dealing with the Soviets, save *Mission to Moscow*, so different from the large genre of resistance films set in Europe in the pre-D-Day period, although many of these films stressed cloak-and-dagger underground activities rather than partisan groups.

Even *Mission to Moscow*, while it presented what was essentially the Soviet government's view of the Moscow trials, concluded with the contention that the alliance with the Soviet Union was necessary to win the war in military terms and to provide postwar peace and prosperity through trade, a position broad enough to appeal to both Wendell Willkie Republicans and popular front leftists.

In the campaigns for the first popular front of the middle and late 1930s, Communist-led or Communist-influenced cultural workers sought consciously to root themselves in the historical traditions of the folk music and popular culture of the working class.[15]

During the war, the muting of class themes and the ability of conservatives also to make use of these national popular democratic symbols, turned the overcoming of cynicism and the revival of commitment into hallmarks of popular front culture. This is seen in films like *Casablanca* and *Action in the North Atlantic*, films in which anti-fascist heroes of the 1930s come back to fight and win the war, or the egalitarian working class of the 1930s, now in fighting units with its diverse ethnicities respected, fights and wins the war.

At the same time, songs like Earl Robinson's 'The House I Live in', celebrating multi-ethnic democracy in the United States, and his 'Ballad for Americans' (so broad it was performed at the Republican National Convention of 1940) became the popular front left's campaign of solidarity through tolerance. This was at a time when the war economy and the demographic shifts it created made the racism associated politically with the fascist enemy more salient in American life. Frank Sinatra's Oscar-winning short film, also called *The House I Live in* (1945), in which Sinatra uses his celebrity to educate working-class kids against prejudice, was a mainstream expression of wartime popular front culture. Ben Shahn's CIO-Political Action Committee poster for Roosevelt's 1944 campaign, showing a black and a white industrial worker together, radiating strength in the present and confidence in the future with the slogan, 'after the war, full employment', captured its political hopes best.

While the Second World War made the United Front against Fascism and an anti-fascist collective security a matter of necessity and survival, the war produced a central contradiction for both the popular front left and its informal coalition partner, the larger New Deal centre in the United States. It began the process of shifting the balance of political forces in the United States to the right, while it strengthened left and revolutionary forces on the world scene as never before.

Thus the United States, historically an anti-colonial power and the champion of liberal anti-imperialism outside of the Western hemisphere, would become the world military and economic foundation for all anti-Communist and counter-revolutionary forces, and the advocate of a doctrine and policy that perhaps with a certain irony might be called 'Trotskyist imperialism', that is, a doctrine of permanent counter-revolution in which revolutions had to be defeated anywhere to keep them from triumphing everywhere, given the changed power relations and power vacuums created by the war.[16]

The extremism that characterized postwar US anti-Communist campaigns also had an important domestic origin. It was the response to the first genuine mass left in US history, the popular front left which had begun a political and cultural reconstruction of democracy and increased the number of workers in unions five times; had built an industrial labour movement; formed connections between it and a rational government; created new networks of mass organizations; and begun to define freedom and democracy in terms of the needs and rights of groups: workers, farmers, city people and oppressed minorities rather than in terms of plucky, small-town, 'Horatio-Alger' individuals.

The latter tradition, represented most forcefully by Frank Capra in *Mr Deeds Goes to Town*, *Mr Smith Goes to Washington* and *Meet John Doe* in the late 1930s and early 1940s, was precisely what the popular front left was transforming, even though conservatives distrusted the

Capra films for challenging authority and a number of their writers and actors would subsequently be blacklisted.[17]

First, the US war economy produced full employment, a doubling of GNP, a huge increase in plant capacity, rising wages, and accumulated savings. That this was accomplished through the most extensive system of state regulation and investment in the economy in US history mattered little to the corporations who saw their profits soar and their executives staff the agencies of a New Deal government that they continued to define as a threat to their wealth and power. Wartime unity, the de-emphasis of class and social conflict themes for a celebration of multi-ethnic, non-class social solidarity in war films, and a revival of traditional small-town, old middle-class values, along with the celebration of the 'miracle of production', all served to strengthen corporate identification with the 'win the war' and 'arsenal for democracy' goals of the administration.[18]

As corporations began both to sanitize and subsume popular front cultural themes during and after the war in portrayals of workers and the work process, of business–labour cooperation and a new sense of corporate national and social responsibility, the popular front left found itself struggling to sustain New Deal labour positions and fearing right-wing reaction at home while it fought an anti-fascist war that it hoped would be a prelude to a postwar revival and internationalization of the New Deal.

While the war economy was most aptly denounced by its critics as 'socialism for the rich', its political effects were to strengthen the conservative coalition in Congress and in the mass organizations of the larger society. Their influence during the war was seen in the pro-business tax legislation, the elimination of New Deal programmes such as the Food Stamp Plan, the Farm Security Administration and the Works Progress Administration on the grounds that the war had made them unnecessary. It was also seen in the abolition of the National Resources Planning Board after that agency had gained national attention with a comprehensive study of US social welfare policies and a call for a postwar welfare state under a New Bill of Rights that was later to be known as 'the Economic Bill of Rights' when Roosevelt adopted the programme as a political platform.

Conservative coalition influence grew substantially during the war, reaching its anti-New Deal zenith in the revolt by Southern and machine Democrats against Roosevelt's left New Deal vice-president, Henry A. Wallace, and his replacement on the national ticket by Senator Harry Truman, a relatively unknown machine politician from Missouri whose voting record made him acceptable to all factions within the Democratic Party. Although the popular front left was able to organize the National

Citizens Political Action Committee and the Independent Citizens Committee of the Arts, Sciences, and Professions, to provide middle-class liberal and cultural allies for the CIO-Political Action Committee's campaign to re-elect Roosevelt in 1944, united front politics and popular front culture, even with their substantial organizational strength, were both in eclipse at the end of the war. They were tied to a Democratic Party which had its feet in both New Deal and anti-New Deal camps while it lived off the political capital created by the New Deal, labour, and popular front left.[19]

The wartime shift to the right was also seen in the Communist Party leadership's advocacy of long-term cooperation with the capitalist class to reconstruct the postwar world, a policy that under Earl Browder's leadership saw the CPUSA establish itself as the Communist Political Association, in effect a Fabian Society-style organization whose fairly obvious function was to work within New Deal coalition politics. Following the death of Roosevelt and the end of the war, the CPUSA reconstituted itself as a political party, by playing a leading role in the postwar CIO industrial strikes, and reasserting a militant position in defence of the rights of the Negro people. However, the party's wartime 'everything for victory' campaign and lack of criticism of many rightward trends in government and politics had given its enemies in the labour movement and in activist organizations ammunition to use against it.[20]

In postwar cultural work, the attempts to develop a militant popular front left could be seen in various 'Win the Peace' rallies; in songs in praise of Roosevelt and the new United Nations organization; in the highlighting of racist atrocities in the South and in campaigns for a permanent Fair Employment Practices Commission. In music the historical connection was drawn between Lincoln and Roosevelt, and between civil rights and peace at the end of two great wars in which the president had perished as the hour of victory approached. There were also attempts to mobilize opposition to the strengthening anti-Communism of the Truman administration as it resisted labour militancy in the 1945–6 CIO strikes, and to continue the labour folk music tradition that was at the centre of the left's cultural solidarity work in the 1930s.

The strikes, whose compromise settlements, coupled with inflation and dramatic consumer goods shortages, helped to mobilize and elect a new wave of conservative politicians, symbolized in 1946 by Richard Nixon and Joseph McCarthy, who used the issue of Communist influence in labour to attack the New Deal more effectively than ever, since that issue was now connected with US–Soviet conflict, new kinds of economic hardships, and a Truman administration seemingly at war with its own core constituencies.[21]

A new era of censorship began with HUAC agents looking at the scripts of B movies with the eyes of clerical inquisitors and FBI agents asking civil servants if they had Paul Robeson records in their homes. The cultural establishment condemned all literature, theatre, cinema, music and art about workers and social struggle as banal, 'kitchen sink', 'party line' and examples of the infiltration of Soviet socialist realism. In this new atmosphere, popular front culture as a culture of mobilization found itself fighting against the most powerful forces of counter-mobilization it had ever faced. These were the forces of the centre-right that represented not only the traditional conservative coalition and its establishment supporters, but the Truman administration and its powerful claims through the Democratic Party to the New Deal's political heritage.

The popularization at the same time of the concept of 'getting tough with the Russians' as the US sought to restore capitalism in Western Europe, aid the Chiang K'ai-shek dictatorship against the Chinese Communist Party and force the Soviets out of Eastern Europe, connected an extreme and open-ended counter-revolutionary foreign policy with anti-labour domestic policies, thus greatly strengthening and legitimizing Red Scare politics.

Blaming all international problems on Communists controlled by Moscow, and portraying the unions as manipulated by Communist cliques serving as fifth columns for Moscow, the Republican Party and the conservative coalition were finally able to win a sweeping victory against the New Deal in 1946, which had become a prisoner of a Democratic Party that it had never really controlled – a Democratic Party that had subsumed and, from the perspective of the popular front left, betrayed both the New Deal centre and the labour-based New Deal coalition under the Truman administration.

That the 1946 Democratic campaign often played recordings of Roosevelt's old speeches and many Democrats in urban areas sought to disassociate themselves from Truman at all costs was perhaps the most powerful example of the debacle that began to reorient postwar politics, one in which the Democrats, in beginning at home the logic that would reflect the Cold War in Vietnam 20 years later, would save the New Deal by destroying it.[22]

'Every liberal is a Socialist, every Socialist is a Communist, every Communist is a spy' a conservative coalition politician argued in the late 1940s, capturing the mindset of the high Cold War period. This period started in earnest in 1947 in the enunciation of the Truman doctrine, the division of Europe under the Marshall Plan, the passage of the Taft-Hartley law, an anti-labour omnibus bill sharply restricting the rights won by trade unions in the 1930s, and in the establishment of the Truman 'loyalty' programme and the Attorney General's list of subversive organizations, seeking to segregate the mass organizations of the popular front left and providing a legitimation for the subsequent industry blacklists.

In corporate-dominated media (motion pictures, radio, and later television) resistance was limited even before the coming of the blacklist and was largely driven underground by the defeat of the Progressive Party in the 1948 elections, the internal purges in the CIO leading to the expulsion of its Communist-led left unions in 1949–50, and the manipulated espionage hysteria that was created by the political show trials of Alger Hiss and Julius and Ethel Rosenberg. In both the mass press, the movies, and on radio, spy stories proliferated, particularly those with plots dealing with nuclear espionage, and became wartime foreign intrigue films and Saturday afternoon adventure serials, along with super-hero radio adventure shows, retooled to fight the Cold War.[23]

The Hiss and Rosenberg cases served as warnings that any attempt to sustain the centre-left coalition could lead the authorities to use a distorted view of the past to destroy activists in the present. By 1948, the world of the popular front left, of marching, demonstrating, signing petitions, engaging in political action through mass organizations – all legal political action – was increasingly seen as subversion and treason. All those with connections to it were placed under surveillance by both the government and the local guardians of respectability. Their past was hurled against them, either to segregate individuals and organizations or to search and destroy any present activities.[24]

The Hiss case, focusing on accusations that a career New Deal functionary, Alger Hiss, president of the Carnegie Endowment for International Peace, and an old or New Deal liberal establishment figure, had passed State Department materials to the Soviet Union, was a message to a generation of establishment liberals in training that anyone with any compromising connection, regardless of his or her political and class credentials, could be destroyed by the cold warriors for any wrong moves.

Also, for the right, Hiss served as both a political and personal surrogate Roosevelt, seen by conservatives as an enemy agent Iago to Roosevelt's malevolent Othello at Yalta, and as an arrogant upper-class traitor who, to paraphrase Joe McCarthy's famous phrase, was born with a silver spoon in his mouth. Now, those who had muttered that Roosevelt was a traitor to his class could use a more commonplace definition of treason to turn the tables on their liberal-labour and left enemies.

The Rosenberg case, connecting lower-middle-class Jews from working-class backgrounds to atomic espionage, provided activists with the message that was trumpeted to the left in all open dictatorships – that anyone could be ensnared in the political dragnets and, with any convenient story line, sent to the electric chair to re-enforce Cold War politics. For a right that had always crudely connected anti-Communism with anti-Semitism, calling Roosevelt 'Rosenfeld' and New York 'Jew York' in emulation of the discourse of those who were hanged at Nuremburg, the Rosenbergs were special targets, even if their prosecutors and judge, though none of their jurors, were Jews.[25]

In the postwar period, the domestic Cold War enabled the government, corporate capital and their allies to accomplish at a much higher level and for a much longer period than the post-First World War Red Scare what might be categorized as surgical strike fascism, segregating and stigmatizing Communist Party activists and their allies from all others and compelling the Party and its allies to function in a political twilight zone bordered by a still functioning, larger liberal democratic society.

In this context, where democratic rights were not generally liquidated as in fascist regimes, resistance took the form of keeping alive protest organizations and the hopes they generated, upholding New Deal values, and warning about the dangers of imperialism and war. Also, as in fascist regimes where political venues were effectively closed and the working class particularly policed, resistance became an all-class phenomenon, and non-monopoly culture a magnet to draw the alienated youth and their politically marginalized elders.

Cultural protest, in small theatres and clubs, especially in the 'free world' of political folk music symbolized in the late 1940s by People's Songs, would continue, and in important ways deepen, as the crisis of civil liberties, civil rights, and peace would bring to national audiences songs like 'If I had a Hammer' and 'We Shall Overcome' and keep alive – in spite of the blacklisting of Pete Seeger and the Weavers and the passport denial of Paul Robeson – songs of protest on the events of the day which would provide either the origins or the inspiration for the songs of social protest generated by the civil rights and peace movements that Bob Dylan, Joan Baez, and Peter, Paul and Mary would bring into a renewed political mainstream in the early 1960s.[26]

Mixed Messages: Hollywood and the Cold War Transition

In the early postwar years, Hollywood films became a political battleground as the New Deal centre began to dissolve and Hollywood made some of the best New Deal social dramas or 'message films' as SOS signals to the labour-based New Deal coalition. *The Best Years of Our Lives* (1946), Walter Wanger's pro-New Deal liberal reconversion film, upheld the broader democratic values for which the war had been fought and looked to a liberal postwar conversion policy providing jobs and social progress, mediating the injustices of the existing class system, in much the same way that decent merchants and businessmen provided happy endings for the victims of industrial capitalism in the novels of Charles Dickens.

Pride of the Marines (1945), written by the soon-to-be blacklisted screenwriter Albert Maltz, looked both to rehabilitating the men crippled by the war and giving them a different America to come home to than they had after the First World War; only, in *Pride of the Marines*, the message was more militant than in *The Best Years of Our Lives*: vets would take things into their own hands rather than permit the gains of the New Deal period to be buried in a new postwar cycle of inflation, union busting, and eventual depression.

Resistance in Hollywood and in the theatre to the emergence and consolidation of Cold War culture, which was built on a policy of political segregation, was also expressed in raising questions about racism and anti-Semitism more openly than Hollywood had ever done earlier, since both the victory against Hitlerism and the shift of African-Americans to urban industrial areas during the war had made both political and labour civil rights policy central to the achievement of a postwar New Deal agenda.

Also, the survival of the New Deal coalition as anything more than a patronage front for the Democratic Party, and of popular front politics, depended on the maintenance of the popular front in CIO labour. To a great extent, this depended both on the success of the CIO's Southern organizing drive and the continuation in Northern urban industrial areas and new areas opening up in the West of depression and wartime labour gains – all of which hinged on the creation of effective forms of white–black unity, which necessitated the elimination of both *de jure* and *de facto* segregation.

Arthur Laurents' successful Broadway play, *Home of the Brave*, dealing with anti-Semitism in the army, became in its 1949 screen version a film about anti-black racism, with the same psychological-social types in conflict. Also, Elia Kazan's adaptation of Laura Z. Hobson's novel, *Gentleman's Agreement* (1947), sought to expose to a general audience both institutional and ideological anti-Semitism through the melodrama of a gentile reporter who pretends to be Jewish. The socially crippling effects of light-skinned blacks passing for white were highlighted in *Pinky* and *Lost Boundaries* (1949). Finally, Edward Dymtryk (soon to be blacklisted as a member of the Hollywood Ten) assayed the acceptance of anti-Semitism by elites and, in effect, the struggle going on in the larger society between those seeking to keep the New Deal alive and those seeking to bury it in *Crossfire*, a film about the murder of a Jewish soldier and subsequent cover-up.

The plot of *Crossfire* may be seen as having some connection to Charles Fuller's *A Soldier's Story*, though unlike *A Soldier's Story*, the military investigator is a clear liberal hero; a non-Jewish New Dealer is fighting anti-Semitism for larger purposes, and the villain is a traditional bigot protected by his associates. In *A Soldier's Story*, where the military investigator is black and the killer turns out to be a militant black, the concept of interethnic unity in the pursuit of justice, even though there are white liberal characters, would be completely out of place.

While a number of these films are today considered stilted, if not camp, they dealt with institutional prejudice more directly than later, far more sophisticated films which became possible with the development of the civil rights movement. Also, while early Cold War films like the *Iron Curtain* (1948) and *Red Danube* (1949) warned of Soviet spy rings stealing atomic secrets in Canada and Soviet aggression in Central Europe, films like *Berlin Story* (1948) written by the soon-to-be imprisoned and blacklisted writer Ring Lardner Jr, and *The Boy with Green Hair* (1948), told of Nazi intrigue in occupied Berlin and the fear of difference that spawns both hatred and war. While the Cold War gangster film – that is, the portrayal of crime not as a vocation of the poor or a system of business but as the domain of evil psychopaths – made its mark in late 1940s films like *White Heat* (1949), the New Deal social drama films in which crime was the arena to look at class questions and urban life moved forward in films like Abraham Polonsky's *Force of Evil* (1948), *Knock on Any Door* (1949) and John Huston's *The Asphalt Jungle* (1950).

In the westerns, which flourished in part because their major genres lent themselves to fighting the Cold War, especially as a frontier struggle in the former colonial regions of the world, the Cold War orientation could be seen in John Ford's *Fort Apache*; while the dangers of dictatorship and a war of generations were expressed in Howard Hawks' *Red River* (1948) which may be seen as a liberal allegory to the development of the Cold War. In seeking a perilous path to the markets of the world, the United States risked turning into the suicidal tyrant that the cattle baron John Wayne nearly becomes as he launches the long drive to bring his herd to market, threatening to destroy his 'liberal' adopted son (Montgomery Clift) who seeks a safer but compatible path.

The struggles to save the centre-left coalition and sustain its open left component were defeated politically in the larger society with the defeat of the Progressive Party in 1948, the CIO purges of 1949–50, the formation of NATO and US intervention in the Korean civil war in 1949–50.

These defeats ended the cinematic debate of the late 1940s. What the conservative press derisively called 'message films' on the themes of New Deal revival, for example, couldn't be made any more. At the same time political 'message films' portraying Communists as spies and gangsters were acceptable. Images of workers as freed from the world of work and living in the realm of consumption, family commitments and countless personal choices (a kind of utopian consumerist 'communism' purchased on the instalment plan) permeated films and particularly television.[27]

However, anti-Cold War resistance themes were expressed in such works as the science fiction film *The Day the Earth Stood Still* (1951), in which the cynicism and corruption of the McCarthy-ridden Korean War era is glimpsed in the story of a visitor from another planet whose mission of peace is threatened by a government that tries to capture him, thus threatening through its venality the destruction of the world.

At the height of the Cold War, blacklisted Hollywood artists and union activists of the Mine Mill and Smelter Workers produced *Salt of the Earth* (1954), a film that raised questions of national and gender oppression in a class context in ways that prefigured later feminist campaigns in the larger society and in the labour movement. *Salt of the Earth* also reflected in the American context under the most extreme conditions the making of a film in the postwar Italian 'neo-realist' tradition (itself influenced by the struggle against fascism and the huge influence of the Communist/Socialist left in Italy) of using both actors and non-actors to explore working-class life. While the harassment of the film's makers by the FBI, other state authorities, and local vigilantes; the collusion to restrict its showing in the United States; even the deportation of its Mexican female star are expressions of what 'freedom and democracy' meant to cold warriors, it still stands as a remarkable expression of resistance and a bridge to themes that would be picked up, albeit in a different context, in the independent film of black life in the United States, *Nothing But a Man* (1964).

The persistence of cultural criticism in the *Daily Worker* and in the *Guardian*, the *New Masses* and its successor *Masses and Mainstream* kept alive left interpretations of trends in movies, theatre and music at a time when the anti-Communist 'caretaker left' centred around *Dissent* magazine was bemoaning the cultural philistinism of a classless, raceless mass society – in essence becoming the official left loyal opposition to the celebration of democratic capitalism and the construction of a suburban substitute for socialism, of classless consumers who had ended the need for all social conflict at home.

Such criticism fostered hope in a period in which those continuing left and labour battles had constantly to read between the lines of the dominant culture. For example one could find in Hollywood films like *Bad Day at Black Rock* (1954), and Fritz Lang's *The Big Heat* (1952) semi-underground messages about societies where the authorities were corrupt.

The folk music magazine *Sing Out*, begun in 1950 following the formal end of People's Songs, became a rallying point for socially active folk music, as did Folkways Records and the left-oriented children's summer camps that continued to exist, and provided jobs for young singers as counsellors.

While the left culture of the 1950s was in effect ghettoized into off-Broadway and Greenwich Village in New York, and into specific clubs and little theatres through the country, making it something for intellectuals and youth as against workers, informal styles were working-class oriented and different from the suburban casual look of the period, which sought to memorialize in loose fitting clothing, short hair and smooth grooming, blonde furniture and banal ballad music Herbert Hoover's dictum that in America there were no social classes, only the middle class.

The political and the anti-political forms of cultural rebellion would both clash and merge in the mid-1950s in the 'discovery' and commodification of Beat literature and poetry, as they would at a much higher level in the relationship of the New Left political culture and the 'counter culture' of the late 1960s. Young men in jeans, and serious women in black dresses and black stockings, made personal and political statements about the bomb, the Cold War, Montgomery, Little Rock, drawing people together in the small places of resistance in the 1950s.

For many, and not only the young, this began the process of thinking again, questioning again, learning to walk politically again, since except for surviving left unions and skeletons of left mass organizations, the community and labour-based forms of activism and protest had been largely shattered by institutionalized repression. While the tactics of political and labour segregation isolated the left, cultural segregation in effect created cultural oases in which issues could be raised, ideas exchanged, and identifications made with people who didn't look, talk, or act like either Richard Nixon, Ozzie Nelson, or Adlai Stevenson.

As the civil rights movement challenged the 'massive resistance' of the segregationist power structure in the South and brought mass political action into the mainstream in the late 1950s, social protest flourished again as expressions of masses in motion around civil rights, anti-war, anti-conformity, and environmental issues.

The influence of the struggles of the popular front left could be seen in the politics of the 1960s, in the attempt to forge a new centre-left coalition and find a new Roosevelt to lead the country and the world away from a Cold War whose only serious possibilities, for those who had abandoned what C. Wright Mills called 'crackpot realism', were national bankruptcy or international genocide. The failure of Lyndon Johnson both to prosecute the Vietnam War and carry through his Great Society programme, in effect to forge a new centre-left coalition at home while expanding the Cold War abroad, was a testament to the revival of political activism, both inside and outside of the Democratic Party, that seemingly had been crushed in the late 1940s.

Everywhere the cold warriors looked, from Bob Dylan singing about Masters of War; to Stanley Kubrick's *Dr Strangelove*, putting on screen the coffee house satires of John Foster Dulles and Werner Von Braun; to 'We Shall Overcome', the words Johnson uttered after Selma which had their origins in the song 'We Will Overcome' published by People's Songs in 1948; to Phil Ochs singing 'Draft Dodger Rag'; to the masses of people marching, petitioning, organizing and educating against their policies, they saw the failure of their domestic Cold War repression confronting them in all areas of US society, just as the failure of their counter-insurgency policy was confronting them in Vietnam. Also, ironically, they saw forms of cultural protest and resistance that would influence peoples throughout the world after the 1960s far more extensively than their myriad of CIA-funded intellectuals' groups, writers, and artists.[28]

Notes

1. See Alistair Cooke, 'Humphrey Bogart: Epitaph for a Tough Guy', *Atlantic*, 199, May 1959, pp. 31-5.

2. Victor Navasky, *Naming Names* (New York: The Viking Press, 1980). For the Bogart cult, see Gerald Weales in Edward Quinn and Paul Dolan (eds), *Sense of the Sixties* (New York: The Free Press, 1968), pp. 163-9.

3. For the battle in the screenwriters' guild, see Lary May, *Screening Out the Past: The Birth of Mass Culture and the Motion Picture Industry* (New York: Oxford University Press, 1985). For an interesting account of the scholarship on and influence of the left in Hollywood in the 1930s and 1940s, see Thom Anderson, 'Red Hollywood', in Suzanne Ferguson and Barbara Groseclose (eds), *Literature and the Visual Arts in Contemporary Society* (Columbus: OSU Press, 1986), pp. 141-96.

4. See C. Wright Mills, *The Power Elite* and C. Wright Mills, *The Sociological Imagination* (New York: Oxford University Press, 1959). For a decent treatment of cultural conflict, see Douglas T. Miller and Marion Novak, *The Fifties* (New York: Doubleday, 1977).

5. Although it does not deal with culture as such, Ann Fagan Ginger and David Christiano (eds), *Cold War Against Labor*, 2 vols (Berkeley: Meikeljohn Institute, 1987) has rich materials concerning both political and cultural resistance to the Cold War, focusing on the experiences of the popular front left, in which it retained its commitment to the working class of the United States and the world against a political background that either celebrated the rise of a majority middle-class society and/or bemoaned working-class authoritarianism and philistinism.

6. For a good introduction to the effects of the Cold War on the civil rights movement and vice versa, see Manning Marable, *Race, Reform, and Rebellion* (Jackson, Mississippi: University of Mississippi Press, 1984).

7. See Cold War sociologist Edward Shils 'The End of Ideology?' in the CIA-funded intelligentsia journal *Encounter* (November, 1955) pp. 52–8. See Daniel Bell's summary work *The End of Ideology* (Glencoe, Illinois: The Free Press, 1960).

8. For an introduction to the functioning of the anti-Communist purge, see David Caute, *The Great Fear* (New York: Simon and Schuster, 1978).

9. In summing up the orientation that was to pervade the 1950s, Eric C. Johnston, who as director of the Motion Picture Producers Association inaugurated the Hollywood Blacklist in 1947, said 'We'll have no more *Grapes of Wrath*, we'll have no more *Tobacco Roads*. We'll have no more films that show the seamy side of American life. We'll have no pictures that deal with labor strikes. We'll have no pictures that deal with the banker as villain.' Quoted in Murray Schumach, *The Face on the Cutting Room Floor: The Story of Movie and Television Censorship* (New York: William Morrow, 1964), p. 129.

10. Derived from German and Italian fascists as essentially a fascist ideal, the concept of a 'totalitarian state/system' was transferred to the Soviets initially by conservative intellectuals, who saw in fascism a more benign form of 'totalitarian' development, and by social democratic rivals of Communists in Germany in the early 1930s who equated the dictatorship of the proletariat with fascist state methods, as a rationale for uncritical alliances with centre forces, as against united front alliances with Communists and centre forces.

11. *Casablanca* is but one cinematic expression of the popular front in mass culture in the United States during the war, especially of the new culture of commitment.

12. For a sympathetic portrayal of this conservative opposition, which has rarely been studied, see George Sirgiovanni, *An Undercurrent of Suspicion: Anti-Communism in America During World War II* (New Brunswick, New Jersey: Transaction Books, 1989).

13. Anti-Soviet stereotypes, like anti-Communist stereotypes generally, bear a strong resemblance to anti-black racism, which has been the model for a wide variety of prejudices in the US. The Soviets as comedy relief characters whom one could tolerate and even work with but never respect (happy non-threatening inferiors or 'Sambos') represented the benign end of this spectrum, while the Soviets as rampaging beasts threatening property and people – in effect 'Red Niggers' – represent its most malign expression in mass ideology. 'Uncle Joe' reached the status of an Uncle Remus, comforting rather than threatening, or at best, a local character in a radio situation comedy of the 1940s, someone from whom Fibber McGee might try to borrow money.

14. Discussion between Herbert Aptheker and the author. Materials relating to the struggle of Communists against discrimination can be found in the Vito Marcantonio Papers (New York Public Library).

15. This was of course a world trend in which historical figures, writers and artists were in effect either reinterpreted or revived in a popular democratic framework, in effect to take the flag out of the hands of the forces of reaction. For the classic expression of the thinking behind the international popular front, see George Dimitrov, *The Working Class Against Fascism and War* (New York: International Publishers, 1987).

16. Two accessible works which capture the theory and practice of this policy of permanent counter-revolution are Richard Barnet, *Roots of War* (New York: Atheneum, 1972) and Philip Agee, *Inside The Company: CIA Diary* (New York: Bantam Books, 1973). See also William Appleman Williams, *Tragedy of American Diplomacy* (Cleveland: World Publishing Co., 1962).

17. The Capra films were often perceived as expressions of New Deal ideology, or even radical by conservatives because, in the context of labour upsurge and anti-New Deal backlash that characterized the late 1930s, even such non-proletarian, non-intellectual anti-establishment figures as the 'Boy Scout' Senator, Jefferson Smith, and the Hobo ex-baseball pitcher transformed into 'John Doe' by a fraudulent newspaper campaign, were challenging established economic and political authorities at a time when business and political conservative coalition forces were conflating many forms of criticism and taking out of context statements in both fiction and real life.

18. An introduction to these general trends can be found in John M. Blum, *V Was for Victory: Politics and American Culture in World War II* (New York: Harcourt, Brace, Jovanovich, 1977).

19. See Norman Markowitz, *The Rise and Fall of the People's Century: Henry A. Wallace and American Liberalism, 1941–48* (New York: Macmillan, 1973), Chapters 2 and 3 for an explication of these trends.

20. No decent history of the CPUSA exists. Philip Bart *et al.* (eds), *Highlights of Fighting History: Sixty Years of the Communist Party USA* (New York: International Publishers, 1979) contains valuable documents, annotations, and commentary on CPUSA history. Maurice Isserman's superficial *Which Side Are You On?* (Middleton, Connecticut: Wesleyan University Press, 1982) is the major general history of the CPUSA dealing with the Second World War, recommended by the traditional and New Left anti-Communist schools whose positions it synthesizes, along with a smug and patronizing view that is reminiscent of Browderism.

21. See Markowitz, *People's Century*, Chapters 4 and 5.

22. See for example, Richard Freeland, *The Truman Doctrine and the Origins of McCarthyism* (New York: Schocken Books, 1971), Athan Theoharis (ed.), *The Truman Presidency: The Origins of the Imperial Presidency and the National Security State* (New York: E.M. Coleman Enterprises, 1979).

23. For the general political climate, see David Caute, *The Great Fear*. Important themes in labour and political culture are highlighted in Marty Jezer, *The Dark Ages* (Boston: South End Press, 1982) and George Lipsitz, *Class and Culture in Cold War America* (New York: Praeger Publishers, 1981).

24. Caute, *Great Fear*; Navasky, *Naming Names*; and Ginger, *Cold War Against Labor*. See also Robert Griffith and Athan Theoharis (eds), *The Specter: Original Essays on The Cold War and the Origins of McCarthyism* (New York: New Viewpoints, 1974).

25. The guilt of both Alger Hiss and the Rosenbergs remains as important to all segments of the United States Cold War establishment and their fans among the general populace as the 'guilt' of Alfred Dreyfus was to the French Right in the 1890s. Unfortunately, no government with an interest in reopening these cases has come to power in the US. Walter and Miriam Schnier, *Invitation to an Inquest* (New York: Doubleday, 1983) 2nd edition, and Athan Theoharis (ed.), *Beyond the Hiss Case* are useful introductions to the two cases from anti-Cold War perspectives. The major Cold War revival interpretations of the cases are Allen Weinstein, *Perjury: The Hiss-Chambers Case* (New York: Alfred Knopf, 1978) and Ronald Radosh and Joyce Milton, *The Rosenberg File* (New York: Holt and Rhinehart, 1983).

26. In 1946, the People's Songs was founded and, in its three years of existence, organized hootenannies, produced records, taught activists how to use folk music, and engaged in labour and civil rights struggles and the Progressive Party campaign of Henry Wallace. Pete Seeger, Lee Hays, Alan Lomax, Woodie Guthrie, Earl Robinson, and the later blacklisted screenwriter, Millard Lampell, were among its National Board members. See Robbie Lieberman, 'My Song is My Weapon'

(Chicago: University of Illinois Press, 1989) for a short history of People's Songs, informed by both sympathies with and for the artists, and a very questionable acceptance of the traditional anti-Communist historiography of Irving Howe and Lewis Coser, Theodore Draper, etc., as modified by the New Left conventional wisdom (good grassroots activists, bad 'Stalinist' national and international leadership) represented best in the documentary film, *Seeing Red*.

27. For a sometimes difficult but stimulating attempt to enter the 1950s according to Hollywood, see Peter Biskind, *Seeing is Believing* (New York: Pantheon Books, 1984).

28. For origins of the song 'We Shall Overcome', see Lieberman, 'My Song is My Weapon', p. 112.

2. So that the Dead may not be Killed Again: Mailer, Doctorow and the Poetics of a Persecuting Society

Richard Godden

> To articulate the past historically does not mean to recognize it 'the way it really was' (Ranke). It means to seize hold of a memory as it flashes up at a moment of danger. Historical materialism wishes to retain that image of the past which unexpectedly appears to a man singled out by history at a moment of danger. The danger affects both the content of the tradition and its receivers. The same threat hangs over them both: that of becoming a tool of the ruling classes. In every era the attempt must be made anew to wrest tradition away from a conformism that is about to overpower it ... Only the historian will have the gift of fanning the spark of hope in the past who is firmly convinced that *even the dead* will not be safe from the enemy if he wins. And this enemy has not ceased to be victorious.
>
> Walter Benjamin, 'Theses on the Philosophy of History' [1]

The Politics of Allegory

Noted postmortems on the Rosenbergs charge the couple with inauthenticity. Warshow and Fiedler, writing in the year of the execution (1953), agree that Julius and Ethel Rosenberg betrayed themselves more importantly than their country, by reading their own lives allegorically. For Warshow the prison letters reveal 'something ... more profound than insincerity', in that as the functionaries of an 'Idea' the correspondents accept themselves 'merely [as] particular objects in which the universal happens at the moment to embody itself': it follows that 'their own experience... did not really belong to them'.[2] Fiedler concurs, arguing that those who think of themselves as political 'cases' become 'official clichés': his Rosenbergs 'blasphemously deny their own humanity'.[3] That noted liberal intellectuals should find the allegorical impulse more culpable than spying or treason is predictable (circa 1953), given that 'truth to self' is a generic moral measure among those of a liberal imagination during the late 1940s and early 1950s. Allegory belongs to the state.

THE DEAD MAY NOT BE KILLED AGAIN 31

In his survey of America's Cold War intelligentsia, Richard Pells speaks of 'lonely and helpless' social critics retreating before 'remote and omnipotent governmental structures',[4] and discovering as their subject the problems of the predominantly affluent private citizen. On a more caustic note Paul Buhle records capital's mass-delivery of suburb and automobile as inducing 'a mood of political futility' among intellectuals,[5] who might either sign up with the American Committee for Cultural Freedom (1951) and celebrate the free and upwardly mobile individual, or attempt some version of 'the great refusal' whereby nay-saying at least leaves a record of personal integrity for future generations. Either option locates its politics in the private life of the mind – a life whose authenticity the Rosenbergs seemingly violated.

Yet privacy is not a safe place in the early 1950s; the 'pragmatic' pleasures of an 'unheroic' denial of ideology (Bell),[6] the espousal of a national genius rooted in an ignorance of political theory (Boorstein),[7] or the 'moral realism' that accepts the insolubility of problems (Trilling),[8] read against the grain become analogous to a suburban accumulation of personal property. None of these moves offers protection should agencies of the state choose to view the life of any particular mind through the stencil of allegory. During the postwar red scare, at its height between 1949 and 1953, guilt by association allowed one thing to become another with a voluptuous and arbitrary allegorical fertility. Witness the following case: a professional-rank employee of a defence agency with access to secret material was charged with writing a PhD thesis (1950–1) based on material largely drawn from the Institute of Pacific Relations: the House Committee on Un-American Activities referred to this institute as a Communist front organization. He was also accused:

> ... of (1) having a close association with a man (2) who wrote a book (3) which was advertised in a publication run by Louis Adamic (4) who had been listed in 1948 as an official of the Progressive Party (5) which was cited as a Communist front (6) by the Tenney Committee in California.[9]

At a more general level, since loyalty boards tested 'tendencies' or 'potentials', and did so via secret files generated by anonymous witnesses, their very existence represented a dramatic extension of the national security state and a politicization of privacy in the name of its defence. As the scare intensified, 'disloyalty' could be interpreted as 'subversion' in a shift that translates 'radical belief' into 'criminal act'.

Such shifts were commonplace: one has only to start a list of federal allegorizers to appreciate the pervasiveness of a Cold War poetics of allegory ... the FBI, the Attorney General's Office, the Department of Justice, a proliferation of Congressional Committees on subversion and a whole range of ad-hoc investigative bodies in schools, universities, libraries ... Membership in part depended on a working, if rudimentary, knowledge of hermeneutics, whereby several interpretations may be offered, but only to establish a pattern of inference that closes in a vicious circle. The inclination of the guesses was predictable: to be affiliated to any organization on the Attorney General's proscribed list was to be a Communist; to be a Communist was to be a spy; to be a spy was to have need of a network of fellow travellers; today's fellow travellers are yesterday's New Dealers, and since New Dealers populate the State Department, China falls and Korea stalemates. Some circles were benign and more simple: to serve on the House Committee on Un-American Activities was to be a Policeman of the Free World,[10] and to live the American High[11] in a white collar was to embody Americanism. For a moment I shall enroll Fiedler as a federal allegorist; his subject, the epistolatory style of Ethel Rosenberg:

> To believe that two innocents had been falsely condemned for favouring 'roses and the laughter of children,' one would have to believe the judges and public officials of the United States to be not merely the Fascists the Rosenbergs called them, but monsters, insensate beasts; and perhaps this was partly their point. But one must look deeper, realize that a code is involved, a substitution of equivalents whose true meaning can be read off immediately by the insider. 'Peace, democracy and liberty,' like 'roses and the laughter of children,' are only conventional ciphers for the barely whispered word 'Communism,' and Communism is itself only a secondary encoding of the completely unmentioned 'Defense of the Soviet Union'.[12]

With two simple steps exegesis releases the text from literal meaning only to discover damnation in plurality.

The disciplines of federal allegory exist primarily to find the enemy. Michael Rogin's recent work on the paranoid style offers insights. He reads paranoia not as a status event but as a structural necessity within a pluralist tradition. Earlier interpreters locate the anxieties of the right and its liberal allies in problems of status, so that the 1950s, as years of high social mobility, are simultaneously a decade in which various interest groups find themselves variously 'dispossessed', and consequently candidates for a simplistic political symbology. Those suffering 'compound strain' (Talcott Parsons)[13] are numerous, ranging from the old middle class (Bell),[14] through the newly regulated business elite (Parsons),[15] to the ethnically insecure (Hofstadter)[16] – all presumably ripe for demonology. Rogin, however, discovers 'dense and massive irrationality' among none of these groups *per se*;[17] instead he situates the counter-subversive impulse within the consensual tradition itself, arguing that liberal emphasis on pluralist melt-down breeds illiberal demons. The myth of America as an exceptional place in which mobility dissolves stratification, and ends ideology, produces 'fears of boundary collapse' and with it the need for categorical enemies:

> Countersubversion can thus function as pluralism's negative underside, constricting legitimate alternatives within the pluralist interest group tradition ... The oscillation between a fear of the breakdown of all difference and a desire for merger lies at the core of American demonology.[18]

It follows that liberal pluralists are always potentially persecutors, the warmth of the suburb has only to chill − a line of thought rather harder on liberals than the claim that, since the mechanics of the loyalty programme were instituted by Truman, the Democratic Party must take some responsibility for the Republican Senator from Wisconsin. Rogin implies that the liberal apologists for the Cold War did not simply deserve McCarthy (in some collective failure of nerve), they birthed him as 'dark double' and 'imaginary twin'[19] from the very centre of their tradition. For good measure, Rogin's indictment continues with the charge that the Cold War's 'demons' are the wrong 'demons', or are at least minor, serving to distract the liberal intelligentsia from the buried history of race and class, and, I would add, from adequate enquiry into an affluence structured on the federal funding of the technology of destruction (the permanent arms economy).

Whatever its roots and its myopics, the politics of security enjoyed a high profile in these years: unsurprisingly, therefore, anti-Communism and its poetics are endemic. In 1949, as China fell, J. Howard McGrath, Truman's Attorney General, insisted: 'Communists are everywhere − in factories, offices, butcher shops, in private businesses, and each carries in himself the germs of death for society.'[20]

He was believed; polls from 1947 had indicated that 57 per cent of the population saw 'a great many' Communists in the US, while two years later 68 per cent would have outlawed membership of the party, yet in 1950 that membership was running at 40,000.[21] A logistical problem is apparent: Communists are almost everywhere and almost nowhere, a problem compounded by a crucial difference between the red scare of the 1950s and earlier versions: where the pre-war working-class red had been an immigrant, visibly different and 'alien', the postwar Communist was an indistinguishable member of the 'mass'. 'Invisibility' generated surveillance, files, eruptions of allegorical interpretation and a concomitant anxiety in large sections of the population. After all, if at any moment the 'particular objects' of any life can be made over into embodiments of 'the universal' (be it the Russian System or the American Way) nervousness may attend life among those objects: as Doctorow puts it in his history of the Rosenbergs:

Of course, there is a slight oddness in the way they reacted to the knock on the door – as if they knew what was coming. But they did know what was coming. And so did everyone else who lived with some awareness into that time.22

The Invasion of the Body Snatchers (1956) focused those nerves; Siegel's pods transform their subjects while they sleep, leaving them apparently themselves, though imperceptibly different, within the body of their small-town families. The pods, be they Communism or Mass Culture, suggest how easily privacy may be invaded, split and devoured while maintaining its superficial integrity.

Barbary Shore and Despair

I have been trying to characterize the aesthetics of a political demonology while glossing some of its institutional roots. The fearfulness of the red scare of the 1950s, whether taking the form of loud accusation or silent conformity, constitutes an atmosphere of mistrust explored by Mailer's second novel *Barbary Shore* (1951). Symptomatically, the first act of the narrator is to doubt the outline of his own face:

> Probably I was in the war. There is the mark of a wound behind my ear, an oblong of infertile flesh where no hair grows. It is covered over now, and may be disguised by even the clumsiest barber, but no barber can hide the scar on my back. For that a tailor is more in order.
>
> When I stare into the mirror I am returned a face doubtless more handsome than the original, but the straight nose, the modelled chin, and the smooth cheeks are only evidence of a stranger's art. It does not matter how often I decide the brown hair and the grey eyes must have always been my own, there is nothing I can recognize, not even my age.23

Mikey Lovett feels that his face is a mask, but he cannot see the join; he is aware that he has been re-made but is uncertain by whom and to what end. The invasion of his integrity is particularly disconcerting in that, having 'no past' (p. 12), he cannot measure what he becomes against what he was. He declares himself able 'to masquerade like anyone else' (p. 12), but, unlike anyone else, in lacking coherent memory he lacks the very staple of that private life of the mind from which the liberal tradition builds its bolt-hole.

Mailer has invented a narrator incapable of liberal self-defence. He sets him up in a Brooklyn boarding house and exposes him to two imperatives; Lovett can write himself as the lover of his landlady, Guinevere – that is to say, he can explore the very many forms of her desire, and so, in Mailer's terms, enter the heart the newly generalized consumer culture.²⁴ Mailer notes in *Advertisements for Myself* (1959), 'sex has become the centre of our economy'.²⁵ Or, he can invent himself as a radical theorist, vanguard leader to an as yet non-existent revolutionary class, through discipleship to the Bolshevik McLeod. His options have allegorical clarity, and the novel is typically and properly read allegorically.²⁶ What is ignored is the political pressure behind Mailer's choice of the allegorical form.

Barbary Shore represents a very considerable shift from the prevalent naturalism of *The Naked and the Dead* (1948), a shift undertaken because of an impasse in Mailer's politics. During the late 1940s, under the informal tutorship of the Marxist philosopher Jean Malaquais (to whom *Barbary Shore* is dedicated), Mailer was reading and discussing 'politics and political economy'.²⁷ The enthusiasm was considerable: a letter of August 1949 has Mailer volunteering to post the three volumes of *Capital* to his friend Fig Gwaltney in Fayetteville, Arkansas.²⁸ But Marxism theory was at more than usual odds with American and Russian practices during the immediate postwar years. At home, peace brought intense labour unrest: in the year after V.J. Day, five million workers joined picket-lines, and by January 1946 the American economy stood close to standstill, with auto, steel, electrical and packing-house workers simultaneously on strike.²⁹ But activist excitement was misplaced: a combination of strike-breaking by Truman and an economic upturn produced a blue-collar rush into the commodity culture. Any American heir-apparent to the Marxist/Leninist tradition was left with the seemingly insurmountable problem of a missing radical agency. Certainly, by 1950, Russia offered no illumination: the onset of the Cold War merely affirmed what some radicals had suspected since the mid-1940s, that socialism had failed in the USSR, which, under Stalin, had been transformed into a nation state with global ambitions. Russia's explosion of a nuclear bomb in 1949 demonstrated her competitiveness. In 1948 Mailer worked for the Wallace campaign, enough to colour him 'red' in the eyes of Truman's liberal allies, but in 1949, at the Cultural and Scientific Conference for World Peace, in a speech in front of the liberal intellectual establishment, he declared that Russia and America exemplified different expressions of 'State Capitalism',³⁰ and that there was no health in either of them. In the same year he broke with Wallace, thereby severing his Marxist, liberal and progressive roots.

The critical argument that fills this political void with existentialism, ignores the fact that his seminal existential text, 'The White Negro', does not appear until 1957, and offers no account of the allegorical impulse behind *Barbary Shore*, save to say that it was an aesthetic mistake. Arguably, however, in 1949 Mailer is quite simply in political despair, and facing it without those liberal comforters, 'irony, paradox, ambiguity and complexity' (Bell).[31] He knows why his world is a fallen world, and, unlike the liberal, he has scant faith that compromise, consensus and Keynesian engineering can deliver an 'eternal affluence[32] whose forms may be vulgar but whose substance cannot, in the last instance, be challenged. Where the liberal may mistrust the materials of affluence, he accepts the social and economic structures that give rise to them, hence his need for the private solace of irony *et al*. Mailer reaches for allegory as the form commensurate with despair.

Reading America through Marx, he has Lovett and McLeod compose a structural account of the history of US capital:

> ... vast armies mount themselves, the world revolves, the traveller clutches his breast. From out the unyielding contradictions of labour stolen from men, the march to the endless war forces its pace ...
>
> But for the present the storm approaches its thunderhead, and it is apparent that the boat drifts ever closer to the shore. (p. 256)

To gloss the theoretical debate contained in Chapters 24 and 29, and summarized in Chapter 33: an economy which in the 1920s fulfilled the growth imperative through designer-Desire (the ubiquitous shop window dressed by the Corporate 'Captains of Consciousness' [33]), in the 1950s recovers growth through manufacture for destruction (the permanent arms economy directed by state capitalism). Production for war renders the Third World War a structural inevitability. Lovett's lyric summation is twice repeated, at the end of the first and last chapters, forming a grim caption to the novel, 'So the blind will lead the blind, and the deaf shout warnings to one another until their voices are lost' (pp. 13, 256). One may dispute the logic, but not the tone – despair is endemic. To take one prevalent metaphor, 'cannibalism', the bureaucracy of state capitalism, as a self-consuming class, produced to administer the flow of profit, sacrificed as the rate of profit falls, 'The first state of cannibalism has been reached' (p. 231). The metaphor is baroque, recording ruinous self-destruction in the body of the state, but it rests on sustained economic analysis. For McLeod, 'monopoly capitalism' has entered 'permanent crisis' (p. 231):

> The productive capacity of monopoly had become so tremendous, its investment in machinery so great in comparison to the labour force it could exploit, that only the opening of the entire world market could solve its search for investment and profit even temporarily. (p. 228)

In other words, investment in constant capital (machinery, buildings, etc.) with its slow yield, far outweighs the surplus that can be extracted from variable capital (the labour force). Monopolies that automate in order to reduce their labour bill, while increasing the output that labour must buy, are engaged in an 'unyielding contradiction': they require the workforce to consume more while depriving them of the means to purchase. More to the cannibalistic point – as capital goes global its incessant technological innovation renders previous 'technological breaks'[34] anachronistic: new machines break old machines, devaluing the capital fixed in them and releasing it in diminished form for future investment. New managerial patterns break old patterns of management, and whole orders of white-collar workers go to the wall for retooling or redundancy. Economists speak of 'creative destruction', Mailer prefers 'cannibalism'. His preference, 'vulgar', 'sententious', 'extravagant' and 'ornamental'[35] is a measure of his despair. He will not read the economy in readily available Keynesian terms, in the manner of Bell or Galbraith, nor can he take more than schematic sustenance from a Marxist tradition whose exemplum is so recently ruined. That is to say, meaning is imminent neither in materials nor in the canonical economic texts: meaning, in this instance the meaning of a moment in the history of a bureaucracy, must ostentatiously be imposed:

> ... in allegory the observer is confronted with the *facies hypocratica* of history as a petrified, primordial landscape. Everything about history that, from the very beginning, has been untimely, sorrowful, unsuccessful, is expressed in a face – or rather in a death's head. And although such a thing lacks all 'symbolic' freedom of expression ... all humanity – nevertheless this is the form in which man's subjection to nature [to nature's decisive category of time] is most obvious and it significantly gives rise not only to the enigmatic question of the nature of human existence as such, but also of the biographical historicity of the individual. This is the heart of the allegorical way of seeing, of the baroque, secular explanation of history as the Passion of the world; its importance resides solely in the stations of its decline. The greater the significance, the greater the subjection to death, because death digs most deeply the jagged line of demarcation between physical nature and significance. But if nature has always been subject to the power of death, it is also true that it has always been allegorical. Significance and death both come to fruition in historical development... (OGTD, p. 166)

I quote at length from Walter Benjamin's *The Origins of German Tragic Drama* (1924–25) because just as Benjamin's interest in the dramatic writings of the Thirty Years War and its aftermath may have granted him insight into Weimar misery,[36] so his model of allegory as *the* aesthetic of a world gone dead (because subject to historical process as destruction) complements Mailer's sense of terminally dark days.

As the narrative of a quasi-dead head, *Barbary Shore* and everything in it is 'subject to the power of death'. Lovett bears witness to a world in decline from a room resembling a long box: 'no more than eight feet wide', its 'blistered' paint and 'fallen' plaster (p. 15) provide apt housing for a mortified head in a boarding-house whose rooms incline to coffins; a co-lodger paints the entirety of her chamber (including the windows) black, and extinguishes the light. Lovett's studies persuade him that the national economy is pump-primed by and for Death, while his teacher (McLeod) confesses to a murderous agent of the surveillance state (Holingsworth) that he too has murdered, though in the name of Stalinist terror. Nor does Lannie, briefly Lovett's lover, release him from mortification: hers is the blackened room in which, driven mad by memories of Trotsky's broken head, she suffers visions of concentration camps. The list could be extended, though to no great point since my concern is less with the thematic, than with its place within Mailer's sense of history. Again Benjamin is helpful – to gloss his elision of 'death' and 'significance' is to point one source for Lovett's wound: death instils significance insofar as termination opens, within a life or a period, a gap which must be explained. Lovett's scar is that gap written into his flesh; through it his own history has seeped toward 'enigma'. Explanation, often a matter of exaggerated caption, strained exegesis and vulgar personification, builds a hermeneutic bridge between reference and significance. The allegorist, dealing with a fallen world, whose details are irrelevant (other than as carriers of death's mark), takes up a detail (often arbitrarily) and brings knowledge (often from elsewhere) to bear on it, so that the detail 'swells up from within' (*OGTD*, p. 183):

> If the object becomes allegorical under the gaze of melancholy, if melancholy causes life to flow out of it and it remains behind dead, but eternally secure, then it is exposed to the allegorist, it is unconditionally in his power. That is to say it is now quite incapable of emanating any meaning or significance of its own. He places it within it, and stands behind it; not in a psychological but in an ontological sense. In his hands the object becomes something different; through it he speaks of something different and for him it becomes a key to the realm of hidden knowledge ... This is what determines the character of allegory as a form of writing. It is a schema. (*OGTD*, pp. 183–4)

The aesthetic consequences of the allegorical gaze are several, all of them present in *Barbary Shore*. I have space only to ghost a list: 'any person, any object, any relationship can mean absolutely anything else' (*OGTD*, p. 175), so a middle-aged Brooklyn landlady is named Guinevere and as an ex-burlesque queen (p. 55) affects the purple (in velvet drapes): she is seduced by a female Lancelot (Lannie). The fact that her real name is Beverley (Hills) and that the knight's profile includes Madison (Avenue) arbitrarily and excessively appoints her the personification of consumer pleasure. Lannie offers herself as a mirror:

> ... we are born to love ourselves and that is the secret of everything. All your life you searched for a mirror to find your beauty, to see how your skin glows and your body swells in rapture ... Caressing, delicate her [Lannie's] voice must seek to create a spell. (p. 215)

Mailer assays a diagram of the erotics of desire in a commodity culture: in it an anorexic (Lannie) becomes a shop window, and a Trotskyite, doubling as a figure from Arthurian myth (Lannie), speaks with the voice of advertising copy, offering the consumer an improved version of herself, at which, 'if it had been possible [Guinevere] would have kissed herself upon her own throat' (p. 215). In order to establish autoeroticism as central to the moment of consumption, Mailer has Guinevere shadowed by an idealized double: her three-year-old daughter, Monina, is rendered pneumatic, and is said to have sprung in an immaculate conception from the material body which she perfects (pp. 61-2). It should be clear from this extended example that where anything be anything else, metaphor will be exuberant and formal tidiness will be minimal. Because the allegorist 'betrays and devalues' (*OGTD*, p. 185) his chosen object even as he reclaims it for his significance (witness Monina's body and Lannie's politics), it is almost inevitable that the work will appear staged, and be given to 'extended explanatory interludes' (*OGTD*, p. 192) as by dint of exegesis it consolidates its own rigidities (*OGTD*, p. 197).

My phrasing derives from Benjamin, but is aimed at Mailer. It has not escaped notice that *Barbary Shore* is organized around a number of 'explanatory' conversations featuring personifications who speak as though they had tracts in their mouths. Chief among these are the exchanges between Lovett and McLeod. McLeod's title is plain, 'Revolutionary Socialist', though as an American of the species, conceived circa 1950-1, he is an anthology of subtitles in transit to nowhere ('Bolshevik', 'Stalinist', 'Fellow Traveller', 'Underground Man', 'Corpse'). Lovett's caption is missing until the novel's close, but Benjamin notes, 'martyrdom prepares the body of the living for emblematic purposes' (*OGTD*, p. 217), in which case Lovett's 'unfertile' wound is allegorically fertile. Certainly, McLeod's will gives Lovett title as 'carrier of the remnants of a socialist culture' (p. 256). At his teacher's death, murdered by an agent of state capitalism, the pupil leaves the novel through a back window, a 'traveller' (p. 256) without fellows, whose role as vanguard theorist to a future revolution awaits only a revolutionary party and a revolutionary class. In the light of such an exit, McLeod's chosen caption may need revision.

My purpose is not to trace the ins and outs of Lovett's crash-course in the Marxist/Leninist tradition, but to fix the peculiar tone of that socialist education. Densely argued, Chapters 22 and 29 represent a structural account of an economy geared to war: McLeod attempts to extract from 'two thousand pages and ... other endless books' (p. 81) a scheme that can trace the determinants of postwar American development. His effort is monumental: he offers his listener a political plot that finally allows a fallen time filled with dead objects to be read. The effect on Lovett is striking: at the outset of the novel, 'no history belonged to me and so all history was mine' (p. 12) ... an uncomfortable position:

> Each time my mind furnished a memory long suppressed it was only another piece, and there were so few pieces and so much puzzle ... Prodigious efforts, but I recovered nothing except to learn that I had no past and was therefore without a future. (p. 12)

His wound renders him incapable not of memory but of narrative; his few recollections, lacking the crudest temporal relation (one thing after another) cannot be grasped together in the crudest of causal relations (one thing because of another). Conversation with McLeod throughout the novel releases some of the materials of Lovett's past; the political vocabulary used triggers his adolescent affiliation to 'a small organization dedicated to workers' revolution' (p. 108). More importantly, he regains a political icon which allows him to draw several events together in a miniature series whose implications are causal:

> ... the sight of a policeman on his mount became the Petrograd proletariat crawling to fame between the legs of a Cossack's horse, and a drunken soldier on a streetcar merged into the dream I was always providing of the same soldier on the breast of the revolution, shaking his fist in an officer's face as he cried, 'Equality'. (p. 109)

Glimpses of the instruments of state power (policeman and soldier) circa 1950, elide with images from the Russian Revolution. This much is obvious: however, since Lovett's 'small organization' follows Trotsky in believing that Russia's revolution 'would beget the others' (p. 109), the image anticipates American labour engaged in revolutionary unrest, such expectation only being possible because of a deep memory of actual blue-collar unrest on a grand scale (circa 1919-22 and 1945). So, past distends present and is further distended by a projected future which rises from the historically repressed knowledge of a radical blue-collar tradition. Through such an icon (care of McLeod) Lovett's experience of time thickens: for a moment he understands two or three or perhaps four events within a single perceptual act; the world is accordingly less dead and his body heals.[37] Nor is this a single instance; when Holingsworth and Lannie combine to expose McLeod, their sado-masochistic alliance is in part founded on Lannie's celebration of her abuser's earlier abuse of a Filipino, as cannon go 'rub dub a dub' (p. 132). Disturbed by this, Lovett recalls his own military service, and more particularly how he and his squad made use of a peasant woman:

> ... I made love from the hip and looked across the meadow with open eyes, for I was also on guard. I never saw the girl. Above my head in magnification of myself the barrel of the machine gun pointed toward the trees, and once, hearing a noise, my fingers stole up to the trigger handle, and I was surprised to find it cold. (p. 135)

The analogy is crude, until informed by McLeod's exposition on the body of labour within a militarized economy, at which point a seemingly casual reference to squad members as 'seven travelling salesmen' (p. 135) receives its logic. To one who believes that the US fought the Second World War for an open door through which to trade on a global scale, military agents are agents of American capital. The temporal network of the metaphor deepens as it is recognized that for McLeod (as for Mailer) the US solved its Depression by going to war, and subsequently substituted a cold war for a hot one, a Cold War that developed not from any real Communist threat, but because 'capitalism would never survive without an economy geared to war'.[38] So, the Second World War implies a Third, and Lovett's experience of time extends through three tenses. With duration comes prognostication: Lovett now knows what kind of war he was, is, and may yet be in.

Such images take their redemptive density from an implied narrative which interanimates personal and historical causality. The master plot informing redemption is McLeod's theoretical transcript (Chapters 22 and 29). To finish the novel is to learn that Lovett has chosen to be the carrier of the theory, and that *Barbary Shore* is itself a memoir produced some time after the theorist's death, 'So the heritage passed on to me, poor hope ... time passes, and I work and I study, and I keep my eye on the door' (p. 256). As Lovett's retrospective narrative, the novel becomes testimony to his lonely salvation within the shadow of a quasi-Marxist paradigm. Quite suddenly, it would appear that Mailer is engaged in a formal volte-face. A death's-head has assumed the countenance of an angel. Where before Lovett saw only 'stations of decline' in 'a realm of dead objects' (*OGTD*, p. 232), he now witnesses intimations of causality by means of which he has recomposed himself as an embodied agent who, having found a past among socialist 'remnants' (p. 256), can 'elect to have a future' (p. 250), albeit grim. Such reversals are latent in the allegorical form: a deep appreciation of the transience of things *can* be ghosted by a need to rescue those things for eternity, as Benjamin notes:

> Ultimately in the death-signs of the baroque the direction of allegorical reflection is reversed; on the second part of its wide arc it returns, to redeem ... Allegory, of course, thereby loses everything that was most peculiar to it: the secret, privileged knowledge ... the supposed infinity of a world without hope. All this vanishes with this *one* about-turn, in which the immersion of allegory ... rediscovers itself, not playfully in the earthly world of things, but seriously under the eyes of heaven. (*OGTD*, p. 232)

The 'heaven' in question, despite being secular and blackened by war and by war production, still holds traces of millennial purpose.[39] Lovett notes as he watches the door, 'perhaps, as the millions will be lost, others will be created, and I shall discover brothers where I thought none existed' (p. 256). From such a perspective, the socialist god has not failed: the very fact that 'the world ... moves forever faster' (p. 75) may yet give rise to as yet untheorized social forms capable of resisting 'the march to endless war' (p. 256). The role of the theorist, in such an eventuality, will be to 'discover brothers' and to direct their actions.

The availability of a redemptive reading rests on considerable inventiveness. Socialist life has to be found where there is next to none. Lovett may have gained his head, but *Barbary Shore* remains a prescient postmortem on the American Communist Party (officially extinct, 1956). By 1951 Truman's prosecution of eleven Party leaders, under the Smith Act, had reached appeal stage: all the defendants were found guilty of conspiracy to advocate forceable overthrow of the American system. In effect, Communism was declared illegal in the US, even as Mailer wrote. More to the point, the Party had not since the experiments of the popular front advocated anything of much relevance to the American working class: without hegemony on the left, and without a version of socialism pertinent to a consumption ethic, 'it staggered through the fifties somnambulantly, a ghost rattling phrases from the past.'[40] The intensification of the Cold War meant that all socialist organizations shrank or went underground. Consequently, in the context of his decade, Lovett has no one to whom he can communicate his text, nor has he access to a collective dissident agency (of class, colour or gender) whose actions might benefit from his knowledge. It would seem that he has regained his life only to play Jeremiah to a terminally sick god. Anticipating the history of the 1950s, Mailer can see only dead and dying things, be they the shadow of Trotsky's spoiled skull or Guinevere's commodified body. Among those objects *Barbary Shore* takes its place as an allegory born of a despair that it can only confirm.

Historiography and Redemption

When Warshow and Fiedler accuse the dead Rosenbergs of crimes against privacy, they repeat the violence of the state, proving beyond doubt, in Walter Benjamin's terms, that 'the dead are not safe' from the historians of the ruling class. Having already signed Fiedler up as a federal allegorist, I have little compunction in reading these essays as part of a larger official history. Central to each is the assumption that privacy is the absolute measure of authenticity. To spin the implicit hermeneutic circle of the Cold War years in a Westerly direction, is to move with speed from 'privacy' to 'individualism' to 'freedom' to 'political democracy' to 'consumer democracy', and so on to those measures and wars that ensure the free individual's right to consume. Depending on how far one wishes to go one may pursue the sequence to a suburban lawn or to Truman's financing of French military action in Vietnam. My point is not just that the celebration of privacy by liberal critics in 1953 is political, but that as such it is part of a much wider cultural narrative whose forms range from TV advertising to the demonology of the surveillance state, and whose very many expressions together constitute what Paul Ricoeur calls 'the prenarrative quality of experience',[41] that serves an '(as yet) untold story'[42] from which a culture's articulated narratives and preferred subjects perforce arise: 'Without leaving everyday experience, are we not inclined to see in a given sequence of the episodes of our lives "(as yet) untold stories", stories that demand to be told, stories that offer anchorage points for narrative?'[43]

Ricoeur's 'inchoate narrativity'[44] is the stuff of the glimpsed headline or the window shopper's gaze, yet for all its latency it tightens, during abject times, into an instrumental historiography within which narrative options narrow dramatically.

Walter Benjamin's 'Theses on the Philosophy of History' illuminates the problem: he argues that historiography is politically instrumental and, as a developed art, rests in the hands of the victors: consequently, to believe the past as given is both to naturalize an interpretation, and to accord with those who have told that particular story in order to keep a world that serves their interests. To move back to Ricoeur, it is possible to argue that the idea of an experiential 'prenarrative' is simply the fossilized or sedimented expression of a pervasive historiography (culture's more or less absolute official stories: titles for the 1950s might include 'Cold War', 'Great Barbecue' and 'American High'). For Benjamin, it follows that the memory of the victim or the endangered person, marginalized and persecuted by a state plot, is the source of images from which may arise an alternative history.

In 1951 Mailer captioned America 'Barbary' because he could find no historiography for redemption. McLeod's theory allows Lovett to recover limited personal memory, insofar as that memory exists causally within a public history of protest and war, but because that history cannot become a ground for collective action, it remains the stuff of private memoir, and so for Mailer, a prompt to further despair.

Narrative, History and the Rosenbergs

In 1967 the narrator of Doctorow's *Book of Daniel* (1971) considers himself a man in danger. His own life seems inextricable from that of his sister: as the children of the Isaacsons (nés Rosenbergs), their childhood during the 1950s has forced them into an absolute dependency:

> All I can say about your voice is that it is so familiar to me that I cannot perceive the world except with your voice framing the edge of my vision. It is on the horizon and under my feet. The world has always been washed in Susan's voice. It breaks where her voice breaks ... It is the feminine voice that passes solidly through ontological mirrors. It lies at the heart of the matter, the nub of the thing, the core of the problem, in the centre, on the bulls-eye, smack in the middle. (pp. 214-15)

His sister cut her wrist on the day before Memorial Day: in December of the same year she kills herself. The two events bracket the novel, which for all its temporal experimentation remains firmly sequential in the matter of Susan's long death: Daniel's Memorial Day visit to his sister in Worcester State mental hospital begins the book, which all but closes on his account of her funeral. Susan's voice is 'the core of the problem' because he senses that her death may stem from her judgement that he 'murdered' their parents again (p. 84). Shortly before her first suicide attempt, she writes to him:

> You think they are guilty. It's enough to take someone's life away.
> Someday, Daniel, following your pathetic demons, you are going to disappear up your own asshole. To cover the time till then, I'm writing you out of my mind. You no longer exist. (p. 79)

Treating the letter as part of the available historical record, Daniel, a graduate student in history, engages in 'annotation' (p. 79). He discerns a lacuna between the penultimate and ultimate sentences: 'writing', rather then 'written', suggests the offer of a brief probation, during which Daniel may save himself ('Because he is not yet beyond redemption?' (p. 84)). The offer is only apparently foreclosed by the final statement, since, in cases of interdependency, the purging of one may well be the destruction of the other. Daniel's annotation concludes, 'there is some evidence that she was finally driven to eradicate him from her consciousness by the radical means of eradicating her consciousness' (p. 84). Susan's death does not destroy Daniel's 'voice' only because, from the moment that his sister put them both at risk, he has been engaged in constructing a narrative that may save her. In effect, he becomes an historian of the Isaacsons, concerned primarily not with 'the way it really was', but with a story that will recover the dead and the soon-to-be-dead from the various official histories of 'the ruling classes'.

His problem is that he needs a story that will prove his parents neither guilty nor innocent: for Daniel Isaacson to find the Isaacsons guilty, would be for the son to kill the daughter, while a verdict of 'innocent' simply renders the parents inconsequential – Daniel imagines his father concluding on the eve of the trial, 'If he [the radical] is found innocent it is the ruling power's decision that he need not be feared' (p. 190). Before tracing how Daniel solves the problem, let me gloss how he experiences the cultural 'prenarrative' of the period (1945–67), since it is that which anchors his eventual historiography. These are abject times: citizens of postwar America are entangled in certain 'inchoate' stories whose aim is not illumination but obscurity. Daniel feels this acutely, in that as an Isaacson he knows himself to be under state surveillance; nor should this be dismissed as paranoia – one of the problems of the term 'McCarthyism' is that it foreshortens America's anti-radical tradition: the politics of loyalty precede both the Cold War and McCarthy, while national security agencies continued greatly to extend their activities under Eisenhower, Kennedy and Johnson.[45] Given that the 1960s proved one of the most turbulent decades of the century, during which state surveillance sought to suggest 'that there is an F.B.I. man behind every mailbox',[46] Daniel is being realistic when he assumes that he is on file. That file is the state's version of his history, and it effectively neutralizes him as an agent of dissent, since should he burn his draft-card or murder the president, his action would merely reaffirm the 'genetic criminality' of his family (p. 74). Further, Daniel recognizes that his being 'totally deprived of the right to be dangerous' (p. 74) is simply a secret example of a more general, though equally secret, incapacitation. As a student of the Cold War, he shares McLeod's structural conviction that the US economy is orientated to a 'militarized ... world' (p. 228) and so to death. Where citizens are implicitly or explicitly 'soldiers', drafted to keep the open door of American trade open to Greece, to Nicaragua, to Vietnam (pp. 241–3), it follows that the state shall necessarily treat the body of the citizen as an extension of its military will. 'All citizens are soldiers. All governments stand ready to commit their citizens to death in the interest of their government' (p. 75). I am guilty of eliding three sub-genres at work in the text, 'A Dictionary of Corporal Punishment', 'A True History of the Cold War' and an essay on popular culture, 'Disneyland at Christmas'. I do so to make a point much brooded over by Daniel, that American war-preparedness curtails individual freedom to a degree synonymous with imprisonment. Pervasive persecution remains unnoticed because it takes the disguised form of consumerism. To enter Disneyland is to submit to 'a radical reduction ... to the nature of historical experience' (p. 295). One ride must make the point: those who travel in the Mad Hatter's Teacup will not have read the book *Alice in Wonderland*, instead they will know Alice through Disney's film, 'if at all' (p. 294), which suggests 'a separation of two ontological degrees' between the Disneyland customer and the ride that she 'treasure[s]' (p. 292). In the place of *Alice* the rider receives 'a sentimental compression' of what is already a 'lie' (p. 295).

The reading of the Teacup may be used more generally as the basis for a critique of the nation's commodity aesthetic, given that for Doctorow the Disney organization has 'pre-emptive powers ... with regard to Western culture' (p. 293). The amusement park is 'womb' shaped, its 'birth canal' formed by 'Main Street', a romantic rendition of 'small-town living at the turn of the century' (p. 292). Doctorow crosses the gynaecological, the historical and the economic to clear purpose. The park features shows and exhibits by a wide range of corporations and a list is included (p. 295): within such a structure, organized by and for Exchange, the child in the Teacup is reborn, possessed of 'a sensuality that is the vehicle of an economic function'.[47] At the moment of purchase, she and her parents make several choices, they choose a 'lie' that appears simply to have perfected an unread original; the perfect lie of the commodity has been described by Jean Baudrillard as central to a consumer culture, which 'liquidate[s] ... all referentials' in order 'to substitute signs of the real for the real itself'.[48] The motive is simple: signs are almost infinitely ductile, and therefore lend themselves to corporations in need of surplus value. Revised signs will generally present an unproblematic past, minus ethnicity and poverty. Certainly, Daniel notes few Mexicans, blacks or hippies among the customers, though he does observe many adults unaccompanied by small children. In a conceptual world where 'the real' may be constructed and torn down whenever the price is right, the child's memory is subject to constant revision. However, it should be recognized that the 'lie' is chosen only because the ride is desired, the rider's body is therefore infiltrated by corporate impulses to which she contributes.

The person in the Teacup bears comparison with Lovett at the start of *Barbary Shore*; both are obscurely wounded in memory and body. Daniel specifies the hurtful agency as 'electricity', describing the frisson of purchase as 'a mindless thrill, like an electric shock' (p. 295). Indeed, General Electric are high on the park's corporate list since all rides are powered by its products. The logic of the essay implies that Corporate Capital tortures the consumer's body, in order to ensure a money flow. For Daniel, more generally, electricity is everywhere, and everywhere a double synonym, standing for that which killed his parents, and that which fuels his culture's growth economy – hence his gnomic gloss, 'The electric chair as methodology of capitalist economics' (p. 33). At one point he goes so far as to root epistemology in electrical discharge; in answer to his own tacit question, 'I wish I knew how education works' (p. 174), he posits an image of the brain as circuitry in which 'small secret chemical switches' are thrown, and 'tiny courses' hang from 'passages of the tissue' (p. 174). In the later Disney piece he will imply that human gynaecology as well as neurology is patterned by the theme park: Disney offers 'culture for the masses', administered electrically, which provides 'a substitute for education' (p. 295). Daniel has answered his own question. In knowing how education works, he knows how the various and dominant prenarratives, within whose tangle he has been trained (Surveillance, Preparedness and Commodity), so structure consciousness that the radical impulse, even where it occurs, can do little more than illustrate state forms, thrown into sudden visibility by the subversive act. Hence, when Daniel 'does' (p. 302) the electrocution (three pages after the completion of the Disney essay), he presents the last 'shuddering spasming movement of his father's life' as 'a portrait of electric current, normally invisible, moving through a field of resistance' (p. 304).

Susan, less aware of the social circuitry (Daniel *does* conclude that 'She died of a failure of analysis' (p. 307)), insists that radical behaviour can be a foundation rather than a conduit. The Christmas before her suicide attempt she proposes to Daniel that they combine their inheritance – the monies of the left, contributed for the children in 1953 – to create 'The Foundation of Revolution' (p. 158). Daniel is sceptical, and on the basis, in part, of that Christmas, Susan cancels him out and threatens her own life. Daniel responds by checking the particular left-wing activist to whom Susan had gone with her suggestion (Abe Sternlicht). He learns that Susan was, in fact, on her way to Sternlicht's when she stopped in a Howard Johnson's to cut her wrist. The unmade second visit was to deliver a political poster of the Isaacsons, for use in a collage made by Sternlicht's partner: the collage is entitled 'Everything that Came Before is All the Same' (p. 141). Consisting of layers of 'pictures, movie stills, posters and real objects' (p. 140), it proposes that the history of the present (or perhaps any history) cannot be written: all that can be offered is an anthology of images lost for causation. Since Susan's plan was to establish her parents' continuity within a left-wing tradition, the collage violates her intention. Indeed, read through the Disneyland piece, were the poster to have reached the wall, the Isaacson's, like Alice according to the Teacup ride, would have suffered 'a reduction' of 'historical content', becoming one sign among many, their presence depending solely upon a capacity to shock. This point is affirmed by the fact than when Daniel first sees the wall it is being photographed for *Cosmopolitan*. On this evidence, the radicalism of the New Left turns into radical chic, even as Daniel watches. Sternlicht intends to use the media, believing that in a culture where 'the commercials are today's school', only the creator of spectacle can break 'the momentum ... of Authority' (pp. 144–5). Hence his plan to levitate the Pentagon (p. 145), and his judgement that the Isaacsons 'didn't know shit' (p. 156); had the Old Left been the New Left, they would have turned the court into theatre, 'overthrow[ing] the United States with images' (p. 146). They would still be dead, but having made the forty-second slot (p. 145).

Daniel's interview with Sternlicht causes him to reappraise Susan's suicide attempt. She too had seen the wall and heard the New Left's version of her parents' death; consequently Daniel reinflects his reading of Susan's brief words to him in the mental hospital:

> *They're still fucking us.* She didn't mean Paul and Rochelle. That's what I would have meant. What she meant was first everyone else and now the Left. The Isaacson's are nothing to the New Left. And if they can't make it with them who else is there? *You get the picture. Goodbye Daniel.* (p. 159)

Arguably, her instruction regarding the picture shifts Daniel beyond victimized autobiography: he must find a just image for his parents by making them part of a more general historiography of the left, within which the deaths will be purposive. If this can be achieved, maybe Susan will live, maybe 'the dead will ... be safe', maybe Daniel's desperate suspicion that his sister's last words to him were 'Good boy' (pp. 9, 16) will be affirmed. To return to Benjamin's terms ... in 'a moment of danger' Daniel 'seizes hold' of spontaneous memory, and struggles to order a phenomenologically dense surge of images into a redemptive plot. He fails, but after Susan's death Daniel reconsiders the months of her incarceration, the deterioration of her condition, and his own actions in her defence. The entire novel is an account of his troubled historiographic effort. What he comes up with is the narrative of the 'other couple'.

The solution runs as follows: if the Isaacsons are guilty, the state is proved correct, and Susan dies. If they are innocent, their deaths lack point, and Susan dies (since her intention with the Foundation was to establish a continuity for their political purpose). Daniel produces a hybrid: he finds his father guilty, but not as accused, and his mother innocent. His materials, at least in their initial form, are memories surprised by danger: 'I have put down everything I can remember of their actions and conversations in this period prior to their arrests ... I find no clues either to their guilt or innocence' (p. 134).

On the basis of this fragmented mental transcript he can dispense with the available histories, and with 'the six books written about the trial' (p. 233); the state has no case, but nor do liberals like his stepfather who wish to reverse the verdict on formal grounds. Robert Lewin's liberal case is that the main prosecution witness was subject to improper pressure: Selig Mindish, Party member and neighbour to the Isaacsons, was persuaded by the FBI to testify to his own and to his friends' subversive activity. The state's weapon against him was his doubtful citizenship which, allied to poor English and ignorance, may have persuaded him either 'to believe in his own guilt ... [or] to believe in the guilt of his friends' (p. 232). Lewin's version rests on proving the accused innocent by establishing the innocence of an accuser who has acknowledged his own guilt. For all its ingenuity it posits an abuse of the system rather than an abusive system. Daniel comments, 'I am beginning to be intolerant of reformers': 'Reform is complicity. It is complicity in the system to be appalled with the moral structure of the system' (p. 233).

I take his emphasis to lie on the word 'moral'.[49] His stepfather, like so many liberal intellectuals during the 1950s, is unwilling or unable to undertake a structural critique of the system. Daniel remains unpersuaded because he needs a story that will at least attempt to break the wall constructed by the system's narratives and by available versions of the couple. On the basis of Susan's need and his own 'clueless' memory he is forced to reach the awkward conclusion, 'Perhaps they are neither guilty nor innocent' (p. 134).

Substantiation involves him in grasping particular memories together. Faced with 'a failure to make connections' (p. 233), he must make new connections involving two glances, a 'big shot' and a rumour. Let me specify: the first glance is exchanged between Mindish and Paul Isaacson, and occurs when a bus in which they are travelling is attacked: their mistake is to have attended a Paul Robeson concert. Isaacson removes his glasses, hands them to Mindish and attempts to open the bus doors in order to remonstrate with a law officer who is standing watching the proceedings. His protruding arm is subsequently broken:

How did I know this? If I was crouched behind a seat, how do I remember this? Calmly, with his right hand, my father removes his glasses, folds them against his chest and hands them up to Mindish. The deliberateness of this act terrifies me. I see something I don't recognize, something I never knew with my child's confidence in my perception of my parents. I am stunned. (p. 52)

In the courtroom, as Mindish is about 'to say the words that will put them in their graves', Rochelle reads in his gaze, 'the message not of a betrayer': in his look she discovers 'the private faith of a comrade, one to another, accomplices in self sacrifice' (p. 287). She is 'stunned', since she is not a party to the 'shared knowledge'. Turning to look at her husband, she meets closed eyes. Mortally threatened by this network of gazes, Rochelle experiences an involuntary recollection in the form of an image from a Communist Party summer camp at Paine Lodge: Mindish, Paul and Rochelle, their hands joined 'in intricate devolving patterns ... dazzling the brothers with a folk dance of infinite beauty, of eternal grace' (p. 287). The memory of the dance is made 'historical' even as it is given significance by the moment in court: each seems incomplete without the other. For Rochelle the 'connections' involve the recognition that she has been betrayed by her husband, whose idealism, rooted in 'the sad determination ... [of] the comrade's life ... one to another' (p. 287), requires that they be found guilty, for 'something ... [he] already knew in himself and for himself' (p. 287). But what? Of course Daniel was not in the court, yet this should not make the second gaze in any easy sense 'fictional': rather, the look is forced from him by the deeply underarticulated image of a moment when his father, sustained by Mindish, was prepared to put his son, his wife and a bus load of companions at grave risk for an idea.[50] The courtroom gaze articulates the earlier gaze, and both came into focus through Susan's condition.[51]

Daniel is left with the problem of purpose: he needs the 'big shot' and the rumour. The former attends the 'shivah' for Rochelle's mother: Daniel's memory of the unnamed figure, who 'talked the way his father talked, but ... was no friend of his father's' (p. 91), is placed directly at the conclusion of his annotation of his sister's pre-suicide note. Nothing separates Susan's threat to herself and Daniel's 'involuntary' memory of an authoritative figure who dominated a party for his dead grandmother, because the former can only be annulled by a saving 'connection'. However, the image is provisional without the rumour of the 'other couple'; Daniel remembers talk among the Bronx membership of a married couple who went underground 'into espionage work' (p. 283). So, the sequence is completed, and the 'something' seen by Rochelle in her husband's refusal of her gaze materializes. Paul Isaacson betrayed his wife in order to protect, by means of Mindish's testimony, another couple – a couple whose existence, for Daniel, is much more than rumour or theory, since he remembers that he saw the 'big shot' who could prove his father guilty (but not in the prosecution's sense) and his mother innocent (but not ineffectually so).[52] Each memory is partial without the others, since each gives to the others vehement persuasive power, even as it takes from the others its own dense historicity.

I am very aware that Daniel's redemptive narrative is open to a charge levelled at historians who acknowledge the instrumentality of the history that they make; Hayden White expresses the charge succinctly:

> It is often alleged ... that those who hold that any historical object can sustain a number of equally plausible descriptions or narratives of its process, effectively deny the reality of the referent, [and] promote a debilitating relativism that permits any manipulation of the evidence as long as the account produced is structurally coherent.[53]

Doctorow approaches this problem in his essay 'False Documents' (1977), which might be read as a fascinatingly aphoristic postscript to *The Book of Daniel*: at times he drifts dangerously close to a less than problematic elision of 'fact' and 'fiction': 'I am thus led to the proposition that there is no fiction or non fiction as we commonly understand the distinction: there is only narrative.'[54]

From such a perspective, since all facts are made from narratives, and 'the available data for the composition' of those narratives 'is greater and more various in its sources than the historian supposes',[55] it would follow that no fact is 'true', and that any fact is simply more or less comprehensive. Elsewhere in the essay Doctorow moves closer to his character's urgency:

> ... we gave it in us to compose false documents more valid, more real, more truthful than the 'true' documents of the politicians or the journalists or the psychologists. Novelists know explicitly that the world that we live in is still to be formed.[56]

Close, but not close enough, since the switching of 'true' and 'false' cannot disguise a hiatus in the argument: the essay lacks an account of what gives 'truthfulness' to the 'truth' of the 'true' historian, or to that of the 'true' novelist whose concern is history.

Daniel does not need 'fiction', nor does he need Doctorow's compelling 'false document'; the imminence of his sister's death, the length and pain of his search for evidence, suggest how much his narrative has finally to ground itself on 'what happened'. His 'theory of the other couple' (p. 284) takes him on a trip to California to confront Mindish; he sees a senile man riding in Disney's 'Tomorrowland': from him he receives one moment of recognition during which Mindish is 'restored to life' (p. 299). The accuser/accomplice touches Daniel's forehead with his lips in what could mistakenly be read as a Judas-kiss. However, given Daniel's memories and their sequences, the kiss is that of a companion: if it were not, how would we explain Mindish's temporary redemption? Daniel restores Mindish by allowing him to acknowledge, albeit mutely, the existence of a radical purpose beyond the circuitry of state capitalism.[57] Funded by Susan's 'Foundation', Daniel discovers his own foundation; threatened, he suffers spontaneous memories whose images force new connections from him, out of which he forms a story that was 'lost for history',[58] but which now, in 1967, speaks for the single remaining agent, Mindish – he who helped to make it 'the way it really was'.

Perhaps the leap from an openly political and instrumental account of the past to the 'truth' about the past can only be made via the historiographer's conviction that his informing vision is true to the general circumstances of his subject. That truth can be measured by how far the narrative of the radical historian articulates the silence of the dead victim: that silence must exist because extant official histories (from right or left) have effectively served the status quo (right), or have modified the balance of forces within the state (left). Given that the state still stands (better or worse for its historical memories), the silence of those who suffer or suffered remains the true historical resource. It follows that radical historiography will not simply 'fit' when put in place, rather it will be forced from lacunae imposed upon the subject by extant accounts. What results may not be 'true' to 'the way it really was', but it will be 'truer' than what has previously passed for history. I am aware of an unfortunate hint of triumphalism here; of course some status quos are better than others, of course some histories discover memories that force a change of circumstance – but I am trying only to fix Daniel's urge to a 'truth' more scrupulous than necessary lie.

Benjamin negotiates the relativist impasse via a network of assumptions: he believes that the evidence of the endangered man, where it takes the form of involuntary memory, cannot be impeached. To this phenomenological security he adds the conviction, born of an idiosyncratic Marxism, that the victim has the privileged view: to the victor goes the official history, to victim goes prostration – a painful perspective, but one demanding utter scepticism as to given reality. Such scepticism, as it occurs endemically in Benjamin's work, avoids cynicism and fends off despair by means of a metaphysical hope rooted in Messianism; for those situated within a Judaic tradition, any moment may prove to be 'the strait gate through which the Messiah might enter'[59] – these are the last words of 'The Theses on History'.

Doctorow, too, ends his work with an oblique appeal to Messianism. Having taken an epigraph from *Daniel* Chapter 3, Verse 4, he closes his book in the manner of his biblical precursor:

> *and there shall be a time of trouble such as never was since there was a nation ... and at that time the people shall be delivered, everyone that shall be found written in the book. And many of them that sleep in the dust of the earth shall awake, some to everlasting contempt. And they that be wise shall shine as the brightness of the firmament, and they that turn many to righteousness, as the stars for ever and ever. But thou, O Daniel, shut up the words and seal the book, even to the time of the end ... Go thy way Daniel: for the words are closed up and sealed till the time of the end.* (p. 309)

From a Christian perspective the passage reads apocalyptically, due warnings of the end are oddly appealing to a traditional that dwells on the last days in their darkness, rather than on the ensuing light. Daniel is not of that persuasion; his Jewish heritage, rooted in the memory of an increasingly mad grandmother, may be fragmented and secularized, but it is present – witness his brief commentary on his post-Alexandrine counterpart (pp. 10–12), and his hiring of old Jews to say 'the prayers the younger Jews don't know' at Susan's funeral (p. 308). Since Daniel Isaacson takes his sense of an ending from the first *Book of Daniel*, thereby playing with ideas of 'first' and 'last', and with the fulfilment of the first by the second, it is necessary to read his concluding instruction remembering that he is a Jew – to do so is to notice hope. From a Judaic perspective, the time of the end is also, and most interestingly, the time of revealed truth, and it may be now. I have neither the space nor the skill to trace the effect on Daniel of a residually Jewish sense of time. I allude to it, as I allude to the parallels between Daniel's and Benjamin's historical practices, in order to focus Doctorow's insistence, at least in this novel, that the true historian is he who tells a radical truth in barbarous times.

I find that I have situated Mailer and Doctorow within a shared problematic, one born perhaps of an intersection between their historical period (the Cold War) and their obliquely shared, obliquely Jewish and obliquely socialist traditions. Both appear to believe that historically truthful and politically useful stories can be told, but both also sense that unless those stories are used they will die. The Cold War curtails faith in radical agency, and leaves these novelists close to despair, in an impasse at once historical and fictional. Without proper use their writings – like the writings of their theorist and their historian – cannot hope to reduce the persecution from which they take their respective forms. I am again reminded of Benjamin's 'Theses on the Philosophy of History':

> ... every image of the past that is not recognized by the present as one of its own concerns threatens to disappear irretrievably. (The good tidings which the historian of the past brings with throbbing heart may be lost in a void the very moment he opens his mouth.) [60]

Notes

1. Walter Benjamin, 'Theses on the Philosophy of History', collected in his *Illuminations* (London: Fontana, 1977), p. 257.
2. Robert Warshow, 'The "Idealism" of Julius and Ethel Rosenberg', collected in his *The Immediate Experience* (New York: Doubleday, 1962), pp. 76–7.
3. Leslie Fiedler, 'Afterthoughts on the Rosenbergs', in *The Collected Essays of Leslie Fiedler, Vol. 1* (New York: Stein and Day, 1971), pp. 38, 45.
4. Richard H. Pells, *The Liberal Mind in a Conservative Age* (Middletown, Connecticut: Wesleyan University Press, 1989), p. 190.
5. Paul Buhle, *Marxism in the USA* (London: Verso, 1987), p. 213.
6. Daniel Bell, *The End of Ideology* (New York: Free Press, 1965), pp. 402–4.
7. Daniel Boorstein, 'Our Unspoken National Faith', *Commentary*, XV (April 1953), pp. 327–9, 333.
8. Lionel Trilling, *The Liberal Imagination* (New York: Doubleday, 1953), pp. 212–15.
9. David Caute, *The Great Fear: The Anti-Communist Purge Under Truman and Eisenhower* (London: Secker and Warburg, 1978), p. 281.
10. In 1953, 185 of the 221 Republican Congressmen asked to serve on HUAC, since it was the place where a political reputation might be made. See Richard M. Fried, *Nightmare in Red* (New York: Oxford University Press, 1990), particularly pp. 144–70.
11. My phrase derives from William L. O'Neill's title, *American High: The Years of Confidence, 1945–1960* (New York: Free Press, 1986).
12. Fiedler, *The Collected Essays of Leslie Fiedler, Vol. 1*, pp. 44–5.
13. Talcott Parsons, 'Social Strains in America', collected in Daniel Bell (ed.), *The Radical Right* (New York: Doubleday, 1964), p. 217.
14. Daniel Bell, 'The Dispossessed', in *ibid.*, pp. 1–45.
15. Talcott Parsons, 'Social Strains in America', p. 223.

16. Richard Hofstadter, *The Paranoid Style in American Politics* (New York: Knopf, 1966), pp. 52–8.

17. The phrasing is Hofstadter's. See Michael Rogin, *Ronald Reagan, The Movie: And Other Episodes in Political Demonology* (Berkeley: University of California Press, 1987), particularly 'Political Repression in the United States', pp. 44–80, and 'Political Demonology: A Retrospective', pp. 272–300.

18. Rogin, 'Political Demonology', pp. 279–80, 284.

19. *Ibid.*, p. 284.

20. Quoted in Rogin, *ibid.*, p. 239.

21. See Richard Fried, *Nightmare in Red*, pp. 87–8, and Richard H. Pells, *The Liberal Mind in a Conservative Age*, p. 263.

22. E.L. Doctorow, *The Book of Daniel* (London: Pan, 1982), pp. 134–5. Subsequent references will be to this edition and will be included in the body of the text. It should be remembered that at its peak the loyalty programme applied to 13.5 million workers in government and 'sensitive' industries – that is, up to 20 per cent of the nation's workforce.

23. Norman Mailer, *Barbary Shore* (St Albans: Panther, 1971), p. 11. Subsequent references will be to this edition and will be included in the body of the text.

24. The term 'Fordism' has been widely applied to that regime of capital where centralized and hierarchic structures are developed to manage not only production but also purchase. During the 1920s the social imperatives emerging from intensified accumulation were a new problem, a matter for market leaders ('partial Fordism'). By the 1940s, and more particularly after the Second World War, issues of labour rationalization, management hierarchy, broadening sales and the control of desire affected the market as a whole ('full Fordism').

25. Norman Mailer, *Advertisements for Myself* (London: Panther, 1972), p. 351.

26. Representative allegorical accounts are Jean Radford, *Norman Mailer* (New York: Barnes and Noble, 1975), pp. 50–4; Stanley Gutman, *Mankind in Barbary* (Hanover, New Hampshire: University Press of New England, 1975), pp. 29–43; Barry Leeds, *The Structured Vision of Norman Mailer* (New York: New York University Press, 1969), pp. 53–103, and Robert Begiebing, *Acts of Regeneration* (Columbia: University of Missouri Press, 1980), pp. 13–32. Begiebing is unusual in that he roots the allegorical in Jungian archetypes.

27. Peter Manso, *Mailer: His Life and Times* (Harmondsworth: Penguin, 1986), p. 113.

28. *Ibid.*, p. 137.
29. See Mike Davis, *Prisoners of the American Dream* (London: Verso, 1986), pp. 85–93.
30. Peter Manso, *Mailer: His Life and Times*, p. 135.
31. Daniel Bell, *The End of Ideology*, p. 300.
32. Richard Pells, *The Liberal Mind in a Conservative Age*, p. 146.
33. The phrase is taken from Stewart Ewen's *Captains of Consciousness: Advertising and the Social Roots of the Consumer Culture* (New York: McGraw-Hill, 1976).
34. David Harvey, *The Limits of Capital* (Oxford: Blackwell, 1982), p. 123.
35. My terms derive from Walter Benjamin, *The Origin of German Tragic Drama* (London: New Left Books, 1977), pp. 184, 187, 191, 192. Subsequent references will be to this edition and will be included in the body of the text. *The Origins of German Tragic Drama* will be abbreviated to (*OGTD*).
36. George Steiner, 'Introduction', *The Origin of German Tragic Drama*, p. 24.
37. My account of the experience of time derives from Paul Ricoeur, *Time and Narrative*, Vol. 1 (Chicago: University of Chicago Press, 1984), pp. 3–30.
38. Norman Mailer, *Cannibals and Christians* (London: André Deutsch, 1967), p. 42.
39. Millennial purpose may be more traceable from within a Judaic account of time. While I would not argue, as I shall for Doctorow's Daniel, that Mailer works consciously from within a Messianic tradition, I would however suggest that his apocalyptic habit of mind has been too readily Christianized. For the Jewish tradition, Messianism ensures that dark days may be 'shot through with chips of Messianic time'; as Benjamin notes, 'the Messiah comes not only as the redeemer, he comes as the subduer of Antichrist' ('Theses on the Philosophy of History', *Illuminations*, p. 257).
40. Paul Buhle, *Marxism in the USA*.
41. Paul Ricoeur, *Time and Narrative*, Vol. 1, p. 74.
42. *Ibid.*
43. *Ibid.*
44. *Ibid.*
45. See Michael Rogin, *Ronald Reagan, The Movie*, pp. 44–80.

46. Quoted, *ibid.*, p. 77.
47. W.F. Haug, *Critique of Commodity Aesthetics* (Oxford: Polity Press, 1986), p. 17.
48. Jean Baudrillard, *Simulations* (New York: Semiotext, 1983), p. 4.
49. Lewin's case 'fits', but for Daniel it fails to be historically persuasive because 'lack[ing] in a knowledge of the old left. The life of embattled Communist Party members in those days. That is what is missing from his analysis' (p. 283). What is missing, as with the New Left's account, is the historical sense.
50. Later, as Daniel recalls FBI surveillance of the house prior to Paul's arrest, he returns to the bus incident. Feeling excluded by Rochelle's attentiveness to his injured father, he observes: 'OH PAULY, OH MY POP, IT'S ALL RIGHT, IT REALLY IS ALL RIGHT. BUT WHY DID YOU HAVE TO GIVE YOUR GLASSES TO MINDISH?' (p. 114). I find neither the statement nor its capitalization comprehensible outside the causal series that I am attempting to trace.
51. My account of how Daniel's memory works owes much to Erich Auerbach, 'Figura', collected in his *Scenes from the Drama of European Literature* (Manchester: Manchester University Press, 1984), pp. 12–98.
52. I am aware that I have skirted the Oedipal question; Daniel's 'other couple' narrative makes Paul the murderer of Rochelle, and allows Daniel to replace his father as the only protector of his mother. Space limits development of the issue, though I would stress that as Deleuze and Guattari have pointed out the Oedipal father is also invariably 'the soldier, the cop, the occupier'. That is to say, he breaks from triangulation. Equally, the triangulated mother may skip the 'Oedipal dragnet' to be the daughter of the blue-collar immigrant workers. I would read Daniel's setting of his parents at eventual odds as his exploration of the tension between vanguard party and proletarian class. See Giles Deleuze and Felix Guattari, *Anti-Oedipus: Capitalism and Schizophrenia* (New York: Viking, 1977), pp. 97, 81.
53. Hayden White, *The Content of the Form* (Baltimore: Johns Hopkins University Press, 1987), p. 76.
54. E.L. Doctorow, 'False Documents', collected in Richard N. Trenner (ed.), *E.L. Doctorow: Essays and Conversations* (Princeton: Ontario Review, 1983), p. 26. In the course of the piece Doctorow acknowledges Benjamin's 'brilliant essay' 'The Story Teller' (p. 18). In the light of this allusion it seems more than likely that Doctorow also knows Benjamin's 'Theses on the Philosophy of History'.
55. *Ibid.*, p. 25.

56. *Ibid.*, p. 26.

57. For an essentially non-political discussion of Doctorow's uses of 'electricity' in the novel, see Geoffrey Gall Harpham's important essay, 'E.L. Doctorow and the Technology of Narrative', *PMLA*, Vol. 100, No. 1, January 1985, pp. 81–95.

58. Walter Benjamin, 'Theses on the Philosophy of History', *Illuminations*, p. 256.

59. *Ibid.*, p. 266.

60. *Ibid.*, p. 257.

3. 1968: The Two Cultures*

Todd Gitlin

There were two different popular cultures in 1968. During the year running from September 1967 through to August 1968, the following events took place in the United States: the Stop the Draft Week demonstrations at the US Army induction centre in Oakland, where several thousand people clogged the streets, fought back against 2000 police officers and spray-painted 'Che is alive and well' on the sidewalks; the Pentagon demonstration, where thousands of demonstrators broke off from the sedate march of tens of thousands and sat down in front of the Pentagon facing fixed bayonets, staying there all night, urging troops to change sides; Senator Eugene McCarthy's campaign for the Democratic presidential nomination; Senator Robert Kennedy's campaign for the nomination; the barely noticed killing of three black students and wounding of 33 others for trying to enter a segregated bowling alley in Orangeburg, South Carolina, four years after the Civil Rights Act had banned segregation; the Tet offensive of NLF and North Vietnamese troops all over South Vietnam; LBJ's decision not to run for president; the assassination of Martin Luther King; the assassination of Robert Kennedy; the riots or uprisings in a hundred black ghettos on the occasion of King's assassination; the demonstrations and police offensive at the Chicago Democratic Convention in August, not to mention the French May, the Prague Spring, the Soviet tanks of August, and the Mexican guns of September.

The most popular movie of 1968 was *The Graduate* and the number one non-fiction bestseller for many weeks was Eldridge Cleaver's *Soul on Ice*. Meanwhile, in the television year running from October 1967 through to April 1968 (I borrow this point from Jeff Greenfield) the top-rated entertainment programmes in prime time were as follows: *The*

---

* An earlier version of this article was presented as a talk at a conference on 'May '68 and Popular Culture', University of Southern California, Cinema Studies, May 1988.

Andy Griffith Show, The Lucy Show, Gomer Pyle USMC, Gunsmoke, Family Affair, Bonanza, The Red Skelton Show, The Dean Martin Show, The Jackie Gleason Show, Saturday Night at the Movies, Bewitched, The Beverley Hillbillies, The Ed Sullivan Show, The Virginian, Green Acres, The Thursday Night Movie, The Lawrence Welk Show, The Smothers Brothers Comedy Hour, Gentle Ben, Rowan and Martin's Laugh In, The FBI, My Three Sons, Walt Disney's Wonderful World of Color.

Despite the ingenious efforts of latter day interpreters to discern vast subversive potential flickering up from these unlikely sarcophagi, and despite the occasional interruptions of the cellophane-wrapped world of these TV shows by unpleasant glimmerings from the streets, I think it is safe to say that the world displayed and mummified on prime time was a world amazingly and almost uncomprehendingly at odds with the world of underground newspapers, newsreel films, the Tet offensive, the Oakland and Pentagon demonstrations, SDS, *Bonnie and Clyde* and *The Battle of Algiers*. Between these two popular cultures there stretched a gulf virtually beyond comprehension.

It is my feeling that this abyss of incomprehension helps to work our way toward an answer to one of the essential political questions about 1968, namely, how two very different social phenomena could happen simultaneously. The first is that the anti-war movement grew from nothing to a sizeable political force between 1964 and 1968: a movement whose force was capable of deposing one president, discrediting his heir apparent, bringing hundreds of thousands of people into political activity for the first time, setting limits on the murderous war in Vietnam, and eventually shattering the governing party of the United States, which has not recovered to this day. The second phenomenon is this; as unpopular as the war had become – and it had become quite unpopular by the end of 1968 – the anti-war movement was detested even more. A Gallup Poll of those who had seen the TV images of the demonstrations and the police response of August 1968 in Chicago revealed that 60 per cent of the viewers felt that the police were right.

How are we to understand this discrepancy? On the one hand, here was the most effective anti-interventionist movement in history, one that was also going to leave behind a shadow force which would keep the brakes on many if not all subsequent expeditionary wars. On the other hand, this movement was not going to leave behind an organized force, let alone a politically mobilized majority. A fire-break was built around the movement which would prevent it from becoming still more popular and more consequential than it already was. It was this failure, as well as the success of the movement, that has to be explained if we are going to learn from the glories of this past, not just sing along with them.

1968: THE TWO CULTURES

I will focus on one aspect of the contradictory terrain of the 1960s. There were by 1968 two nations that wanted to obliterate each other. There was an American majority that wanted to imagine itself into the world of *Andy Griffith, Gomer Pyle* and *Green Acres*. It yearned to be there, adorably managing the contradictions of its life. It thought that it could lean back and breathe in the world – if only those uppity blacks, hippy freaks, student radicals, Viet Cong Commies and (if all that wasn't bad enough) hypothetically bra-burning women would vanish.

None of the above were ready for prime time. This majority hoped to keep them contained on the news, if anywhere. (Its leaders, Richard Nixon and Spiro Agnew, were not even willing to concede that much.) This not-so-silent American majority was belatedly repelled by the war, not because it thought the war immoral or imperial or that it killed too many Vietnamese. This America turned against the war because it concluded that the war was foolish, ineffectual, excessively divisive, expensive, and killed too many Americans. This is why the Tet offensive resounded throughout the media and throughout the country – it refuted the Johnson administration's claim that the light of victory was visible at the end of that famous and interminable tunnel.

The other America, the American that wasn't watching those 25 shows, the America of black militants, freaks and radicals, was trying to express a very different sort of identity and a very different set of hopes. It also had a base in popular culture. By 1968 it had seized that part of popular culture which stands closest to popular feelings among the young: music. This America was saying things like, 'Come on Baby, Light My Fire', 'Break on Through to the Other Side', 'Dance in the Streets', 'Fight in the Streets' (or, at least if you weren't listening to Mick Jagger's irony, that's what you thought you heard). Instead of a slap on the back and the wave of a glad hand and what Hubert Humphrey called the politics of joy (only three weeks after the assassination of Robert Kennedy), this other America offered the clenched fist and sometimes, increasingly, the Viet Cong flag or the televisual hodgepodge image of warpaint bandolier and toy machine gun given us by the yippie leader, Jerry Rubin – pure television in its incoherence. It was also saying, 'Say it loud, I'm black and I'm proud.' It offered the revolutionary black image, also right out of Central Casting, of the Black Panther leader, Huey Newton, posed in a black beret, seated in a fan-shaped wicker throne, a spear upright in his left hand and a rifle in his right.

How a great deal of the anti-war movement moved from the politics of strategy against the war to the politics of expressing itself is a long story. It has a lot to do with the growing rift between radicals and liberals, which I think was heavily and tragically the doing of the liberals. I have written extensively on this subject in my *The Sixties: Years of Hope, Days of Rage* (1987). Radicals and liberals, having been symbiotic to each other throughout the early 1960s, became the unintentional casualties of 1968. Because the liberals were too enamoured of power during the Democratic years when they were riding high, and because the radicals were sometimes too hopeful and sometimes too desperate and there were not enough of us, the partial liberal/radical alliance of the early 1960s broke down. This dissolution of the liberal/radical alliance led to the abandonment of the idea of a strategic politics – a politics that you enter into because of its ends and because of your belief that it can produce those ends, as opposed to a politics that you enter in order to feel good. Strategic politics came to be replaced by an expressive politics where you let your disgust, your fear, your loathing and your jubilation show, hang out, and you shake, rattle and roll along with it.

Of course, it wasn't only the anti-war lefties who were in that frame of mind by 1968. There were others who felt the same way. Primary among them were the hippies and freaks who wanted to put their bodies on the line, not just once in a while in order to accomplish some specific political end, but spiritually every day, as if they believed, as Sartre once said about his generation, that 'the world was new because we were new in the world.' I would like to take a moment to consider the power of the images that were put forward in the name of this 'expressive politics'. How did these images work their way into the national mainstream? Certainly one central channel was television news. It bears remembering that although we sometimes think that broadcast news programmes have been with us since at least the days of the Old Testament, one of the things that was interesting about television in the 1960s was that television news was essentially new – that is, they didn't know quite how to do it yet.

Television news adopted the half-hour format in the autumn of 1963 on CBS and NBC. ABC didn't move to a half-hour format until 1967. Television news, not quite knowing what it was, was feeling its way, interestingly enough, just as the anti-war movement was feeling its way, and the two surged up in an intimate relationship to each other. Television news helped tear America in half, or rather 60:40, if we go back to that 1968 Gallup Poll. TV news polarized America into the country of *The Red Skelton Show* and that of 'Break on Through to the Other Side'.

For most people, in most living rooms, the images that pass for reality on television are pried out of narrative context and the ones that register best are the lurid ones. As Paul Krassner and the other founding yippies understood in 1967–8, the nation is wired; as much as any force, television sets the emotional agenda. Those who knew how to produce the most vivid images got space because the producers of television for the most part heeded the call from Central Casting: get us some freaks. Statesmen are expected to look statesmanlike, demonstrators are supposed to look demonstrative. Presidents call press conferences (most of them do, anyway). Movements, in order to express themselves, call demonstrations. This is the half-truth in the right-wing attack on the media – that the media do in this curious way relay a certain version of anti-authority.

Knowing these principles of newsworthiness, enter the opposition's media geniuses. They cracked the code and turned it to their own use. There were the bearers of Viet Cong flags, for example, and the burners of American flags, knowing full well that if one American flag was burning and a hundred were being carried upright, it would be the spectacle of the burning flag which would make an impression and end up on the evening news. In 1968 there were scads of anti-war projects and leaders, quiet and patient and unsung, but the celebrities were the likes of Mark Rudd and Abbie Hoffman (whose *shtick* was at least genuine and original in many ways) and Jerry Rubin, a truly manipulative worker of the television news routines.

Abbie and Jerry, to give them their due, had a theory. The theory was that the young were a revolutionary constituency. Young people flocking into Venice or the Lower East Side were, in Abbie's terminology, 'runaway slaves' who would be radicalized by billy clubs and by emulation. If you showed them the image of what a revolutionary looked like on television, then they would spring into action – a sort of rural electrification theory which led to meteoric careers in revolution but a very poor idea of the staying power, let alone the strategy, that serious politics requires. Needless to say, mainstream television had very little interest in conveying the texture of the opposition. There were some exceptions in public television, which was not yet old enough or absorbing enough to be of interest to corporate sponsors.

Mainstream television had very little interest in conveying what the interior of the opposition was about. It had very little interest in conveying the intense and growing disaffection that was spreading through American colleges – not simply the elite Harvards and Stanfords, but down the class ladder to San Francisco State College, Kent State University, etc. Nor was it capable of conveying the intense longing of white freaks who were looking for some kind of God, 'lost in a Roman wilderness of pain', as Jim Morrison sang it, in a country whose leadership had gone mad with the belief that it was saving a nation that they had invented, South Vietnam, by sprinkling it with napalm. Mostly television news gave us not that famous 'substance' only recently outfoxed by pretty-face 'flash' in the world according to *Broadcast News*, but surges of electrons on the surface of things.

So television news played a part in amplifying this sense of a divided country. The cut-loose style, the *Wild in the Streets* style (to name yet another cult film of 1968), ultimately made for a kind of politics which imploded, a kind of desperado politics, self-destructive politics, because, finally, self-expression is no substitute for strategy. What made you feel good was not necessarily what was going to help end the war or transcend the misery of the ghetto. From the broadcasting of lurid images came an aestheticization of politics, politics as theatre, feel-good politics, be-bad politics, which helped isolate the anti-war militants. In 1936 Walter Benjamin decried this kind of aestheticizing of politics, which he said was the business of fascism, when he wrote: 'All efforts to render politics aesthetic culminate in one thing: war.'

By the late 1960s, a fair part of the left had devolved into dadaistic and violent gestures claiming to be the politics of revolution, which they were not. Whereupon the dominant culture was able to describe the left in terms used by the cops in Arthur Penn's version of *Bonnie and Clyde*: 'They ain't got no respect.' To which we said, 'Right on.'

I don't want to be entirely dismissive of youth and identity politics, because there was really something quite wonderful about that sense of starting history again, which was so widespread in 1968. Whether it took the form of drug experience or political epiphany, a sense of revelation, the sense that the final days were coming due – that sort of millennarian feeling was everyday stuff and it was exhilarating. What prevailed was audacity, thinking that you could transcend limits by thinking your way past them – a kind of politics of the will, in which limits were just some grown-up bad-vibes bring-down. We – and I mean this globally, not just me and my friends, but Jerry Rubin and his friends and Andy Warhol and his friends – are all children of the cornucopia which was the longest, giddiest boom in American history.

The rallying cry of 1968 in the US and Europe was becoming 'Master the Impossibilities'. The idea was that you could act as if the world were other than it is, and make it so. That was an amazing concept based on one of the founding ideas of the 1960s as a whole, which was one of direct action: the idea that you could sit-in at a lunch counter and act as if segregation didn't exist. The idea of the sit-in was not to go and make a demand, knock on somebody's door and say, 'You're doing something bad, we humbly petition you to stop it.' No, the idea of the sit-in was that you imagined yourself to be living already in a world in which segregation didn't exist – and, by God, if you suffered enough then you could bring it about. Or you could take a pill and think as if God were already radiating through a burning bush and damned if paradise weren't already here, 'Come on baby, let the good times roll.' 'Remember what the dormouse said, "Feed your head".'

You could follow Marx and say, 'Change the world', or Rimbaud and say, 'Change life', or you could search, as so many did, for a sort of rapprochement and say, 'Change both', or even, 'Changing life *is* changing the world.' This kind of politics refused to take anything for granted. It said, 'Express yourself'; it said, 'Make the decisions that affect your life.' It said with Bob Dylan, 'If they ask you for some collateral, pull down your pants' (which L.A.'s great Jim Morrison did on more than one occasion). Ultimately the great allure – and delusion – of this visionary strain of politics was the belief that if you demanded the future vehemently enough, the millennium would be at hand.

This style of politics had touchstones, not only in the underground press where you would expect to find it, and of course in music, where the apocalyptic mood was enormous, but in another sector of popular culture, the arena of commercial cinema. I would like to talk about two films that circulated in 1968: *Bonnie and Clyde* and *The Battle of Algiers*.

Compared with television, commercial cinema offered a very different way of thinking about what was and wasn't 'commercial'. In cinema the image of doomed noble outsider outlaws was marketable, as could be seen from the success of Brando's *Wild One* and James Dean's *Rebel Without a Cause* in the 1950s. But the 1968 hero had something distinct to offer: only in 1967 and 1968 did the outsider hero relish the purity of the blood bond that kept him an outsider. Only in 1968 was blood essential to the tragic and exhilarating fate of the outsider. I'm going to quote Abbie Hoffman, who wrote very perceptively in his 1968 book, *Revolution for the Hell of It*: 'America lost its balls in the frontier and since then there have been no mighty myths and now we hunt for them in lonely balconies watching *Bonnie and Clyde*.'

He was on to something. Arthur Penn understood something of the sensibility that was coming into being. *Bonnie and Clyde* launched not only new fashions, but a kind of hero cult, a stylized great plains myth version of Huey Newton and Che Guevara, in gripping colour.

As Pauline Kael wrote at the time, there had been earlier movie versions of the real life story of Bonnie Parker and Clyde Barrow in 1937 and 1949. These films were more or less Depression-style social realism. They were films about hard times forcing people to commit crime in order to get back at the banker or simply to scrape up a living. Penn's versions of Bonnie and Clyde were very different. They were 1960s people set back in the 1930s. They were creatures of will, free-standing angels of revolt, without regrets, no looking back, no alibis. Crime for them wasn't compelled by poverty or foreclosure; it was chosen. Bonnie and Clyde went on the run because that was the way to be young. The gun wasn't an instrument of redistributive justice, it was a fetish, an instrument of pure bleeding death, a shocker, a prick, no apologies given or received. They lived and died by aesthetics. The rest of the people were thick-headed rubes. We, together with Bonnie and Clyde, were 'the people'. Anybody with spunk would go off with Bonnie and Clyde. Gerald Long, who then reviewed films for the *National Guardian*, and later went off with the Weathermen, wrote at the time that Bonnie and Clyde were like Frantz Fanon and an NLF hero named Nguyen van Troi. Long said more or less, 'If a car full of revolutionaries like them, pulled up at the gas station where you pumped gas for a living, wouldn't you go off with them?' It was the *New York Review* caricaturist, David Levine, who understood that the issue brought to the surface by the film was the enormity of violence – he drew Lyndon Johnson as Clyde and Secretary of State, Dean Rusk, as Bonnie.

The effects of a movie are always complicated, confused and ultimately unknowable. But I do know the absurd effect that Bonnie and Clyde had on me. In the summer of 1967, after the first time I saw the film, I happened to be walking past the National Guard Armory in Manhattan. It was the summer of 1967, a summer of great upheavals, violent upsurges in black communities. I was so angry at the police that I reached into my pocket for an absurd little tourist pocket knife that my mother had brought back from a trip to Italy. I desperately wanted to have that knife so that I could rip a hole in the tyre of the National Guard jeep that was parked in front of the Armory. Mysteriously, anti-climatically, I was missing the knife that night, so I didn't get to do the deed. But I wanted to.

Another film that was significant in the psychic life of the movement in 1968 was Gillo Pontecorvo's *The Battle of Algiers*. Beloved by black and white revolutionaries, it offered a brilliant re-enactment of an actual anti-colonial uprising. There were groups in 1968 who used this film virtually as a sort of study group curriculum – out of context. They neglected the fact that the actual battle of Algiers, the one that was re-enacted in the film, presupposed years of organization and a broad anti-colonial spirit whose successful revolution was not based on the simple act of picking up a gun. They weren't going to drive 'the man' out of the ghetto with war whoops.

The main movement reading of the film went like this: 'Don't bother to organize', as Mark Rudd said to me at an SDS meeting after the Chicago demonstrations in 1968, 'Organizing is just another word for going slow.' Another reading of *The Battle of Algiers* was: If you're going to organize, organize cadres only. And then, once you've gotten the organization together, it is justifiable to plant bombs in cafés. (Fortunately, there was a lot more talk about that than there was imitation.)

1968: THE TWO CULTURES

I want to come back now to the paradox that I pointed to earlier: that the radical movement accomplished as much as it did, and yet isolated itself at the moment of its apparent triumph. This has political relevance today, for one consequence of the movement's self-enclosure and final isolation is the awful delusion that the movements of the 1960s, which may or may not have been noble and well intentioned, were in any case futile; you can't change history.

Interestingly, it is the right which seems to have a very different understanding of the events. What the right begins to understand is that, despite the movements' failures and shortcomings, they have a sort of shadow presence, even today, 20 years on, one that makes itself felt. There are many ways in which it is a cultural presence, but it is also a political one. It is easy to forget in a culture that is systematically amnesiac, that the 1960s did bring blacks and women into political citizenship, and that while many specific accomplishments have been eroded and repealed, all has not been lost. Even after a decade of Republican rule in the 1980s, the right was not able to impose most of its social agenda.

The shadow movement is also an anti-war force. That shadow movement in fact defeated aid to the Nicaraguan contras. It was part of what made possible an end to the Cold War. I'm very far from arguing that this represents the millennium or that it comes anywhere near close to what, in 1968, we thought might be possible. The influence of US finance continues abroad in Guatemala, Iraq, the Israeli-occupied territories, and elsewhere. The left, such as it is today, is contained, timid, marginal. There are many important movements of ethnic groups; there are local organizing projects; there are ecological and environmental groups. There are all kinds of people doing all kinds of sensible things in the professions, continuing the values on which they acted in 1968. But for all the achievements, I think it should not have been surprising that the movements of the 1960s fell short of the millennium, and the reason is that what the movements of the 1960s really propounded was a radical reworking of values, not a revolution but something both more primitive and basic, a reformation.

I think that is what the 1960s were all about; a fundamental reworking of values toward three principles. We were pursuing a politics of limits with three dimensions to it. The first places a limit on what the species, or any of its representatives or would-be representatives, are entitled to do to the world as a whole, to the planet. You are not entitled to blow it up, you are not entitled to poison it and make it uninhabitable. Second, any collective, whether nation, gender, or ethnic group, is not entitled to do certain things to another nation, gender, and ethnic group – there is a limit to what one gang is permitted to do to another gang. Third, there are limits to what any collective is entitled to do to an individual. You are not permitted to torture that individual, to deprive that individual of livelihood or the power of speech. I believe that these are the three principles around which the movements of the 1960s clustered and on which they agreed. These are subversive principles. Collisions are possible between them – on the planet Earth this is the nature of all sets of principles – but as a whole they are clearly set against the prevailing order. They may sound pious, but if you follow their logic, they are deeply disturbing to the culture in which many people have many privileges and investments. It is therefore no surprise that the reformation of the 1960s led eventually to what we have been living through, namely the counter-reformation of the 1980s and 1990s.

Like many others, I did not quite understand in 1968 that you do not propound the need for reformation without expecting a counter-reformation. After all, we were accusing those in power of committing atrocities, of getting fat from them, of having unearned privileges. We accused them of inheriting wicked ways from a system deeply rooted in history. We insisted that they cease their wicked ways – immediately. What did we think the system was going to do in response? Congratulate us? It hit us over the head. It tried to roll us back. In the person of Ronald Reagan and his co-conspirators, that is what it did.

I don't feel gloomy about what was not accomplished in 1968. The best of the spirit of 1968 was the generosity, the passion, the community, the ingenuity, the urgency, the insistence on testing limits (even if they weren't always tests that I approved of) and, to use a very old-fashioned word, the love. It is that totality that has receded, but it is still a presence in American life. I don't refer to the stock images cryogenically preserved in films and books. I mean something more spectral than that, that in curious ways is among us, but has yet to find its political expression so that we are inundated instead with various adulterated forms. Whether the letter of 1968 can be repeated is doubtful – the conditions are too different. But the best and the wisest of its spirit can be neither repealed nor repeated. The reformation, in its complicated and mysterious forms, continues, and its destiny is known to none of us.

4. The World Turned Upside Down: The Alternative Press and Visionary Politics in the US in the 1960s

Jackie Di Salvo

> The 60s was, then, the period in which all these 'natives' became human beings, and this internally as well as externally: those inner colonized of the first world ... fully as much as its external subjects and official 'natives.'
>
> Fredric Jameson, in *The 60s Without Apology*

> Oh, these are the people that would turn the world upside down, that make the nation full of tumults and uproars, that work all the disturbance in church and state. It is fit that such men and congregations should be suppressed ... that we may have truth and peace and government again.
>
> William Dell (1646)[1]

In 1968 revolting students had scrawled on the walls of Paris the Blakean aphorism, 'All power to the Imagination', for they had suddenly stumbled into one of those historical moments when rapid shifts in the constellations of power made almost anything seem possible. Cuba had somehow snuck past the US imperial guards to establish the first socialist state in the West. Mao's 'Great Proletarian Cultural Revolution' was proposing to skip a whole historical stage by unleashing the militant power of its masses and going directly from feudalism to the withering away of the state. Suddenly, Western democracies, smug in the welfare–warfare state's muffling of class struggle, were startled by calls to revolution from the most unexpected quarters. For Third World insurgencies were creating an historical opening much like the English, French and Russian revolutions. Like the Jacobin revolt, which moved from Paris to London in 1793, the anti-imperialist upsurges in Asia, Africa and Latin America would evoke radical aspirations that went far beyond both their local domains and the political possibilities of the actual historical situation, producing rumbles along the fault lines which had long existed under the surface of Western liberal republics.

In the 1790s, hoping the English people would follow the French in their sudden surge into the political arena, William Blake hailed the awakening of Albion (the empowered and creative masses) from a deathly sleep and envisioned a drastic alteration not only of politics and economics but of culture, family, religion and even personality in the building of that 'Jerusalem which is called Liberty among the sons and daughters of men'. The plebeian poet had inherited that apocalyptic dream directly from seventeenth-century Puritan revolutionaries like Milton who had believed the Civil War of the 'Saints' against king and bishops might be that final battle prophesied by the Book of Revelations to initiate a return to Eden for a millennium of peace and justice. Even more, as one of the first to appreciate the entry of a huge, new, disenfranchised working class into the age of democratic revolutions, Blake hailed the revival of the more radical versions of that myth which had appeared when those middle-class religious radicals and republicans had so disrupted mechanisms of censorship and control that a horde of newly articulate lower-class Levellers, Diggers and Ranters could begin preaching a gospel of democracy, Communism and a liberation completely opposite to the Puritan exaltation of family and property in its ethic of hard work and self-denial. Appropriately then, it would be the proclamation of Blake's *Milton* that 'We shall not cease from mental fight / Nor shall my sword sleep in my hand / Till we have built Jerusalem / In England's green and pleasant land' that would echo through the streets of London as the anthem of the British Labour Party when it first took power in 1945.

The aim of reactionaries from King Charles II to Ronald Reagan has been to bury that radical tradition by trumpeting the inevitability and universality of the existing order of inequality and deprivation, be it oligarchic government or the free market, and to cast cynical scorn on its 'utopian' challengers. But the reappearance of such agendas, not just in the fantasies of poets, but on the banners of mass movements from the peasant revolts in the fourteenth, seventeenth and eighteenth centuries to the 1960s shows that history which buries such dreams also brings them back to life. For, as Lenin insisted, history is characterized not just by gradual increments of change but by the drastic leaps and reversals possible at such times when the oppressed can no longer live in the old way, or the rulers rule in the old way – and the intelligentsia switches sides. Wordsworth captured the spirit of such a time when artists and intellectuals are buoyed by mass insurgency and vision seems suddenly wed to power in *The Prelude*, recalling how 'the inert / Were roused and lively natures rapt away' and both found 'helpers to their hearts desire ... For mighty were the auxiliars which then stood / Upon our side.' His exclamation that 'Bliss was it in that dawn to be alive / But to be young was very Heaven!' anticipates the manic optimism and apocalyptic fervour that would break out again in the 1960s when young radicals felt once more 'called upon to exercise their skill / Not in Utopia – subterranean fields – / Or some secreted island ... / But in the very world, which is the world / Of all of us' for 'the whole Earth / The beauty wore of promise ... (As at some moments might not be unfelt / Among the bowers of Paradise itself.' Book 11, pp. 133–7, 105–9, 139–44.)

'A New F**k Censorship Press' 2

According to the 1950s reigning myth, however, since America was already paradise, and its economic and military domination of the rest of the world a triumph for freedom and democracy, dissent could only be a demonic plot of foreign agents whose suppression all patriots must support. This pretty delusion was shattered by the struggle of African-Americans against second-class citizenship and the proto-fascism which had maintained it. Their militancy destabilized political controls and embarrassed the apologists for extending democratic imperialism throughout the non-white world. So too did the continuation for the McCarthyite repression originally necessary to the establishment of the national security state after the Second World War. Early Berkeley protests targeted hearings of the House Un-American Activities Committee and university loyalty oaths, and when white students there sought to support the struggles of blacks in the South, they first had to overturn censorship and secure the right to organize on campus through the Free Speech Movement (FSM). Into this newly cleared political space, the underground press was born when a survivor of an earlier radicalism, Art Kunkin, a former Trotskyist, started the *Los Angeles Free Press* in 1964, followed by Max Scherr, who founded the *Berkeley Barb* in 1965. The *Barb's* first issue, reporting student attempts to stop troop trains in Oakland, prophetically headlined what the regular press ignored – GIs' signs in the windows: 'We don't want to go!' [3] The new papers covered an opposition rendered invisible by the mainstream capitalist press: demonstrations against racism, war and repression and the creations and spokespersons of an oppositional counterculture: black culture, folk music, art films, experimental drama, radical comics, Lenny Bruce, Dick Gregory, Leroy Jones, Franz Fanon, Allen Ginsberg, Paul Goodman, Herbert Marcuse and, increasingly, that satanic trilogy: sex, drugs and rock and roll. Ignoring the more moderate liberal elite, they opened their pages to a new audience in the youth and college ghettos.

FSM leader Jack Weinberg's admonition, 'Don't trust anyone over 30' drew the infamous generation gap between them and a 1950s 'silent generation' complicit in Cold War reaction and repression.

The new papers offered an engaged, participatory, and frequently first person reportage of, say, a draft resistor at the induction centre.[4] Unafraid, even eager to give offence, they immediately distinguished themselves from the mass media by presenting urban riots from a black perspective as a revolt of the oppressed. They defined themselves by divergence from a mainstream media which, according to Herbert Gans, only projected 'the social order of public, business, professional, upper-middle-class, middle-aged and white male sectors of society'.[5] Thus they deliberately rejected 'the rhetoric of objectivity' which Jack Newfield described as 'belief in welfare, capitalism, God, the West, Puritanism, the Law, the family, property, the two party system and ... the notion that violence is only defensible when employed by the state'.[6] As the civil rights and anti-war movements shredded the myth of America as a bastion of democracy, the underground press grew with the rising disgust at official deceit about almost every aspect of the Vietnam War – from the Gulf of Tonkin incident justifying the war's expansion to the phoney casualty figures predicting victory. That radicalizing suspicion was captured well by Robert Bly:

> The ministers lie, the professors lie, the television lies, the priests lie
> . . .
> Now the Chief Executive enters; the press conference begins:
> First the President lies about the date the Appalachian Mountains rose. Now he lies about the population of Chicago ... he has private information about which city is the capital of Wyoming; he lies about the birthplace of Attila the Hun. He lies about the composition of the amniotic fluid, and he insists that Luther was never a German, and that only the Protestants sold indulgences. That Pope Leo X *wanted* to reform the church but the 'liberal elements' prevented him, that the Peasants War was fomented by Italians from the North.
> And the Attorney General lies about the time the sun sets.[7]

Also at stake, as Marty Glass explains in *Dock of the Bay*, were different conceptions of what was 'news':

> The daily papers convey a very strong and indirect message ... Life is good ... 'News' is what deviates from the ordinary and the normal; 'news' is what someone else decides is important. This is pure bullshit. The real news isn't in distinct, bizarre events. The real news is what happens 24 hours a day all day long everywhere. This is the news we don't read about in the daily papers because the people who control those papers don't want us to know about it ... The real news is the expression on the faces of children sitting in tenement door-

ways with nothing to do. The real news is the tenement itself. The real news is the despair and humiliation on the faces of people waiting for hours for a lousy check in the unemployment offices. And it's also on the emptied faces of people who have jobs ... where their creative potential is stifled and crushed under the weight of meaningless labor performed to make enough money to survive. The real news is jobs created solely to provide profits for those who don't work at all ... The precious unredeemable time of our lives is sacrificed for numbers in bankbooks ... The real news is that guys are being forced to kill their brothers in Vietnam. The real news is that all the important decisions made in this country are made by maniac insects with dollar bills engraved on their beady, inhuman plastic eyeballs. [8]

The underground press expanded with the movement; by 1969 there were 456 papers with a circulation of well over a million (Free Press – 95,000). They soon spawned both the Underground Press Syndicate which implemented the slogan 'no copyrights on the left' through the exchange of articles which gave local papers access to national news, and Liberation News Service, which sent out twice weekly packets of stories and graphics – typically news of a college strike, a trial of draft resistors, an NLF offensive, a black uprising, and movement photos. Radical journalism celebrated and instigated radical action. New York's *Rat* printed inspirational accounts of communal life inside the occupied buildings of the Columbia strike and reprinted stolen documents detailing the university's financial links not only to the military industrial complex but to the *New York Times* – thus discrediting its attacks on the strike. Papers soon sprang up everywhere – on over 40 GI bases, in high schools, prisons (San Quentin's *Outlaw*), minority communities (*La Raza, El Gallo*) and even the deep South where young intellectuals allying with the black movement risked constant harassment to put out Atlanta's *Great Speckled Bird*, Mississippi's *Kudzu*, New Orleans' *Nola Express*, Dallas's *Space Notes*, the *Miami Herald* and the *Southern Patriot*. The *Black Panther* promoted the party's ten-point reform programme of equal education, housing, jobs, justice and the right to armed self-defence, reported attacks by 'pig' police, caricatured in lurid porcine graphics, advocated GI organizing, reprinted accounts of imperialism from Cuba, North Korea, Guinea-Bissau and Vietnam and presented the African-American movement as part of a worldwide revolution. In Chicago *Rising Up Angry* adapted the Panthers' celebration of the outlaw, its message of 'Power to the People', and SDS politics of anti-racism, anti-sexism and anti-imperialism to 'greasers' – poor, alienated white teenagers from the streets of Chicago. And, by 1970, former SDSers seeking to radicalize labour were putting out over a dozen local papers aimed at the working class: Detroit's *RPM*, Madison's *We the People*, St Louis's *On the Line*, Dayton's *Worker's Voice*.

These papers benefited from the new technology of the offset press which slashed publication costs to a mere $100 for 3000 eight-page papers and made possible a multi-media, McCluhanesque visual spectacle through creative graphics and layout. In 1965 the *East Village Other* reinvented the newspaper as an art form, mixing journalism with bohemian art and poetry. Believing with Tuli Kupferberg that 'the true work of art is the infinite body of man moving in harmony through the incredible changes of his particular existence', the underground adopted Herbert Marcuse's elevation of the pleasure principle over repressive rationalism, and revived Blake's vision of the revolutionary potential of liberating the imagination and the unconscious.[9] Hence, just as Blake's famous revolutionary aphorism would be adapted to a contemporary context on a poster proclaiming 'The Panthers of wrath are wiser than the horses of instruction', so too would the poet's unaccomplished dream of creating a multi-media art which would put the power of the imagination in the hands of the masses through giant murals, popular songs and mass-produced illustrated texts finally be achieved.

The desire both to shock people into consciousness and *épater la bourgeoisie* produced a penchant for surrealist effects in the San Francisco *Oracle* and other counterculture newspapers. Collage and montage critiqued mainstream icons – ironically juxtaposing images of politicians, government, police, the military and the flag with obscenity, violence, money and advertising symbols: phallic missiles captured the displacement of sexual energy to military aggression in a sadistic, macho culture; LBJ's head on a Nazi body excoriated the proto-fascism of imperialism; Nixon as a Mafia gun-moll exposed the criminality of the state; Santa Claus crucified on a dollar sign, the hypocrisies of a commodity culture; while other associations exalted the heroes of the counterculture: a dope-smoking hippie as an American Indian, Santa as 'Ho Ho Ho' Chi Minh, San Francisco as the 'wild west' frontier of a new consciousness; the 'Pepsi generation' with a molotov cocktail in hand! Berkeley's *Yellow Dog* pronounced itself the 'paper that pisses on the American establishment'. Satire and parody reigned, pelting the establishment with ridicule and subjecting all aspects of mainstream culture and middle-class lifestyle to a contemptuous, acerbic humour. Headlines screamed the news behind the news – the historical dialectic: 'Elvis Presley Killed Ike Eisenhower'; graphics refuted the dominant propaganda – Marx and Engels with the logo 'We Found It', mocking both Jesus freaks and left dogmatists. Thus it was the underground, employing a 'double-voiced discourse' which echoed mainstream rhetoric while critiquing it, that actually invented deconstruction in practice; post-1960s intellectuals merely abstracted and theorized it.

'Revolution in Our Lifetime' [10]

Like the civil rights movement that inspired it, 1960s activism began as a democratic reform movement (Students for a 'Democratic Society'), demanding that America live up to its own propaganda. But political praxis increasingly radicalized both the analysis and the political agenda. As activists found themselves facing a wall of indifferent and oppressive authority, dramatic photos of repression filled their press: the bloodied Columbia student flashing a peace sign as he was arrested; army bayonets framing the door of the Wisconsin Education building; troops and artillery lining Chicago's Michigan Avenue as police rampaged outside the 1968 Democratic convention – street signs changed to 'Welcome to Prague'. In implementing the slogan 'Question Authority', activists went from identifying the cops, the CIA, the military and university administrations as their enemy to exposing authoritarianism throughout society. Radicals etched out a critique which incorporated the schools, the Church, the media, the professions, political parties and government in this picture of illegitimate power. Inevitably the trail of intransigence and tyranny led to an indictment of underlying corporate control. The highly undemocratic 1968 convention put to rest liberal assumptions about the American state. For it was the Johnson administration, the most liberal in US history, that had trampled upon the popular will and escalated the war in Vietnam. The underground no longer treated the war as a mistake, an exception, or the folly of a few men, but rather as an indictment of 'The System' whose fraudulent liberal façade hid pervasive imperialism and dictatorship abroad, economic exploitation, political oligarchy and racism at home. Political authority was now seen to be based not on popular support or elections but on courts and jails at home, military force and CIA counter-insurgency abroad. 'Bring the Boys Home' was replaced by 'Victory to the NLF' and 'Bring the War Home'. The agitation of Communist groups like Progressive Labor in SDS finished off the 1950s' alleged *End of Ideology* and hastened the new turn toward Marxism.

Out of this radical opposition to the status quo came a search for alternatives which spawned, along with the anarchist and utopian perspectives of the counterculture, a new generation of socialists. If most students were radicalized by the horror of imminently being drafted to fight a war for the profits of the multinationals, the Draft Resistance slogan, 'Not with my life you don't' soon extended to most social roles. Jerry Farber's 'The Student as Nigger' was reprinted nationwide as rebellious students and youth drew parallels between themselves and other oppressed groups. Schools were depicted as prisons, mental institutions or factories grinding out like-minded robots to fit the various strata of the capitalist workforce. A common epigram protested sardonically 'I am student 6579208; do not fold, spindle or mutilate.' Young radicals adopted a Great Refusal to be good students, workers, soldiers, citizens or consumers. Jerry Rubin's invitation to the Chicago protest announced, 'Let's have a party that expresses our values which are don't go to Vietnam; don't work for the large corporations; don't do everything that our parents say', while the *Barb* denounced 'the brain-washing, fingernail cutting mass production of junior cops for tight-assed America's old age home war machine'.[11]

Two cultures were in conflict, that of an adult world resigned to the limits of capitalism and a new generation paused at the threshold of maturity, refusing to be integrated into the discipline of alienated labour or to trade life, leisure and creativity for merely earning a living. A manifesto in the *Madison Kaleidoscope* proclaimed:

> American capitalism says graduate and leave; we want $10 million to build a community. American capitalism says tear down the [food] Coop for a left turn lane; we say tear down all the left turn lanes, all the used car lots ... in one night of frenzied dadaistic energy, plant trees, flowers, make Madison beautiful ... We want the feel of life in a young girl's sweatshirt and jeans, not the feel of death on the dashboard of an Olds ... We will throw off the yoke of oppression. We will have poets in our drugstores and supermarkets ... and we will have workers control, students control, women's control, lovers control, and children's control. We need to found a left which speaks to each corner of our existence, a *Marxism of everyday life*, an understanding and self-perception of every wheeze of existential desperation, every half-smile of satisfaction of our meagre pleasures, every movement of our tepid and boring days. We need a left that can speak to our dream-fantasies and *make them come true*.[12]

The rise of capitalism in the seventeenth century had required a psychological as well as a political/economic revolution. Puritanism had imposed a repressive self-discipline, reconfiguring the family as an institution for 'moulding the man' through a cruel socialization of children that policed even the most innocent pleasures.[13] Despite the weakening of religion, capitalist work discipline had continued to demand this neurotic conditioning. The first children of affluence, born after the Second World War, could not comprehend the material basis of such self-sacrifice – either in working-class survival or bourgeois accumulation. Julius Lester said youth were 'on strike against the way of life America was presenting them'.[14] Jerry Rubin declared it a 'post-industrial age' and called for a 'politics of ecstasy'. The *Oracle* issued Timothy Leary's call to 'tune in, turn on and drop out' as the gospel of a new age of human liberation based on sexual freedom, the expansion of consciousness through hallucinogenic drugs and Eastern religious practices, a return to the primitive wisdom of the American Indian, and a lifestyle freed from the obligations of the workaday world by communal living and voluntary poverty. Living between two worlds, 'hippies' saw the revolution in Blakean terms transpiring within their psyches as much as in society. Drugs seemed to open another dimension of consciousness in which one could observe and thus alter the workings of the mind. Timothy Leary urged them to 'blow your minds', using hallucinogens as tools for undoing one's social programming and 'freeing the self from the symbolic & destructive games of everyday life'.[15] Under their influence, 'hippies' reported experiencing tremendous energies, surges of love and joy and mystical experiences of 'divinity' and oneness with the cosmos which made the little life of the workaday world seem trivial and misguided. If nothing else, LSD and marijuana were certainly powerful aphrodisiacs which instantly overthrew years of sexual conditioning. The underground's flaunting of nudity was at once an anarchist violation of societal taboos and a finger in the face of middle-class respectability. At the same time it preached a romantic primitivism (as old as medieval Adamites) of getting away from the artificial constraints of civilization, the enslavements of commodity culture and its inhibiting social disguises and back to authentic human needs, the truth of the body and the simple, natural pleasures of the naked self.

The counterculture rediscovered the old anarchist idea of building a new society within the shell of the old and resurrected a long American history of utopian communes. As the press primarily of voluntary youth ghettos in Berkeley, Madison, the East Village, etc., the underground fostered an ideology of ghetto self-rule. They promoted a network of food co-ops, free clinics, drug crisis centres, free schools, women's centres, cultural cooperatives (like the papers themselves), and other self-help institutions as well as the giant communal assemblies represented in both demonstrations and mammoth Be-Ins and rock concerts like Woodstock. This utopian communalism was facilitated by access to the university, a semi-public space, uniquely communal in being site of home, work and culture. All this constituted a rebellion against the contradictions centred upon the divisions of public and private in allegedly democratic societies based upon private property. In seizing university buildings students spontaneously created a *polis* not accessible in the wheeling and dealing of politics as usual. All-night sessions and endless meetings with open mikes provided an exhilarating experience of empowerment. Michael Rossman, who witnessed its birth in Berkeley's Free Speech Movement, describes such a moment as for hours students blocked the police car containing one of their leaders: 'The sockfooted solemn file at the microphone atop the car was the first real public dialogue I had ever heard, speaking of ideas as though they had real substance and meaning ... relevant to the lives clustered there.' [16] The occupation of Columbia buildings by SDS 'communes', and the People's Church by the Young Lords, the battles over Madison's Mifflin Street party and Berkeley's People's Park were symbolic reappropriations of public space, expressed in the common battle cry, 'the streets belong to the people'. The concomitant rock refrain 'Why don't we do it in the road?' as well as the orgies and crash pads, group houses, communal tripping, affinity groups and collectives sought to transcend what Allen Ginsberg bemoaned as the 'deathly public solitude' of a society which had marginalized all creativity in isolated work, all relationship and fulfilment in privatized love and marriage.[17] Against this the youth culture and its 'Shadow University' tried to create a new public sphere of participatory democracy, cooperative labour, communal living and populist culture. While on some levels it was a Peter Pan movement, implementing the romantic poets' call for a recovery of the joy and spontaneity of childhood, much of that joy resided in the sense of solidarity, and the feeling of enormous possibility which arose from the experience and expectation of power which came from participation in the movement.

Where Have All the Flowers Gone?

With hindsight we can see the inadequacy of this strategy, pointed out at the time by a growing number of Marxists who recognized the limitations of a communalism which tried to appropriate cultural production without challenging private control of economic production. The sexual revolution had provided a metaphor for the 1960s' apocalyptic demand for a culture of gratification rather than exploitation. But to the extent that sex became a synecdoche, it was deceiving, for while people owned their own bodies and nothing but inhibition (and the abortion laws) might obstruct their liberation, they didn't own anything else – certainly not the resources for transforming work, education, media, housing or the environment. The underground press and the counterculture were destroyed partly by harassment (bombings, FBI dirty tricks, obscenity and drug charges) but mostly by economic conditions. Most of the papers folded after the FBI persuaded record companies to remove their ads.[18]

As hard times returned in the 1970s, the young grew up into the stagflation which crippled counter-institutions, put an end to the subsistence lifestyle of 'drop-outs' and forced them into the compromises of the capitalist work world. Their nemesis finally was the economic reality which the petty bourgeois left, living on the fringe of the surplus of a uniquely prosperous post-Second World War guns-and-butter boom economy, had too much ignored. For the counterculture's apocalyptic understanding of its historical stage had not been particularly accurate. What some had presumed to be a post-industrial society was only the end of the primitive accumulation which built its industrial base. True, the possibility now existed for redirecting the vast resources of capitalism to human fulfilment but not until an economic, a socialist, revolution could put an end to the surplus accumulation of private profit and the 'surplus repression' its labour discipline demanded. [19]

Finally, neither objective nor subjective conditions were ripe for that kind of revolution. Politically, power in the university did not translate into power in the larger society. Utopian strategies failed to construct the broader political alliances - with workers, farmers and the middle class - required seriously to contest the power of the oligarchy. Sectarian squabbles over black nationalism, radical feminism and violent sabotage decimated even the mass student and youth organizations. And, as Norm Fruchter insightfully argued, the underground undermined its own base by promoting media and culture as a substitute for organization.[20] Much was pure posturing - whether the Panthers' guns or People's Park reclaiming the land stolen from the Indians. But since it was movement as street theatre, spectacle and vision, judging it as that - a mass collective act of revolutionary propaganda, creating the news, as the Yippies did in Chicago by calling for action, doing it, and publicizing one's own version - we must appreciate it as a major break in the history of contemporary capitalism whose cultural legacy still reverberates. The Zen poet Gary Snyder identified it as a resurgence of the 'Great-Sub-Culture', which went back to the spirituality, freedom and matrilineal communalism of tribes which had existed long before class society and had survived under its surface in the visions of subaltern visionaries from the seventeenth-century Diggers to the Haight-Ashbury ones.[21] In its modern context I see it as an enduring counterculture in a permanent cultural revolution - the popular, mass revolutionary romanticism in practice prophesied by William Blake when he envisioned the imagination in power.[22]

Notes

1. William Dell, 'The Building, Beauty, Teaching and Establishment of the Truly Christian and Spiritual Church' (1646) in *Several Sermons* (1709), p. 109; cited in Christopher Hill, *The World Turned Upside Down: Radical Ideas During the English Revolution* (New York: Viking, 1972), p. 16.
2. John Wilcock cited in Abe Peck, *Uncovering the Sixties: The Life and Times of the Underground Press* (New York: Pantheon, 1985), p. 40.
3. New York's *Village Voice* had provided a model and harbinger for a personal and committed journalism, but its quest for commercial profitability had confined it politically within the liberal wing of the Democratic Party.
4. Books on the underground press include Abe Peck, *Uncovering the Sixties*; Laurence Leamer, *The Paper Revolutionaries: The Rise of the Underground Press* (New York: Simon and Schuster, 1972); Robert J. Glessing, *The Underground Press in America* (Bloomington: Indiana University Press, 1970). Sixties' anthologies include Jesse Kornbluth (ed.), *Notes From the New Underground: An Anthology* (New York: Viking, 1968); Mitchell Goodman (ed), *The Movement Toward A New America: The Beginnings of A Long Revolution* (New York: Alfred A. Knopf, 1970); Judith Clavir Albert and Stewart Edward Albert (eds.), *The Sixties Papers: Documents of a Rebellious Decade* (New York: Praeger, 1984). An assortment of underground papers are available in *The Underground Newspaper Collection, 1963-75* (microfilm), 1976 ed. and 1980 & 1985 supplements (Wooster, Ohio: Bell & Howell); many papers are available from University Microfilms (Ann Arbor, Michigan) and individual libraries such as Tamiment Institute Library, New York University.
5. Herbert Gans, *Deciding What's News* (New York: Pantheon, 1979).
6. Jack Newfield, 'Journalism: Old, New and Corporate – The Reporter as Artist: A Look at the New Journalism', in Michael Schudson, *Discovering the News: A Social History of American Newspapers* (New York: Basic Books, 1978), p. 184.
7. Robert Bly, *The Teeth Mother Naked at Last* (San Francisco: City Lights, 1970).
8. Marty Glass, 'What's News?', *Dock of the Bay* 1:3 (18 August 1969), p. 4.
9. Tuli Kupferberg, 'Life as art', *Barb* (4 August 1967).
10. Frequent slogan of the *Black Panther* paper.
11. Quoted by Peck, *Uncovering the Sixties*, p. 118.

12. 'Manifesto: Toward a New Culture', *Madison Kaleidoscope*, Vol. 1, No. 1 (23 June–6 July 1969), p. 4.
13. I tell this story in *War of Titans: Blake's Critique of Milton and the Politics of Religion* (Pittsburg: University of Pittsburg Press, 1984).
14. Julius Lester, 'Yippie as Effective', *Seed*, Vol. 2, No. 6.
15. Timothy Leary, quoted from a speech at *Oracle's* 'Human Be-In', *Barb* (27 January 1967).
16. Michael Rossman, 'Look, Ma: No Hope, A Multiple Memoir of the New Left', *Commonweal* (12 April 1969).
17. Allen Ginsberg, 'Renaissance or Die', quoted in Peck, *Uncovering the Sixties*, p. 54 from the *East Village Other* (10 January 1967).
18. Geoffrey Rips *et al.*, *Un-American Activities: The Campaign Against the Underground Press* (San Francisco: City Lights, 1981).
19. Herbert Marcuse, *Eros and Civilization* (New York: Vintage, 1962).
20. Norman Fruchter, 'Games in the Arena: Movement Propaganda and the Culture of the Spectacle', *Liberation* (May 1971), pp. 4–17.
21. Gary Snyder, 'Why Tribe', in *Earth House-Hold* (New York: New Directions, 1969); 1960s' Diggers believed that in distributing free food and clothing and burning money at the Stock Exchange they were following the seventeenth-century Communists.
22. At the time of writing Vol. 1, No. 1 of the *Black Panther* was published again by former Panthers and a fifth alternative paper, *The Madison Insurgent*, was launched in Wisconsin after a hiatus of 15 years.

5. The Meaning of the 1960s

Abbie Hoffman

People came to a crossroads in their lives and they said 'are we going to go for prime time culture and politics and accept all the mythologies handed down by the powers that be, or are we going to strike out another way?' The most activist decade in the century was born out of a rejection of prime time culture and politics.

There was moral outrage against apartheid, that is, legal segregation in the South. There was inspiration: seeing black students in Greensboro, North Carolina, sit-in, take chances. Feeling and knowing that we were part of a great historical process inspired us. We also responded to the cultural renaissance that was exploding around us – beat poetry, rock and roll, a sense of liberation. We felt that we had been cheated in our education, not having been told about the other America; about poverty and injustice in the past. And of course later there was the war, the immoral barbaric war in Vietnam.

Black people weren't able to vote. Poor people were in the streets. There had been an attempt to invade Cuba. We felt it was our responsibility to take on City Hall. Before the 1950s we wouldn't have known where City Hall was.

In a strange way we were responding to John Kennedy's 'ask not what your country can do for you but what you can do for your country'. We were volunteers fighting for a New America. We were going to remake the country so that the reality would fit closer to the myths about equality, and about being peaceful and fair in international relations.

There was also a sense that we were a break from the previous generation culturally and politically. We felt connected to youth around the world, in the sense that it was youth that was making the revolution, that youth would change things. So we didn't feel alone. We practised civil disobedience, fought in the streets, and also worked inside the system.

At the beginning of the 1960s I worked for the peace candidate H. Stewart Hughes, who was running as an independent in Massachusetts, and in this way was working through the system. I also worked with black people for voter registration in the South, which was certainly as far outside the system as you could get in Mississippi. The question of being legal or illegal, of being inside or outside the system, has always seemed to me to be merely metaphysical. The CIA, for example, operates outside the system, as do the utilities companies which have been violating the laws for years.

We saw the correct stance as having one foot out in the streets, which is outside the system. That is the foot of courage because you have to make a break with the system within which you have been raised. You put your whole heart into it. That is where you set out your visions of an alternative. This is where you show what the Emperor looks like without clothes, where you are confrontational.

The other foot is the foot of intelligence. It is inside the system. That is where you learn to build strategies, to form coalitions, to fundraise, etc. You learn how to institutionalize the changes that you are fighting for in the streets. So the correct stance is important; one foot outside, one foot inside. You have to do both. Young people like the confrontational part, but experiences teach us that you have to do both. It is not enough to be on the side of the angels. Success is important.

Our country was built by people at first operating outside the system. That was something we re-learned in the 1960s. That America was born in revolution. By breaking laws. By dumping tea in the Boston Harbor. By burning down Tory newspapers. Then they had to work inside the system in order to build coalitions, to pass the Bill of Rights, etc.

There were two lasting victories achieved in the 1960s. One was the legacy that you could fight the powers that be. There was little sense of this in the Cold War generation. The consciousness didn't exist that you had the ability to go out on to the streets and succeed, and effect decisions at the highest level. Today when there is intervention in Latin America we see thousands of people protesting in the streets. When there is obvious injustice there is massive organizing throughout our country, using technology to its fullest. The realization that you can fight this way rather than waiting every four years to vote for the lesser of two evils is the legacy of the 1960s.

The second legacy is that youth are in the forefront. Young people now are nostalgic for the 1960s and can understand why it was a great time to be young. Throughout the world. Chicago. Paris. Prague. Peking. Belfast. South Africa. We knew all about each other. Young people were fighting. They took a hell of a lot of risks with their careers, with their marriage plans, with their freedom (when they went to jail), with their lives. We were part of a cultural revolution. We made a break from the old styles of communication that the captains of industry and the Pentagon were using. The alternative was entering some faceless bureaucracy, and becoming a cog in a big machine. Taking orders from the power structure. That is not any fun. Doing things as they were always done simply because they say it should be that way, when you internally feel that something is not right. It's not good to live that way. It is better to act on your impulses, your heart, and then later to learn how to control those impulses, to control that energy, that moral outrage, that willingness to defy authority, and then to make yourself into a good organizer.

I'd like to correct one misconception about the period. People today often look at the 1960s as if viewing a video. Lots of chants, energy, excitement. They think of the 1960s as a spontaneous happening. That is an illusion. They don't think of it as grassroots organizing, coalition building, developing strategies. They don't see the hard work that went on behind the scenes. I can tell you that behind the scenes we had plenty of structure, plenty of leaders. The idea of a spontaneous movement takes many many leaders, and involves many structures. It's just that the structures were not hierarchical, like they are at IBM, and in corporate society.

You can't win a local issue without outside agitators, outside help, as well as with good local grassroots organization. It is always a minority that starts things happening. Stands on the street corner claiming the Emperor has no clothes. In the 1960s there were two cultures. We didn't have everybody on our side but we had more than nobody. We were creative, and we were flexible, and we were out to win. We learned how to use the opposition to expose its own stupidity and its own brutality.

Today looking at the world I'm pessimistic about some things and optimistic about others. The democratic institutions of our society have been virtually destroyed. The political process is little more than television advertisements. Our sense of reality is manipulated by special effects: 'We're number one. Rah rah'; 'If you are poor you should feel lucky to be poor in America.'

People are scared, unlike in the 1960s. There is little analysis of the existing society, economy and culture. We also have to construct a counter-reality of hope and belief in positive change; to envision alternatives, to organize. One of the lessons of the 1960s is that change can happen. It was taught in Mississippi by signs that said 'colored only'. Everybody said, 'You'll never change things, it's been the way for two hundred years.' But we did.

Of course many mistakes were made in the 1960s. But think of it in this way. If I was talking to Thomas Jefferson today I think he would have second thoughts about having had 75 slaves. But it wouldn't be right to start with this. I'd want to start with where he got the idea of public education, with how he came to write the Declaration (with its vision of human equality and of the social rights of 'life, liberty and the pursuit of happiness'), with how did he work to beat the British. I'd want to dwell on the achievements not the shortcomings.

What were the mistakes we made? We didn't do it long enough and hard enough. We became middle aged. We didn't make it stick enough. The mistakes were a result of issue-oriented politics as opposed to building parties. Once we won the issue and the Vietnam War was over, the anti-war movement was over. Once the Jim Crow signs came down and the battle against the obvious evil of legal segregation was over we could not sustain a protracted attack about the fundamentals.

We also weren't very sophisticated about government infiltration, about what the FBI was doing to divide us, to destroy our unity. I've come to rue consensus as a curse of the left, as minority rule. People who believe in universal consensus in decision-making should try it when four FBI agents and eight schizophrenics are part of a group. It is hard to maintain unity because in America we are trained to act only as individuals, not as a community.

Thomas Paine, my favourite amongst the Founders (he wrote *Common Sense*), said that 'generations can't lay their trip on later generations; each has to find their own way'. That is also part of the legacy of the 1960s. A very important part.

6. Students, Capital and the Multiversity:
Radical Challenges to the Dominant Pattern of American Higher Education from Berkeley to Livingston

Michael Klein

Capital and the Structure of American Education

> There is a natural alliance between business and academe.
>> The President of New England Telephone, speaking at a
>> US College Commencement exercise (October, 1989)

There is a contradiction in that the more a state claims to be 'free' the more the ruling class employs sophisticated means to limit choices in order to retain a monopoly of power. Control of the boundaries of good taste in thought – and limitation of the range of acceptable options for social action – are key aspects in the way that hegemony is maintained in a state capitalist democracy. The dominant institutions of education and the media attempt to ensure that a consensus is constructed that restricts our sense of what is possible and desirable to the ideological imperatives of the dominant classes and groups. Yet often within these institutions we begin to develop a critique, begin to see through the process, begin to set out alternative visions of education, culture and society – and inevitably challenge not only the consensus but the authority and interests of the power structure it legitimizes.

In *The Higher Learning in America* (1918), writing in the early days of the establishment of the modern form of the system of higher education in the US, Thorstein Veblen observed that 'discretionary control in matters of university policy now rests finally in the hands of businessmen' and politicians.[1] Veblen noted that this was facilitated by the direct and indirect control of the finance of education by boards of trustees, foundations and vested interests in government; 'which comes to saying that they exercise a pecuniary discretion in ... the way of deciding what the body of academic men that constitutes the university may or may not do'.[2] The resultant equation of business values and educational goals fostered a 'conservative habit of mind', both in educational policy and in framing the structure and content of education.[3] The system was also, for the most part, segregated according to race and class.

These developments can be traced back to the origins of public education in the US – a system for provision of skills and socialization for the children of workers and immigrants – at the start of the industrial revolution. The roots of the development of the educational rebellions of the 1960s go back to the type of system of education that was being established in the US by the late 1860s.

By the late nineteenth century higher education in America was being increasingly shaped by the needs of industrial capitalism. The most obvious aspect of this adaptation to commercial culture was the incorporation of vocational training into the curriculum of higher education. Equally important, the structure of educational discourse was fragmented, a process that occurs parallel to the division and atomization of labour on the assembly line in the factories and in the modern office. Knowledge becomes specialized, alienated, segregated. By the start of the First World War faculties of Arts and Sciences tended to be subdivided into departments, each specializing in a particular discipline, specialists communicating to fellow specialists in professional languages that outsiders – whether other specialists or the general public – can seldom understand. Engaged in a process of intellectual piecework, teachers and students lose control of the social function of their labour, which tends either to be appropriated by the needs of capital or to be reduced to decorative impotence. The connections between science and the humanities and between education and society are diminished.

Richard Ohmann and Russell Jacoby have traced some of the adverse effects of compartmentalization and professionalism in higher education: the erosion of critical intelligence; marginalization of the civic function of the intellectual. [4] Parallel to this process, and to the development of large-scale industrial corporations, higher education becomes increasingly subject to labour discipline, to cost-accounting and quantitative modes of assessment, and to business standards of management. Business jargon for review and control of intellectual work – 'periodic performance review system', 'self and peer appraisal', 'post-tenure evaluation', 'measurable standards of performance', [5] – both signify and mask a process of constraint that ensures the ideological domination of capital at all levels in the educational system. With the advent of Fordism the state begins to play an increasingly important role in regulating the economic and cultural life of the nation, ideologically defining the boundaries of legitimate inquiry, interpretation, debate and choice. The university soon takes the form of a corporation, organized according to the standardized norms of business management, the economic, political and cultural imperatives of the market, as well as prevailing constructions of the 'national interest'. Moreover, within the educational system as a whole cultural hegemony tends to be regulated by a complex process of coercion, constraint and reward.

> The doctrine of 'scientific management' [was] borrowed from industry where the work of Frederick Taylor in time and motion studies and other attempts to ensure cost-effectiveness and accountability was rapidly gaining ground ... Closely allied to ... scientific management ... one centered on 'social efficiency ...' To some tendencies in ... educational sociology it meant ... the schools as unparalleled instruments of social control ...[6]

The first empirical studies of the power elite that controls higher education in the US date back to the mid-1930s. Hubert Beck's study *The Men Who Control Our Universities*[7] focused upon 30 of the most prestigious private and public institutions: Beck discovered that half of the largest industrial and financial corporations were represented on the boards of trustees; one-third of the trustees of key universities were on the *Social Register*; the trustees held 54 directorships in 29 major educational foundations.[8] A parallel study by Merle Curti and Roderick Nash focused upon the role of foundations and private philanthropy – including the Carnegie and Rockefeller funds – in shaping the structure and educational policies of US universities.[9] David Caute has estimated that by 1950 80 per cent of trustees or regents of US universities were businessmen, bankers or politicians.[10]

In Cold War America pressures on education to conform were immense. The cultural life of the nation was regulated by outright coercion. By 1947 36 states had introduced loyalty oaths for teachers, 13 prohibiting employment to educators who had been affiliated with any of the several hundred organizations on the Attorney General's list.[11] In 1949 the House Un-American Activities Committee (HUAC) contacted 81 colleges and high schools, requesting information about textbooks used in the fields of literature, economics, history, political and social science.[12] Most boards of trustees, regents and administrators not only complied but also instituted actions of their own ranging from a purge of faculty (perhaps 1000 people lost their jobs and were blacklisted) to revision of teaching material in accord with Cold War ideological imperatives. Universities barred controversial speakers, in some cases checking their credentials with HUAC. President James Conant of Harvard declared that Communist Party members were 'out of bounds as members of the teaching profession'.[13] The first dismissals of faculty who cited the Fifth Amendment when called before the US Senate Internal Security Subcommittee took place at Rutgers University in 1952.[14] At the University of California action was initiated against 44 professors by the Board of Regents after they refused to sign a non-Communist loyalty oath. While the faculty as a whole expressed their displeasure with the oath, the academic Senate of the University of California passed a resolution declaring that Communists should not be allowed to teach at UC.[15] As late as 1956, the American Association of University Professors – a relatively liberal civil liberties-oriented organization – declared:

> The academic community has a duty to defend society and itself from subversion of the educational process ... including ... false causes. Any member of the academic profession who has given reasonable evidence that he uses such tactics should be proceeded against forthwith and should be expelled from his position if his guilt is established ...
>
> The administrations of colleges and universities should, of course, take note of the possible unfitness of faculty members. If a Faculty Member invokes the Fifth Amendment when questioned about Communism, or if there are other indications of past or present Communist associations or activities, his institution cannot ignore the possible significance ...[16]

One would have thought that testing received wisdom and putting forward new and perhaps controversial ideas were fundamental to the process of education. However, in higher education in America, from the time of Veblen, the parameters of intellectual enquiry have been closely structured and regulated in line with the dominant ideology. In the decade of the onset of the Cold War syllabuses that had been set in the New Deal era and the wartime alliance against fascism were revised. Students who entered university at the end of the 1950s and the early 1960s thus found themselves in institutions where there were severe constraints upon intellectual freedom, in which education was specialized and compartmentalized, and in which restrictions against political advocacy masked an institutional commitment to the economic, political and military prerogatives of the power elite.

The Berkeley Rebellions and the Cultural Revolution in Education

> There is a time when the operation of the machine becomes so odious, makes you feel so sick at heart that you cannot take part, you can't even tacitly take part. And you've got to put your body on the gears, and upon the wheels and upon the levers and upon all the apparatus and you've got to make it stop. And you've got to indicate to the people who own it, and the people who run it, that unless you are free their machine will be prevented from operating at all.
>
> Mario Savio, Sproul Hall Sit-In, December 1964[17]

The revolt of students at the University of California at Berkeley in 1964, which was one of the sparks of the student movement of the 1960s, took place at a university that was the epitome of higher education in America. Mario Savio's call to resistance conflated two revolutions: a social and political revolution (the civil rights movement, opposition to the war in Vietnam, struggles against poverty and injustice); and an educational revolution against the structure and ideology of the modern American multiversity.

The term 'multiversity' is Clark Kerr's. Kerr was president and chief administrative officer of the University of California at Berkeley in 1964. He was also the author of a book that set out a theory of the university that was a distillation of corporate state liberalism – the ideology of a society that was the subject of radical challenge in the 1960s.

In *The Uses of the University* (1963) Kerr set out a philosophy of a university as a compliant junior partner to business and government that was all too willing 'to adapt' [18] to the demands of its patrons, including the federal government, which by 1961 was financing 75 per cent of all university expenditures on research, 40 per cent of which were directly linked to Cold War-related military projects and, as the decade unfolded, to military projects related to the war in Vietnam.[19] In short, as Kerr noted and affirmed, the university had become an instrument of the Cold War liberal consensus since the Second World War and the emergence of the US as the dominant world power:

> So many of the hopes and fears of the American people are now related to our educational system ... our fears of Russian or Chinese supremacy ... of individual loss of purpose in the changing world. For all these reasons and others, the university has become a prime instrument of national purpose. This is new. This is the essence of the transformation now engulfing our universities ... Basic to this transformation is the growth of the 'knowledge industry,' which is coming to permeate government and business ...
>
> Intellect has also become an instrument of national purpose, a

component part of the 'military-industrial complex...' In the war of the ideological worlds, a great deal depends upon the use of this instrument ... It only pays to produce knowledge if through production it can be put to use better and faster.

The process cannot be stopped ... It remains to adapt.[20]

It is this conception of the university, and of education as merely training, that was challenged by Mario Savio during the sit-in in Sproul Hall: 'One conception of the university ... is that it be in the world but not of the world. The conception of Clark Kerr by contrast is that ... it stands to serve the need of American industry ... or government.' [21]

The critique was further rooted in student experience of the multiversity by Brad Cleaveland, in an education manifesto that was widely distributed in leaflet and pamphlet form in Berkeley in 1964 and 1965:

The multiversity is not an Educational center ... it produces enormous numbers of safe, highly skilled and respectable automatons to meet the immediate needs of business and government ...

In the name of human learning you acquire the capacity to be docile in the face of rules. While you are training, the rules which tell you how to go about your training are displacing your freedom to think ... skill and obedience are what you acquire.[22]

Cleaveland's intervention was extended by Paul Goodman in a general call to restructure the form of the American university:

Thus far in the Berkeley revolt, two new factors have emerged: [1] The students want to extend the concept of Academic Freedom from *Lehrfreiheit* (freedom of professors to teach according to their lights) to include *Lernfreiheit* (freedom of students to ask for what they need to be taught, and if necessary to invite teachers, including advocates of causes).[23]

It is also significant that Cleaveland regarded overcoming the constraints of the form of higher education in the modern multiversity as an integral part of a challenge to the hegemony of Cold War ideology. His education manifesto prodded the students to attempt to see beyond the confines of the Second World War establishment consensus:

You will not learn that, at home, here in the good ole USA, in the civil rights revolution which is now going on, the phrase 'white backlash' ... used by 'scholars,' so-called liberals, advocated by conservatives, is the simplistic way to say 'the bigotry of the majority' ...

And you will learn most of all not to entertain so much as the possibility that American foreign policy in Korea and South Viet Nam are precisely counter-revolutionary ... That the American nation is involved in destroying popular national revolutions, and appears to be getting itself locked more and more in that suicidal and inhumane policy ...[24]

The debate can only be fully understood in the context of the times. At the dawn of the 1960s the student movement, in launching demonstrations against the House Un-American Activities Committee in the San Francisco Bay Area, had begun to challenge Cold War politics. The on-campus activities of Turn Toward Peace, the Student Peace Union and SANE were challenges, in varying degrees, not only to Cold War policies (nuclear testing, the arms race) but to the ideological assumptions that underpinned those policies. Student opposition to the US-sponsored invasion of Cuba at the Bay of Pigs in 1961, solidarity with the civil rights movement and its tactics of civil disobedience and mass protests, and opposition to the war in Vietnam in 1965, marked a sharp break from the Cold War liberal consensus and the policies of the mainstream of the Democratic Party. Insofar as these demonstrations were often discussed, debated, organized and launched on campuses they were a direct challenge to the ideological foundations and ethos of the multiversity: research divorced from social value; service to the military, government and capital within the norms of the postwar ruling class consensus; specialization of function by discipline ('intellectual', 'human being', 'revolutionary', 'citizen', being moral and political but non-academic categories, unlike 'political scientist' or 'English major'.)

When 814 students sat-in at Sproul Hall of the University of California at Berkeley in the autumn of 1964, organized a successful strike of 20,000 students in support of their demands, and for a brief time won near unanimous backing of the faculty, the immediate issues were: the university's prohibition of on-campus advocacy and of organization of off-campus political activity; the arrest of the 814 students as well as of other students who had set up literature tables and given out leaflets on previous occasions. However, the free speech and civil liberties issues were related to regional and national concerns. The subtext of the Free Speech Movement (FSM) campaign was solidarity and involvement with campaigns against discrimination in hiring black people in San Francisco, Oakland and Berkeley. By May of 1965, when the Vietnam Day Committee (VDC) organized a two-day teach-in about the Vietnam War, which was attended by 30,000 people, and followed by a demonstration at the Selective Service office near campus at Shatuck Avenue at which several students burned their draft cards, the political agenda had broadened to include opposition to the war in Vietnam and to the US invasion of the Dominican Republic. Three months later students gathered to protest the war at the railroad tracks in the environs of Berkeley where soldiers were being shipped off to Vietnam. They were greeted with solidarity by the young conscripts.[25]

I had the good fortune of being a student in Berkeley and of having a role in the FSM campaign as well as in the activities staged by the Vietnam Day Committee. These events were holistic moments of liberation. The sit-in at Sproul Hall on 2-3 December 1964 was on one level a protest against university actions in disciplining students and in forbidding meetings and rallies at which advocacy of off-campus political action might occur. When the 800 marched into the building their actions also signified solidarity with the civil rights movement, and opposition to racism and discrimination in US society. Within Sproul Hall the students established the seeds of an alternative or counter-university. We were creating the future within the shell of the old institutions. Or so it seemed. Classes were held on literature and sociology and history, but viewed from new and different perspectives. The insights of previous generations were rediscovered as if they were new.

The new curriculum was further advanced when the Vietnam Day teach-in assembled on 21-2 May 1965. The teach-in was a great academic festival. While the primary focus was the war, there were also sessions on poor people's projects and campaigns for integrated education, lectures on the global dynamics of capitalism and imperialism and workshops on the cultural politics of literature, folk and rock music. The speakers were not specialists from the faculty of the University of California (those who were invited refused to attend) but intellectuals who had been blacklisted and marginalized during the Cold War era (Harry Magdoff, Isaac Deutscher, I.F. Stone) as well as a new generation of radicals who were challenging not only government ideology and policy on the issue of the war but the academic establishment's definitions of expert and expertise.

Equally important, the students who participated in these events had forged a sense of community in the midst of the alienation that pervaded not only the multiversity but also the atomized, individualistic and materialistic society in which it was situated: a sense of empowerment, of being able to shake a structure that had seemed fixed and immutable since the Eisenhower and McCarthy eras, of being able to change the world. We had dared to struggle and to change the rules of the game. For we had not only challenged the police, the state and the most reactionary sectors of the media (the Hearst and Knowland press); we had proved that we were right; we had out-organized and outmanoeuvred the Governor, the Board of Regents, Clark Kerr, the campus administration and their advisers from the Political Science and Social Science faculties. In the midst of the struggles we had created poetry (Ken Sanderson's 'Multiversity Lost'); drama (Barbara Garson's *MacBird*); songs and oratory (FSM's *Sounds and Songs of the Demonstration* album, the speeches of Mario Savio and Lenny Glaser); produced documentary phonograph records of the events at Berkeley as well as several films (*Berkeley Vietnam Day 1965*, *An American Dream*), and published political analyses of the links between the university and the power structure that confirmed and extended the pioneer studies of Veblen, Beck and Curti (Hal Draper's 'The Mind of Clark Kerr', Marvin Garson's 'The Regents', Bettina Aptheker's 'Big Business and the American University', Brad Cleaveland's 'Education Manifesto', FSM's 'We want a University'). The movement itself was a great university, a new community. [26]

The movement seemed to be engaging Goliath on all fronts, like the Sons of Liberty in 1776 or the NLF in Vietnam. Throughout the 1960s it influenced (and in turn was influenced by) events that ranged from the student–worker rebellion in Paris of May 1968 and anti-Vietnam War student unrest in England and Germany, to the student phase of the cultural revolution in China and, at the end of the decade, the student-led People's Democracy marches of the civil rights movement in the north of Ireland. It was a time when everything seemed possible.

Student consciousness challenged the ideological foundations of the universities of the *ancien régime* on all fronts. At the level of theory Martin Nicolaus, Herbert Gintis, Martin Sklar and Richard Flacks argued that students, and educated labour in general, occupied a strategic position in post-industrial capitalist society, in which unfulfilled desire and the liberating ideals of democracy are frustrated, not by the capacity of the system to satisfy needs but by the imperatives of profit which engender a network of irrationalities, injustices, barbarities, oppressions and alienations. [27] Thus there was a certain logic in the university becoming a locus of the contradictions of US society in the 1960s.[28] However the student revolt of the 1960s was interpreted by the scribes and pharisees of the dominant culture in a different way. *The Report of the President's Commission on Campus Unrest*, echoing the mentality of the great purge of the McCarthy era, maintained that militant campus dissent was primarily the result of 'a small minority of politically extreme students and faculty members', and that these neo-subversives should be 'identified, [and] removed from the university as swiftly as possible'.[29] The Commission insisted that 'universities as institutions must remain politically neutral.' [30] Given the context of their report – nationwide campus involvement in anti-Vietnam War, civil rights and other radical reform activities – this was an injunction to turn the clock back and maintain the status quo *ante bellum* in the sphere of higher education in America.

The intensity of the negation of Cold War ideology on campus in the US in the 1960s can be illustrated by reference to a survey that was conducted in Berkeley of 570 of the 814 students who took part in the FSM occupation of Sproul Hall in December 1964. The students filled out a 53-page survey (279 questions) in February 1965 that was concerned not only with the circumstances of the sit-in, but also with their family background, the nature of their involvement in previous student protests, their experience of education at the university, and their cultural and political perspectives.[31]

Judith Radu is a fairly typical representative of the students who identified with the FSM from the inception of the conflict and took part in the sit-in. Judith reported that she studied 30–40 hours a week, read 20 or so books a year in addition to her required assignments, listened to FM radio 10–20 hours a week, preferred small classes and seminars, and believed that awareness, individual discovery and self-insight were the most important goals in education. She was somewhat alienated from education at the large, impersonal and bureaucratic University of California. Judith Radu's family was geographically mobile, having moved from Ohio to San Jose, California. Both parents were from immigrant stock (Romania, Russia). They had a high school education, were skilled working class (her father was an electrician), and had a family income of US$3000 in 1964. There was, perhaps, a certain amount of self-perceived upward mobility: the family, once Greek Orthodox, had become Unitarians. Judith had made an effort to register as a voter. Her party preference prior to 1964 was Democrat (the party of Kennedy and Johnson). Her parents were independent voters.

Thus far this is a somewhat typical profile of a serious middle-American student in the early 1960s. Then, after involvement in the praxis of FSM, there is a significant change. It is dramatically registered in her reply to the following questions:

'Do you feel the Court has a moral right to sentence you to jail?'
'No. We were constitutionally justified in sitting-in.'
'Would you ever again subject yourself to arrest for some act of civil disobedience?'
'Yes.'
'What University political organizations do you belong to?'
'Campus CORE [a civil rights organization]; Campus Women for Peace.'
'What candidate did you favor in the Presidential election last fall?'
'DeBerry.' [Socialist Workers' Party]
'In terms of political ideology, how would you classify yourself?'

She had a choice of: 'Conservative'; 'Moderate'; 'Liberal'; 'Reform Socialist'; and 'Revolutionary Socialist'. She chose to identify herself as 'Revolutionary Socialist'.

A sampling of students who were significantly involved throughout the FSM events shows a similar profile: 50 per cent identified themselves as 'Revolutionary Socialist'; 25 per cent as 'Reform Socialist'; 20 per cent as 'Liberal'; 5 per cent did not indicate; 0 per cent indicated 'Moderate' or 'Conservative'.[32]

In November of 1964 35 per cent of this group voted for a protest candidate for president of the United States (most often Clifton DeBerry of the Socialist Workers' Party, in several cases Dizzy Gillespie who was a SLATE choice for write-in candidate in the Berkeley area). Those protesting the limitations of the two-party system by not casting a vote constituted 25 per cent; and 35 per cent voted for the Democratic Party, often as a protest against Goldwater and the ultra-right. The GOP obtained 5 per cent of the vote. In the next presidential election in 1968, 38 per cent of the Sproul Hall students voted for alternative protest candidates (Peace and Freedom Party, etc.); 22 per cent deliberately refused to vote; 34 per cent voted for the Democratic Party.

By 1968 the changes in consciousness that had been initially registered at Berkeley (as well as at Harvard, Columbia, Wisconsin, Michigan, and San Francisco State) had achieved a certain hegemony on campuses throughout the nation. Detailed surveys of student opinion on 94 campuses conducted by Daniel Yankelovich for *Fortune* magazine, CBS Network News and the John D. Rockefeller Fund in 1968, 1970 and 1971 are an index of the consciousness that existed on campus at the end of the 1960s.[33] Counter to the ethos of the multiversity only 18 per cent indicated that money was a significant goal in life or education. The students' responses to a series of overtly political questions were also a challenge to Clark Kerr's concept of a multiversity in service to government and the military-industrial complex, as well as to the dominant ideology of the nation and of the educational system during the period of the Cold War consensus.

- Institutions that most need change: the Universities (85% agree); the Political Parties (92% agree); the FBI (74% agree).
- Tactics that are sometimes justified: sit-ins (91% agree); shielding political prisoners and fugitives (71% agree); resisting or disobeying the police (65% agree); bombing or setting fire to buildings owned by large corporations (15% agree).
- Groups that are not likely to have a fair trial: Black Panthers (71%); Radicals (60%); Weathermen (49%); Vietnam War Crimes criminals (16%); Slumlords (11%).
- What is wrong with our society?: the Vietnam War (76%); pollution (71%); racial prejudice (62%); poverty (60%).
- If the Vietnam War was to end similar military involvements are inevitable if present policies continue (68% agree).

AMERICAN HIGHER EDUCATION

- US foreign policy is based upon our own narrow economic and power interests (88% agree).
- The war in Vietnam is pure imperialism (79% agree).
- Business is too concerned with profits and not public responsibility (95% agree).
- The US is basically a racist nation (89% agree).
- The establishment unfairly controls every aspect of our lives: we can never be free until we get rid of it (58% agree).
- The real power in this country lies with the giant corporations not the government (51% agree).
- Our present system of government is democratic in name only, and the mass of the people are propagandized that what they say really counts (51% agree).
- The two-party system offers no real alternative (84% agree).
- A mass revolutionary party should be created (33% agree).
- A total change in the American system is needed, not just significant reforms (31% agree).

From the Teach-In to the New Curriculum

> We have striven to produce an unconventional and contemporary ... view of American culture in a period of unprecedented conflict and change by choosing works from the very best and most committed writers today.
>
> *Voices of Concern*

The students on campuses throughout the US at the end of the 1960s did not want higher education in America simply to 'adapt' to the imperatives of the corporations, finance and the establishment. There were significant demographic changes taking place in the student body as well. For example, in the City University of New York 42 per cent of the first year students in 1971 came from families with incomes below US$7,500; 20 per cent were black or Hispanic.[34] With the advent of Open Admissions policies the population of some state university systems doubled in a few years.

For the most part the new students were: (a) blacks; (b) Vietnam War veterans; (c) 'non-traditional' or white working-class students.

Moreover, by 1971 the new teachers in the community colleges, colleges and universities were often graduates of the movement and of the struggles of the 1960s, about to undertake what Rudi Dutschke, in adapting Mao to the realities of the 1970s, had called 'a long march through all the institutions of society'. They and the new students often had some experience of the *geist* of the anti-Vietnam War, of civil rights/black liberation and educational reform movements, of teach-ins and ad-hoc free universities. As the political struggles of the 1960s waned a cultural revolution was lodged within the institutions of US higher education.

A renaissance had quietly taken place. Between 1962 and 1965 the core texts of New Left radicalism were produced or discovered: Marcuse's *One-dimensional Man: Studies in the Ideology of Advanced Industrial Society*; C. Wright Mills' *Power, Politics and People*; the *Port Huron Statement*; Leo Marx's *The Machine in the Garden: Technology and the Pastoral Idea in America*; Fanon's *The Wretched of the Earth*; Williams' *The Contours of American History*.

Between 1968 and 1971, as movement and anti-war activity peaked and then began to decline, a number of key books were published. Taken together they define a new political orientation, a new sensibility, a new consciousness. In a sense the Great Books of the late 1960s can be regarded as the start of a new humanities curriculum. For example: Kampf's *The Politics of Literature*; Silberman's *Crisis in the Classroom: The Remaking of America*; Green's *The Enemy: What Every American Should know About Imperialism*; Malcolm X's *By Any Means Necessary*; Jackson's *Soledad Brother*; Gitlin's *Campfires of Resistance* (movement poetry); Barry's *Winning Hearts and Minds* (Vietnam veteran anti-war poetry); Hayden's *Rebellion and Repression*; Magdoff's *The Age of Imperialism: the Economics of US Foreign Policy*; Domhoff's *Who Rules America*; Rubin's *Do It*; Reich's *The Greening of America*; Hoffman's *Woodstock Nation*; Roszak's *The Making of a Counter Culture*; Toffler's *Future Shock*; Millett's *Sexual Politics*.

Equally important, changes in the syllabuses of required courses taken by most first-year students, especially in 'readers' – that is, collections of essays designed to be the basic text in large introductory courses in literature, history, and social science – are a significant index of a transformation in consciousness within US higher education that was a fruit of the struggles of the 1960s.[35] Multidisciplinary in orientation, these texts extended an opportunity to students to transcend the alienated piecework structure of the established disciplines and to link their academic study to comprehension of the world. Moreover, the content of these readers was revolutionary in that they reconstructed from the historical memory of world culture a counter-hegemonic and liberating tradition of dissent and insurgence, from classical antiquity and the enlightenment to the nineteenth and twentieth centuries. Classes organized in study of the cultural politics of the new syllabus shattered the restrictive, traditional definition of academic freedom in higher education in America. Remember that the American Association of

University Professors (AAUP) had warned professors 'not to introduce into teaching material controversial matter' that fell outside 'the limits' of their discipline'.36 By Cold War consensus standards the new syllabuses constituted 'subversion of the educational process'.37 A cultural revolution was underway that challenged bourgeois hegemony within higher education and opened up space for consideration of liberating perspectives.

As a good deal of the new curriculum was revised or modified in the Reagan era and thus may not be familiar I will illustrate it in some detail. The readers fall into several categories. First of all there are a number of anthologies that draw upon American or popular cultural material in establishing a new curriculum. Robert Uphaus's *American Protest in Perspective* (1971) announces in the introduction that it is one of many new 'protest anthologies'.38 It contains essays by Thomas Jefferson (the 'Declaration'), Thomas Paine, Henry David Thoreau ('Civil Disobedience'), Frederick Douglass, W.E.B. Dubois, James Baldwin, LeRoi Jones, Martin Luther King ('Letter from Birmingham Jail'), and Eldridge Cleaver of the Black Panther Party. Morris Friedman and Carolyn Banks' *American Mix: The Minority Experience in America* (1972) was similar in orientation – contributions by Jefferson, King, the Black Panther Party, the Young Lords, etc.39 Barbara Graves and Donald McBain in *Lyric Voices: Approaches to the Poetry of Contemporary Song* (1972) selected material from the protest music of the 1960s as the basis for the new syllabus. Writers featured include Bob Dylan, Pete Seeger, Phil Ochs, Tom Paxton, Buffy Sainte Marie, Donovan, Grace Slick, Tim Hardin and Carl Oglesby (the SDS activist).40

Other readers were drawn from oppositional material that had appeared in mass market magazines such as *Esquire* and *Playboy*. For example *Voices of Concern: The Playboy College Reader* (1971) included interviews with Eldridge Cleaver and Marshall McLuhan as well as articles by Paul Goodman ('The Deadly Halls of Ivy'), Frank Donner ('Spies on Campus'), Jon Waltz ('13 Legal Questions Raised by the Trial of the Chicago 8'), and Alan Watts ('Wealth vs Money').41 Edward Quinn and Paul Dolan's *The Sense of the Sixties* included widely published material by Paul Goodman, Michael Harrington, Staughton Lynd, Susan Sontag, Martin Luther King and Stokely Carmichael, all of whom had been active in either the civil rights or anti-Vietnam War protest movements.42

Charles Muscatine (distinguished professor of English at UC Berkeley and Chair of the UC Berkeley Academic Senate Select Committee on Education that produced the study *Education at Berkeley*)43 and Marlene Griffith's *The Borzoi College Reader* (1971) included articles by Theodore Roszak, LeRoi Jones, Haig Bosmajian ('The Language of

White Racism'), James Baldwin, Malcolm X ('The Bullet or the Ballot'), as well as the key texts by Jefferson, Thoreau, Martin Luther King and Mao Zedong.[43] *The Devil's Party* (1970), edited by Tim Drescher and Glen Miller, was derived from the English syllabus at the University of Wisconsin at Madison.[44] Contributors included Jefferson, Ho Chi Minh, Jean Paul Sartre and Frantz Fanon. Sheila Delaney's *Counter-Tradition: The Literature of Dissent and Alternatives* (1971), focused on the 'tradition which opposes', and featured texts by Spartacus, John Ball, Gerrard Winstanley, Thomas Paine, Mary Wollstonecraft, Karl Marx, Thoreau, Frederick Douglass, W.E.B. DuBois, Elizabeth Cady Stanton, Malcolm X, Mao Zedong, Ho Chi Minh and Marshall McLuhan.[45] *Counter-Tradition* had an endorsement by Louis Kampf, who was at that time president of the Modern Language Association of America:

> Freshman courses and textbooks are usually an introduction to the dominant culture ... and to the going ideologies masking societies' real concerns ... Here finally ... is a long overdue alternative ... This collection invites us to get into the habit of studying what really matters to us – and that is the beginning of real education.[46]

Kampf's own anthology, *The Politics of Literature* (1970), was intended as a guide to both the teaching and reading of literature.[47] In his Preface Kampf noted that most of the contributors had been 'deeply transformed' by the events of the 1960s, and that nearly all the academics who wrote material for the book had been involved in 'civil disobedience in protest against the war and domestic oppressions'.[48] Kampf's book set out a new definition of an academic: he/she should be an 'organic intellectual' (Gramsci), in touch with the national-popular movements of the time, not a cog in the wheel of the establishment multiversity.

Several other books aimed at the social science and history student also became set texts in English and Humanities first-year university courses: John Leggett's *Taking State Power* (1971); Bruce Franklin's anthology *From the Movement Toward Revolution* (1971); Felix Greene's *The Enemy: What Every American Should Know About Imperialism* (1971).[49] By the end of the 1960s a different kind of student, teacher and syllabus had been created.

The Livingston Experiment

> Those who profess to favor freedom yet deprecate agitation, are men who want crops without plowing the ground; want rain without thunder and lightning ...
> Frederick Douglass

> Livingston College cannot ignore the society of which it is a part. It is in a context of a world torn by grave problems that higher education takes place today ... Livingston ... questions ... the very goals of the society ... From this perspective the college intends to enable students not only to perceive societal needs but to affect their environment and shape their own development ... At Livingston, the arts are not seen as an escape from reality, but as a means of bearing witness to the crises of the times. In essence, that is the basic role of the college.
>
> From the Livingston College Catalog

There is a tradition of violation of academic freedom at Rutgers. The first Fifth Amendment dismissals in the US occurred there in 1952.[50] In 1990 the distinguished black writer and activist Amiri Baraka was denied tenure by the Rutgers English Department.[51] However at the end of the 1960s a beachhead of educational liberation was established at Livingston College, which for slightly more than a decade was a college within Rutgers, the federated state university of New Jersey.

The educational mission of Livingston was set out clearly in its prospectus. The quotation from Frederick Douglass on the first page of the 1972 Livingston Catalog was a double-edged sign. On the one hand it signified the college's general endorsement of movement activism of the 1960s, of an ideology of activism and struggle, of 'agitation' for 'freedom', which in the context of the 1960s would have been understood as a nexus of demands that included civil rights/black liberation and non-compliance with the war in Vietnam. Reference to Douglass, a former slave and the foremost nineteenth-century black radical leader, was also a clear sign that the college welcomed Afro-American students, and was committed to a policy of hiring minority faculty.

The statement of educational policy that followed placed the college in an oppositional position to the goals of establishment society, encouraged students to adopt critical perspectives and to intervene to promote positive social and cultural change. A negative reference to 'knowledge factories' [52] was a further indication that the founders and faculty of Livingston had been profoundly influenced by the critiques of Clark Kerr's concept of 'the multiversity'. Reforms of the structure of education went beyond the recommendations of the UC Berkeley Muscatine report, moving toward the ideal of 'tutorial'-based 'mass, noncoercive higher education' that Mario Savio championed in the 1960s. For example, the standard system of grading was abolished; in the early years the college was governed by a bicameral chamber that gave equal power to students and faculty, and some courses were taught collectively by the students who were taking them with faculty guidance. Students also had significant representation on course and hiring committees.

When I was hired to teach at Livingston many of the questions at the interview were asked by student members of the panel.

The Livingston student body included a large number of 'non-traditional' (that is working-class) students. A quarter of the student population was drawn from the Afro-American community and received significant financial aid. The faculty (white, Afro-American and Hispanic) was a diverse mixture of young scholars as well as community and labour activists, practising poets, playwrights, musicians, journalists and educators.[54] Some of the best, most dedicated and creative teachers in the country migrated to Livingston in the early years of the experiment.

Equally important, programmes and courses that had been initiated in the radical teach-ins and the pioneer ad-hoc free universities of the 1960s were incorporated in the accredited BA degrees of the college. For example, the syllabus of an introductory college-wide course in Class and Race given by the Philosophy Department included readings from Marx, Lenin, Garvey, Fanon, Malcolm X and Che Guevara. A course in the Anthropology Department began with an examination of 'the impact of capitalism, colonialism and imperialism on the peoples of the Third World' and concluded with 'an examination of the reactions to conquest ... armed resistance and wars of liberation'. A course offered by the English Department in seventeenth- and twentieth-century Prose and Poetry studied 'John Donne's sermons alongside Malcolm X's speeches'. Physical Education was organized on an 'alternative' and non-competitive basis.[55] Marxist theory was studied in a wide range of disciplines. African as well as European languages and literatures were taught in the liberal arts programme.

Very little of this sort of material was taught in a positive way to undergraduates at the University of California at Berkeley in 1964, although Berkeley was many times larger than Livingston. Livingston, founded in 1969 under the direction of its first Dean, Ernest Lynton, was one of many US colleges and universities that took on board the thrust of the progressive cultural revolution of the 1960s. The significance of Berkeley lay not only in the events that took place there but in the praxis of the struggle being fought out by antagonists who articulated fundamentally opposed theories of education and society (Savio and Cleaveland/Clark Kerr). The history of Livingston is significant in that the struggles that erupted there, in the mid-1970s when the college came under attack, were also theorized by the participants: on the one hand the mission and ethos of the college; on the other an antagonistic ideology of education and society articulated by Emmanual Mesthene, who replaced Ernest Lynton as Dean of the college in 1974, coming to Livingston from Harvard Business School to restore establishment hegemony.

Days of Restoration: Deconstructing Livingston

> First, the Program was set up ... under a $5,000,000 grant from the IBM Corporation ... We have recently announced formation of a high-level Advisory Committee of eminent figures from industry, government and the universities ... I am suggesting that my titular idea of Social Heracliteanism might serve as an organizing function in the area of technology and education.
>
> Emmanual Mesthene

Whereas Clark Kerr's writings, especially *The Uses of the University*, were public documents readily available in most libraries and campus bookshops, like John Silber's influential radical-baiting article 'Poisoning the Wells of Academe', which was published in *Encounter* in 1974, Mesthene's interventions were often covert, semi-private studies commissioned by the ruling class for their own guidance. From 1957 until 1974 Mesthene was employed as a consultant by RAND corporation, a Santa Monica think-tank linked to the US military, which in the 1950s commissioned studies on the feasibility of nuclear war, and in the next decade turned its attention to Vietnam, to strategies of counter-insurgency in the south of Vietnam and of containment of the student anti-war movement at home. In 1971 a RAND report advised curtailment of open admissions policies in higher education and phasing out of compensatory education of minority and working-class students.

Prior to becoming a theorist on education and social control Mesthene's work for RAND in the Cold War era of the 1950s and during the war in Vietnam was primarily concerned with military matters and the cultural infrastructure to sustain war: 'Planning for research and development ... is very much like planning for war.' [56] His research interests included a controlled experiment in the utilization of electronic surveillance devices, and a study of community higher education in the New York metropolitan area. Our interest is in his theory of education as behaviour modification, a strategy for 'training wants, needs and preferences' to conform to the needs of advanced technocratic capitalism.

I came across some of Mesthene's work for RAND in his office by chance shortly after he became Dean and announced his intention to 'turn Livingston around'. Additional information was supplied by students following an occupation of the Dean's office that was organized by an emerging student union. This was augmented by material acquired through collaborative research by faculty and students. The findings were the subject of a pamphlet entitled 'The Mesthene Papers' that was widely circulated, read and discussed at Livingston.[57] All my quotations from Mesthene's writings are cited from this document. While

Mesthene's theory of education and society owed something to scientific management social control theories that were developed in Veblen's time,[58] as well as to the work of Clark Kerr, it exceeded the brief of his predecessors in that education for Mesthene was the primary site for the maintenance of the ideological hegemony of capital, in the face of changes engendered by economic decline, automation, de-industrialization and global realignment of investment.

It is this aspect of Mesthene's work that I would like to explore for a moment, and the 'late capitalist' (the term is Mandel's) assumptions that underlie it, some of which became a commonplace of postmodernist media pronouncements on social, educational and cultural policy in the 1980s in the US and the UK, both within establishment and some 'left' oppositional circles. Mesthene defined his philosophical stance as 'social heracliteanism', in opposition to humanism ('Romantic Idealism') and 'Marxian materialism'. 'Social heracliteanism' – somewhat like social darwinism – posits the existence of an irrepressible force ('technology' rather than 'nature') that transforms society and culture through a variant of natural selection: the promotion of continuous change; apparent obsolescence; pragmatic accommodation. Upon closer inspection the dynamic of this process turns out to be the changing needs of business and the military, the anarchy of the market, and the policy decisions of finance capital.

Education and the media have a crucial role to play in Mesthene's scenario. Extending Alexander Pope's eighteenth-century apology for emerging capitalism, *whatever is is right*, to a cultural imperative for a post-industrial society in crisis, *whatever is must be*, Mesthene argued that the role of education is to construct value systems, modes of consciousness and identity functional to the requirements of the 'heraclitean' process of change: 'Emphasis will have to shift ... from values to valuing ... guiding us to the reformulation of our ends ... Choice behavior must be somehow attuned to the new options ... altering value predisposition and attitudes ... so they will be chosen.'

Writing during the ferment of the late 1960s, Mesthene expressed concern that 'negative political reaction by certain groups in society' (presumably radical coalitions of students and national minorities as well as sectors of the workforce who would be made redundant by automation, de-industrialization and the flight of capital) would lead to long-term political 'uncertainty', advised the use of techniques of 'systems analysis' to identify potential problems, and looked forward to a time when 'personal identity' based upon 'identification with a particular social group, trade or profession' (that is, class and national consciousness) would be 'subject to Heraclitean flux' and disappear. In the future the triumph of 'heraclitean flux' and of establishment hegemony (over traditional humanist values, radical dissent, class consciousness, etc.) might be ensured by scientific management of consciousness: 'Increasing knowledge of the chemical basis of memory raises the theoretical possibility of implanting learning or information in individuals with no effort or even awareness of the fact on their part.' In the present, however, the maintenance of hegemony, or in Mesthene's words, the training of functional 'needs, wants and preferences', is the primary mission of education, a task to be undertaken in partnership with business and government. Education of a particular sort is of crucial importance to capital so that its hegemonic position can be maintained. During the Vietnam War radical attacks on the links of education with the military-industrial complex had disturbed this special relationship. Thus traditional links had to be restored throughout all levels of the educational system: 'The government must finance it and set its standards, industry will enter into it ... That education is on the way to becoming big business is perhaps the most encouraging trend I see on the horizon.'

For Clark Kerr the university was a 'knowledge factory' to provide a broad range of services to business and industry. Mesthene gives greater emphasis to the ideological function of the multiversity, as by the late 1960s and early 1970s the hegemony of capital in educational institutions throughout the nation had been challenged, and their ability to train future ruling and managerial elites compromised, by the content of the new radical syllabuses, by new patterns of education, and by a democratic spirit that had been fostered by open admissions policies and which facilitated the entry of minorities and youth from working-class backgrounds to radicalized sectors of higher education. Mesthene, an advocate of hierarchical education for a stratified society, had applauded the 'increasing relegation of questions which used to be matters of political debate to professional cadres of technicians and experts which function almost independently of the democratic political process', regarding the rest of the population as 'natural slaves, who have little of value to contribute to themselves or to society except their mechanical ability', although they might be capable of technological upgrading, providing they were socialized into the appropriate consciousness and skills. Thus open admissions and ideological dissonance were the first targets of his campaign at Livingston.

As the whole thrust of the cultural revolutions on campus in the 1960s had been democratic and oppositional, the encounter at Livingston took the form of a struggle between two vanguards. The encounter was emblematic of a general trend in education and society in the mid-1970s. By 1974 the American war in Vietnam was over, the peace movement had not developed into a mass-based progressive alliance and the civil rights movement was in disarray. Unlike 1964, when the Berkeley rebellion began, or 1969, when Livingston was founded, right-wing forces had regained the initiative in many sectors of the society and culture. The process of restoration of normalcy at Livingston and other advanced sectors of education was a sophisticated version of a *Thermidor* that took the form of military intervention at Kent State and Jackson State universities, and of FBI and COINTELPRO counter-insurgency in the black community and in movement and liberal circles.

Soon after Mesthene became Dean he proclaimed his intention to 'turn Livingston around'. Frederick Douglass's creed and the radical humanist statement of Livingston's mission disappeared from the catalogue, the honours grading system was modified, the student chamber and student representation on course and hiring committees were abolished, a pilot project to establish a compulsory programme of courses on 'technology and culture' (a version of the IBM-funded social heraclitean project) was set in motion, and a series of skills tests were proposed that would have seriously modified Livingston's *de-facto* open admissions policy and excluded minority students from the benefits of a four-year degree programme in liberal arts education.

There was considerable debate, discussion and struggle on all these issues. As the events at Livingston were representative of a larger trend in US culture and society there is no need to recount all the details. To be brief: after the 'Mesthene Papers' were distributed and a series of teach-ins and public meetings about the threat to Livingston were held there was significant resistance to many of his proposals to change the character of the college; and after a protracted series of intense faculty chamber meetings his plans to employ basic skills tests to alter the composition of the student body were modified. A stalemate of a sort existed. In an effort to maintain the distinct quality of the college, progressive faculty at Livingston proposed that it be renamed in honour of one of Rutgers University's most distinguished graduates, the black activist, socialist and artist Paul Robeson.

The campaign to rename Livingston Paul Robeson College received nationwide support, including endorsements from Coretta King, Angela Davis and Leonard Bernstein, as well as from faculties throughout the country. Unfortunately, the proposal was not ratified by the Livingston faculty assembly. Although Mesthene abandoned his plans to transform Livingston and resigned the following year, plans to liquidate the college through centralization into the State University of New Jersey system had been set into motion, with his approval. The struggle over proposals to liquidate the college raged from 1979 to 1981. By 1982 the Livingston experiment was over. Few, if any, Livingston courses could be found in the 1989–91 Rutgers University prospectus. Visitors to the site of the experiment today are welcomed by signs pointing the way to 'Kilmer Campus'.

The Long March

Every night we does the tell ... and keeps on the track.[59]

There is a good deal more to tell. It is often assumed that the 1960s' generation of education activists and teachers vanished from sight on a 'long march through the institutions' when the forces of reaction reasserted their dominance in the late 1970s. This is true to a certain extent. At the same time a purge somewhat more sophisticated than that which occurred during the Cold War era and the McCarthy period took place in academe. There is a need for research comparable to that which David Caute, Paul Tillett and others have conducted on dismissals and blacklisting in Cold War America.[60] My comments on the purge at Livingston are an attempt to illustrate a larger trend in US society that occurred in the wake of the defeat and disintegration of 1960s radicalism, that is, as the nation staggered towards the Reagan and Bush eras.

Most of my information about the pattern of dismissals of members of the faculty of Arts and Science at Livingston comes from the files of the Rutgers AAUP.[61] I will focus upon the years when the liquidation of Livingston was imminent. In 1979–80 68 per cent (46 out of 68) faculty at Rutgers Arts and Sciences up for tenure were successful and were retained.[62] In contrast only three out of 16 applicants from Livingston were retained, a success rate of only 18 per cent. Or to put it another way, 82 per cent of the applicants for tenure from Livingston were dismissed in 1979–80! *In addition* in 1979–80 11 Livingston faculty on one- and three-year contracts were not renewed (including two teachers of Africana Studies, one lecturer in Puerto Rican Studies, a faculty member of the Equal Opportunity office, and two members of the faculty who would have been perceived as being 'radical'). In contrast, in 1978–9 only one person in Arts and Sciences at Rutgers on a one- or three-year contract did not have their contract renewed. The purge of Livingston faculty was equally severe the following year. In 1980–1 78 per cent of Rutgers applicants (46 out of 59) for tenure were successful. By then the Livingston faculty was somewhat diminished in size. Eight out of ten (including re-reviews) were denied tenure and dismissed. Only 20 per cent were successful. The following year at least five faculties of Livingston origin were denied tenure.

The purge struck particularly hard at the Livingston English Department whose faculty had tended to oppose Mesthene on a range of issues, including the use of assessment of writing skills as a means to eliminate black students from the college at the end of their first year of study. From 1978 to 1981 only two out of twelve candidates for tenure as Associate-Professor were successful. No black candidates received tenure. In addition, five faculty on one- or three-year contracts were denied reappointment. Some related statistics are also of interest. For example, from 1979–81 no person from the Livingston English Department received tenure, although there were five applicants. In contrast, in the same period, all of the candidates from the Rutgers English Department were awarded tenure and achieved job security, which enhances academic freedom. During the time I taught at Livingston no black member of the English Department survived the 'probationary period', and the core of the senior black faculty (Toni Cade Bambara, A.B. Spellman, Addison Gayle, Nathan Heard) in the Department left in protest or out of disappointment.

Once the purge and restoration of normalcy began, neither teaching ability nor publications nor outside evaluations had any bearing on whether radicals or minorities at Livingston were awarded tenure. For example, the first three recipients of an award for excellence in teaching that was bestowed by the Livingston faculty chamber (in 1979, 1980 and 1981) were subsequently denied tenure by the Rutgers boards.[63]

In the years following the purge, through protracted grievance proceedings and utilization of the courts, some of the negative decisions were modified.[64] But on the whole right-wing forces succeeded in turning back the clock, at Livingston and elsewhere, restoring the basic pattern of education and enlarging and re-consolidating their sphere of hegemony in the universities and throughout the culture. So did we go full circle from the state of education and culture in the US in the 1950s? Perhaps what happened in the period of restoration in the late 1970s and 1980s was somewhat more dialectical. There are signs that their victory is far from final. Something still remains: a sense of historical memory, of heritage and tradition, of typology, of a Good Old Cause.

For example, a lead editorial in the Rutgers University student newspaper, in November 1989, was concerned with the Livingston experiment, commenting that 'The mission of the college was ... to place strong emphasis on ... the general phenomena of social change ... and "strength through diversity".' Near it, a letter to the editor in support of an 'emergency teach-in' noted that that event was 'reminiscent of the Vietnam era', and went on to argue that the 'parallels between El Salvador and Vietnam have been clearly drawn in the last few weeks'.[65] That same week in New York City, near Columbia University, there were posters on the walls announcing a forthcoming demonstration. A slogan on the poster defined the area of immediate concern, and at the same time set it in historical context: 'No Vietnam War in El Salvador'.

What is striking is not so much the persistence of radical political activity on campuses but the consciousness of history (the Vietnam War/the cause of national liberation) that is being manifested *and* the ways that the symbolism and the forms of the campus rebellions of the 1960s are being appropriated in new situations.

The telling, or the discovery, of narratives of our suppressed/repressed historical experience is also part of this liberating process. They are a reminder that things are problematic and that what we desire is possible. Writing in the period of the *ancien régime* in France, Rousseau observed that 'there is no subjugation so perfect as that which keeps the appearance of freedom, for in that way one captures volition itself'. This is also a persistent theme in Marx's writing. Education may be a link in the transparent chain of oppression but it can be a weak link, for colleges and universities are places where youth has the opportunity to critique received notions of freedom and social practice, to envision alternatives other than those that are dictated by the dominant culture and to test its ideals in practice. This is what happened in the radical thrust of the 1960s and early 1970s. That is the essence of what struggles against the thrust of capital for monolithic hegemony in colleges and universities in the US have been all about.

The operative word for education in the US in the waning years of the twentieth century seems to be 'diversity'. From the perspective of the establishment, 'diversity' is newspeak that celebrates the ghettoization and disempowerment of everything that is stratified as subordinate and positioned as 'other' in US society. Perhaps this is a realistic assessment of the relation between the ruling classes and broad sectors of US society today. However, for those of us who retain a sense of nature's history, 'diversity' also signifies habitat, spaces to live and to learn and perhaps to teach. Granted, within a territory that has again come under the intensified occupation of capital. But that is an old condition. Livingston and Berkeley were under continual attack. Walden and Yenan were places of retreat.

Notes

1. Thorstein Veblen, *The Higher Learning in America* (1981), in Max Learner (ed.), *The Portable Veblen* (New York: Viking Press, 1958), p. 508.

2. Veblen, *The Higher Learning in America*, p. 509.

3. Veblen, pp. 513–14.

4. Richard Ohmann and Russell Jacoby have called attention to the adverse effects of professionalism and compartmentalization on higher education. See: Richard Ohmann, 'English Departments and the Professional Ethos', in Rosemary Bergstrom and Paul Olson (eds), *A Time Half Dead at the Top: The Professional Societies and the Reform of Schooling in America: 1955–1975* (Lincoln, Nebraska: Study Commission on Undergraduate Education, 1975); Russell Jacoby, *The Last Intellectuals: American Culture in the Age of Academe* (New York: Basic Books, 1987). Ohmann notes that 'specialism – the dividing up, of productive technique into small units, and apportioning these skills to narrowly trained workers' conforms to 'the conditions of work in capitalist society' (p. 292). Jacoby links this to the production of a generation of 'missing intellectuals' (p. 4).

5. Christine M. Licata, *Post-tenure Faculty Evaluation* (Washington DC: ASHE-ERIC Higher Education Reports, 1986), pp. xiii, 54, 123.

6. Hazel Hertzberg, 'History and Progressivism: A Century of Reform Proposals', in Paul Gagnon (ed.), *Historical Literacy: The Case for History in American Education* (New York: Macmillan, 1989), p. 81.

7. Hubert Beck, *The Men Who Control Our Universities* (London: Kings Crown, 1947).

8. Beck quoted in G. William Domhoff, *Who Rules America?* (New Jersey: Prentice Hall, 1967), p. 79.

9. Merle Curti and Roderick Nash, *Philanthropy in the Shaping of American Higher Education*, quoted in Domhoff, p. 78.

10. Curti, p. 78.

11. David Caute, *The Great Fear: The Anti-Communist Purge under Truman and Eisenhower* (London: Secker and Warburg, 1978), p. 404. For additional information on aspects of the purge in US universities in the Cold War era see also: Sigmund Diamond, confessional narrative and letters, *The New York Review of Books*, 28 April/26 May/9 June/14 July 1977; *Freedom at Harvard*, reprinted from *Harvard Alumni Bulletin* (25 June 1949); Leo Huberman, 'The Daggett-Sweezy Case', *Monthly Review*, Vol. 6, No. 4 (August 1954); 'It Also Happened at Harvard', *The Educational Record*, Vol. 34, No. 4 (October 1953); 'It Did Happen at Rutgers', *The Educational Record*, Vol. 34, No. 2 (April 1953); Robert MacIver, *Academic Freedom in our Time* (New York: Columbia University Press, 1955).

12. Caute, p. 204.

13. Caute, p. 405.

14. Caute, pp. 414–15.

15. Caute, pp. 422–4.

16. Louis Joughin (ed.), *Academic Freedom and Tenure: A Handbook of the American Association of University Professors* (Madison: The University of Wisconsin Press, 1969), pp. 51–3.

17. Mario Savio quoted in Paul Jacobs and Saul Landau (eds), *The New Radicals* (New York: Vintage, 1966), p. 69.

18. Clark Kerr, *The Uses of the University* (Cambridge: Harvard University Press, 1964), p. 124. In Kerr's view education becomes merely training; see Hal Draper, *The Mind of Clark Kerr* (Berkeley: 1964).

19. Kerr, p. 53.

20. Kerr, pp. 87, 124.

21. Mario Savio, 'An End to History', reprinted in Seymour Lipset and Sheldon Wolin (eds), *The Berkeley Student Revolt* (New York: Doubleday Anchor, 1965), p. 218.

22. Brad Cleaveland, 'A Letter to Undergraduates', *The Berkeley Student Revolt*, p. 75; first presented in *SLATE Supplement Report*, Vol. 1, No. 4 (Berkeley: September 1964). See also Brad Cleaveland, 'Education, Revolution, and Citadels' (September 1964), also reprinted in *The Berkeley Student Revolt*. There Cleaveland contrasts 'education as revolution' with 'education as cold war' (pp. 82–7). Cleaveland's Education Manifesto and the better known Port Huron Statement are essential reading for an understanding of this aspect of 1960s oppositional culture.

23. Paul Goodman, 'Thoughts on Berkeley', *The New York Review of Books*, 14 January 1965; reprinted in Lipset and Wolin, p. 315. My memory of conversations with Goodman, at the time of his visit to Berkeley, is that he viewed the on-going process of self-determination, participation and democracy at Berkeley as a model for social transformation of the US.

24. Cleaveland, quoted in *The Berkeley Student Revolt*, p. 73.

25. See my accounts of FSM and the Vietnam Day Committee Teach-In: 'Cultural Narrative and the Process of Re-Collection', in Michael L. Klein (ed.), *The Vietnam Era: Media and Popular Culture in the US and Vietnam* (London: Pluto Press, 1990), pp. 3–38; 'Scenes from the Politics and Culture of the Movement in the Beginning and the End', in John Dumbrell (ed.), *Vietnam and the Antiwar Movement: An International Perspective* (Aldershot: Avebury, 1989), pp. 82–101. The first Vietnam Day Committee troop train demonstrations took place during the first week of August 1965.

26. There is little real sense of the *geist* of the FSM Berkeley revolution in investigative reports produced by the University of California, however sympathetic and reform-minded sectors of the faculty were. For example, both the Byrne and Muscatine reports reduced the

radical ethos of the movement to a limited agenda for reform: *Byrne Report to the Forbes Committee of the Board of Regents*, reprinted in *People of the State of California versus Mario Savio and 571 Others: Appellants' Opening Brief* (1965), pp. 329–93; Charles Muscatine et al., *Education at Berkeley: Report of the Select Committee on Education* (Berkeley: University of California Press, 1966). In contrast, the writings and commission work of Nathan Glazer, Sidney Hook, Daniel Bell, Louis Feuer and Seymour Martin Lipset tend to portray the movement as deviant and marginal in relation to US society, and focus on 'unrest', protest 'disruptive' of law and order and campus 'terrorism'. See, for example, *The Report of the President's Commission on Campus Unrest* (New York: Arno Press, 1970) and a 43-volume study also published by Arno Press entitled *Mass Violence in America*. Also *Crisis at Columbia: Report of the Fact-Finding Committee Appointed to Investigate the Disturbances at Columbia University* (New York: Vintage, 1968). For alternative sources of information from left movement perspectives see Bettina Aptheker (ed.), *Higher Education and the Student Rebellion in the United States: 1960–1969; a Bibliography* (New York: American Institute for Marxist Studies, 1969). Also for an adaptation of the Domhoff-Mills-Curti-Beck thesis to the study of higher education and data on the influence of finance and corporate capital on policy boards of the University of California and Harvard University in the 1960s see Bettina Aptheker, *Big Business and the American University* (New York: New Outlook Publishers, 1966).

27. Richard Flacks has focused on an aspect of the dynamic of student protest in the 1960s. Flacks argues that many student activists came from liberal or progressive family backgrounds (often 1930s New Deal or anti-fascist in origin); that a radical humanist set of values fuelled their revolt against segregation in education and other aspects of life, a competitive technological society, the military-industrial complex, and a foreign policy based upon the assumptions of the Cold War era. Richard Flacks: 'The Liberated Generation: An Exploration of the Roots of Student Protest', *Journal of Social Issues*, Vol. 23, July 1967: pp. 52–75; 'Social and Cultural Meanings of Student Revolt', *Social Problems*, Vol. 7, winter 1970: pp. 340–57. Also see Philip Altbach and Robert Laufer (eds), *The New Pilgrims: Youth Protest in Transition* (New York: David McKay, 1971), which contains articles by Flacks and by advocates of the generational conflict theory. Flacks' article contains a cogent summary of the work of Martin Sklar, Martin Nicolaus and Herbert Gintis on the intelligentsia, 'new working class', and 'a deep, far-reaching crisis in advanced capitalism' in the 1960s (pp. 86–90).

28. *The Byrne Report* (1965) was one of the first studies to comment upon the generational aspects of youth and student revolt in the

1960s. Byrne (pp. 352–6) calls the reader's attention to a gulf between the social and political ideals of the students and those of the '1950's generation'; Louis Feuer and the popular media tended to characterize this in glib and reductive Freudian terms. From another perspective, insofar as the dominant ideology of the 1950s had a distinct political character, generational contradictions in the next decade can be regarded as a sign that youth and students were in revolt against certain aspects of the value system of the Cold War era, and that they were rejecting the assumptions and cast of characters of Cold War global narratives.

29. *The Report of the President's Commission on Campus Unrest*, p. 7.

30. *Ibid.*, p. 14.

31. I am in debt to John Leggett for access to the questionnaires (each of which consists of 53 pages and 279 questions about family background, political and social attitudes, experience of education at UC Berkeley as well as about the police action against the student occupation of Sproul Hall) and to related material from his Berkeley FSM files. Most of the 571 questionnaires are in the files and still intact.

32. Judith Radu (#038); Michael Klein (#134) FSM Executive Committee; Jackie Goldberg (#274) FSM Ex Com; Stephanie Coontz (#517) FSM Ex Com; Syd Stapleton (#587); David Bills (#017) sat at illegal literature tables; Bettina Aptheker (#516) FSM Ex Com/Steering Committee; Sandor Fuchs (#003) FSM Ex Com; Stephen Murphy (#039); Richard Schmorleitz (#538) illegal tables; Sherril Jaffe (#100); Peter Wiesner (#530) illegal tables; Margaret Klein (#595); Sylvia Kalitansky (#173) illegal tables; Alice Huberman (#590); Arthur Goldberg (#699) FSM Ex Com/Steering Committee; Allan Paulson (#663) Graduate Student Coordinating Committee; Karen Mark (#328) petitions; David Geneson (#294); Sharon Ferguson (#036) illegal tables.

33. Daniel Yankelovich, *The Changing Values on Campus: Political and Personal Attitudes of Today's College Students* (New York: Washington Square Press, 1972).

34. David Rosen, Seth Bruner, Steve Fowler, *Open Admissions: The Promise and the Lie of Open Access to American Higher Education* (Lincoln: University of Nebraska, 1973).

35. Michael L. Klein, *The Vietnam Era*, pp. 29–34.

36. *Academic Freedom and Tenure/AAUP*, p. 36.

37. *Ibid.*, p. 50.

38. Robert Uphaus (ed.), *American Protest in Perspective* (New York: Harper and Row, 1971).

39. Morris Friedman and Carolyn Brooks (eds), *American Mix: The Minority Experience in America* (New York: J.B. Lippincott, 1972).
40. Barbara Graves and Donald McBain (eds), *Lyric Voices: Approaches the Poetry of Contemporary Song* (New York: John Wiley, 1972).
41. *Voices of Concern: The Playboy College Reader* (New York: Harcourt Brace Jovanovich, 1971).
42. Edward Quinn and Paul Dolan (eds), *The Sense of the Sixties* (New York: The Free Press, 1968).
43. Charles Muscatine and Marlene Griffiths (eds), *The Borzoi College Reader* (New York; Alfred Knopf, 1971).
44. Tim Drescher and Glen Miller (eds), *The Devil's Party* (Waltham Massachusetts: Ginn and Co., 1970).
45. Sheila Delaney (ed.), *Counter-Tradition: The Literature of Dissent and Alternatives* (New York: Basic Books, 1971).
46. Louis Kampf in Delaney (ed.), *Counter-Tradition*, p. vii.
47. Louis Kampf and Paul Lauter (eds), *The Politics of Literature: Dissenting Essays on the Teaching of English* (New York: Vintage, 1970).
48. *Ibid.*, p. 9.
49. John Leggett (ed.), *Taking State Power: The Source and Consequences of Political Challenge* (New York: Harper and Row, 1973); Bruce Franklin (ed.), *From the Movement Toward Revolution* (New York: Van Nostrand and Reinhold, 1971); Felix Greene, *The Enemy: What Every American Should Know About Imperialism* (New York: Vintage, 1971).
50. Caute, pp. 414–15. Moses Finley and Simon Heinlich were dismissed in 1952.
51. *THES*, 20 April 1990, p. 11.
52. *This is Livingston* (New Brunswick: Rutgers University, 1972), p. 17.
53. Mario Savio, 'The Uncertain Future of the Multiversity: A Partisan Scrutiny of Berkeley's Muscatine Report', *Harper's Magazine* (October 1966), pp. 88–94. See Leo Marx, 'Pastoralism in America', in Sacvan Bercovitch and Myra Jehlen, *Ideology and Classic American Literature* for an evaluation of Berkeley vis-à-vis the traditions of radicalism.
54. Livingston Faculty included: Miguel Algarin; Toni Cade Bambara; Jackie DiSalvo; Addison Gayle; Gwendolyn Hall; Nathan Heard; Michael Klein; John Leggett; Norman Markowitz; James Roy McBean; Carey McWilliams Jr; Marty Oppenheimer; Sonia Sonchez; A.B. Spellman; Ann Snitow; Betty Taylor; Richard Wasson.

55. *This is Livingston* (1971-2 catalogue): pp. 31, 48, 106, 143.

56. Mesthene contributed to the following RAND studies: 'Military Research and Development Politics' (RAND document R# 333, 4 December 1958) which advocated neo-Cold War massive US rearmament, especially in the field of guided nuclear missiles; 'Organizing for National Security' (1961) which was written in the period of the rise of the civil rights movement and of peace movement opposition to nuclear testing and US policy toward Cuba; 'Defense Strategy' (April 1970), a document prepared for a seminar at the National War College in Washington DC during the height of the Vietnam War. The quotation from Mesthene on the relation of R&D to war was taken from RAND document R# 333. In 1968 Mesthene contributed to a RAND study of educational policy in conjunction with the New York Community Education Corporation. Four years later he became Dean of Livingston.

57. 'The Mesthene Papers' (pamphlet, 1975). All quotations from Mesthene's writings cited in this chapter are reproduced from this collection of leaflets and documents without additional footnotes. It was a collaborative effort involving faculty, myself included, and students. Oppositional research sometimes takes the form of liberation, as well as interpretation, of privileged material or of material that is not in the public domain.

58. For example, Edward Ross and David Snedden. Snedden 'envisioned the schools as unparalleled instruments of social control, hierarchically organized and scientifically managed, with separate schools for rulers and ruled, or what he called the "consumers" (the elite) and the "producers" or the "rank-in-file" ... Schools were to engineer pupils to fit neatly into the status quo.' Hazel W. Hertzberg, in Paul Gagnon (ed.), *Historical Literacy* (New York: Macmillan, 1989), p. 81. In many respects Mesthene's cultural politics participates in a trend that Bertram Gross characterizes as 'friendly fascism'. See Bertram Gross, *Friendly Fascism: The New Face of Power in America* (Boston: South End Press, 1980). In other respects it participates in postmodernist and related 'new times' assessments of culture and society in the US and Europe. The correspondences are especially suggestive! As are the parallels of Kerr and Mesthene's writings with Thatcher-period education 'reforms' in the UK. The Savio/Cleaveland–Kerr debate also has certain parallels with the Leavis/Snow debate in the UK in the early 1960s.

59. *Road Runner/Mad Max 3: Beyond Thunderdome*. The quote comes from the last part of a series of three films, made in 1979, 1981 and 1983 – at the start of the Reagan era. It is the motto of a tribe of survivors who live in a junk-filled wilderness after a global holocaust. Retelling the narrative of their collective experience sustains them and prepares them for the future.

60. David Caute's *The Great Fear*, not only Part Six 'The Purge of the Professions', but also the appendix which contains the information gathered in 'The Tillett Survey: The Predicament of the Discharged Teacher'. See also Lary Ceplair and Steven Englund, *The Inquisition in Hollywood* (New York: Doubleday, 1980).

61. My research at the Rutgers office of the AAUP was conducted in September 1989. Unfortunately they did not have tabulated comparative data about non-retention at greater Rutgers and at Livingston for the period prior to 1978-79, and their files for this year are not entirely complete. The statistics placed at my disposal thus, if anything, most likely underestimate the full extent of the elimination of non-tenured Livingston faculty from the State University of New Jersey system in the final years of the college. The files for the key years of the administration's successful effort to liquidate Livingston (1979-80/1980-1) are complete. The hit list in the English Department from 1976-82 included: Pepsi Charles; Marc Crawford; Jackie DiSalvo; Hattie Gossett; Arnold Henderson; Michael Klein; Barbara Masakela; James Roy MacBean; Peter Parisi; Manny Peluso; Gerry Peary; Al Prettyman; Connie Pohl; Ann Snitow; Steve Zemmelman.

62. By 'Rutgers' I mean the Faculty of Arts and Sciences (FAS) at Rutgers University in New Brunswick, excluding applicants from Livingston College.

63. Jackie DiSalvo (1978); Betty Taylor (1979); Mary Gibson (1980).

64. For example, after protracted struggles involving both university grievance procedures and the courts, Mary Gibson was awarded tenure and Ann Snitow damages for having improperly been denied tenure. Jackie DiSalvo and Michael Klein won re-reviews for having improperly been denied tenure.

65. *The Daily Targum*, 28 November 1989, p. 8.

7. 'The Deep Immortal Wish':
Radicalism in Modern American Poetry

Jeffrey Walsh

> A poet ... presupposes the existence of an ideal reader, and the poetic act both anticipates the future and speeds its coming.
> Czeslaw Milosz, from *On Hope* (1983)

> The poet is a born democrat not thanks to the precariousness of his position only, but because he caters to the entire nation and employs its language.
> Joseph Brodsky, from *The Keening Muse* (1986)

It may seem paradoxical that a study of poetry is included in a collection of essays that examines radical culture and political institutions in modern America. Poetic discourse is different, for example, from narrative fiction in its more intense linguistic self-consciousness; the 'literariness' of poetic utterance is perhaps its most pre-eminent signifying feature. Yet there are perfectly good reasons for suggesting that the artifice of poetry enhances its communicative powers. A command of prosody and formal rhythm may render the civil meanings of a poem all the more cogent. Although poetry has become a minority taste, its community of regular readers is still an influential one. Poetry still matters in modern American culture.

In the networks of a culture responsibility for the maintenance and purity of a written language falls most significantly to the poet, and, by extension, to his or her readers. Poetry has a moral function also, which is not the same as a narrowly didactic one. There is truth in the claim that poets are far sighted in discerning social problems, and intuitively perceive what the rest of us are inclined to miss. How far a particular poet is 'ahead' of his or her time is a matter for critical discrimination. 'Referentially', the 'application' of poetry to its context and contemporary history is also a separate issue which varies from poet to poet. In the essay that follows emphasis is placed equally upon 'radical values' as well as upon aesthetic ordering. Enduring poetry possesses artistic integrity in addition to moral insight.

Critics and theorists, among them T.S. Eliot, Orwell, Sartre, Lukacs and Adorno, have conducted during the second half of the twentieth century a sophisticated debate about the relationships and competing claims between 'commitment' and 'autonomy' in literature. The poles of this debate are now well known; at one extreme, the modernist emphasis upon the self-referential aspects of writing; at the other, the idea that literature involves not merely aesthetic objectification but also a common concern with meanings that are socially significant. Perhaps the most famous example of the social realist position was Lukacs' critique of modernist writing when he criticized such writers as Kafka, Faulkner and T.S. Eliot for representing man as a being trapped in an apolitical and ahistorical vacuum. Such a vision, Lukacs argued, eliminated potential for decisive action and attenuated actuality; it thus substituted an 'angst-ridden vision of the world for objective reality'.[1]

The contours of this dispute and of others similar in kind are relevant in an evaluation of American poetry from the 1940s to the present because of the importance of modernism's legacy. The four most distinctive modernist poets are American – Eliot, Pound, Stevens and William Carlos Williams – and their work has had immense influence. Their descendants include many of the finest poets of the modern generation; the list could be a very long one and would certainly include a 'canon' of poets studied on university syllabuses: such figures as Robert Lowell, Sylvia Plath, Richard Wilbur, Charles Olson, John Berryman, James Merrill, John Ashberry – all among the most celebrated figures of their time. Inevitably, trying to classify poets as diverse as the above, and to sort them into a category labelled 'modernist' is a reductive exercise. While it is true that some of the poets mentioned above such as, say, Berryman or Lowell are relentless experimenters and high formalists, whose work consistently foregrounds technique and innovation in a broadly autotelic fashion, this does not mean that they do not frequently write poems which address urgent political and social matters. Robert Lowell is a poet whose work developed in spectacular formal fashion; indeed he has claims with the British poet W.H. Auden to be the finest and truest descendant of the modernist revolution. Yet Lowell, despite his secure class position, embodied in his work and in his life radical causes. His sequence of anti-war poems in the 1940s and 1950s exemplify his pacifism, and in 1943 he was sent to jail as a conscientious objector. Later, during the Vietnam era, he protested angrily against what he saw as America's imperialist war in Asia.[2]

Weighing up the equivalences between 'autonomy' and 'commitment', then, necessitates discrimination. Poetry, perhaps of all literary genres, is ostensibly the most 'subjective' and 'personal', and obliges the poet rigorously to refine and condense language. Do we measure radicalism in terms of content or form? If the latter then the 'conservative' poets Eliot and Pound are significant radicals. The terminology is fraught and problematical, yet clearly merits attention. One influential attempt to examine the nature of committed writing, and indeed to explore its political dimension is Italo Calvino's elegant essay 'Right and Wrong Uses of Literature'. Here he attempts to codify how writing may speak what is repressed and thereby articulate for those unable to do so for themselves. This role of expressive advocacy he summarizes eloquently thus: 'Literature is necessary to politics above all when it gives a voice to whatever is without a voice, when it gives a name to what as yet has no name.' Calvino extends such a concept of 'truth-telling' to include the writer's creation of 'a model of values that is at the same time aesthetic and ethical, essential to any plan of action, especially in political life'.[3]

Calvino's conceptualization raises issues of empowerment and challenge. It has particular relevance, for example, for some of the poets whose work will be considered in this essay and who are not included in the neo-modernist canon mentioned above. It may be that a poet's work will address the matter of historical representation and perhaps ask awkward questions such as 'Whose history are we talking about when we refer to the nation's history?' or 'Is the experience of this particular class or ethnic group adequately acknowledged?' Sartre referred to the writer as someone who 'functionally moves in opposition to the interests of those who keep him alive'. In asking such difficult questions about gender, historical concealment or cultural neglect a poet may fulfil the Sartrean role of becoming through the poem an attacking agent who radiates 'destructive powers' towards dominant ideology and thereby subverts facile consensus.[4]

Such heavyweight claims for the poet may seem absurd and run counter to the saying that to write lyric poetry after Auschwitz is itself barbaric. While acknowledging the force of such a warning it is possible to discover modern American poets who strike a delicate balance between 'commitment' and 'autonomy', and do represent in memorable form and language elements of suffering and injustice which call for social change. The poet who quietly celebrates neglected cultural values through the conduit of the crafted poem raises consciousness; the poem of integrity, through its rhythmical density and beauty, is a medium resistant to crude dogmatism, impervious to slurs of 'idealist' or 'essentialist' or to the deconstructive attacks of the most outlandish of postmodernists. The latter, an intellectual movement which attempts to map out a 'condition' of contemporary civilization, emphasizes randomness, chaos, superficiality, disruption, formlessness, pastiche, the dubiousness of proclaimed 'value' and the problematic of contradiction; such a perspective seems unlikely to commend the ordered occasion of the single poem.

One recent critic, Paul A. Bové, has nevertheless tried to review certain aspects of modern American poetry through the prism of postmodernism. In an interesting study which examines the work of such poets as William Carlos Williams and Charles Olson he outlines a poetic line or 'open' way of seeing that represents man as 'decentred', and describes a context where the traditional world view is replaced by a 'more truly human universe, in which man and his work are only objects'.[5] Bové considers the seminal influence of Heidegger on American poets, a thinker who was anathema to Lukacs for his statement that man is 'meaninglessly thrown into the world'. Clearly the postmodernist debate, especially in the work of Fredric Jameson, is of great significance in the study of modern poetry, and Bové's book is extremely interesting, yet the work of the poet of radical sensibilities is premised upon a different ontology. He or she is likely to see man as not merely a passive victim of forces, cast randomly into a chaotic and meaningless world, but as a being situated in history, capable of self-government, rational control and positive action. From such a viewpoint poetry as a discursive practice, to borrow Foucault's term, becomes a discourse of power where values are represented, challenged and legitimized.

In radical poetry of the modern era there are four central areas of concern; the struggle for historical truth and the expression of neglected historical narrative; the demythologizing of gender; the criticism of material values and environmental pollution; and the opposition to expansionist wars.

'The Timeless Will': The Struggle for Historical Truth

Old-style American studies courses in British universities used to organize their syllabuses around the concept of a united America. Themes such as the birth of the nation, the fight to end slavery, the frontier, immigration and the growth of cities structured a vision of one-ness, representing a monolithic and easily identifiable culture free from contradiction or conflict. In such a unified reading of Americanness modern poetry would usually be allocated to such Euro-centred poets as Pound, Eliot and Lowell with perhaps those of a more 'American' flavour such as e.e. cummings, William Carlos Williams and Wallace Stevens placed in the second rank. Such a conceptualization of American 'nationhood', 'culture' or civilization', which had powerful resonances in the academy of 20 or 30 years ago is now no longer tenable, and even a cursory glance at poetry written during the last two or three decades shows this view to be flawed and misleading. Modern poetry written in the United States over the last 40 years or so represents struggle, disunity, urgent questioning of the idea that America is a united country, and doubt about the United States' historic European role in foreign affairs. It focuses much more widely upon the growth of interest in cultures non-European in origin and upon intergenerational conflict; poets have also engaged in intense debate about the construction of gender, class and ethnicity within cultural discourse.

History, that comfortable narrative of the past, telling stories of such great men as Benjamin Franklin, George Washington and Abraham Lincoln, is now likely to include many hitherto unacknowledged and unpalatable facts about the massacre of native Americans, the deaths of Africans in slave ships and the murder of black Americans in the South; or it will criticize the United States' role abroad, either burning civilians in Vietnam or assisting tyrants in South or Central America. Poets have placed such truths on the agenda.

The multiplicity of America's racial mix inevitably leads to a plurality of histories represented in poetry. The evidence points to cultural diversity, to poets aware of different ethnic cultures enriching their imagination. It would be relatively easy to construct a list of such poets, all of whom are American poets and yet carry with them a sense of being 'other', of non-European descent, usually from Asia, Central or South America; those whose work is most interesting include the Chicano, Alberto Rios, Lorna Dee Cervantes, a Chicana poet whose grandmother was Mexican; Cathy Song from Hawaii whose work is distinguished by oriental imagery; and Simon J. Ortiz, a native American born in New Mexico who attended school within the bureau of Indian affairs on the Acoma Reservation. The visionary perspectives of such poets, although enormously varied, challenge the notion of a European or Western mind with common cultural values, and signify also the efflorescence of minority voices and poetic discourses. It is natural and common, for example, for poets of Mexican descent to collaborate on joint projects and to provide a focus for Chicano culture. Beth Brant's excellent anthology of writing by North American Indian women, *A Gathering of Spirit* (1988), is an example of such multi-ethnic writing and includes a range of poetry of considerable interest.

Perhaps the most significant affirmation and oppositional current of thought in the competing strands for authentic historiography is the rescue of Afro-American history and its resultant revisionism. In this restoration of forgotten or wilfully ignored histories three poets have written major works: Robert Hayden, one of America's greatest poets; Michael Harper, a New Yorker, who is now a professor at Brown University; and the younger formalist poet, Rita Dove.

Robert Hayden's work demonstrates the inappropriateness of classifying radical poets as being more interested in 'content' than in formal experiment, as his poetry exhibits considerable technical virtuosity and a high degree of linguistic and formal innovation.[6] His two most important poems, 'Middle Passage' and 'Elegies for Paradise Alley', especially the former, draw freely upon such modernist strategies as multiple voices, fragmentary narration, free association, typographical variation and intertextual allusion. 'Middle Passage' is a cunningly crafted poem comprising a number of voices giving different accounts of various incidents involving slave ships sailing through the south Atlantic between Africa and the West Indies. The voices, ranging from the narrator's all-seeing and knowing historical sweep to those of crew members, suborned witnesses, or ship's captains, whose words are often carefully placed in quotation marks, convey the barbarities of the voyages, commingling metaphor and symbolism with factual and documentary detail. There is an outbreak of blindness on the ship which signifies moral evil; a crew member describes:

> ... A plague among
> our blacks – Opthalmia: blindness – & we
> have jettisoned the blind to no avail.
> It spreads, the terrifying sickness spreads.
> Its claws have scratched sight from the Captain's eyes
> & we must sail 3 weeks before we come
> to port.   (1962)

In this passage many of the poem's language effects may be seen working to create historical meaning. The speaker is one of the oppressors, a white crew member who callously mentions how they jettisoned the blinded blacks. He seeks the reader's sympathy by foregrounding his own fear that he may catch the plague and by recounting starkly the tragedy of the captain's blindness. Drawing upon the Machereyan concept of textual 'silences' it is obvious that the history being narrated is ironically one-sided and biased, a white man's account oblivious to the deeper significance of the events. What is missing is the record of how the black slaves experienced the voyage, how they endured the fire that broke out on another ship, *The Bella J* or how the negresses who had been raped faced their death with the drunken captain.

'Middle Passage', as the above extract illustrates, incorporates many passages that purport to be factual. It refers to actual place names in the Gambia, to precise voyages and ships and to a court case where mutinous slaves were defended by the former president, John Quincey Adams. At the heart of the poem is an account of a rebellion led by a slave 'prince', Cinquez, on a vessel, *The Amistad*. Two perspectives on the rebellion are juxtaposed by the narrative; first the white slave owner's version of events:

> ... our men went down
> before the murderous Africans. Our loyal
> Celestino ran from below with gun
> and lantern and I saw, before the cane –
> knife's wounding flash, Cinquez,
> that surly brute who calls himself a prince,
> directing, urging on the ghastly work.

and second the narrator's more detached and interpretive framing of the episode; Cinquez embodies an historical law:

> The deep immortal human wish,
> the timeless will:
>
> Cinquez its deathless primeval image,
> life that transfigures many lives
>
> Voyage through death
>   to life upon these shores.

The poet's transcendent voice places the events in a timescale that translates them into America's primal experience: the slave voyage unequivocally is destined to 'these shores', part of the nation's ineluctable history. The trope of the perilous voyage, recalling Coleridge's *Ancient Mariner*, symbolizes the journey to American nationhood, an evil and unwholesome 'middle passage'.

Similar concerns are located in the work of Michael Harper and the Pulitzer prizewinner, Ruth Dove, two Afro-American poets with an interest in reconstituting historical truth. Michael Harper in several poems such as 'American History', 'History as Apple Tree', 'Martin's Blues' and 'Tongue Tied in Black and White' addresses head-on the problematic of writing in a truthful historical register.[7] 'American History', for example, problematizes the history of civil rights by associating the deaths of four black girls blown up by white racists in Alabama with a continuum stretching to the slave days,

> These four black girls blown up
> in that Alabama church
> remind me of five hundred
> middle passage blacks,
> in a net, under water
> in Charleston harbor
> so *redcoats* wouldn't find them
> Can't find what you can't see
> Can you?   (1970)

The last two lines of this succinct poem, resonant with irony, subtly interlink the notion of hiding and persecution, and produce a double meaning. Society frequently 'can't see' racism and 'can't find' its perpetrators: while racists, to the contrary, can see and *can* find victims.

American history is a muddied dangerous pool or, as Harper prefers to call it, an apple tree with roots in people's skeletons. In his poem, 'History as Apple Tree', he conflates the history of Native Americans, Afro-Americans and the white man, Roger Williams, who founded Rhode Island in 1636. The poem's conclusion theorizes about origins, history and myth,

> As black man I steal away
> in the night to the apple tree,
> place my arm in the rich grave,
> black sachem on a family plot,
> take up a chunk of apple root,
> let it become my skeleton,
> become my own myth.
> My arm the historical branch,
> my name the bruised fruit,
> black human photograph: apple tree.   (1972)

Certainly the confidence of such a stance is impressive as is Harper's sophistication and intellectuality in debating about the dialectic of historical representation. Such a theme is crystallized in another poem, 'Tongue Tied in Black and White', where he takes to task the famous poet, John Berryman, for misrepresenting black speech in his portrayal of Mr Bones in 77 *Dream Songs*.[8] He argues that Berryman 'lied' and derided black utterance in his poems,

> you wrote in that needful black idiom
> offending me, for only inner voices
> spoke such soft tongues, your father's soft prayers
> in an all black town in Oklahoma; your ear lied.
> *That slave in you was white blood forced to derision,*
> those seventeenth-century songs saved you from review.   (1975)

The kernel of Harper's criticism is that Berryman's historicism, evident in *Homage to Mistress Bradstreet*, was compromised by his representation of black language in *Dream Songs*.

Behind Harper's poem, 'Tongue-Tied in Black and White', is a consciousness of the politics of language, and, equally as important, an instinct to forgive; Harper's tone is composed of affection for the older poet, reprimand with a hint of subdued anger, and sorrow shading into forgiveness that Berryman's gifts, his poet's ear, betrayed him into damaging cliché. Harper's seizing of the ideological significance of language is replicated in a much more tragic and grave poem by Rita Dove, 'Parsley'.[9] Like Harper, whose imagination turned to other cultures such as that of South Africa where persecution was commonplace, Dove widens the frame of her work to include an actual incident in the Dominican Republic. The country's dictator, Rafael Trujillo, ordered 20,000 blacks killed because they could not pronounce the letter 'r' in the Spanish word for parsley (*perejil*). Dove's poem seeks to represent the madness and barbarity of the act.

Walter Benjamin, in his *Theses on the Philosophy of History*, has argued that the 'image' briefly seized is the only way that we can grasp the past, and connect it with our present reality.

> The true picture of the past flits by. The past can be seized only as an image which flashes up at the instant when it can be recognised and is never seen again ... For every image of the past that is not recognised by the present as one of its own concerns threatens to disappear irretrievably.[10]

'Parsley' narrates through metaphor; its fictionality, based upon verifiable historical fact, creates, in Benjamin's words, 'an image which flashes up'. Divided into two parts, of three and seven or eight line stanzas, it offers two ways of experiencing reality, that of the peasants, 'The Cane Fields', followed by 'The Palace' which renders the consciousness of the dictator. Linking the two parts is the symbol of the parrot and the presence of spring as a season of verdant growth. The parrot is the dictator's treasured love object, replacing his dead mother; it is forever 'imitating' and 'practising' spring, literally and figuratively, because its feathers are 'parsley green', and it can 'roll an r' unlike the cane-cutters, who sing 'Katalina' instead of 'Katarina'. The general orders them dead for no reason other than 'Who Can I kill Today?' The effect of his action is adumbrated in the first section of the poem,

> El General has found his word: *perejil*.
> Who says it, lives. He laughs, teeth shining
> out of the swamp. The cane appears
>
> In our dreams, lashed by wind and streaming.
> And we lie down. For every drop of blood
> there is a parrot imitating spring.
> Out of the swamp the cane appears. (1983)

Subtly, the poem here plays upon the associations of 'swamp' and 'cane', swamp signifying both the terrain of their physical labour and also the primeval; 'cane' similarly refers not only to the sugarcane, but to the walking cane that the dictator planted at his mother's grave and also to the brutality of caning as punishment. The 'teeth' which are shining carry similar overtones of menace, playing off handsome cleanliness against cannibalism. 'Parsley' is a powerful treatment of dictatorship, rooted in a precise historical incident yet communicating a cross-cultural charge starkly reminding us of the reality of political dictatorship. The language theme, that they died 'for a single beautiful word' is a disturbing one, reminding us perhaps of George Steiner's famous essay, 'The Hollow Miracle', which links Nazism to the corruption of language.[11] 'Parsley', then, is a fine and sophisticated artefact, recalling other antifascist poems such as Philip Levine's 'On the Murder of Lieutenant José de Castilo by the Falangist Bravo Martínez, July 12, 1936'.

'I am She': Demythologizing the Construction of Gender

A major difference between poetry written over the last five decades or so and that published in previous eras has been the steady growth in poems written by women. While from the nineteenth century perhaps only Emily Dickinson has become a canonical figure, any list of distinguished poets from the 1940s onwards is likely to include Elizabeth Bishop, Anne Sexton, Sylvia Plath, Denise Levertov, Adrienne Rich, Gwendolyn Brooks, Audre Lorde, and in recent years, Rita Dove. Making sense of the field of women's poetry is a formidable task; its themes are as diverse as the poets themselves. What is most impressive about this development is that new areas of experience have been treated poetically from a female perspective; for example, motherhood, female sexuality, marriage, women's history.

Cora Kaplan, surveying the field, has argued, in a seminal article, that a high proportion of poems written by women share a common concern with access and the right to speak. Because the poet has traditionally been male, speaking from a man's viewpoint, a woman faces an inherent problem,

> To be a woman and a poet presents many women poets with such a profound split between their social, sexual identity (their 'human' identity) and their artistic practice that the split becomes the insistent subject, sometimes overt, often hidden or displaced, of much women's poetry.[12]

Kaplan's perceptive observation offers a useful starting point for an analysis of the politics of women's poetry because it marks out a recurrent problematic that is found both in the work of conscious 'feminist' poets such as Rich, Brooks, Pat Parker and Lorde and other poets such as Levertov or Dove who are seemingly less overtly politicized feminists.

The gifted woman poet extends the agenda of poetry, and 'gendered writing' (to use a cliché) is likely, as Kaplan has argued, to be addressed in her work. Perhaps the most effective way of analysing the issue is to try to explore how it is treated in the work of singular poets such as Denise Levertov or Adrienne Rich who came to prominence in the 1960s and 1970s at the height of the women's liberation struggle.

The work of Denise Levertov is richly rewarding, encompassing a wide range of material and theme. She is an intellectual poet whose intellectuality is lightly worn, as well as being a deeply emotional one whose emotionalism is shaped and distanced by her verbal craft. Her political position is broadly radical; during the Vietnam War, as *The Sorrow Dance* (1967) and *Footprints* (1972) demonstrate, she protested vigorously against American involvement. In poems such as 'The Day the Audience Walked Out on Me, and Why' she records her commitment to civil rights. Levertov's best known poems are probably those written to other women, especially to her sister, Olga, from *The Sorrow Dance*, and to her mother, 'The 90th Year', 'Death Psalm', 'A Soul Cake', from *Life in The Forest* (1978), and 'Visitant' from *Candles in Babylon* (1982). These poems and others in their sequences are as good as any in American poetry in communicating the love and respect sister has for sister or daughter for mother; their power resides in their individuality of utterance and in precision of imagery and rhythm.

The theme of writing poetry, especially focusing on the role of the woman poet, is a recurrent one throughout Levertov's *Selected Poems* (1986).[13] Its composite nature is explored variously, describing how the woman poet works, how she is receptive to inspiration; and the manner in which she marks out an independent spirit from men and also from the powerful influence of her own mother. Frequently the contextual imagery of the poems, their ethos, is either the home, the ambience of the family or the world of the fairy tale. All of these features cohere in 'The Acolyte', a representative poem from *Candles in Babylon*. The poem is set in a kitchen, the woman is baking; she is an acolyte, presumably voyaging out from her mother's influence, and the process of baking becomes a metaphor for the creation of poetry. The imagery drawn upon in 'The Acolyte' combines the ordinary and the magical. She stands in domestic fashion,

> At the table, floury hands
> kneading dough, feet planted
> steady on flagstones,
> a woman ponders the loaves-to-be.
> Yeast and flour, water and salt,
> have met in the huge bowl. (1982)

She is not, however, thinking merely of making bread, but of how the dough is transformed and 'has a life of its own'. In the two final stanzas the analogy with poetry is made central: the woman's role is that of ambitious magician of words,

> She wants to put
> a silver rose or a bell of diamonds
> into each loaf;
> she wants
>
> to bake a curse into one loaf,
> into another, the words that break
> evil spells and release
> transformed heroes into their selves;
> she wants to make
> bread that is more than bread.

The relationship of such a poem to the feminist theory of Hélène Cixous, Simone de Beauvoir and Juliet Mitchell is interesting and highly ambiguous. How we read the poem ultimately depends upon whether we judge that the woman's 'wants' are likely to be fulfilled. Is the traditional role of baking *necessarily* a restrictive one or can it be 'transformed' like the heroes. Can 'writing the self' for a woman be linked with older 'female' activities? Certainly the aesthetic overtones implied in 'the soul smell changes/to fragrance' suggests that it *can* be changed.

In 'She and the Muse', 'The Soothsayer' and 'The Dragonfly-Mother' there is a more confident reiteration of the woman poet's urgent need to write in full self-expression of identity. 'The Dragonfly-Mother', a beautiful fairytale poem, envisages the woman poet keeping trust with her own destiny 'poem by poem'. To fulfil this 'tryst' or 'long promise' she must keep faith with her mythical mother,

> Dragonfly-Mother's
> a messenger,
> if I don't trust her
> I can't keep faith   (1982)

Levertov's ascription of a central role to the soothsayer matriarch or 'weaver of fictions' is a delicately implied statement about the significance of gender in her work. Without stridency she dismisses the male 'the hour's delightful hero', in 'She and the Muse' in humorous fashion. He 'rides off in dustcloud' while the woman clears the kitchen table and enters a room of her own,

> ... here is her lectern,
> here her writing desk. She picks a quill,
> dips it, begins to write. But not of him.

A sentiment that is without rancour yet all the more effective for being so!

While Denise Levertov's poetry is feminist in the broader conceptual sense, Adrienne Rich's work, especially from the 1970s onwards, is more specifically addressed to the concerns of women in their struggle to attain independence within their lives. Rich's early volumes diagnose the contradictions experienced by herself and other women in attempting to conform to social expectations.[14] In a series of poems from *The Diamond Cutters* (1955), such as 'Autumn Equinox' or 'The Perennial Answer', the institution of marriage is portrayed as repressive where it curtails a woman's freedom of action. A later volume, *Snapshots of a Daughter in Law* (1963), extends the analysis, particularly in the title poem, one of her most celebrated meditations upon the roles of mother, daughter and wife. The weight of culture and institutions is represented as oppressive, felt all the more intensely by the intelligent woman,

> A thinking woman sleeps with monsters.
> The beak that grips her, she becomes. And Nature,
> that sprung-lidded, still commodious
> steamer-trunk of *tempora* and *mores*
> gets stuffed with it all: the mildewed orange-flowers,
> the female pills, the terrible breasts
> of Boadicea beneath flat foxes' heads and orchids.   (1963)

Such 'snapshots' of women's lives supply the impetus for a politics of change.

Her early work thematizes the divisions enforced upon women through established constructions and conventions of gender, and her response is a complex and radical one, signified in her prose manifestos, for example, *Of Women Born, Motherhood as Experience and Institution* (1976), and in her volume of poems, *The Will to Change* (1971).[15] A typically combative poem from this latter collection is the much-praised 'Planetarium', written in homage to Caroline Herschel, a woman astronomer denied the fame accorded to her brother William. 'Planetarium' wittily conjures up a universe full of 'monster women', galaxies of females 'doing penance for impetuousness'. The poem's conclusion turns to the creative activity of the woman poet,

> ... I am an instrument in the shape
> Of a woman trying to translate pulsations
> into images for the relief of the body
> and the reconstruction of the mind.
>   (1968: published 1971)

Astronomer-like, the poet focuses empirical truths in the cause of healing.

One of Rich's favourite images is that of the woman as experimenter, she who dares to defy convention for her beliefs. Many of her heroines fall into this category such as Emily Dickinson, the 'half-cracked' poet whose integrity irritated her publisher, Higginson, in 'I Am in Danger – Sir – '.

A related poem is 'For Ethel Rosenberg' in which Rich tackles a dangerous subject, that of a woman who betrays her country.[16] Ethel Rosenberg is an anti-heroine whose fate was exemplary. Her mother and brother testified against her (they needed her to be a 'female monster'), and she believed in the possibility of revolution. Like the hero of Albert Camus's novel *The Outsider*, her true crime was to violate social taboos. Posterity judged Ethel Rosenberg adversely because she wanted to be 'distinguished', to be a woman of distinction. Like Camus's hero who is condemned to death because he showed no emotion at his mother's death, she is castigated for being 'a bad daughter a bad mother'. The poem allows Adrienne Rich to reflect upon her own nonconformism,

> And I walking to my wedding
> by the same token a bad daughter   a bad sister
> my forces focussed
>
> on that hardly revolutionary effort
> Her life and death   the possible
> ranges of disloyalty
>
> so painful   so unfathomable
> they must be pushed aside
> ignored for years.   (1981)

'For Ethel Rosenberg' is an uncomfortable poem, which asks disturbing questions about public morality. Its linking of gender with 'the selling of secrets to the Communists' is particularly disorientating.

Feminism, then, is a constituent of Adrienne Rich's poetry, a thread giving her work depth and consistency. It is not, however, an ideological scheme that narrows the breadth of her imagination. Her best work has a density that locates it in the quotidian world, free from 'argument and jargon' as in the magnificent concluding passages of 'Transcendental Etude' (1978).[17]

'Transcendental Etude', in its conclusion, affirms new directions, 'a whole new poetry beginning here'. Its celebration of the potentialities of vision hinges upon the radiances that may be perceived and experienced in the here and now. Rich dismisses the abstract notion of 'eternity'; the experience of feeling and seeing is of the moment, not transhistorical, timeless or eternal, but specific, the product of active care for the present life. Woman may transcend, in some significant way, the confines of being:

> becoming now the sherd of broken glass
> slicing light in a corner, dangerous
> to flesh, now the plentiful, soft leaf
> that wrapped round the throbbing finger, soothes the wound;
> and now the stone foundation, rockshelf further
> forming underneath everything that grows.   (1978)

The metaphors of change, growth, process, amplitude and strength are wholly characteristic of Rich's poetry.

The Fall of America: False Ideologies and Radical Critiques

Radicalism in modern American poetry is, above all, characterized by a sense that, in the post-1945 world, the country has lost its way and turned uglier. Allen Ginsberg encapsulated this in the apocalyptic title of one of his books, *The Fall of America* (1972), a critique outspoken in its loathing of the spread of materialism and the dominance of the Pentagon throughout the 1960s.[18] Bob Dylan (said by Professor Christopher Ricks to be perhaps the century's finest poet) wrote, 'The Times They Are A-Changin''' in 1963, which suggested prophetically the momentous events of the 1960s and 1970s, civil rights, women's liberation and the anti-war movements, for example. Other poets responded to what the counterculture named 'Amerika', the intolerant downside of capitalist ideology, in more elegiac terms. Regional poets, such as Richard Hugo or James Wright, observe run-down and loss, yet also resistance, symbolized in the places they know intimately, Montana, Nebraska, Ohio and West Virginia.

In a consideration of 'the poetry of protest' written during the 1960s, Robert B. Shaw has commented upon the prophetic nature of Allen Ginsberg's poem, 'Howl', published in 1956.[19] Shaw suggests that its esoteric vision, which initially seemed extreme and arcane, was transformed by historical events into 'everyone's daily reading' a decade or so later. The 'myth of the apocalypse' came to symbolize certain dominant features of mid-century American social life.

Like all effective art, 'Howl' challenges the dominant ideologies of its time at every level of its expressivity. It is radical in both form and content. Reading the poem again, after a number of years, the reader is likely to have absorbed its influence: the spiritual desolation it represents is as far removed from the illusory world of the advertising man as it is possible to be. 'Howl' signifies the alternative experience of America, that of the drop-out, the victim, the drug addict, the deviant, the psychologically disoriented, the man or woman driven to behave self-destructively. It is a world the reader recognizes even if he or she pretends to be separate from it.

In formal terms Ginsberg's poem subverts many of the constraints commonly found in poetry admired during the early 1950s, the strain of academic wit and self-conscious literary allusion, for example; its raw language employs diction that often shocks, and its long drawn-out lines have a revolutionary fervour about them. Almost any passage registers this rhetorical mix of iconoclasm and lofty truth-seeking. Speaking of the 'best minds' of his generation in 'Howl' Ginsberg laments those

> who chained themselves to subways for the endless ride
> from Battery to Holy Bronx on benzedrine until the noise
> of wheels and children brought them down shuddering
> mouth-wracked and battered bleak of brain all
> drained of brilliance in the dream light of Zoo.   (1956)

An analysis of this passage is likely to focus on the cumulative effects of the long lines, the drawn-out phrasing, the difficulty of achieving pauses for breath and the feeling that movement is shaped for public effect. It is clearly meant to be spoken, and suggests a quasi-liturgical rhythm. In her book *Paterfamilias: Allen Ginsberg in America* (1970) Jane Kramer informs us of the occasion when part of the poem was first read aloud to the poet's friends at a gathering in San Francisco.[20] It is no surprise to learn that Ginsberg was interested in Buddhism and meditative practices. 'Howl' is a communal poem, which consciously speaks for a generation that anticipated the counterculture: its resonant power is partly dependent upon this cultural nexus of sympathetic sharing and a residual mantra-like quality.

Many of the most acute Marxist theorists of literature such as Althusser have acknowledged the relative autonomy of literature to transcend a merely reflective mirroring of its context. Its fictive or imaginary power distances it from the constraints of its time, allowing it to comment upon aspects of social reality that are frequently concealed. In this manner Ginsberg's 'Howl', although related to San Francisco, the beat culture of Haight Ashbury, etc., illuminates what we may for convenience refer to as the 'historical unconscious' of the 1950s. It has a wider frame of cultural reference. Similarly, in the case of Bob Dylan his songs reach out beyond the 1960s counterculture that they represent so admirably.

Like Ginsberg, Bob Dylan has become an American institution, his songs deeply embedded in our consciousness. His status as a 'classic' popular entertainer, though, may easily prevent academic critics from according his lyrics their due as poems in their own right.

Bob Dylan's poems, influenced by folk and blues (Woody Guthrie and Leadbelly are among his heroes), are the nearest cultural equivalents in modern American poetry to the ballad. [21] His lyrics, of love, war, injustice and calamity, are in significant ways comparable to traditional songs. They share with the traditional song the concept of destiny, how reckless action, fate, chance, accident bring forth severe consequences. Most of Dylan's songs of the 1960s and 1970s have a compelling narrative power; they tell an exemplary story of how we should or should not behave. Frequently they are characterized by an abiding sense of mystery, displaying a lack of connectives; the lack of explanation makes them resistant to facile deciphering. They challenge the listener, usually leaving him or her with a feeling of threat or anxiety because something irreversible is about to happen.

A famous example 'It's All Over Now, Baby Blue' (1965) recalls the apocalypse of Ginsberg in one respect. A hint of the surreal, communicated through narrative detail and imagery, intensifies the warning,

The Highway is for gamblers, better use your sense.
Take what you have gathered from coincidence.
The empty-handed painter from your streets
Is drawing crazy patterns on your sheets.
This sky, too, is folding under you
And it's all over now, Baby Blue.

The reader does not know who is speaking and to whom. Baby Blue, clearly a symbolic figure, remains anonymous. Why the sky is folding remains an enigma. Only a new identity, a life change, will appease the imperatives of destiny.

By being unspecific 'It's All Over Now, Baby Blue' achieves a more potent impact; it is not reductively tied to its context. Dylan's more socially orientated, historically pointed lyrics also retain a sense of 'relative autonomy' and transhistorical appropriateness, although it is clear that they are positive anti-war poems or humanitarian protests against the injustices of the law. His group of civil rights poems, which includes 'The Death of Emmet Till' (1963), 'Only a Pawn in their Game' (1963), 'The Lonesome Death of Hattie Carroll' (1964) or 'Talkin' John Birch Paranoid Blues' (1970), address in overt narrative fashion issues of persecution and racial oppression. What is impressive is that his analysis of abuse is presented not in a pessimistic, defeatist mode, but framed by poems that point to the victory of the civil rights movement. Such poems as 'Paths of Victory' (1964) or 'Chimes of Freedom' (1964) are lyrics of hope and democratic struggle.

Perhaps Dylan's most lasting achievement as a poet is to signify in a cluster of his songs an intuition of popular history, how powerful processes are at work in widely disseminated ways. The best of these are justly admired, such works as 'The Times They Are A_Changin" (1963), 'Blowin' in the Wind' (1962) or (the present author's favourite) 'With God on Our Side' (1963). The latter, making use of a refrain and of an intricate rhyme or rhythmic scheme, has a restraint and economy that recalls the terse satire of Blake's lyrics in his *Songs of Experience*. America's history is celebrated in a tone of wry irony,

> Oh the history books tell it
> They tell it so well
> The cavalries charged
> The Indians fell
> The cavalries charged
> The Indians died
> Oh the country was young
> With God on its side

In the way that William Blake 'extended' his satire by setting his verse within his illuminated books, Dylan's work, drawing on the twentieth century's primary youth cultural mode of expression, is intensified by its musical form. Both lyric and music are inseparable.

Whereas in Bob Dylan's work place is represented in broadly symbolic terms, in other poets landscape is a significant index of human life, signifying failure or endurance. Richard Hugo's poetry, for example, makes specific reference to the regional culture of the north-west. His landscapes, of Dakota, Montana, Nebraska, Iowa and Washington State, seem to overwhelm their inhabitants. Hugo's poems are unsentimental records of the harshness of life in the wide open spaces.[22]

He is especially interested in how such vast plains and mountains bear the marks of American history beyond the prosperous cities. Having himself worked as an industrial writer for Boeing, Hugo is intensely aware of how the frontier myth has obscured the reality of regional depression, slump and cyclic decay. His poems record how history has treated the descendants of the settlers. In 'Graves at Elkhorn' a cemetery testifies to the deaths of over a 100 children in a severe year. Kicking Horse Reservoir, on the Flathead Indian reservation, inspires Hugo to reflect upon the drowning of a woman and boy, but the poem's speaker, as if unconsciously, admits, 'No one liked our product and the factory closed.' Industrial reality is never far away in his work. He celebrates the stoicism of those men and women in 'Degrees of Gray in Philipsburg' who find themselves stranded in a town which is still yoked to the silver industry whose boom time was in the early years of the century. Frustration and boredom are the legacy of 50 years' collapse in the mining of minerals.

Aesthetics After War

The title, from a poem by Richard Eberhart, comments on the implicit aesthetics of war poetry, the best of which demonstrates a level of artistic detachment from the chaos and political confusion immediately occasioned by the conflict itself. War is such a dramatic and momentous acting out of a nation's ideologies that it tends to overwhelm poetic artifice, sweeping the poet along in its turbulence. As James Mersmann has shown in his book *Out of the Vietnam Vortex* (1974), this is broadly what happened in the 1960s and early 1970s when heated debate and the political imperatives of opposing the war tended to take precedence over the measured distance and autonomy of art.[23] Some of the most interesting of contemporary poets failed to respond to America's Asian war in terms beyond agit-prop. Despite the occasional exception in an odd poem or passage, such volumes as Denise Levertov's *The Sorrow Dance* (1967), Robert Bly's *The Teeth Mother Naked at Last* (1970) or Robert Duncan's *Bending the Bow* (1968) fail to go beyond the confines of the narrowly political.

Geoffrey Thurley in *The American Moment* (1977) has suggested how intense political agitation may militate against the poem's power to suborn the immediate political issue,

> The Vietnam involvement has given American poets a dangerous weapon – dangerous, that is, to the survival of their own integrity. The Vietnam war was something on the face of it quite easy to be simply 'right' about. Yet poetry is not the same as political action. To march against the war, to agitate against it was one thing; to write a 'poem' either about it or touched off by it, quite another.

Thurley's point does seem valid; the flood of 1960s and 1970s anti-war poetry is often complacent, self-congratulatory and lacking in either historical or literary context.[24]

As in the case of the eagerly awaited 'definitive 'Nam novel', no major Vietnam War poetry has yet been produced to equal that, for example, written by Randall Jarrell, perhaps America's finest war poet, about the 1939–45 war. Jarrell's treatment of that war, in which he himself participated, is complex and philosophically ambitious. In plain, democratically accessible language he ranges discursively over a wide theatre, taking in precise geographical zones and actual historical situation. The epic sweep of his coverage is signified within *The Complete Poems* (1977) through his subheadings, 'Bombers', 'The

Carriers', 'Prisoners', 'Camps and Fields', 'The Traders', 'Children and Civilians', 'Soldiers'.25

In Jarrell's war poems the condition of war symbolizes emergent historical change, emblematic of how the century will develop. He is interested in both the wider repercussions of 'the world's war, just or unjust' and also the 'separate war' of the individual soldier who bears the brunt of such forces. A poem such as the restrained lament for Jews who are persecuted by the Nazis, 'A Camp in the Prussian Forest', demonstrates Jarrell's repudiation of fascism; it is one of the handful of American poems to treat the holocaust effectively in poetic terms. From this starting point, however, his poems represent the Allies as complicit in some of the war's barbaric actions. A recurrent image is that of the 'overkill' bombing of cities, which is referred to again and again in such poems as 'Losses' or 'Siegfried'.

Jarrell's poems portray fundamental truths about modern warfare, especially apt when such philosophers as Baudrillard are suggesting that the Gulf War of 1991 did not actually happen if the media are to be believed, and that the war's 'reality' and 'truths' will *never* be uncovered in discourse. For Jarrell such truths are manifest; that the soldier or airman is merely a pawn, the hapless instrument of formidable technology, certainly no mythical Rambo, but a frightened human being, disorientated and yearning to be at home with his family. This is memorably expressed in such poems as 'Pilots, Man Your Planes', 'A Pilot from the Carrier' or 'The Dead Wingman'. Such poems represent the disruption occasioned by war, its overturning of lives and frontiers: the locations of Jarrell's poems include transient barracks, prisoner of war stockades, refugee zones and concentration camps.

The wide angle of Jarrell's poems takes in also the emotional pain of soldiers and their families, and of other civilians, especially children, affected by war. Several poems focus upon bereavement, notably 'Burning the Letters'; others upon how children are inevitably pulled into war's vortex, for example, 'The State', 'The Truth' and 'Come to the Stone'. Although Jarrell's poems explore the war at home in the US and in the Pacific, in the section of his *Complete Poems* subheaded 'The Trades' his vision is based most extensively upon images of a Europe dismembered and in deep crisis; the places he draws upon as settings, for example Hamburg, Odessa and Haifa, are pressure points signifying territorial and psychological breakdown.

Poetry is never totally divorced from ideology, although a poet's politics are not usually foregrounded in poems. In Jarrell's case the moral underpinning of his work may be examined most clearly in the ways in which he represents the individual soldier. In 'The Sick Nought' the poem's speaker reiterates a common theme, the dispensable and

unremarkable fate of one man when empires are at stake,
> ... You are a ticket
> Someone bought and lost on, a stray animal
> You have lost even the right to be condemned
> I see you looking helplessly around, in histories,
> Bewildered ...   (1945)

Indeed, it seems from Jarrell's analysis that the experience of war is exemplary, dramatizing issues of power, hegemony and socialization in lessons easily digested. In 'Prisoners' such an indoctrination process is visibly formulated,
> The prisoners, the guards, the soldiers – they are
> all, in their way, being trained.
> From these moments, repeated forever, our own new world
> will be made.   (1945)

In such representation the 'separate war' of the soldier becomes part of a much more significant sociopolitical process closely related to the operations of finance capitalism.

From the Vietnam era only John Balaban's poems come near to the philosophical and historical cogency of Jarrell's. Balaban's knowledge of Vietnamese language and culture sets him apart, giving his work a cognate resilience and intellectuality in *After Our War*, his 1974 volume.[26] Of the more established canonical figures who wrote of America's conflict Robert Duncan's variations on Robert Southwell's 'The Burning Babe' are most likely to endure. Duncan's long poem 'Seventeenth Century Suite' was originally printed privately in 1973, and is included in his 1984 volume, *Ground Work: Before the War* (1984).[27] Two of the variations, Sections 4 and 5 of 'Seventeenth Century Suite', reflect upon the burning of children by napalm. In majestic and sombre language, drawing upon formal Catholic diction, the poet accepts both his own and his nation's culpability for the atrocity,
> From the broiled flesh of these heretics,
> by napalm monstrously baptized
>   in a new name,   every delicate and
> sensitive curve of lip and eyelid
>   blasted away, surviving ...
>   eyes? Can this horror be called their
> fate? Our fate grows a mirroring face
> in the accusation beyond accusation
>   of such eyes,
> a kind of hurt that drives into the root
> of understanding,   their very lives
>   burnd into us   we live by.   (1984)

The controlled rhetoric, slotted into a timescale stretching back to Southwell and Elizabethan England, enables urgent questions to be asked about the spiritual values of our civilization.

Conclusion: A Brief Note on Radicalism in Poetry

Radicalism in modern American poetry is a problematic issue. Poets are rarely radical in the sense of being militants or extremists who believe that their poems will change society irrevocably. Poetry is a much more sophisticated and contradictory form. More often than not radicalism is allied with a looking back to older forms and modes. Langston Hughes was an earlier example of a writer with such a stance because he preferred to cultivate the speech, songs and myths of his own black culture in his work, setting it apart from the dominant white poetic discourse. The black poet Margaret Walker drew upon Hughes's legacy, differing from him in that her radical agenda was more prominently displayed. Her volume *Prophets for a New Day* (1970) is perhaps the most impressive poetic response to the civil rights disturbances of the 1960s.[28] Interestingly, though, Margaret Walker draws upon the resonances of biblical language to express her sense of outrage. She therefore borrows from a conservative and apocalyptic tradition of language to make overtly political statements.

It is probably fair to say that most good poets are progressively attuned to impending historical change. Most often their prescience is expressed in seemingly occasional or minor poems that, with the passage of time, turn out to be prophetic. A relatively neglected example of such intuitive awareness is the way a number of poets have addressed what has come to be termed animal liberation or animal rights. Galway Kinnell is the most celebrated poet to do so, but the theme is subtly adumbrated in the work of other poets. Philip Levine's 'Animals are Passing from Our Lives' (1968) and W.S. Merwin's 'For a Coming Extinction' (1967) are examples of attunement to an issue that has become increasingly heated, and has generated bomb attacks on stores and research laboratories.

To borrow Ezra Pound's phrase, poets act as the 'antennae' of our race, and perform a public if often obscure role in raising consciousness. We may speculate that there will be a re-evaluation of past work as the radical themes poets have addressed come increasingly to seem 'relevant'. Perhaps the present intense public concern for environmental issues, for example, will alter the way we read the work of poets who have written sensitively upon such themes: the late James Wright and A.R. Ammons may attract such a reassessment. Radicalism, then, is an elusive concept, resistant to facile definition: poetry, likewise, is a meditative art affecting its readers in complex and mysterious ways. There is no doubt, though, that poems with radical energy and precise verbal beauty compel the reader's mind and senses.

Notes

1. Georg Lukacs, 'The Ideology of Modernism', from *The Meaning of Contemporary Realism*, trans. E. Bone (first pub. 1957). This quotation is included in D. Walder (ed.), *Literature in the Modern World* (Oxford: Oxford University Press, 1990), p. 163.

2. An account of Lowell's participation in peace marches is given in Norman Mailer's book, *The Armies of the Night: History as a Novel, The Novel as History* (London: Weidenfeld and Nicolson, 1968).

3. Italo Calvino, *The Uses of Literature: Essays*, trans. Patrick Creagh (1986). Quotation is from D. Walder (ed.), *Literature in the Modern World*, pp. 101–2.

4. Jean Paul Sartre, 'Writing, Reading and the Public', from *What is Literature?* (first pub. 1948), trans. B. Frechtman (1967). Included in Walder, *Literature*, pp. 88–9.

5. Paul A. Bové, *Destructive Poetics: Heidegger and Modern American Poetry* (New York: Columbia University Press, 1980). See introduction for a summary of this argument.

6. Quotations from the work of Robert Hayden (1913–80) are from *The Norton Anthology of American Literature*, third edition, Volume 2, ed. N. Baym *et al.* (New York and London: W.W. Norton and Co., 1989, first pub. 1979), pp. 2449–58.

7. Quotations from the poetry of Michael Harper (b. 1938) are from Baym (ed.), *ibid.*, pp. 2752–63.

8. See John Berryman's *Homage to Mistress Bradstreet* (1956) and *77 Dream Songs* (1964).

9. Quotations from the poems of Rita Dove (b. 1952) are from Baym, *The Norton Anthology of American Literature*, pp. 2773–82.

10. Walter Benjamin, 'Theses on the Philosophy of History', from *Illuminations* (first pub. 1955), trans. H. Zohn (1968). Quotations from Walder, *Literature*, p. 362.

11. George Steiner, 'The Hollow Miracle', from *Language and Silence: Essays 1958–1966* (Harmondsworth, Middlesex: Penguin Books, 1979), first pub. 1959.

12. Cora Kaplan, 'Language and Gender', from *Sea Changes: Culture and Feminism* (London: Verso, 1986). Quotation from Walder, *Literature*, p. 312.

13. Quotations are from Denise Levertov's *Selected Poems* (Newcastle upon Tyne: Bloodaxe Books, 1986).

14. Quotations from Adrienne Rich's poems dated up to 1974 are from Adrienne Rich, *Poems, Selected and New, 1950–1974* (New York: W.W. Norton & Co, 1975).

15. Adrienne Rich, *Of Woman Born: Motherhood as Experience and Institution* (1976), contrasts the myth of motherhood with the actuality of giving birth and of rearing children.

16. Quotations from Baym, *The Norton Anthology*, p. 2709.

17. *Ibid.*, p. 2703.

18. Quotations from Allen Ginsberg's poetry are from Allen Ginsberg, *Collected Poems, 1947–1980* (Harmondsworth, Middlesex: Viking, 1985).

19. Robert B. Shaw, 'The Poetry of Protest', from Robert B. Shaw (ed.), *American Poetry Since 1960: Some Critical Perspectives* (Cheadle Hulme, Cheshire: Carcanet Press, 1973), p. 50.

20. Jane Kramer, *Paterfamilias: Allen Ginsberg in America* (London: Victor Gollancz, 1970), pp. 47–8.

21. Quotations from the work of Bob Dylan are from *Writings and Drawings by Bob Dylan* (London: Jonathan Cape, 1973).

22. A selection of Richard Hugo's (1923–82) work from which quotations are taken is included in Baym, *The Norton Anthology*, pp. 2563–8.

23. James Mersmann, *Out of the Vietnam Vortex: A Study of Poets and Poetry Against the War* (Lawrence, Kansas: University of Kansas Press, 1974).

24. Geoffrey Thurley, *The American Moment, American Poetry in the Mid-Century* (London: Edward Arnold, 1977).

25. Quotations are from Randall Jarrell, *The Complete Poems* (London: Faber and Faber, first pub. 1971), 1981 edition.

26. John Balaban, *After Our War* (Pittsburg: University of Pittsburg Press, 1974).

27. Quotations from Robert Duncan (1919–88) are from Baym, *The Norton Anthology*, pp. 2525–6.

28. Margaret Walker, *Prophets for a New Day* (Detroit: Broadside Press, 1970).

8. Side Saddle on the Golden Calf: Moments of Utopia in American Pop Music and Pop Music Culture

John Storey

Writing in 1950, David Riesman more or less predicted a major feature of the subsequent development, the ebb and flow, of American pop music and culture following its tidal upsurge in 1956. Riesman argued that the audience for popular music could be divided into two groups, 'a majority one, which accepts the adult picture of youth somewhat uncritically, and a minority one in which certain socially rebellious themes are encapsulated'.[1] As Riesman pointed out, the minority group is always small. Its rebellion takes a symbolic form:

> an insistence on rigorous standards of judgement and taste ... a preference for the uncommercialized, unadvertised small bands rather than name bands; the development of a private language and then a flight from it when the private language (the same is true of other aspects of private style) is taken over by the majority group.[2]

What Riesman identified, what he called simply the minority group, is, after 1956, better understood as a *radical music subculture*.[3] What I want to suggest is that the history of American pop music has been generated (and will probably continue to be generated) by such subcultures. Although the two histories are not the same, without radical music subcultures there would not be a general history. Put simply, they are the dynamo which has powered the historical development of pop music.

Radical Music Subcultures

Consuming a particular music is a *way of being* in the world. Music is a sign by which the *young* judge and are judged by others. To be part of a radical music subculture is to display one's musical taste, and to claim that its consumption is an act of communal creation. It doesn't matter whether the community is real or imagined. What is important is that the music provides a *sense* of community. It is a community created in the act of consumption: 'When he (sic) listens to music, even if no one else is around, he listens in a context of imaginary "others" – his listening is indeed often an effort to establish connection with them.' [4]

The music doesn't just provide a symbolic form of cultural self-expression, it constructs a certain subjectivity. To be part of a radical music subculture is to become (for limited duration) a particular type of subject. The music operates as a sort of singing mirror, interpellating the young as subject to, and subjects of, its discourse. It is the passport to what George Melly called 'the country of the Now'.[5] The music is the articulating principle of the subculture. It is the communication through consumption of difference and identity; its binaries are *us* and *them*. To belong is to celebrate both identity and difference; to be dancing in a state of internal exile within a world of conformity and consensus. Radical music subcultures represent a temporary refusal of the drab conformity of the everyday; a refusal to assume the subject position of 'the gray flannel dwarf'.[6] It is a symbolic form of resistance to what is perceived as the commercial incorporation and ideological defusion of the *threat* and *promise* of pop music and pop music culture. But above all, it is an insistence on the geographic integrity of the country of the Now. So attractive has the country become that *adult society* has attempted, often with great success, to colonize it, claiming its music and general culture as its own. Commitment to a radical music subculture is above all a commitment to the notion that *being young* is a necessary and absolute condition of meaningful consumption of the music.

> Not only does the rock audience have a particular identity, that of youth, but that identity 'bleeds' into the very definition of the music itself. (In what other cultural setting would it make sense to tell someone that they are too old to understand or enjoy it?)[7]

Consumption is thus an act of defiance against *adult society's* attempt at the commercial incorporation and ideological defusion of the elusive spirit of rock'n'roll. What this elusive spirit communicates is *youth*.[8] A radical music subculture is both a celebration of youth and a resistance to the music industry's pan-generational colonization of pop music culture. The rhetoric of radical music subcultures is thus generational; a rhetoric of generational conflict. This does not mean that each radical music subculture actively propagates in any thorough theoretical fashion the view that the major division in American society is generation rather than class, race or gender. What it does mean is that each operates a certain utopian blindness which acts to obscure other divisions and enacts only generational conflict as significant. To trace the history of this struggle is to hear a voice singing on behalf of different generations, from within different historical moments, singing of the time before the emergence of each new radical music subculture, two lines from Bob Dylan's 'My Back Pages':

> Ah, but I was so much older then,
> I'm younger than that now.[9]

One might object that I am ignoring the determinant role of the record industry. Patterns of consumption are formed out of patterns of production. This is true, but as Simon Frith points out, 'Despite the difficulties of the calculations ... most business commentators agree that about 10 percent of all records released (a little less for singles, a little more for LPs) make money.'[10] Frith also estimates that 'only another 10 percent cover their own costs'.[11] In other words, the vast majority of records released don't make money, they actually lose money. Given this situation it is obvious that pop music's audience does not passively consume what the industry produces; there is a great deal of active selection involved. Radical music subcultures represent this selection process at its most critical.

> For, after the commercial power of the record companies has been recognised, after the persuasive sirens of the radio acknowledged, after the recommendations of the musical press noted, it is finally those why buy the records, dance to the rhythms and live the beat who demonstrate, despite the determined conditions of its production, the wider potential of pop.[12]

It is the wider, if ultimately limited, potential of pop music which is displayed in the distinctive patterns of consumption of radical music subcultures. What follows is by necessity, given the space available, a brief and schematic account of the significance of radical music subcultures in the history of American pop music and pop music culture.

Rock'n'Roll

The explosion of rock'n'roll in 1956 was the beginning of a revolution in popular music. It marked the emergence of *pop* as opposed to *popular* music. Pop meant youth music; a music which claimed *youth* as central to its definition. Rock'n'roll produced the first radical music subculture. 'A new generation identified itself by the seriousness with which it regarded the feelings and experiences described in the songs.'[13]

What was first called rock'n'roll by disc jockey Alan Freed and music store owner Leo Mintz was in fact rhythm and blues.[14]

> 'Rhythm and blues' had meant music by black people for black people. Rock'n'roll meant at first only that this music was being directed at white listeners, but then, as the people producing the music became conscious of their new audience, they changed the character of the music, so that rock'n'roll came to describe – and be – something different from rhythm and blues.[15]

The rock'n'roll revolution changed the relationship between audience and popular music. It produced an audience that reacted to the music in ways only previously witnessed in audiences for jazz, folk or classical music. Being *unpopular* had guaranteed their seriousness. Rock'n'roll suggested that being popular did not necessarily mean not being taken seriously. There are of course definite limits to a radical music subculture's engagement with popularity. Too much popularity usually means the disintegration of the subculture.

Like all revolutions, rock'n'roll was attacked by those in old positions of power. The British popular music establishment attacked rock'n'roll for being 'the antithesis of ... good taste and musical integrity'. Elvis Presley's 'Hound Dog' was singled out for displaying 'sheer repulsiveness coupled with the monotony of incoherence'.[16] As Ian Chambers points out, 'The majority of objections raised by the popular music establishment insisted that rock'n'roll was loud and brash, that, quite simply, it was not music but a noise, and worse still, a vulgar commercial noise.'[17]

To deny a new music the very status of being *music* is a common strategy. The teenage chronicles of Chuck Berry, the hiccuping enunciation of Elvis Presley and Gene Vincent, the peculiar pronunciation of Buddy Holly, the stage antics of Little Richard and Jerry Lee Lewis, the rhythmic invitations of Bill Haley and the Comets to dance and more – all helped increase the hostility of the popular music establishment. When appeals to musical consensus failed, coercion was applied. For example, the BBC banned Gene Vincent's 'Be Bop A Lula', Elvis Presley was only allowed on the 'Ed Sullivan Show' after he agreed to wear a dinner suit. Sullivan also insisted that the camera must remain above his waist. Presley's 'subversive hips'[18] were considered too much for American television.

Rock'n'roll's moment was brief: 1956–8. By 1958 rock'n'roll was becoming gentler, less emphatic, less aggressive; rebellion was being replaced by 'innocuous adolescent sentimentality'.[19] In short, rock'n'roll was being overwhelmed by High School pop. The new stars were a collection of manufactured teenage Sinatras: Paul Anka, Frankie Avalon, Fabian, Rick Nelson, Bobby Rydell. Elvis Presley's meek acceptance of the draft in 1958 seemed like a symbolic act of incorporation. Of far greater significance was the death of Buddy Holly, still only 22, in a plane crash in February 1959. The sense of loss was compounded when a Congressional inquiry, completed in 1959, found that bribery ('payola') was commonplace throughout American radio. Alan Freed, rock'n'roll's first great disc jockey, was prosecuted. The inquiry disclosed that certain rock'n'roll records had been promoted in return for money, expensive gifts and sexual favours. One common technique had been to credit disc jockeys with co-authorship of records to encourage airplay.[20]

Despite its apparent commercial incorporation and ideological defusion, rock'n'roll had made fundamental changes in the relation between youth and popular music: 'Absorbing this music without necessarily thinking much about it, the generations of popular music audiences since 1956 have formed quite different sensibilities from the preceding generations which were raised on sentiment and melodrama.' [21] As the sentiment and melodrama returned, the radical music subculture went underground.

West Coast Rock

Bob Dylan's response to rock'n'roll was the typical response of an enthusiast of a radical music subculture. A former classmate remembers Dylan's reaction to 'Rock Around the Clock' as being 'almost explosive' as Dylan shouted, 'Hey, that's our music. That's written for us.' [22]

With the commercial incorporation and defusion of rock'n'roll, Dylan looked elsewhere for its spirit of rebellion. Folk music seemed to embody some of this spirit. In some respects its rebellion seemed less symbolic, more concrete. From 1961 to 1964 Dylan worked in this form. In 1964 the 'British Invasion' (the success of the Beatles and other British groups in the American charts) brought the original spirit of rock'n'roll back to America. Dylan recognized the return of the repressed dialectic: youth/music. He responded with the album *Bringing It All Back Home*. 'The album title is a fine colloquial phrase tattooed onto our language. It reminds Beatles' and Stones' fans, who vaguely thought rock was a British invention, that it all started in America.' [23]

Dylan attempted to resuscitate the oppositional spirit and rhythms of his youth. He was bringing the music back home to America and back home to his youth. It was a move from the rhetoric (and by 1964, the clichés) of 1930s radicalism, to a language and style to suit the changed conditions of the 1960s. Dylan had stopped pretending that he was *ramblin'* through the 1930s with Woody Guthrie, and recognized instead that his time was *Now* – he was 30 years younger in an instant. To the folk song establishment the transition meant only one thing: Dylan had sold out. The truth was that Dylan had embraced a different revolution; one he had embraced briefly as a teenager. It had been the Beatles who had reminded Dylan of his rock'n'roll heritage.[24] Their success prompted his return to his youth. But the music Dylan returned to was a rock'n'roll refracted through the lyrical concerns and complexities of folk music. The fusion resulted in the creation of a new form: folk-rock. In January 1965, Dylan recorded 'Subterranean Homesick Blues', the keynote song on *Bringing It All Back Home*. 'A bluesy, amplified rhythm section blasted away while Dylan shouted the lyric almost too fast to catch, sounding all the world like Chuck Berry singing "Too Much Monkey Business" back in 1956.' [25]

A phrase from the lyrics of 'Subterranean Homesick Blues' – 'You don't need a weatherman to know which way the wind blows' – was taken up as the motto of a radical underground political organization active in the US in the late 1960s and early 1970s. In a seemingly revolutionary era, the very titles of Dylan's songs signified an alternative cultural politics: 'The Times They Are A-Changing"; 'Masters of War'; 'Gates of Eden'. The lyrics were often visionary and oppositional:

> There's a battle outside
> And it is ragin' ...
> For the loser now
> Will be later to win ...
> The times they are a-changin'

and proclaimed that something alternative and important was happening. For a time they became the anthems of the civil rights and anti-war movements, and later of a sector of the youth counterculture. The Dylan look, the Dylan sound, even his way of dealing with press conferences, signified a deep suspicion about the claims of the dominant culture. Lines like 'It's easy to see ... that not much is really sacred' in their time seemed to radicals to convey a new left and counterculture criticism of consumer capitalism, as well as of the hypocritical stance of the institutions of the dominant culture on civil rights, racism and the war in Vietnam.

'Subterranean Homesick Blues' presents a picture of a society where to be young is to be in trouble. The police plant drugs, the phones are tapped, school is nothing more than a preparation for dead-end jobs. Its key phrase is 'Look out kid', but the song's power is as much to do with the *grain* [26] of Dylan's voice, the pure physicality of its protest, as with the words he sings. The impact of the song was immediate. Dave Harker remembers that 'Simply to play "that noise" in a middle-class, or aspiring working-class, living-room was itself a minor act of subversion, a symbolic defiance.' [27]

Dylan's return to his roots had created 'the potentially radical, if not revolutionary, force of folk-rock'.[28] It was this new form which formed the basis of what became known as West Coast rock, the sound of the American counterculture.[29] The music of the counterculture was, at least initially, the product of men and women who, like Dylan, had grown up musically during the folk revival. Folk music had been their first music. However, when Dylan went electric in 1965, his example was quickly followed by the musicians who were to form the core of the counterculture. Coming out of the folk revival they carried with them its political concerns: its belief that music was politics by other means. Self-expression and social commentary were seen as complementary. Another influence, carried over from folk music, was the belief that they belonged to an alternative community rather than to an entertainment industry. For the political folk singers music had been a means of class mobilization, of organization, the muse of solidarity. For the counterculture it was the central and unique mode of political and cultural expression. Put simply, the culture was built around the music. It was not possible to be a hippie and not hear West Coast rock as deeply pleasurable and profoundly political. It was the music that produced and promoted the lifestyle; it was the means by which it discovered and reproduced itself. The music wasn't an appendage to the lifestyle, it was its central articulating principle. Rather than mass meetings and rallies, its organizing events were festivals and dances. The fact that the West Coast musicians were, in the main, of the same class and age (middle class and under 25) as their audience reinforced the sense of community within the culture. As with all radical music subcultures, the music was seen as a collective event (even if consumed in the presence of only imaginary others). Its favourite pronoun was 'we', its favourite adverb 'together'.

Of radical music subcultures, West Coast rock undoubtedly produced the most politically motivated and articulate. All radical music subcultures operate with an implied politics. Sometimes it is little more than the demand for the freedom to party. West Coast rock, however, posed an alternative culture to 'straight Amerika'. It was music to win the world to the ways of the counterculture. As Grace Slick of Jefferson Airplane told Ralph Gleason, 'Music makes it easier to get your ideas across.' [30] One of the key ideas, perhaps *the* key idea, was encapsulated in the slogan: 'Make Love, Not War'. To be part of West Coast rock's radical music subculture was to be against 'straight Amerika's' war in Vietnam.

> Rock music must not be seen apart from the movement among young people to reshape their lives ... As such it is a profoundly *political* form of music, one that opts for a different form of social organisation, one that lets people love rather than makes them go to war.[31]

West Coast rock's opposition to 'straight Amerika' also manifested itself as a reluctance to meet the normal imperatives of the music industry. Bands made albums without having made a single. Other bands became nationally known without having even signed a recording deal. Commercial success always threatened to break up the sense of community. But the problem was this: in order to make records, musicians, however alternative, had to engage with the profit-making concerns of the music industry. If you want to continue making records you have to continue making profits. The audience is no longer the community, but the marketplace. The defusion that radical music subcultures fear most becomes inevitable. The contradictions become unbearable. While Jefferson Airplane sang;

> All your private property is target for your enemy
> And your enemy is *We* ...

RCA made money. In other words, the proliferation of Jefferson Airplane's anti-capitalist politics increased the profits of their capitalist record company. 'Turn on to profit power' was the slogan for the 1968 ABC distributors' conference. And profits certainly flowed. Marketed under slogans such as 'The revolutionaries are on Columbia', 'The man can't bust our music' (Columbia), 'It's happening on Capital', and 'Psychedelia – the sound of the Now generation' (MGM), the new music helped to increase record sales from US$862 million in 1965 to US$1660 million in 1970.

The commercial incorporation of its music and festivals, the Manson murders, the death of Meredith Hunter at the Rolling Stones concert at Altamont Speedway, the killings at Kent State University, all contributed to the collapse of the radical music subculture of West Coast rock.[32]

Punk Rock

The collapse of West Coast rock produced the self-conscious spectacle of progressive rock. This deformed offspring of the American counterculture was seen by punk rock as a betrayal of the original spirit of rock'n'roll.

> Punk attacked rock and roll[33] for having grown old and fat,[34] for having lost that which puts it in touch with its audience and outside the hegemonic reality. It attacked rock and roll in the guise of megagroups and arena rock, hippies and baby boomers who had

clearly become part of what was supposed to be outside of rock and roll.[35]

Against this the punks returned to basics. And though they ransacked the available wardrobe of subcultural style to put together the punk look, musically they represented a leap back across the 1970s and 1960s to the elemental power of rock'n'roll.[36]

Punk rock produced a mini reprise of the 'British Invasion' of the 1960s. It emerged in Britain in the hot, sweaty summer of 1976: 'a dramatic illustration of the alarming advancement of Britain's diseased state'.[37] It had developed out of 'pub rock', a London-based music scene. Pub rock had itself represented a refusal of the increasing pretentions of progressive rock. It was a metropolitan return to the spirit of 1962–4, which had produced the Beatles. But what pub rock inspired was a great deal less acceptable to the British pop musical establishment. Punk bands, unlike the Beatles, would not be invited to play the Royal Variety Performance.

Defining itself against the excesses of the 'technobores' of progressive rock, the bombastic technical sophistication of bands such as Yes, Genesis, Pink Floyd[38] and Led Zeppelin, punk rock had nowhere to go but back to basics, to a music which was loud, crude and direct. The February 1977 issue of *Sniffin' Glue*, punk rock's principal 'fanzine', featured a diagram of three chords with the caption: 'This is a chord. This is another. This is a third. Now form a band.' It was a 'noise' that anyone could play, a do-it-yourself culture. As with all radical music subcultures, minimal distance was maintained between producers and consumers. All that was necessary (or so it seemed) was to look and behave in ways that were unacceptable to the rest of society. Their hostility and disgust was part of punk rock's self-definition. It prided itself that 'its music [was] the summation of all rebellious youth "noise", its social manners the perverse opposite of normal conduct.' [39] Such a radical music subculture would inevitably be greeted with hostility. The Sex Pistols, with their mixture of dole queue anger and art school bohemia, provoked and received more hostility than most. It was the attitude of their sound and the mood of their performance that both attracted and repelled. Part of the lyric of 'Anarchy in the UK', banned, like most of their singles, by the BBC and others, might suggest some of their positive/negative power:

> Right now I am an antichrist
> I am an anarchist
> Don't know what I want
> But I know how to get it
> I wanna destroy
> Because I wanna be anarchy ...

But of course, the lyric only really comes alive when it is articulated by the band's raucous rhythm, and the threatening physicality of Johnny Rotten's voice.

Punk rock was a radical music subculture with a shared knowledge that the music outraged and scandalized those outside the subculture. Thus a sense of belonging was established by the shared knowledge of the disgust of others. Records were banned, concerts cancelled, police prosecutions brought, contracts ended, sections of the pop music press offended. The Chairperson of the Greater London Council's Arts Committee called punk 'the negation of culture'.[40] Even Members of Parliament joined the hostilities. Conservative MP Marcus Lipton declared: 'If pop music is going to be used to destroy our established institutions, then it ought to be destroyed first.' [41]

Despite the consolidating effect of such opposition, the moment of punk rock as a radical music subculture was brief. The end came, more or less, with the break up of the Sex Pistols, following their American tour, in January 1978. The band which had for the many symbolized the energy and scandal of punk rock, brought it to a close for the few.

American punk tended to be imitative. Bands wanted to be like the Clash or the Sex Pistols in much the same way as bands a decade or so earlier had wanted to be like the Beatles or the Rolling Stones. American punk quickly gave way to the more sophisticated New Wave. The exception was the Dead Kennedys. The name alone was enough to outrage and annoy. Songs such as 'Too Drunk to Fuck' confirmed their distance from any notion of a consensus of good musical taste. When the band's leader, Jello Biafra, was in legal difficulties in 1987, it was European punk bands who raised most of the money for his defence costs.[42]

A Few Drops in the Ocean for Change [43]

The 1980s were a remarkable decade for 'political pop'.[44] The decade began with the release of the *No Nukes* film and triple album featuring the performances of members of Musicians United for Safe Energy. The appearance of Crosby, Stills and Nash on the same bill as Bruce Springsteen suggested a symbolic suturing of the countercultural rock of the 1960s and the political pop of the 1980s. The Sun City project established in 1985 united musicians in opposition to apartheid in a declared refusal to play the Sun City entertainment complex in South Africa. The result was a single, a video and an album featuring performers such as Dylan, Bono and Springsteen. Live Aid, perhaps the key political pop event of the 1980s, reached an audience in excess of 2 billion. It gave famine both money and publicity. A few remarks from Dylan were enough to produce Farm Aid. The following year, Amnesty International's 'Conspiracy of Hope' tour featured Dylan, Tom Petty, Peter Gabriel, Jackson Browne, Lou Reed, Joan Baez, Sting and U2 on a week-long tour across America from San Francisco to New York. As a result Amnesty International doubled its membership in the US. Two years later it organized the Amnesty International World Tour. The event was headlined by Springsteen.

Such endeavours are not without contradictions. Pop music's political maturity (if that's what it is), it might be argued, has been gained at the cost of its generational radicalism. This might seem a curious claim. After all, what is rebellious style when compared with a starving or tortured human being? Nevertheless, pop music's role as charitable body or political publicist could be seen as a sign of its incorporation into the very adult society it has always struggled to resist. Certainly it is a happier collision than that between RCA and Jefferson Airplane in the 1960s. But as Robin Denselow points out, 'Live Aid helped to make pop music – the "rebel" music of previous eras – seem ... respectable.' [45]

Perhaps it is not a question of contradictions, but the sign of the rather shaky formation of a new radical music subculture, one that defines itself in terms of political pop. U2's tour of the US, the year following the 'Conspiracy of Hope' tour, certainly seemed to suggest this might be the case. Audiences turned up with anti-apartheid banners and Amnesty International posters calling for the release of political prisoners around the world. Bono's comments certainly support the suggestion:

> When we first came here five years ago, there was this incredible entrenchment, and a broken spirit, made up for by an arrogance and a right-wing prevalence through the colleges and schools, and a feeling not just that rock'n'roll couldn't change anything but that the individual couldn't change anything. But now there is a turning of the tides.[46]

One can of course be cynical and suggest that some of the performers who have been supporting political campaigns have done so simply to sell records. Well founded or not, such cynicism should not survive the witnessing of the deeply moving reception Nelson Mandela received at Wembley, London, in April 1990. However the performers were defining their presence that day, the audience clearly wanted to be part of a utopian/political moment when pop music mattered enough for the world's most famous political prisoner (released only two months earlier) to thank a pop music audience because they 'chose to care'.

Against Pessimism

> Rock'n'roll is not revolutionary but it is a form of struggle against a certain debilitating organisation of pessimism.⁴⁷

What pop music asserts at its moments of greatest radicalism is that the limits of the ordinary, the everyday, are not the limits of experience. Radical music subcultures open up a gap between what is and what might be. Springsteen remembers the rock'n'roll of his youth as offering

> the promise of something else. Not the politicians' promise, y'know, that everything is gonna be alright ... that would be a false promise anyway. I mean the promise of *possibilities*, the promise that the search and the struggle matter, that they affirm your life. That was the original spirit of rock'n'roll ... a message that no one has the right to tell you gotta forfeit.⁴⁸

It is the very vagueness of the promise of possibilities, the promise of something else, which gives the ideology ('the original spirit of rock'n'roll) its power to persuade that the temporary can be permanent and more. Myths of course don't have to be true to be powerful, they have only to be acted on. The ideology that binds together each radical music subculture, constantly articulating the difference between *us* and *them*, has the status of such myths. What isn't a myth, however, is the terrain on which radical music subcultures operate:

> The truth of youth culture is that the young displace to their free time the problems of work and family and future. It is because they *lack* power that the young account for their lives in terms of play, focus their politics on leisure.⁴⁹

It is also true that: 'Youth cultural styles may begin by issuing symbolic challenges, but they must inevitably end by establishing new sets of conventions; by creating new commodities, new industries or rejuvenating old ones.' ⁵⁰

And as John Muncie points out:

> Pop does not undermine capitalism, it merely makes it function more disparately, and ultimately more effectively. Although the total and passive integration of 'pop' is never achieved, it is consistently reduced to being a reflection of, rather than a reaction to, the structural inequalities of contemporary capitalism.⁵¹

Despite this – and much of this falls outside the ideological vision of radical music subcultures, their *generational consciousness* – there is pleasure and there is the struggle for pleasure; dancing in a fleeting hedonistic moment of utopia in a generational struggle to sustain the youth specificity of *pop* against the adult generality of the *popular*. If we want more than this we must look elsewhere.

Notes

1. David Riesman, 'Listening to Popular Music' in Simon Frith and Andrew Goodwin (eds), *On Record: Rock, Pop, & The Written Word* (London: Routledge, 1990), p. 8.

2. *Ibid.*, pp. 9–10.

3. Charlie Gillett, *The Sound of the City* (London: Souvenir Press, 1983), pp. 12–13, glosses Riesman's argument thus:

   Riesman's observations that no matter what the majority choose, there will be a minority choosing something different explains how popular music continues to change, no matter how good – or bad – the dominant types of music are at any particular period. And because the minority audience defines itself as being radical within the music audience, its taste is likely to favour, consciously or unconsciously, music with some element of social comment or criticism in.

4. 'Listening to Popular Music', p. 10.

5. George Melly, *Revolt into Style* (Oxford: Oxford University Press, 1989) p. 6.

6. Bob Dylan, *Writings & Drawings* (London: Granada, 1974), pp. 283–4.

7. Lawrence Grossberg, 'Rock and Roll in Search of an Audience' in James Lull (ed.), *Popular Music and Communication*, (Beverley Hills: Sage, 1987), p. 180.

8. 'Being young', 'youth' and 'adult society' are ideological terms that don't necessarily have a generational fix. They indicate attitude as much as age.

9. Dylan, *Writings & Drawings*, p. 215.

10. Simon Frith, *Sound Effects: Youth, Leisure, and the Politics of Rock'n'Roll* (London: Constable, 1983), p. 147.

11. *Ibid.*, p. 101.

12. Iain Chambers, *Urban Rhythms: Pop Music and Popular Culture* (London: Macmillan, 1985), p. xii.

13. Gillett, *The Sound of the City*, p. 44.
14. See *The Sound of the City* for the origins of the term, and Freed and Mintzer's use of it.
15. *Ibid.*, p. 22.
16. *Melody Maker*, 5 May 1956 and 10 October 1956.
17. Chambers, *Urban Rhythms*, p. 24.
18. Dave Harker, *One for the Money: Politics and Popular Song* (London: Hutchinson, 1980), p. 56.
19. Chambers, *Urban Rhythms*, p. 40.
20. For example, Chuck Berry's 'Maybellene' credited Alan Freed as co-author to encourage the disc jockey to promote the record.
21. Gillett, *The Sound of the City*, p. xii.
22. Quoted in Antony Scaduto, *Bob Dylan* (London: Sphere, 1973), p. 6.
23. Robert Shelton, *No Direction Home: the Life and Music of Bob Dylan* (London: New English Library, 1986), pp. 270–1.
24. Dylan in turn introduced the Beatles to marijuana.
25. Gillett, *The Sound of the City*, p. 299.
26. See Roland Barthes, *Image-Music-Text* (London: Fontana, 1977).
27. Harker, *One for the Money*, p. 133.
28. Gillett, *The Sound of the City*, p. 335.
29. Folk rock became acid rock and then simply rock.
30. Ralph Gleason, *The Jefferson Airplane and the San Francisco Sound* (New York: Ballantine Books, 1969), p. 159.
31. Jonathan Eisen (ed.), *The Age of Rock: Sounds of the American Cultural Revolution* (New York: Vintage Books, 1969), p. xiv.
32. See John Storey, 'Rockin' Hegemony: West Coast Rock and Amerika's War in Vietnam', in Alf Louvre and Jeff Walsh (eds), *Tell Me Lies About Vietnam* (Milton Keynes: Open University Press, 1988) for a more detailed account of West Coast rock's confrontation with straight Amerika. See John Storey, 'Bringing It All Back Home' in Michael Klein (ed.), *The Vietnam Era* (London: Pluto, 1990) for a general account of the American musical response to the war in Vietnam.
33. Grossberg's use of the term 'rock and roll' demonstrates the diffi-

culty of finding a general term to denote pop music which isn't simply pop.

34. Paul Weller, then of the Jam, on Roger Daltry of the Who: 'you can't play rock'n'roll with a beer-gut' (*New Musical Express*, 7 May 1976).

35. Lawrence Grossberg, 'Is There Rock After Punk', in Simon Frith and Andrew Goodwin (eds), *On Record: Rock, Pop & the Written Word* (London: Routledge, 1990), p. 117.

36. The Sex Pistols recorded an excellent version of Eddie Cochran's 'Something Else'. Punk rock seems to have relocated Gene Vincent, Eddie Cochran and the early Elvis Presley as proto-punks.

37. Chambers, *Urban Rhythms*, p. 175.

38. The lyrics of Pink Floyd's *Wish You Were Here*, recorded in 1975, the year before punk, suggest a certain awareness of the cost of their drift from Britain's premier 'Underground' band to elite and remote megagroup:
    Did you exchange
    A walk on part in the war
    For a lead role in a cage?
    Punk Rock's answer would be a raucous 'Yes'.

39. Chambers, *Urban Rhythms*, p. 185.

40. Quoted in Chambers, *Urban Rhythms*, p. 175.

41. Quoted in Dick Hebdige, *Subculture: the Meaning of Style* (London: Methuen, 1979), p. 158.

42. See Robin Denselow, *When the Music's Over: The Story of Political Pop* (London: Faber and Faber, 1990).

43. This is taken from a quotation from Peter Gabriel: 'Music can create awareness ... and if people become politically engaged, that's a few drops in the ocean for change.' *When The Music's Over*, p. xvii.

44. I use the term as employed by Denselow in *When The Music's Over* to denote pop music which explicitly aligns itself with political groups or movements. I do not, however, accept Denselow's implicit distinction between political and non-political pop music: the view that pop music or pop music culture not defined by Denselow as political is therefore non-political. I find the distinction both limited and limiting. This is particularly apparent in his critique of what he calls John Lennon's 'media politics'.

45. Denselow, *When the Music's Over*, p. 248.

46. *Ibid.*, p. 260.
47. 'Rock and Roll in Search of an Audience', p. 180.
48. Quoted in Stephen Barnard, *Rock: An Illustrated History* (London: Guild Publishing, 1986), p. 236.
49. Frith, *Sound Effects* p.201.
50. Hebdige, *Subculture: The Meaning of Style*, p. 96.
51. John Muncie, 'Pop Culture, Pop Music and Post-war Youth: Subcultures', in *Popular Culture*, block 5, unit 19 (Milton Keynes: Open University Press, 1981), p. 61.

9. What Feminism has said about Motherhood

Ann Snitow

> Modern feminism in the US, of course, predates the 1960s. We can trace it back to the Seneca Falls conference in the mid-nineteenth century and its convergence with the broad abolition movement. There were important moments of flowering before the First World War and during the struggles of the 1930s. However, the roots of modern feminist consciousness were to a great extent forged in the mid- to late 1950s and early 1960s. It was at this time that key texts began to be written and received and widely read in the US. For example, works such as Simone de Beauvoir's *The Second Sex* (1955) had a significant impact upon the consciousness of a new generation. Betty Friedan's *The Feminine Mystique* (1963) was one of the first oppositional text of the 1960s New Left.
>
> Thus, we can say that the new feminist consciousness in the US developed prior to and together with the civil rights, anti-war and other liberation movements of the 1960s – not in their aftermath. In a sense the struggle to obtain an equal rights amendment (ERA) to the US Constitution in the 1970s was the final major statement of the 1960s movement.
>
> In the 1970s and the 1980s many significant debates about feminism centred upon the ways that motherhood is constructed by the dominant and oppositional cultures.
>
> *Michael Klein*

I've just emerged from a bout of reading, a wide eclectic sampling of what the current wave of US feminism has had to say about motherhood. My conclusions are tentative, and there's another study that I've learned arises directly out of this one – a study of how feminists have *misread* our own texts on this subject. My reading came as the end point of a year and a half of infertility treatments, and though I see now how heavy that experience lies on my own readings, perhaps my misreadings, I've also come to see that *anyone* doing this work is likely to worry about where to stand. I want to criticize the pervasive pronatalism that has so shaped my recent experience – a pronatalism not only in the culture at large but also within feminism – but this desire inevitably raises the question: who is allowed to criticize pronatalism, to question the desire for children? The mothers might feel it disingenuous to take on this task; they have their children after all. And the childless are bound to feel that their critique is a species of sour grapes. Certainly, women like me who have tried so hard to have babies late might well feel sheepish and hypocritical about mounting a heavy critique of pronatalism. Will the lesbian community speak up with unembarrassed enthusiasm for the child-free life? Not now. Far more typical at the moment is the recent book *Politics of the Heart: A Lesbian Parenting Anthology*. (Though I find there Nancy D. Polikoff's question to the community: 'Who is talking about the women who don't ever want to be mothers?' Her answer: 'No one.')[1]

In one of the best collections of essays about the decision to mother I've found, *Why Children?*, the editors say they searched for mothers unhappy with motherhood and they found them: but they could not get these mothers to write.[2] The dissatisfied mothers feared hurting their children if they admitted how little they had liked mothering. And what about the mothers who had children against their will? Are they in a position to complain? Not really, once again: it will hurt the children to know they were unwanted. Besides women have made an art of turning these defeats into triumphs; women have made a richer world out of their necessities. And so the children rarely hear a forthright critique of how women come to mother in a patriarchy – though of course they usually know all about it at one level or another, and guilt is left to fill in the holes of the story.

Women with children and women without them have been bristling at each other for years over the question of authenticity. The fight over the ERA was a national example of this kind of warfare, but even inside feminism there's no particularly friendly entry point for this discussion. Which speaker has the necessary experience, hence the authority, to speak? Mothers can say they've seen both sides, can make judgements about what motherhood is like. Initiates, they are the ones who can measure the true dimensions of the choice. It's harder to imagine what the non-mothers can tell about their condition. One rises each morning to children – and often, of course, all through the night – but does one rise to the counter-condition – ah, another day without children? The two conditions are not precisely parallel. And each one has its own narrative taboos.

What I want to argue today is that feminism set out to break *both* sets of taboos – those surrounding the experiences of the mothers and of the non-mothers, but for reasons I find both inside our movement and even more in the American society in which that movement unfolded, in the long run we were better able to attend to mothers' voices (or at least to *begin* on that project) than we were able to imagine a full and deeply meaningful life without motherhood, without children. Finally, in the defensive Reagan years, feminist ambivalence and guilt about blaming mothers, and our ambivalence about becoming mothers ourselves, toned down and tuned out a more elusive discussion of what choice might mean if there were really two imaginable lives for women – with and without children.

Building a supportive culture for both the mothers and the non-mothers – both are crucial feminist tasks – but in the rising national babble of pronatalism in the 1980s, listening to the mothers was a project subtly susceptible to cooptation. Meanwhile, though I certainly felt that feminism was my shield at the infertility clinic, and that the often desperate women I met there were relatively lucky to be experiencing this loss of a baby now, when feminism is in the air, when middle-class married women work, when the birthrate is 1.9 children per woman, not the 3.7 of 1956, nonetheless feminist culture didn't seem to be producing alluring images or thinkable identities for the childless. What feminist idea about independence of work or political life seemed bracing enough to counter the yearning miasma of the infertility clinic? Could one turn to the feminist critique of the new reproductive technologies? Middle class and well informed, the women in my infertility support group (set up by the US national organization, Resolve) had already intimated most of the useful social and medical feminist analysis in books such as those by Andrea Eagan, Barbara Katz-Rothman, Gina Correa and Barbara Stanworth. Certainly, we all knew we were test animals (for example, record keeping was the major undertaking at the clinic I attended), but this knowledge of the down-sides of medicalization had little bearing on the questions of our desire and need. Where was the feminist critique of our motivation? Why were we such eager consumers of twice daily injections of pergonal, and mood-altering progesterone?

In 1970 feminism would have been quite hostile to these extreme undertakings, but that can't help anyone now. Indeed, it may well be that that earlier reaction to the pressure to mother was so historically specific that it can have no direct descendants. Young women now can be angry about the threat to abortion without feeling the terrible claustrophobia about the future my generation felt as children of the 1950s. All the same, historical shifts like these cannot fully explain the current flaccidity of the critique of motherhood in feminism.

Surely we can't claim that young women have made peace with mothers, or that mothers now have social services or more help, so where has the rage gone? Why does the pronatalism of our period flourish with so little argument from us, the feminists?

To answer questions like these, I've begun to construct a time-line of feminism on motherhood. (This research is very much in progress, and I hope readers will suggest titles, key moments, significant shifts as you experienced them.) Here are the main features of the line as it has emerged so far.

Though the record is complex, and though my generalizations are often contradicted by important exceptions, I see three distinct periods along the time-line. First, 1963 (Friedan, of course) to about 1974 – the period of what I call the 'demon texts', for which we have been apologizing ever since. Second, 1975 to 1979, the period in which feminism tried to take on the issue of motherhood seriously, to criticize the institution, explore the actual experience, theorize the social and psychological implications. In this period, feminists began on the project of breaking the first of the two taboos I mentioned earlier – the taboo on mothers' own descriptions of the fascination and joy of mothering (even in a patriarchy) and also the pain, isolation, boredom, murderousness.

By 1979, in a massive shift in the politics of the whole country, some feminist work shifts, too, from discussing motherhood to discussing families. Feminism continues to anatomize motherhood, but the movement is on the defensive. Certain, once desired-changes recede as imaginable possibilities. In this period, feminists speak of 'different voices' and 'single mothers by choice'; the feminist hope of breaking the iron bond between mother and child seems gone, except in rhetorical flourishes, perhaps gone for good in this wave.

I'm going to try – briefly – to substantiate this periodization, but first a reminder: precision about generations is particularly important in a discussion of motherhood. In Paula Gidding's fine phrase, 'when and where I enter' matters. Each one has her own point of entry on this line. Nonetheless, the line has its own power to impose similar conditions, pressures, meanings on women of different ages, races, classes. The particular piece of feminist intellectual history I'm exploring here follows quite closely the trajectory of the baby boom generation, what demographers call the mouse in the python, a large bulge travelling down the decades.

As Atina Grossmann has pointed out, this bulging generation is very powerful and continues to set its own rules. Its late childbearing has made an upward blip on the generally descending graph of births per thousand. Its experiences disproportionately influence the social atmosphere. When it has babies, the stores are flooded with baby food. The culture this group creates, including the culture of feminism, shapes the era I'm describing here. For the young, the next bit of the line remains a mystery. Current debates about the real meaning of black teenage pregnancy and the low rate of marriage and fertility among college students give hints of how women may now be experimenting with the placement of children in their life cycles. It's a cheerful thought that many younger women will have experiences that don't correspond to this outline.

The Period from 1963 to 1975

It was in 1963 that *The Feminine Mystique* first appeared. The inadequacies of that book are well-known. For example, in *From Margin to Center*, bell hooks flips Friedan's story of the homebound misery of the suburban housewife: for black women of the same period, paid work (which Friedan recommends for middle-class women) was usually drudgery, alienated work; work in the home seemed far more satisfying. Many have criticized Friedan's classism, racism, homophobia, her false universals. But Friedan herself has ignored all this and criticized *The Feminine Mystique* herself on different grounds altogether. In *The Second Stage* of 1981, Friedan blames her earlier book of being anti-family, for trying to pry women away from children, and for overemphasizing women as autonomous individuals. In fact, *The Feminine Mystique* is rather mild on these points; it says nothing most feminists wouldn't agree to today about the need for women to have some stake in the world beyond their homes.

The Feminine Mystique is the first of my demon texts, by which I mean books demonized, apologized for, endlessly quoted out of context, to prove that the feminism of the early 1970s was, in Friedan's words of recantation, 'strangely blind'.[3] She excoriates her earlier self for thinking too much about 'women alone, or women against men', but not enough about 'the family'. In retrospect, it is an amazing thing that books in the early 1970s dared to speak of 'women alone, or women against men'. It was, plain and simple, a breakthrough. Yet we've been apologizing for these books and often misreading them as demon texts ever since.

The most famous demon text is Shulamith Firestone's *The Dialectic of Sex: The Case for Feminist Revolution* of 1970. This book is usually the starting point for discussions of how feminism has been 'strangely blind' about motherhood. Certainly there are few of its sentences that Firestone would leave unmodified if she were writing with the same intent today. Her undertheorized enthusiasm for cybernetics, her self-hating disgust at the pregnant body ('Pregnancy is barbaric'), her picture of the female body as a prison from which a benign, non-patriarchal science might release us have all dated. Her call for an end to childhood – though more interesting, I think, than scoffers have been prepared to grant – doesn't resonate with any experience of children at all. Finally, though, it is her tone we can't identify with, the 1960s-style atmosphere of free-wheeling, shameless speculation. Part of the demonizing of this text arises out of a misreading of genre. *The Dialectic of Sex* is an example of utopian writing. (Some of this atmosphere has now been reclaimed – at least for academic feminism – in such work as Donna Haraway's *Manifest for Cyborgs*.)

Besides this tendency by feminists as well as non-feminists to misread the tone and genre of *The Dialectic of Sex*, everyone colludes in calling it a mother-hating book. Search the pages; you won't find the evidence. I find instead:

> At the present time, for a woman to come out openly against motherhood on principle is physically dangerous. She can get away with it only if she adds that she is neurotic, abnormal, childhating and therefore 'unfit' ... This is hardly a free atmosphere of inquiry. Until the taboo is lifted, until the decision not to have children or not to have them 'naturally' is at least as legitimate as traditional childbearing, women are as good as forced into their female roles.[4]

In other words, Firestone's work is reactive and rhetorical. The point is always 'smash patriarchy', not mothers.

Of course there are real demon texts inside feminism, callow works like a few of the essays in the collection *Pronatalism: The Myth of Mom and Apple Pie* of 1974, which reject childbearing in favour of having unsoiled white rugs and the extra cash to buy them. There's also some panic during this period about what was then a new term, the 'population explosion'. An ecology influenced by feminism has reinterpreted this material for us since, but some of the early essays talk as if once again it is up to women to populate the world properly, this time by abstaining from a killing *over*production of children.

But, inside feminism, such moments are rare. Instead I found extreme rhetoric meant to break the inexorable tie between mothers and children. For example, Lucia Valenska, in *Quest* (1975): 'All women who are able to plot their destinies with the relative mobility of the childfree should be encouraged to take on at least one existing child ... to have our own biological children today is personally and politically irresponsible.'[5] In the demonizing mode it is easy to hear this as a party line with biological mothers as self-indulgent backsliders. I hear in it, too, an effort to imagine a responsibility to kids which is not biological. The early texts are trying to pull away from the known, and like all utopian thinking, they can sound thin, absurd, undigested. But mother-hating? No.

The real demon texts I've found in my first period are works of social science outside feminism like the Moynihan report of 1965 on the so-called 'tangled pathology' of the black family. Mother really *is* named as the problem there, and the cure? More power for fathers! Black feminists often have to wrestle with this text when they set out to write about the motherhood experience. Ambivalence about the culture of black mothering is hard to express in the same universe where one has also to find ways to contradict the Moynihan report.

Finally in my search for early feminist mother-hating what I found was – mostly – an absence. In the major anthologies like *Sisterhood is Powerful*, *Women in a Sexist Society*, and *Liberation Now!* there are hardly any articles on any aspect of mothering. Nothing strange, really, about this blindness. The mouse had only just started down the python; most of the writers were young.

The exceptions, such as several articles in Leslie Tanner's *Voices from Women's Liberation* of 1970, offer a programme that is unexceptionable even today – for example, Vicky Pollard's 'Producing Society's Babies' or the much reprinted 'On Day Care' by Louise Gross and Phyllis MacEwan. This second piece argues mildly that women shouldn't just want day care because it will liberate *them*, but also because day care is good for kids, too.

The revisions between the *Our Bodies/Ourselves*, which was a newsprint booklet in 1971, and the glossy tome *Ourselves and Our Children* of 1978 reveals, I think, the hidden dynamics of our alienation from that earlier time. Under the section 'Pregnancy' the early newsprint says such things as: 'We, as women, grow up in a society that subtly leads us to believe that we will find our ultimate fulfillment by living out our reproductive function and at the same time discourages us from trying to express ourselves in the world of work.' Only after pages and pages of reassurance, that 'we as women can be whole human beings without having children' does the 1971 text finally ask, 'What are the positive reasons for having children?' [6] The feminism of 1970 established a harsh self-questioning about a motherhood which formerly had been taken for granted.

But soon, very soon, this peremptory and radical questioning was misread as an attack on housewives. This has been as effective an instance of divide and conquer as I know. By the late 1970s, both the mothers and the non-mothers were on the defensive. What a triumph of backlash, one with internal dynamics which have been fully explored by

Faye Ginsburg (1989) and others – feminists seeking to understand the special bitterness among women in our era.

The rewriting of the material on whether or not to have a child, in the *Ourselves and Our Children* of 1978, carries me into my second period, 1976 to 1980.

The Period from 1976 to 1980

The 1978 text couldn't be more different from the newsprint of *Our Bodies/Ourselves*. It acknowledges that 'until quite recently' having a baby was not really considered a decision, but then goes on to assume that all that has changed, ending with this sentence: 'Now almost 5% of the population has declared its intentions to remain child-free.' [7]

This is a liberal text, celebrating variety without much concern for uneven consequences. People who have decided to have children and people who have decided against are quoted at some length; but the effect is false symmetry, with no dialectic tension. The proliferation of people's reasons here is useful and instructive, an effort to get at difference, but the structural result is an aimless pluralism, a series of lifestyle questions, no politics.

But if in my description of *Ourselves and Our Children* I am using the word liberal pejoratively, this, my second period, is also liberal in the best sense of the word: a time of freer speech, wider enquiry, a refusal of orthodoxy, an embrace of the practical reality. In these years the feminist work of exploring motherhood took off, and books central to feminist thinking in this wave were written, both about the daily experience of being a mother and about motherhood's most far-reaching implications.

In 1976 several key texts were published: Adrienne Rich's *Of Woman Born*, Dorothy Dinnerstein's *The Mermaid and the Minotaur*, Jane Lazarre's *The Mother Knot* and Linda Gordon's *Woman's Body, Woman's Right*. Also in that year French feminism began to influence American feminist academic thinking. *Signs* published Hélène Cixous's *The Laugh of the Medusa* which included these immediately controversial words: 'There is always within [woman] at least a little of that good mother's milk. She writes in white ink.' [8] Mysteries and provocations – which introduced a flood!

Then in 1977: *My Mother/Myself* appeared. Nancy Friday's book popularized the motherhood discussions in feminism, though it has often been criticized as essentially a daughter's book. Julia Kristeva split the page of *Tel Quel* down the middle in that year in 'Love's Heretical Ethics'; she was digging for the semiotic, the mother language of the body before speech. And 1978: Nancy Chodorow's *The Reproduction of*

Mothering and Michelle Wallace's *Black Macho and the Myth of the Super-Woman*. These books were events. The intellectual work of feminism has its renaissance in these years. Not only does this period give rise to important work but also to fruitful debate.

Rachel DuPlessis introduced the brilliant special issue of *Feminist Studies* on motherhood in 1978 with an encomium to Rich's *Of Woman Born*. She honoured what Rich was trying to do – to pry mothering away from the patriarchal institution, *motherhood*. But then, DuPlessis went on to worry that Rich might be over-reacting, over-privileging the body. DuPlessis wrote, 'If, by the process of touching physicality, Rich wants to find that essence beyond conflict, the place where all women necessarily meet, the essence of woman, pure blood, I cannot follow there.' Discussions like these inaugurate our continuing debates about essentialism, the body, and social construction.

DuPlessis says she will not discuss practical politics, but she does ask the larger political question that nags throughout the period but is rarely addressed: which construction of motherhood is productive for feminist work? If we take Dinnerstein at her word, we're trying to get men to be mothers. If we follow Rich, our energies move towards building a female culture capable of the support not only of women but also of their children. Neither author would put these implications so baldly, without shading. Yet these texts create rival political auras and feminist theory is still far from sorting out the implications for activism of this great period of groundbreaking work.

It is important to add, though, that right in the middle of this period, in 1977, the first Hyde amendment was passed; we in the US lost medicaid abortion. Abortion – the primal scene of this wave – won to our amazement in 1973, was only affordable for all classes for four years before this barely established right began slipping away again. While feminist thinkers were elaborating on the themes of motherhood, that other question – whether or not mothering is to remain a female universal – was slipping away. Feminist work of this period largely ignores the subject of my second taboo, the viability of the choice not to mother. Meanwhile the New Right was mounting a massive offensive against all efforts to separate women and mothering.

My second period ends – and my third begins – with the important threshold article by Sara Ruddick in 1980, 'Maternal Thinking'. This piece pushed the work of the late 1970s to some logical conclusions. Ruddick took seriously the question of what women actually *do* when they mother. She developed a rich description of what she called 'maternal practice' and 'maternal thinking'. A whole separate study deserves to be made of how this much reprinted article has been read, re-read, misread, and appropriated into a variety of arguments. Ruddick herself says that the implications for feminism of her splendid anatomy of mothering are unclear. Is motherhood really a separable practice? Are its special features capable of translation into women's public power? Does motherhood have the universality Ruddick's work implies? Does the different voices argument (also developed by Carol Gilligan in 1982) lead to a vigorous feminist politics?

This is not even the beginning of a proper discussion of Ruddick, but for my purposes here, it is important to point out that Ruddick herself says that her book is not really about what feminism should say or do about mothering. Rather, it provides one of the best descriptions feminism has of *why* women are so deeply committed to the mothering experience, even under very oppressive conditions. Ruddick's work is a song to motherhood – multiphonic, without sugar – but still a song. 'Maternal Thinking' is the fullest response since Adrienne Rich to the call to end my first taboo, the taboo on speaking the life of the mother.

It leaves my other taboo untouched, but this might well have seemed benign neglect in any other year but 1980. It was not part of Ruddick's intention to publish her work in the same year Reagan was elected, yet the meeting of the twain is, I think, part of this small history of feminism on motherhood.

Ruddick argues – with much reason – that hers is a specifically anti-Reagan text. It includes men as mothers; it includes lesbians as mothers; it demands public support for women's work. But it is extremely difficult to do an end run around Reaganism by a mere proliferation of family forms. The left tried it; feminism tried it; everyone failed. (I'm thinking of Michael Lerner's Friends of Families organizing between about 1979 and 1982. I'm thinking of NOW's National Assembly on the Future of the Family in November of 1979. I'm thinking of Betty Friedan's retreat in *The Second Stage* of 1981.) As Barbara Ehrenreich and others pointed out, the word 'family' was a grave in which the more autonomous word 'women' got buried. The problem with defining any cohabiting group as family and leaving it at that was the disappearance of any discussion of power within that group. Arlie Hochchild's *The Second Shift* reaffirms what we already intimate from experience: women, not families, continue to do almost all domestic work.

My time-line for the 1980s is a record of frustration, retrenchment, defeat and sorrow. Out of the Baby M case in 1986-7 comes Phyllis Chesler's *Sacred Bond*, the very title unthinkable a decade earlier. Certainly things were not going our way, and the studies to prove it poured out. In 1986 and 1987 we get Chesler on the injustice of child custody laws, including feminist initiated reforms, and Lenore Weitzman's frightening figures about what happens to women after no-fault divorce.

My peak year for backlash that was at least partially internalized by feminism was 1986, the date of publication of Sue Miller's novel *The Good Mother* and Sylvia Ann Hewlett's *Lesser Lives*. *Lesser Lives* concerns itself with the horrendous struggle of working mothers, that is of most mothers now. Hewlett, once a self-defined feminist, is now against the ERA and sees nothing but liberal blarney in legal equality models. In this particularly mean season, in which mothers do everything without social supports, Hewlett wants protection. She simply cannot imagine social support of childrearing except as special programmes for women, whom she assumes will be the main ones responsible for children for evermore. Hewlett blames feminism for not making demands on the state. Of course we *did* make them. Our failure to win is a complex, historical event Hewlett oversimplifies. Further, one might argue that Hewlett's assumption, that women will inevitably do most of the childrearing, is broadly shared by the men in power, too, and that this attitude itself is one reason it is hard to coerce the state to do the work.

These are exceptions to backlash thinking on the 1980s time-line, of course, though several turned out to be books and articles published elsewhere (I find my line doesn't work outside the US). Kathleen Gerson's *Hard Choices: How Women Decide About Work, Careers and Motherhood* (1985) tried to get at how profoundly women's lives are being changed by work. Sacred bond or not, women are simply spending less of their lives on mothering, more and more on a variety of other things. This book was among the very few I found that tried to address my second taboo, to take seriously the idea that women may well come to see mothering as one element in life, not its defining core. However raggedly, the women Gerson interviewed are already living out basically new story lines, making piecemeal changes over which feminism must struggle to preside.

Also during this period have come the great books on abortion: Rosalind Petchesky's *Abortion and Women's Choice*, Kristen Luker's *Abortion and the Politics of Motherhood* in 1984 and Faye Ginsburg's *Contested Lives* in 1989. Reading these, one would never guess that – on the political front – it has been some time since feminists demanding abortion have put front and centre the idea that one good use to which one might put this right is to choose not to have kids *at all*. Chastised in the Reagan years, pro-choice strategists – understandably – have emphasized the right to wait, the right to space one's children, the right to have each child wanted. They feared invoking any image that could be read as a female withdrawal from the role of nurturer.

Broad societal events like the steady rise in divorce and women's increasing workplace participation collide with women's failure to get day care, child support, fair enough custody laws, changes in the structure of a work day and a typical work life, and finally any reliable, ongoing support from men. Our discouragement is, in my view, the subtext of most of what we have written about motherhood in the past decade. I think women are heartbroken. Never has the baby been so delicious. We are – in this period of reaction – elaborating, extending, reinstitutionalizing this relation for ourselves. Mary Gordon writes in the *New York Times* book review (1985): 'It is impossible for me to believe that anything I write could have a fraction of the importance of the child growing inside me.' A feminist theorist tells me she is more proud of her new baby than of all her books.

I don't mean to criticize these deep sentiments but to situate them. They are freely expressed now; in 1970, feminist mothers, like all mothers, were briefly on the defensive, and ecstatic descriptions of mothering were themselves taboo. But now, since 1980, that brief past, with whatever its excesses or limitations, feels long gone. Even the still acceptable project of elaborating the culture of motherhood tends now to leave out the down part of the mother's story – her oppression, fury, regrets. One can't speak blithely of wanting an abortion any more nor sceptically about the importance of motherhood. In the 1980s we apologized again and again for ever having uttered what we now often name a callow, classist, immature or narcissistic word against mothering. Instead, we praised the heroism of women raising children alone, or poor, usually both. We embraced nurturance as an ethic, sometimes wishing that men would share this ethic without much hoping they will, and we soldiered on, caring for the kids (in the US more first children were born in 1988 than in any year on record), and continue to do 84 per cent of the housework. Complaints now have a way of sounding monstrous, even perhaps to our own ears. For here the children are, and if we are angry, in backlash times like these it is easy for feminism's opponents to insist that anger at oppression is really anger at children or at mothers. The New Right has been brilliant at encouraging this slippage, making women feel that being angry at the present state of mothering will poison the well of life. Guilt complicates feminist rage – and slows down feminist activism. There is the mother's guilt towards her children, and the non-mother's guilt that she has evaded this mass sisterhood now elaborated for us all as full of joy and pain, blood and passion, that she has evaded the central life dramas of intimacy and separation described so well in feminist writing about motherhood.

So, in conclusion, what? I hope it is clear that it is no part of my argument to say women should not want children. This would be to trivialize the complexity of wishes, to call mothering a sort of false consciousness – a belittling suggestion. Women have incorporated a great deal into their mothering, but one question for feminism should surely be: 'Do we want this presently capacious identity, mother, to expand or to contract?' How special do we want mothering to be? In other words, what does feminism gain by the privileging of motherhood? My reading makes more obvious than ever that feminists completely disagree on this point – or rather that there are many feminisms, different particularly on this point. And here is another viper's nest: Do feminists want men to become mothers, too, that is, to have primary childcare responsibilities?

Again, the feminist work on this point veers wildly, is murky. Women disagree about what we should want – also about what we can get – from men, and bell hooks thinks we are afraid to let men know how mad we really are, afraid finally to confront them. That may be one reason we falter; but there are others: women ask, for example, 'Can men really nurture?' And behind that doubt, or that insult, hides our knowledge of what psychological power mothers have. Why give that up, we may well ask. I suspect that in addition, in our period, women are eager to establish that we do not really need men. This wave of feminism was a great outburst of indignation, and it is important for us to feel that men are no longer necessary, particularly since lots of men are gone before the baby is two. Insofar as patriarchy means the protective law of the father, patriarchy is over.

I find a great cynicism among us about ever getting men's help, or the state's. Because we have won so few tangible victories, women tend to adopt a sort of Mother Courage stance now – long suffering, almost sometimes a parody of being tireless.

But it occurs to me that, finally, this picture I am painting is much too bleak. One can ask other questions that hint at a more volatile situation altogether. The low spirits of recent movement history are an irony. Actually, we are living in a moment in which women's identities are extremely labile and expanding. How do we feminists greet and interpret the fact that women are voting with their feet, marrying later, using contraception and abortion and having fewer children? Do we look forward to some golden age when parental leave, childcare and flexi-time will have helped women so much that the birthrate will rise again? Such a thought seems buried in the current feminist piety about abortion, that we want not only the right to abort but also the right to have children, etc. A worthy thought, but one that has not yet been fully examined. Are we to consider the lowered birthrate as merely one more proof that women are so overworked they are ready to drop, or might there be some opportunities for feminism buried in these broad, demographic changes?

Under what banner are we going to fly our demands for mothers? I like best the gender-neutral constructions of this cohort of the brilliant feminist lawyers. Yet as they would be first to point out, gender-neutral demands – for parenting leaves, disability, gender-blind custody, have their short-term price. We give up something, a special privilege wound up in the culture-laden word 'mother' which we will not instantly regain in the form of freedom and power. We are talking about a slow process of change when we talk about motherhood; we are talking about social divisions which are still fundamental. Giving up the exclusivity of motherhood is bound to feel to many like loss. Deirdre English called this 'the fear that feminism will free men first'. Men will have the power of the world and the nurturant experience, the centrality to their children. Only a fool gives up something present for something intangible and speculative, Jack exchanging the cow for a couple of beans. But even if we can't yet imagine our passage from here to there, from control over motherhood to shared, socialized parenthood, couldn't we talk about it, structure demands? An epigram keeps forming in my mind: 'Just because you can't have something doesn't mean you don't want it or shouldn't fight for it.'

Let me end with a cautionary analogy: in the nineteenth century, feminism's *idée fixe* was the vote. We won it, but it was hard to make it mean something larger than mere voting, to make it into a source of public authority for women. In our wave, the *idée fixe* has been abortion. If we are lucky, and if we work very hard, we may win it. But just like the vote, there will be much resistance to letting the right to abortion expand to its larger potential meaning. We seem – this time around – really to want abortion. And this right carries within it the seed of new identities for women.

Notes

1. Sandra Pollack and Jeanne Vaughan (eds), *Politics of the Heart: A Lesbian Parenting Anthology* (Ithaca: Firebrand Books, 1987).

2. Stephanie Dowrick and Sibyl Grundberg, *Why Children?* (New York: Harcourt Brace Jovanovich, 1981).

3. Betty Friedan, *The Feminine Mystique* (New York: W.W. Norton, 1963), p. 83.

4. Shulamith Firestone, *The Dialectic of Sex: The Case for Feminist Revolution* (New York: William Morrow, 1970), pp. 199, 200.

5. Lucia Valenska, 'If All Else Fails, I'm Still a Mother', *Quest*, Vol. 1, No. 4, 1975, pp. 82–3.
6. Boston Women's Health Collective, *Our Bodies/Ourselves* (Boston: New England Free Press, 1971), pp. 73, 74, 76.
7. Boston Women's Health Book Collective, *Ourselves and Our Children: A Book by and for Parents* (New York: Random House, 1978), p. 17.
8. Hélène Cixous, 'The Laugh of the Medusa', in *Signs*, Vol. 1, No. 4, summer 1976, p. 251.

10. Black Women: Constructing the Revolutionary Subject

bell hooks

Sitting in a circle with black women and one black man, children running in and out, on a hot Saturday evening at the office of the Council on Battered Women, after working all day, my spirits are renewed sharing with this group aspects of my development as feminist thinker and writer. I listen intently as a sister comrade talks about her responses to my work. Initially she was disturbed by it. 'I didn't want to hear it', she says. 'I resented it.' The talk in the group is about black women and violence, not just the violence inflicted by black men, but the violence black women do to children, and the violence we do to one another. Particularly challenged by the essay in *Talking Back*, 'Violence in Intimate Relationships: A Feminist Perspective', because of its focus on a continuum of dominating violence that begins not with male violence against women but with the violence parents do to children, individual black women in the group felt they had to interrogate their parental practice. There is little feminist work focusing on violence against children from a black perspective. Sharing our stories, we talked about how styles of parenting in diverse black communities support and perpetuate the use of violence as a means of domestic social control. We connected common acceptance of violence against children with community acceptance of male violence against women. Indeed, I suggested many of us were raised in families where we completely accepted the notion that violence was an appropriate response to crisis. In such settings it was not rare for black women to be verbally abusive and physically violent with one another. Our most vivid memories (in the group) of black women fighting one another took place in public settings where folks struggled over men or over gossip. There was no one in the group who had not witnessed an incident of black women doing violence to one another.

I shared with the group the declaration from Nikki Giovanni's 'Woman Poem': 'I ain't shit. You must be lower than that to care.'

This quote speaks directly to the rage and hostility oppressed/ exploited people can turn inward on themselves and outwards towards those who care about them. This has often been the case in black female encounters with one another. A vast majority of black women in this society receive sustained care only from other black women. That care does not always mediate or alter rage, or the desire to inflict pain; it may provoke it. Hostile responses to care echo the truth of Giovanni's words. When I first puzzled over them, I could hear voices in the background questioning, saying: 'How can you be worth anything, if you care about me, who am worth nothing.' Among black women, such deeply internalized pain and self-rejection informs the aggression inflicted on the mirror image – other black women. It is this reality Audre Lorde courageously describes in her essay 'Eye to Eye: Black Women, Hatred, and Anger'. Critically interrogating, Lorde asks:

> Why does that anger unleash itself most tellingly against another Black woman at the least excuse? Why do I judge her in a more critical light than any other, becoming enraged when she does not measure up? And if behind the object of my attack should lie the face of my own self, unaccepted, then what could possibly quench a fire fueled by such reciprocating passions?

I was reminded of Lorde's essay seated among black women listening to them talk about the intensity of their initial 'anger' at my work. Retrospectively, that anger was vividly evoked so that I would know that individual black women present had grappled with it, moved beyond it, and come to a place of political awareness that allowed them openly to acknowledge it as part of their process of coming to consciousness and go on critically to affirm one another. They wanted me to understand the process of transformation, the movement of their passions from rage, to care and recognition. It is this empowering process that enables us to meet face to face, to greet one another with solidarity, sisterhood and love. In this space we talk about our different experiences of black womanhood, informed by class, geographical location, religious backgrounds, etc. We do not assume that all black women are violent or have internalized rage and hostility.

Lorde writes in 'Eye to Eye':

> We do not love ourselves, therefore we cannot love each other. Because we see in each other's face our own face, the face we never stopped wanting. Because we survived and survival breeds desire for more self. A face we never stopped wanting at the same time as we try to obliterate it. Why don't we meet each other's eyes? Do we expect betrayal in each other's gaze, or recognition?

Lorde's essay chronicles an understanding of ways 'wounded' black women, who are not in recovery, interact with one another, helping us to see the way in which sexism and racism as systems of domination can shape and determine how we regard one another. Deeply moved by her portrait of the way internalized racism and sexism informs the formation of black female social identity, the way it can and often does affect us, I was simultaneously disturbed by the presumption expressed by her continual use of a collective 'we' that she was speaking to an experience all black women share. The experience her essay suggests black women share is one of passively receiving and absorbing messages of self-hate then directing rage and hostility most intensely at one another. While I wholeheartedly agree with Lorde that many black women feel and act as she describes, I am interested in the reality of those black women, however few, who even if they have been the targets of black female rage do not direct hostility or rage towards other black women.

Throughout 'Eye to Eye' Lorde constructs a monolithic paradigm of black female experience that does not engage our differences. Even as her essay urges black women openly to examine the harshness and cruelty that may be present in black female interaction so that we can regard one another differently, an expression of that regard would be recognition, without hatred or envy, that not all black women share the experience she describes. To some extent Lorde's essay acts to shut down, close off, erase and deny those black female experiences that do not fit the norm she constructs from the location of her experience. Never in Lorde's essay does she address the issue of whether or not black women from different cultural backgrounds (Caribbean, Hispanic, etc.) construct diverse identities. Do we all feel the same about black womanhood? What about regional differences? What about those black women who have had the good fortune to be raised in a politicized context where their identities were constructed by resistance and not passive acceptance. By evoking this negative experience of black womanhood as 'commonly' shared, Lorde presents it in a way that suggests it represents 'authentic' black female reality. Not to share the critique she posits is to be made yet again 'outsider'. In Donna Haraway's essay 'A Manifesto for Cyborgs' she warns feminist thinkers against assuming positions that 'appear to be the telos of the whole', so that we do not 'produce epistemologies to police deviation from official women's experience'. Though Haraway is speaking about mainstream feminist practice, her warning is applicable to marginalized groups who are in the process of making and remaking critical texts that name our politics and experience.

Years ago I attended a small gathering of black women who were meeting to plan a national conference on black feminism. As we sat in a circle talking about our experiences those individuals who were most listened to all told stories of how brutally they had been treated by 'the' black community. Speaking against the construction of a monolithic experience, I talked about the way my experience of black community differed, sharing that I had been raised in a segregated rural black community that was very supportive. Our segregated church and schools were places where we were affirmed. I was continually told that I was 'special' in those settings, that I would be 'somebody' someday and do important work to 'uplift' the race. I felt loved and cared about in the segregated black community of my growing up. It gave me the grounding in a positive experience of 'blackness' that sustained me when I left that community to enter racially integrated settings, where racism informed most social interactions. Before I could finish speaking, I was interrupted by one of the 'famous' black women present, who chastised me for trying to erase another black woman's pain by bringing up a different experience. Her voice was hostile and angry. She began by saying, 'She was sick of people like me ...' I felt both silenced and misunderstood. It seemed that the cathartic expression of collective pain wiped out any chance that my insistence on the diversity of black experience would be heard.

My story was reduced to a competing narrative, one that was seen as trying to divert attention from the 'true' telling of black female experience. In this gathering black female identity was made synonymous again and again with 'victimization'. The black female voice that was deemed 'authentic' was the voice in pain; only the sound of hurting could be heard. No narrative of resistance was voiced and respected in this setting. I came away wondering why it was these black women could only feel bonded to each other if our narratives echoed, only if we were telling the same story of shared pain and victimization. It was impossible to speak an identity emerging from a different location.

A particular brand of black feminist 'essentialism' had been constructed in that place; it would not allow for difference. Any individual present who was seen as having inappropriate thoughts or lingering traces of politically incorrect ideas was the target for unmediated hostility. Not surprisingly those who had the most to say about victimization were also the ones who judged others harshly, who silenced. Individual black women who were not a part of the inner circle learned that if they did not know the 'right' thing to say, it was best to be silent. To speak against the grain was to risk punishment. One's speech might be interrupted or one might be subjected to humiliating verbal abuse.

At the close of this gathering, many black women gave testimony about how this had been a wonderful experience of sisterhood and black woman bonding. There was no space for those individuals whose spirits had been assaulted and attacked to name their experience. Ironically, they were leaving this gathering with a sense of estrangement, carrying with them remembered pain. Some of them felt that this was the first time in their lives that they had been so cruelly treated by other black women. The oldest black woman present, an academic, an intellectual, who had often been the target for verbal assault, who often wept in her room at night, vowed never again to attend such a gathering. The memory of her pain has lingered in my mind. I have not forgotten this collective black female 'rage' in the face of difference, the anger directed at individual black women who dared to speak as though we were more than our pain, or any collective pain black females had historically experienced.

I was reminded of this earlier gathering, sitting at the offices of the Council on Battered Women. After many years of feminist movement, it seemed to me that black women can now come together in ways that allow for difference. There women could speak openly and honestly about their experience, describe their negative and positive responses to my work without fear of rebuke. They could name their rage, annoyance and frustration and simultaneously critique it. In a similar setting where black women had talked openly about the way my work 'enraged' them, I had asked a sister if she would talk about the roots of her hostility. She responded by telling me that I was 'daring to be different, to have a different response to the shit black women were faced with everyday'. She said,

> It's like you were saying, this is what the real deal is and this is what we can do about it. When most of us have just been going along with the program and telling ourselves that's all we could do. You were saying that it don't have to be that way.

The rage she articulated was in response to the demand that black women acknowledge the impact of sexism on our lives and engage in the feminist movement. That was a demand for transformation. At the offices of the Council on Battered Women, I was among black comrades who were engaged in a process of transformation. Collectively, we were working to problematize our notions of black female subjectivity. None of us assumed a fixed essential identity. It was so evident that we did not all share a common understanding of being black and female, even though some of our experiences were similar. We did share the understanding that it is difficult for black women to construct radical subjectivity within white supremacist capitalist patriarchy, that our struggle to be 'subject', though similar, also differs from that of black men, that the politics of gender create that difference.

Much creative writing (fiction, plays, poetry) by contemporary black women authors highlights gender politics, specifically black male sexism, poverty and black female labour, the struggle for creativity. Celebrating the 'power' of black women's writing in the essay 'Women Warriors: Black Women Writers Load the Cannon' (*Voice Literary Supplement*, May 1990) Michelle Cliff asserts:

> There is continuity in the written work of many African-American women, whether writer is their primary identity or not. You can draw a line from the slave narrative of Linda Brent to Elizabeth Keckley's life to *Their Eyes Were Watching God* to *Coming of Age in Mississippi* to *Sula* to *The Salteaters* to *Praisesong for the Widow*. All of these define a response to power. All structure that response as a quest, a journey to complete, to realize the self; all involve the attempt to break out of expectations imposed on black and female identity. All work against the odds to claim the I.

Passionate declarations like this one, though seductive, lump all black female writing together in a manner that suggests there is indeed a totalizing telos that determines black female subjectivity. Narratively, it constructs a homogeneous black female subject whose subjectivity is most radically defined by those experiences she shares with other black women. In this declaration, as in the entire essay, Cliff glorifies black women writers even though she warns against the kind of glorification (particularly that accorded a writer that is expressed by sustained academic literary critique of their work) that has the potential to repress and contain.

Cliff's piece also contains. Defining black women's collective work as a critical project that problematizes the quest for 'identity', she subsumes that quest solely by focusing on rites of passage wherein black women journey to find themselves. She does not talk about whether that journey is fruitful. By focusing attention primarily on the journey, she offers paradigms for understanding and reading black women writers that invite readers of that work (critics included) to stop there, to romanticize the journey without questioning the location of that journey's end. Sadly, in much of the fiction by contemporary black women writers, the struggle by black female characters for subjectivity, though forged in radical resistance to the status quo (opposition to racist oppression, less frequently to class and gender) usually takes the form of black women breaking free from boundaries imposed by others only to practise their newfound 'freedom' by setting limits and boundaries for themselves. Hence though black women may make themselves 'subject' they do not become radical subjects. Often they simply conform to existing norms, even ones that they once resisted.

Despite all the 'radical' shifts in thought, location, class position, etc. that Celie undergoes in Alice Walker's novel *The Color Purple* – her movement from object to subject, her success as a capitalist entrepreneur – by the novel's end, Celie is reinscribed within the context of family and domestic relations, and the primary change is that those relations are no longer abusive. Celie has not become a 'feminist', a civil rights activist or a political being in any way. Breaking free from the patriarchal prison that is her 'home' when the novel begins, she creates her own household, but radical politics of collective struggle against racism or sexism do not inform her struggle for self-actualization. Earlier writing by black women, Linda Brent's slave narrative for example, records resistance struggles where black women confront and overcome incredible barriers in the quest to be self-defining. Often after those barriers have been passed, the heroines settle down into conventional gender roles. No tale of woman's struggle to be self-defining is as powerful as the Brent narrative. She is ever conscious of the way in which being female makes slavery 'far more grievous'. Her narrative creates powerful groundwork for the construction of radical black female subjectivity. She engages in a process of critical thinking that enables her to rebel against the notion that her body can be sold and insists on placing the sanctity of black ontological being outside modes of exchange. Yet this radical, visionary 'take' on subjectivity does not inform who she becomes once she makes her way to freedom. After breaking the bonds of slavery, Harriet Jacobs takes on the pseudonym Linda Brent when she writes about the past, and falls into the clutches of conventional notions of womanhood. Does the radical invented self 'Linda Brent' have no place in the life of Harriet Jacobs? Once she is free, descriptions of her life indicate no use of the incredible oppositional imagination that has been a major resource enabling her to transgress boundaries, to take risks and dare to survive. Does Jacobs's suppression of the radical self chart the journey that black women will follow both in real life and in their fictions?

More than any other novel by a contemporary black woman writer, Toni Morrison's *Sula* chronicles the attempt by black females to constitute radical black female subjectivity. Sula challenges every restriction imposed upon her, transgressing all boundaries. Defying conventional notions of passive female sexuality, she asserts herself as desiring subject. Rebelling against enforced domesticity, she chooses to roam the world, to remain childless, unmarried. Refusing standard sexist notions of the exchange of female bodies, she engages in the exchange of male bodies, as part of a defiant effort to displace their importance. Asserting the primacy of female friendship, she attempts to break with patriarchal male identification and loses the friendship of her 'conservative' buddy Nel, who has indeed capitulated to convention. Even though readers of *Sula* witness her self-assertion and celebration of her autonomy, which she revels in even as she is dying, we also know that she is not self-actualized enough to stay alive. Her awareness of what it means to be a radical subject does not cross the boundaries of public and private; hers is a privatized self-discovery. Sula's death at an early age does not leave the reader with a sense of her 'power'; instead she seems powerless to assert agency in a world that has no interest in radical black female subjectivity, one that seeks to repress, contain and annihilate it. Sula is annihilated. The reader never knows what force is killing her, eating her from the inside out. Since her journey has been about the struggle to invent herself, the narrative implies that it is the longing for 'selfhood' that leads to destruction. Those black women who survive, who live to tell the tale, so to speak, are the 'good girls', the ones who have been self-sacrificing, hardworking black women. Sula's fate suggests that charting the journey of radical black female subjectivity is too dangerous, too risky. And while Sula is glad to have broken the rules, she is not a triumphant figure. Sula, like so many other black female characters in contemporary fiction has no conscious politics, never links her struggle to be self-defining with the collective plight of black women. Yet this novel was written at the peak of contemporary feminist movement. Given the 'power' of Sula's black female author/creator Toni Morrison, why does she appear on the page as an 'artist without an art form'? Is it too much like 'treason' – like disloyalty to black womanhood – to question this portrait of (dare I say it) 'victimization', to refuse to be seduced by Sula's exploits, ignoring the outcome?

There are black female characters in contemporary fictions who are engaged in political work. Velma, the radical activist in Toni Cade Bambara's *The Salteaters*, has grounded her struggle for meaning within activist work for black liberation. Overwhelmed by responsibility, by the sense of having to bear too much, too great a weight, she attempts suicide. This novel begins with older radical black women problematizing the question of black female subjectivity. Confronting Velma's attempt at self-destruction and self-erasure, they want to know 'are you sure, sweetheart, that you want to be well?' Wellness here is synonymous with radical subjectivity. Indeed, the elders will go on to emphasize that Velma's plight, and that of other black women like her, reflects the loss of 'maps' that will chart the journey for black females. They suggest that it is the younger generation's attempt to assimilate, to follow alien maps, that leads to the loss of perspective. Velma comes back to life (for though she fails to kill herself, she is spiritually dead) only when she testifies to herself that she indeed will choose wellness, will claim herself and nurture that radical subjectivity. Like in Paule Marshall's *Praisesong for the Widow*, in Gloria Naylor's *Mama Day*, the 'radical' black women elders with fresh memories of slavery holocaust, of the anguish of reconstruction, who sustain their courage in resistance, live fruitfully outside conventional gender roles. They either do not conform or they acknowledge the way conformity rarely enables black female self-actualization.

Representing a new generation of 'modern' black women, Velma, even as she is in the process of recovery, critiques her desire to make a self against the grain, and questions 'what good did wild do you, since there was always some low-life gruesome gang-bang raping lawless careless pesty last straw nasty thing ready to pounce – put your shit under total arrest and crack your back ...' 'Wild' is the metaphoric expression of that inner will to rebel, to move against the grain, to be out of one's place. It is the expression of radical black female subjectivity.

Law professor Regina Austin calls for black women to cultivate this 'wildness' as a survival strategy in her piece 'Sapphire Bound'. Significantly, she begins the essay by calling attention to the fact that folks seem to be more eager to read about wild black women in fictions than to make way for us in real life. Reclaiming that wildness, she declares:

> Well, I think the time has come for us to get truly hysterical, to take on the role of 'professional Sapphires' in a forthright way, to declare that we are serious about ourselves, and to capture some of the intellectual power and resources that are necessary to combat the systematic denigration of minority women. It is time for Sapphire to testify on her own behalf, *in writing*, complete with footnotes.

If the writers of black women's fiction are not able to express the wilder, more radical dimensions of themselves in sustained and fruitful ways, it is unlikely that they will create characters who 'act up' and flourish. They may doubt that there is an audience for fictions where black women are not first portrayed as victims. Though fictions portray black women being wild in resistance, confronting barriers that impede self-actualization, rarely is the new 'self' defined. Though Bambara includes passages that lets the reader know Velma lives, there are no clues that indicate how her radical subjectivity will emerge in the context of 'wildness'.

Consistently, contemporary black women writers link the struggle to become subject with a concern with emotional and spiritual well-being. Most often the narcissistically based individual pursuit of self and identity subsumes the possibility of sustained commitment to radical politics. This tension is played out again and again in Alice Walker's *The Third Life of Grange Copeland*. While the heroine, Ruth, is schooled by her grandfather to think critically, to develop radical political consciousness, in the end he fights against whites alone. It is not clear what path Ruth will take in the future. Will she be a militant warrior for the revolution or be kept in her place by 'strong' black male lover/patriarchs who, like her grandfather, will be convinced that they can best determine what conditions are conducive to producing black female well-being? Ironically, *Meridian* takes up where Ruth's story ends, yet the older black woman activist, like Ruth, remains confined, contained by a self-imposed domesticity. Is Meridian in hiding because there is no place where her radical black subjectivity can be expressed without punishment? Is the non-patriarchal home the only safe place?

Contemporary fictions by black women focusing on the construction of self and identity break new ground in that they clearly name the way structures of domination, racism, sexism and class exploitation oppress, making it practically impossible for black women to survive if they do not engage in meaningful resistance on some level. Defiantly naming the condition of oppression and strategies of opposition, such writing enables the individual black woman reader who has not yet done so to question and/or critically affirm the efforts of those readers who are already involved in resistance. Yet these writings often fail to depict any location for the construction of new identities. It is this textual gap that leads critic Sondra O'Neale to ask in her essay 'Inhibiting Midwives, Usurping Creators: The Struggling Emergence of Black Women in American Fiction':

> For instance, where are the Angela Davises, Ida B. Wellses and Daisy Bateses of black feminist literature? Where are the portraits of those women who fostered their own action to liberate themselves, other black women, and black men as well? We see a sketch of such a character in *Meridian*, but she is never developed to a social and political success.

In an earlier essay 'The Politics of Radical Black Subjectivity' I emphasize that opposition, resistance, cannot be made synonymous with self-actualization on an individual or collective level: 'Opposition is not enough. In that vacant space after one has resisted there is still the necessity to become – to make oneself anew.' While contemporary writing by black women has brought into sharp focus the idea that black females must 'invent' selves, the question – what kind of self? – usually remains unanswered. The vision of selfhood that emerges now and then is one that is in complete concordance with conventional Western notions of a 'unitary' self. Again it is worth restating that Donna Haraway challenges feminist thinkers to resist making 'one's own political tendencies to be the telos of the whole' so that we can both accept different accounts of female experience and also face ourselves as complex subjects who embody multiple locations. In 'A Manifesto for Cyborgs' she urges us to remember that 'The issue is dispersion. The task is to survive in diaspora.'

Certainly, collective black female experience has been about the struggle to survive in diaspora. It is the intensity of that struggle, the fear of failure (as we face daily the reality that many black people do not and are not surviving) that has led many black women thinkers, especially within the feminist movement, to assume wrongly that strength in unity can only exist if difference is suppressed and shared experience is highlighted. Though feminist writing by black women is usually critical of the racism that has shaped and defined the parameters of much of the contemporary feminist movement, it usually reiterates in an uncritical manner major tenets of dominant feminist thought. Admonishing black women for wasting time critiquing white female racism, Sheila Radford-Hill in 'Considering Feminism as a Model for Social Change' urges black feminists

> to build an agenda that meets the needs of black women by helping black women to mobilize around issues that they perceive to have a direct impact on the overall quality of their lives. Such is the challenge that defined our struggle and constitutes our legacy ... Thus, black women need to develop their own leadership and their own agenda based on the needs of their primary constituent base: that is, based around black women, their families, and their communities. This task cannot be furthered by dialoguing with white women about their inherent racism.

While I strongly agree with Radford-Hill's insistence that black critical thinkers engaged in the feminist movement develop strategies that directly address the concerns of our diverse black communities, she constructs an either/or proposition that obscures the diversity of our experiences and locations. For those black women who live and work in predominantly white settings (and of course the reality is that most black women work in jobs where their supervisors are white women and men) it is an appropriate and necessary political project for them to work at critical interrogations and interventions that address white racism. Such efforts do not preclude simultaneous work in black communities. Evocations of an 'essentialist' notion of black identity seek to deny the extent to which all black folk must engage with whites as well as to exclude individuals from 'blackness' whose perspectives, values, lifestyles may differ from a totalizing notion of black experience that sees only those folk who live in segregated communities or have little contact with whites as 'authentically' black.

Radford-Hill's essay is most insightful when she addresses 'the crisis of black womanhood' stating that 'the extent to which black feminists can articulate and solve the crisis of black womanhood is the extent to which black women will undergo a feminist transformation'. The crisis Radford-Hill describes is a crisis of identity and subjectivity. When the major struggle black women addressed was opposition to racism and the goal of that struggle was equality in the existing social structure, when most black folks were poor and lived in racially segregated neighbourhoods, gender roles for black women were more clearly defined. We had a place in the 'struggle' as well as a place in the social institutions of our communities. It was easier for black women to chart the journey of selfhood. With few job options in the segregated labour force, most black women knew that they would be engaged in service work or become teachers. Today's black woman has more options even though most of the barriers that would keep her from exercising those options are still in place. Racial integration, economic changes in black class relations, the impact of consumer capitalism, as well as a male-centred contemporary black liberation struggle (which devalued the contributions of black females) and a feminist movement which called into question idealized notions of womanhood, have radically altered black female reality. For many black women, especially the underclass, the dream of racial equality was intimately linked with the fantasy that once the struggle was over, black women would be able to assume conventional sexist gender roles. To some extent there is a crisis in black womanhood because most black women have not responded to these changes by radically reinventing themselves, by developing new maps to chart future journeys. And more crucially, most black women have not responded to this crisis by developing critical consciousness, by becoming engaged in radical movements for social change.

When we examine the lives of individual black women who did indeed respond to contemporary changes, we see just how difficult it is for black women to construct radical subjectivity. Two powerful autobiographies of radical black women were published in the early 1970s. In 1970 Shirley Chisholm published *Unbought and Unbossed*, chronicling the events that led to her becoming the first black congresswoman. And in 1974 *Angela Davis: An Autobiography* was published. Both accounts demonstrate that the construction of radical black female subjectivity is rooted in a willingness to go against the grain. Though many folks may not see Chisholm as 'radical', she was one of the first black female leaders to speak against sexism, stressing in the introduction to her book: 'Of my two "handicaps," being female put many more obstacles in my path than being black.' An outspoken advocate of reproductive rights for women, specifically abortion, Chisholm responded to black males who were not opposed to compulsory pregnancy for black women by arguing:

> Which is more like genocide, I have asked some of my black brothers – this, the way things are, or the conditions I am fighting for in which the full range of family planning service is fully available to women of all classes and colors; starting with effective contracep-

tion and extending to safe, legal termination of undesired pregnancies, at a price they can afford?

Militant in her response to racism, Chisholm stressed the need for education for critical consciousness to help eradicate internalized racism:

> It is necessary for our generation to repudiate Carver and all the lesser-known black leaders who cooperated with the white design to keep their people down. We need none of their kind today. Someday, when, God willing, the struggle is over and its bitterness has faded, those men and women may be rediscovered and given their just due for working as best they could see to do in their time and place, for their brothers and sisters. But at present their influence is pernicious, and where they still control education, in the North or the South they must be replaced with educators who are ready to demand full equality for the oppressed races and fight for it at any cost.

As a radical black female subject who would not allow herself to be the puppet of any group, Chisholm was often harassed, mocked and ridiculed by colleagues. Psychological terrorism was often the weapon used to try to coerce her into silence, to convince her she knew nothing about politics, or worse yet that she was 'crazy'. Often her colleagues described her as mad if she took positions they could not understand or would not have taken. Radical black female subjects are constantly labelled crazy by those who hope to undermine our personal power and our ability to influence others. Fear of being seen as insane may be a major factor keeping black women from expressing their most radical selves. Just recently, when I spoke against the omnipresent racism and sexism at a conference, calling it terroristic, the organizers told folks I was 'crazy'. While this hurt and angered, it would have wounded me more had I not understood the ways this appellation is used by those in power to keep the powerless in their place. Remembering Chisholm's experience, I knew that I was not alone in confronting racist, sexist attacks that are meant to silence. Knowing that Chisholm claimed her right to subjectivity without apology inspires me to maintain courage.

Recently re-reading the autobiography of Angela Davis, I was awed by her courage. I could appreciate the obstacles she confronted and her capacity to endure and persevere in a new way. Reading this work in my teens, her courage seemed like 'no big deal'. At the beginning of the work, Davis eschews any attempt to see her as exceptional. Framing the narrative in this way, it is easy for readers to ignore the specificity of her experience. In fact, very few black females at the time had gone to radical high schools where they learned about socialism or had travelled to Europe and studied at the Sorbonne. Yet Davis insists that her situation is like that of all black people. This gesture of solidarity, though important, at times obscures the reality that Davis's radical understanding of politics was learned, as was her critical consciousness. Had she voiced her solidarity with underclass black people, while simultaneously stressing the importance of learning, of broadening one's perspective, she would have shared with black females tools that enable one to be a radical subject.

Like Chisholm, Davis confronted sexism when she fully committed herself to working for political change:

> I became acquainted very early with the widespread presence of an unfortunate syndrome among some Black male activists – namely to confuse their political activity with an assertion of their maleness. They saw – and some continue to see – Black manhood as something separate from Black womanhood. These men view Black women as a threat to their attainment of manhood – especially those Black women who take initiative and work to become leaders in their own right.

Working in the radical black liberation movement, Davis constantly confronted and challenged sexism even as she critiqued the pervasive racism in the mainstream feminist movement. Reading her autobiography, it is clear that reading and studying played a tremendous role in shaping her radical political consciousness. Yet Davis understood that one needed to go beyond books and work collectively with comrades for social change. She critiqued self-focused work to emphasize the value of working in solidarity:

> Floating from activity to activity was no revolutionary anything. Individual activity – sporadic and disconnected – is not revolutionary work. Serious revolutionary work consists of persistent and methodical efforts through a collective of other revolutionaries to organize the masses for action. Since I had long considered myself a Marxist, the alternatives open to me were very limited.

Despite limited options, Davis's decision to advocate Communism was an uncommon and radical choice.

When the Davis autobiography was written, she was 30 years old; her most militant expression of subjectivity erupted when she was in her twenties. Made into a cultural icon, a gesture that was not in line with her insistence on the importance of collectivity and fellowship, she came to be represented in mass media as an 'exceptional' black woman. Her experience was not seen as a model young black women could learn from. Many parents pointed to the prison sentence she served as reason enough for black women not to follow in her footsteps. Black males who wanted the movement to be male-centred were not trying to encourage other black women to be on the left, to commit themselves fully to a revolutionary black liberation struggle. At public appearances, Angela Davis was not and is not flanked by other black women on the left. Constantly projected as an 'isolated' figure, her presence, her continued commitment to critical thinking and critical pedagogy has not had the galvanizing impact on black females that it could have had. Black women 'worship' Davis from a distance, see her as exceptional. Though young black women 'adore' Davis, they do not often read her work and seek to follow her example. Yet learning about those black women who have dared to assert radical subjectivity is a necessary part of black female self-actualization. Coming to power, to selfhood, to radical subjectivity cannot happen in isolation. Black women need to study the writings both critical and autobiographical of those women who have developed their potential and chosen to be radical subjects.

Critical pedagogy, the sharing of information and knowledge by black women with black women, is crucial for the development of radical black female subjectivity (not because black women can only learn from one another, but because the circumstances of racism, sexism and class exploitation ensure that other groups will not necessarily seek to further our self-determination). This process requires of us a greater honesty about how we live. Black females (especially students) who are searching for answers about the social formation of identity want to know how radical black women think but they also want to know about our habits of being. Willingness to share openly one's personal experience ensures that one will not be made into a deified icon. When black females learn about my life, they also learn about the mistakes I make, the contradictions. They come to know my limitations as well as my strengths. They cannot dehumanize me by placing me on a pedestal. Sharing the contradictions of our lives, we help each other learn how to grapple with contradictions as part of the process of becoming a critical thinker, a radical subject.

The lives of Ella Baker, Fannie Lou Hamer, Septima Clark, Lucy Parson, Ruby Doris Smith Robinson, Angela Davis, Bernice Reagon, Alice Walker, Audre Lorde and countless others bear witness to the difficulty of developing radical black female subjectivity even as they attest to the joy and triumph of living with a decolonized mind and participating in the ongoing resistance struggle. The narratives of black women who have militantly engaged in radical struggles for change offer insights, let us know the conditions that enable the construction of radical black female subjectivity as well as the obstacles that impede its development. In most cases radical black female subjects have been willing to challenge the status quo, to go against the grain. Despite the popularity of Angela Davis as cultural icon, most black women are 'punished' and 'suffer' when they make choices that go against the prevailing societal sense of what a black woman should be and do. Most radical black female subjects have never been caught up in consumer capitalism. Living simply is often the price one pays for choosing to be different. It was no accident that Zora Neale Hurston died poor. Radical black female subjects have had to educate ourselves for critical consciousness, reading, studying, engaging in critical pedagogy, transgressing boundaries to acquire the knowledge we need. Those rare radical black women who have started organizations and groups are attempting to build a collective base that will support and enable their work. Many of these black women create sites of resistance that are far removed from conservatizing institutions in order to sustain their radical commitments. Those of us who remain in institutions that do not support our efforts to be radical subjects are daily assaulted. We persevere because we believe our presence is needed, is important.

Developing a feminist consciousness is a crucial part of the process by which one asserts radical black female subjectivity. Whether she has called herself a feminist or not, there is no radical black woman subject who has not been forced to confront and challenge sexism. However if that individual struggle is not connected to a larger feminist movement, then every black woman finds herself reinventing strategies to cope when we should be leaving a legacy of feminist resistance that can nourish, sustain and guide other black women and men. Those black women who valiantly advocate feminism often bear the brunt of severe critique from other black folks. As radical subject the young Michelle Wallace wrote one of the first book-length, polemical works on feminism that focused on black folks. She did not become a cultural icon; she was to some extent made a pariah. Writing about her experience in 'The Politics of Location: Cinema/Theory?/Literature/Ethnicity/Sexuality/Me', she remembers the pain:

> I still ponder the book I wrote, *Black Macho and the Myth of the Superwoman*, and the disturbance it caused: how black women are not allowed to establish their own intellectual terrain, to make their own mistakes, to invent their own birthplace in writing. I still ponder my book's rightness and wrongness, and how its reception almost destroyed me so that I vowed never to write political and/or theoretical statements about feminism again.

Wallace suffered in isolation, with no group of radical black women rallying to her defence, or creating a context where critique would not lead to trashing.

Without a context of critical affirmation radical black female subjectivity cannot sustain itself. Often black women turn away from the radicalism of their younger days as they age because the isolation, the sense of estrangement from community, becomes too difficult to bear. Critical affirmation is a concept that embraces both the need to affirm one another and to have a space for critique. Significantly, that critique is not rooted in negative desire to compete, to wound, to trash. Though I began this piece with critical statements about Audre Lorde's essay, I affirm the value of her work. The 'Eye to Eye' essay remains one of the most insightful discussions of black female interaction. Throughout the essay Lorde emphasizes the importance of affirmation, encouraging black women to be gentle and affectionate with one another. Tenderness should not simply be a form of care extended to those black women who think as we do. Many of us have been in situations where black females are sweet to the folks in their clique and completely hostile to anyone deemed an outsider.

In 'Eye to Eye' Lorde names the problem. Offering strategies black women might use to promote greater regard and respect, she says that 'black women must love ourselves'. Loving ourselves begins with understanding the forces that have produced whatever hostility towards blackness and femaleness that is felt but it also means learning new ways to think about ourselves. Often the black women who speak the most about love and sisterhood are deeply attached to essentialist notions of black female identity that promote a 'policing' of anyone who does not conform. Ironically, of course the only way black women can construct radical subjectivity is by resisting set norms, challenging politics of domination, race, class, sex. Essentialist perspectives on black womanhood often perpetuate the false assumption that black females simply by living in white supremacist, capitalist patriarchy are radicalized, they do not encourage black women to develop their critical thinking. Individual black women on the left often find their desire to read or write 'theory', to be engaged in critical dialogues with diverse groups (reading the literature, talking, etc.) mocked and ridiculed. Often, I am criticized for studying feminist theory, especially writing by white women. And I am seen as especially 'naive' when I suggest that even though a white woman theorist may be 'racist', she may also have valuable information that I can learn from. Until black women fully recognize that we must collectively examine and study our experience from a feminist standpoint, there will always be lags and gaps in the structure of our epistemologies. Where are our feminist books on mothering, on sexuality, on feminist film criticism, etc.? Where are our autobiographies that do not falsely represent our reality in the interest of promoting monolithic notions of black female experience, or celebrating how wonderfully we have managed to overcome oppression?

Though autobiography or any type of confessional narrative is often devalued in American letters, this genre has always had a privileged place in African-American literary history. As a literature of resistance, confessional narratives by black folks were didactic. More than any other genre of writing, the production of honest confessional narratives by black women who are struggling to be self-actualized and to become radical subjects are needed as guides, as texts that affirm our fellowship with one another (I need not feel isolated if I know that there are other comrades with similar experiences. I learn from their strategies of resistance and from their recording of mistakes.) Even as the number of novels published by black women increases, this writing cannot be either a substitute for theory, or for autobiographical narrative. Radical black women need to tell our stories; we cannot document our experience enough. Works like *Lemon Swamp*, *Balm in Gilead*, *Ready from Within*, and *Every Goodbye Ain't Gone*, though very different, and certainly not all narratives of radical black female subjectivity, enable readers to understand the complexity and diversity of black female experience. There are few contemporary autobiographies by black women on the left. We need to hear more from courageous black women who have gone against the grain to assert non-conformist politics and habits of being, folks like Toni Cade Bambara, Gloria Joseph, Faye Harrison, June Jordan and so many others. These voices can give testimony, sharing that process of transformation black women undergo to emerge as radical subjects.

Black females need to know who our revolutionary comrades are. Speaking about commitment to revolution Angela Davis declares:

> For me revolution was never an interim 'thing-to-do' before settling down: it was no fashionable club with newly minted jargon, or new kind of social life – made thrilling by risk and confrontation, made glamorous by costume. Revolution is a serious thing, the most serious thing about a revolutionary's life. When one commits oneself to the struggle, it must be for a lifetime.

The crisis of black womanhood can only be addressed by the development of resistance struggles that emphasize the importance of decolonizing our minds, developing critical consciousness. Feminist politics can be an integral part of a renewed black liberation struggle. Black women, particularly those of us who have chosen radical subjectivity, can move us towards revolutionary social change that will address the diversity of our experiences and our needs. Collectively bringing our knowledge, resources, skills and wisdom to one another, strategies for how we dare to be 'different', the ways we construct identity in resistance, we make the site where radical black female subjectivity can be nurtured and sustained.

Selected Reading List

Toni Cade Bambara, *The Salteaters* (New York: Random House, 1981).

Shirley Chisholm, *Unbought and Unbossed: An Autobiography* (New York: Avon, 1971).

Michelle Cliff, *The Land of Look Behind: Prose and Poetry* (New York: Firebrand Books, 1985).

——, *No Telephone to Heaven* (New York: Random House, 1988).

Angela Y. Davis, *An Autobiography* (New York: International Publishers, 1974, reprinted 1988).

——, *Women, Race and Class* (New York: Vintage, 1983).

Nikki Giovanni, *Black Feeling, Black Talk, Black Judgement* (New York: Morrow, 1970).

Donna Haraway, *Primate Visions: Gender, Race and Nature in the World of Modern Sciences* (London: Routledge, 1989).

bell hooks, *Ain't I a Woman: Black Women and Feminism* (Boston: South End Press, 1982).

——, *Talking Back: Thinking Feminist, Thinking Black* (Boston: South End Press, 1988).

Zora Neale Hurston, *Dust Tracks on a Road: An Autobiography* (Urbana: University of Illinois Press, reprinted 1984).

——, *Their Eyes Were Watching God* (Urbana: University of Illinois Press, reprinted 1978).

Gerda Lerner (ed.), *Black Women in White America* (New York: Random House, 1973).

Audre Lorde, *A Burst of Light* (New York: Firebrand Books, 1988).

——, *The Black Unicorn* (New York: Norton, 1978).

——, *Sister Outsider: Essays and Speeches* (New York: Feminist Services, 1984).

——, *Zami: A New Spelling of My Name* (New York: Feminist Services, 1983).

Paule Marshall, *Brown Girl, Brownstones* (New York: Feminist Press, 1983).

——, *The Chosen Place, The Timeless People* (New York: Random House, 1984).

Toni Morrison, *Sula* (New York: Knopf, 1973).

——, *Beloved* (New York: Knopf, 1987).

Gloria Naylor, *Mama Day* (New York: Random House, 1989).

Michelle Wallace, *Black Macho and the Myth of the Superman* (New York: Riverrun Press, 1989).

Alice Walker, *In Search of Our Mother's Gardens: Womanist Prose* (London: The Women's Press, 1984).

——, *Meridian* (New York: Simon and Schuster, 1976).

——, *The Color Purple* (London: The Women's Press, 1983).

——, *The Third Life of Grange Copeland* (London: The Women's Press, 1984).

11. Malcolm X and the Crisis in Black America

Manning Marable

A spectre is haunting black America – the seductive illusion that equality between the races has been achieved, and that the activism characteristic of the previous generation's freedom struggles is no longer relevant to contemporary realities. In collective chorus, the media, the leadership of both capitalist political parties, the corporate establishment, conservative social critics and public policy experts, and even marginal elements of the black middle class, tell the majority of African-Americans that the factors which generated the social protest for equality in the 1950s and 1960s no longer exist. The role of race has supposedly 'declined in significance' within the economy and political order. And as we survey the current social climate, this argument seems to gain a degree of credibility. The number of black elected officials exceeds 6600; many black entrepreneurs had achieved substantial gains within the capitalist economic system by the late 1980s; thousands of black managers and administrators appeared to be moving forward within the hierarchies of the private and public sector. And the crowning 'accomplishment', the November 1989 election of Douglas Wilder as Virginia's first black governor, was promoted across the nation as the beginning of the transcendence of 'racial politics'.

The strategy of Jesse Jackson in both 1984 and 1988, which challenged the Democratic Party by mobilizing people of colour and many whites around an advanced, progressive agenda for social justice, is dismissed as anachronistic and even 'reverse racism'. As in the Wilder model, racial advancement is projected as obtainable only if the Negro learns a new political and cultural discourse of the white mainstream. Protest is therefore passé. All the legislative remedies which were required to guarantee racial equality, the spectre dictates, have already been passed.

It is never an easy matter to combat an illusion. There have been sufficient gains for African-Americans, particularly within the electoral system and for sectors of the black petty bourgeoisie in the last decade, that elements of the spectre seem true. But the true test of any social thesis is the amount of reality it explains, or obscures. And from the vantage point of the inner cities and homeless shelters, from the unemployment lines and closed factories, a different reality emerges. We find that racism has not declined in significance, if racism is defined correctly as the systemic exploitation of blacks' labour power and the domination and subordination of our cultural, political, educational and social rights as human beings. Racial inequality continues albeit within the false discourse of equality. Those who benefit materially from institutional racism now use the term 'racist' to denounce black critics who call for the enforcement of affirmative action and equal opportunity legislation.

Behind the rhetoric of equality exist two crises, which present fundamental challenges to African-Americans throughout the decade of the 1990s. There is an 'internal crisis' – that is, a crisis within the African-American family, neighbourhood, community, cultural and social institutions, and within interpersonal relations especially between black males. Part of this crisis was generated, ironically, by what I term the 'paradox of desegregation'. With the end of Jim Crow segregation, the black middle class was able to escape the confines of the ghetto. Black attorneys who previously had only black clients could now move into more lucrative white law firms. Black educators and administrators were hired at predominantly white colleges; black physicians were hired at white hospitals; black architects, engineers and other professionals went into white firms. This usually meant the geographical and cultural schism of elements of the black middle class from the working-class and low-income African-American population, which was still largely confined to the ghetto. As black middle-class professionals retreated to the suburbs, they often withdrew their skills, financial resources and professional contacts from the bulk of the African-American community. There were of course many exceptions, black women and men who understood the cultural obligation they owed to their community. But as a rule, by the late 1980s, such examples became more infrequent, especially among younger blacks who had no personal memories or experiences in the freedom struggles of two decades past.

The internal crisis is directly related to the external, institutional crisis, a one-sided, race/class warfare which is being waged against the African-American community. The external crisis is represented by the conjuncture of a variety of factors, including: the deterioration of skilled and higher paying jobs within the ghetto, and the decline in the economic infrastructure; the decline in the public sector's support for public housing, health care, education and related social services for low-to-moderate income people; the demise of the enforcement of affirmative action, equal opportunity laws and related civil rights legislation; the increased racial conservatism of both major political parties and the ideological and programmatic collapse of traditional liberalism; and most importantly, the conscious decision by the corporate and public sector managerial elite to 'regulate' the black population through increasingly coercive means.

The major characteristic of the internal crisis is the steady acceleration and proliferation of *violence*, in a variety of manifestations. The most disruptive and devastating type of violence is violent crime, which includes homicide, forcible rape, robbery and aggravated assault. According to the *Sourcebook of Criminal Justice Statistics* for 1991, the total number of Americans arrested was nearly 9.5 million. Blacks comprise only 12.5 per cent of the total US population, but represented 2.3 million arrests, or about *one-fourth of all arrests*. Black arrests for homicide and non-negligent manslaughter were 8693, or about 48 per cent of all murders committed in the US. For robbery, which is defined by law as the use of force or violence to obtain personal property, the number of blacks arrested was 74,275, representing 57 per cent of all robbery arrests. For aggravated assault, the number of African-Americans arrested was 94,624, about 29 per cent of all arrests in this category. For motor vehicle theft, the number of blacks arrested and charged was 38,905, about 27 per cent of all auto theft crimes. Overall, for all violent and property crimes charged, blacks totalled almost 700,000 arrests in the year 1979, representing nearly one-third of all such crimes.

One of the most controversial of all violent crimes is the charge of forcible rape. Rape is controversial because of the history of the criminal charge being used against black men by the white racist legal structure. Thousands of black men have been executed, lynched and castrated for imaginary rape offences. Yet rape or forcible sexual violence is not imaginary when African-American women and young girls are victimized. In 1979, there were 29,068 arrests for forcible rape. Black men comprised 13,870 arrests, or 48 per cent of the total. Within cities, where three-fourths of all rapes are committed, blacks total 54 per cent of all persons arrested for rape.

The chief victims of rape are not white women, but black women. The US Department of Justice's 1979 study of the crime of forcible rape established that overall most black women are nearly *twice* as likely to be rape victims than are white women. The research illustrated that in one year, about 67 out of 100,000 white women would be rape victims; but the rate for black and other non-white women was 115 per 100,000. In the age group 20 to 34 years, the dangers for black women increase dramatically. For white women aged 20 to 34, 139 out of 100,000 are rape victims annually. For black women the same age, the rate is 292 per 100,000. For attempted rape, white women are assaulted at a rate of 196 per 100,000; black women are attacked sexually 355 per 100,000 annually.

There is also a direct correlation between rape victimization and income. In general, poor women are generally the objects of sexual assault; middle-class women are rarely raped or assaulted, and wealthy women almost never experience sexual assault. The statistics are clear on this point. White women who live in families earning under US$7,500 annually have a 500 per cent greater likelihood of being raped than white women who come from households with more than US$15,000 income. The gap is even more extreme for African-American women. For black middle-class families, the rate of rape is 22 per 100,000. For welfare and low-income families earning below US$7,500 annually, the rate for rape is 127 per 100,000. For attempted rape, low-income black women are victimized at a rate of 237 per 100,000 annually.

The type of violence which most directly impacts black men is homicide. Nearly half of all murders committed in any given year are black men who murder other black men. But that is only part of the problem. We must recognize, first, that the homicide rate among African-Americans is growing. Back in 1960, the homicide rate for black men in the US was 37 per 100,000. By 1979, the black homicide rate was 65 per 100,000, compared to the white male homicide rate of 10 per 100,000. In other words, a typical black male has a *six to seven times* greater likelihood of being a murder victim than a white male.

The chief victims of homicide in our community are young African-American males. Murder is the fourth leading cause of death for all black men, and the leading cause of death for black males age 20 to 29 years. Today in the US, a typical white female's statistical chances of becoming a murder victim are one in 606. For white men, the odds narrow to one chance in 186. For black women, the odds are one in 124. But for black men, the chances are one in 29. For young black men living in cities who are between age 20 and 29, the odds of becoming a murder victim are *less than one in 20*. Young blackmen in American cities today are the primary targets for destruction – not only from drugs and police brutality, but from each other.

The dynamics of violence within the African-American community which represent this 'internal crisis' are propelled by the institutions of class and racial inequality within the society as a whole. Indeed, there would be no internal crisis among blacks if the political economy and social institutions within American society were designed to foster the conditions for human development and social justice. Massive unemployment in the rotten, industrial cores of the central cities exceeded 20 per cent for African-American adults and over 50 per cent for workers below the age of 24. In the early 1990s nearly one-third of the total African-American population exists below the federal government's official poverty level. Three-fourths of this impoverished population consists of African-American women and their children. Conservatively, three-quarters of a million blacks are homeless, dwelling in the urban streets, alleys and gutters, searching garbage cans for food. The median income level of African-American households compared to white households has declined sharply since 1975, from 63 per cent to 54 per cent. The violence between human beings is essentially a manifestation of the normative cruelty of poverty, eroding incomes, substandard housing and inferior education.

Perhaps the best single example of the institutionalized violence which characterizes the crisis within the African-American community is the criminal justice system. With the election of Ronald Reagan as president in 1980, his conservative Republican administration pursued a policy of appointing reactionaries and racists to the federal district courts and the US circuit courts of appeal. By 1989 Reagan had appointed over 425 federal judges, more than half of the 744 total judgeships. Increasingly, the criminal justice system was employed as a system of social control, for the millions of unemployed and underemployed African-Americans. The essential element of coercion within the justice system, within a racial context, is of course the utilization of the death penalty. According to one statistical study by David C. Baldus based on over 2000 murder cases in Georgia during the 1970s, people accused of killing whites were about eleven times more likely to be given the death penalty than those who murdered blacks. Even factoring for 230 different variables, the death sentence was still 4.3 times more likely to be rendered if a victim was white. Over half of the defendants in white-victim crimes would not have been ordered to be executed if their victims had been African-Americans. Research on the death penalty in Florida during the 1970s illustrates that Florida blacks who are accused and convicted of murdering whites are five times more likely to be given the death penalty than whites who murder other whites.

As of 30 June 1989, the entire prison population of the US reached 673,565 inmates, more than double the figure of 1980. At the current rate, just to keep pace with the increased penal population, authorities have to add 1800 new prison beds *each week*. At the current rate, the African-American prisoner population by the year 2000 will exceed 600,000, or about one in 60 African-American men, women and children. Under the conditions of race/class domination, prisons are the principal means for group social control, in order to regulate the labour position of millions of black workers.

The contemporary crisis within African-American life has also given birth to a rethinking of collective political memory. Since the current crisis has not generated the type of uncompromising, visionary leadership which millions of low-income, unemployed and young people desire, there has been a renaissance of the rhetoric of protest which was characteristic of the Black Power period in the 1960s. Since 1989, moreover, a new generation of African-Americans has 'rediscovered' that period's most dynamic militant leader, Malcolm X. Malcolm's image and words have been popularized in film, music videos, posters, poetry and political literature. Spike Lee's controversial 1989 film, *Do the Right Thing*, depicting race relations in Brooklyn, ended with a Malcolm X quotation. In 1992, Lee released a film biography of Malcolm X. Students on university campuses are now wearing T-shirts with Malcolm's portrait or his uncompromising slogan, 'By Any Means Necessary'. Louis N. Jackson, a black student union leader at Stanford University, speaks for his generation: 'Malcolm's picture is in everybody's room. He embodies people's rage over the struggles African-Americans have had to bear. He was an inspiration to those who didn't turn the other cheek. He gave us the spirit to fight back.'

Many black communities and college campuses hold public forums and cultural events on 19 May to commemorate Malcolm X's birthday. For nearly two decades, a 'Malcolm X Day Celebration' has been held in mid-May in Washington, DC. For six years, Andrea Brown and a group called 'Sisters Remember Malcolm' have organized an observance in Philadelphia. In Harlem, black nationalist Preston Wilcox has created a 'Malcolm X Lovers Network'. In 1989, a Cleveland, Ohio, coalition led by Omar Ali Bey held a major series of events on Malcolm X's birthday. Black nationalist scholar James Turner of Cornell University has initiated a National Malcolm X Holiday Commission. Ron Daniels, the former head of Jesse Jackson's National Rainbow Coalition, explains this renaissance of interest:

> Malcolm X was an excruciating critic of America's system of virulent racism, oppression and Euro-American domination and economic exploitation of Africa and the Third World ... [His] voice is claiming renewed expression in a new generation that finds the continuing reality of racism, poverty, drugs, violence and oppression of African people in America intolerable. Especially among the youth there is an increasing resolve to 'fight the power.' Malcolm's 'fighting spirit' has spread.

Much of the acclaim around the figure of Malcolm X has assumed an uncritical, reverential character, a tendency to transform a dynamic activist into a political icon. This tendency has also occurred with the gradual ossification of Martin Luther King, Jr, his ideological and political development frozen on the steps of the Lincoln Memorial, on that hot August afternoon in 1963, at the March on Washington DC. Half-forgotten and deliberately obscured are the final radical years of King's public life, his commitment to the struggle against the Vietnam War, his embrace of social democratic economic positions, and his mobilization of a poor people's march on Washington in 1968.

Similarly, the prophetic and charismatic figure of Malcolm X has experienced a series of misinterpretations and partial distortions years since his assassination, which have undermined his actual political significance within black history. With the exception of Martin Luther King, Malcolm X certainly ranks as the most influential African-American political figure of the mid-twentieth century. In the general public mind, and in most textbooks, there is a regrettable pattern of juxtaposing King versus Malcolm, which emphasizes the former's philosophy of nonviolence and commitment to racial integration against the Black Muslim's verbal militancy and demands for 'the ballot or the bullet'. King's peaceful methods are praised, while Malcolm is still frequently attacked as a racial demagogue or dangerous nihilist.

But the actual historical record points toward greater ideological affinity between these two central political figures. Both men were profoundly religious activists whose critique of both institutional racism and, subsequently, American capitalism, was rooted in an ethical and moral opposition to all forms of human domination. Both Malcolm and Martin became gradually disillusioned with their earlier ideologies – conservative black nationalism and reformist, petty bourgeois integrationism – and moved decisively to the left in their final two years. Long before King uttered any public criticisms against the Johnson administration's escalation of American military involvement in southeast Asia, for example, Malcolm had denounced the war in anti-imperialist terms. Before King assumed the leadership in the domestic peace movement, calling for a greater internationalist perspective among African-Americans, Malcolm had already charted the way by advocating that African-American formations make direct contacts with African revolutionaries, and seek to obtain official status within the United Nations. Malcolm comprehended that American capitalism and the state could not be opposed effectively without building solidarity and support among other progressive forces throughout the world. This common political insight of both individuals, the realization that the domestic struggle for democratic rights and self-determination by African-Americans was directly linked with the larger international struggle of exploited classes and colonized nations, was ultimately the central factor which made them dangerous to the American government. Both Martin and Malcolm had become powerful and threatening symbols of resistance which could have culminated in more radical and unpredictable movements.

Part of the present difficulty in refocusing the actual political legacy and relevancy of Malcolm X to contemporary struggles is the confusion generated by much of the literature written about him since 1965. There is a massive and eclectic corpus of commentary and historical writing about King; progressive historian Clayborne Carson, author of an excellent study of the Student Nonviolent Coordinating Committee, is in the process of organizing the civil rights leader's personal archives. King was also a frequent contributor to periodicals, and authored several books before his death. By contrast, the great bulk of primary literature on Malcolm X is extremely fragmented. Only a portion of the thousands of speeches and interviews given by Malcolm during his public career have been reproduced and printed. The FBI documents on Malcolm track his extensive surveillance by the Bureau, but much sensitive information is still unavailable. There have been fewer than twelve dissertations to date on or about Malcolm, and most of the 200 articles published on the subject in academic journals are narrowly focused, looking at only partial aspects of Malcolm's political rhetoric or ideas. There is no comprehensive theoretical analysis which combines an extensive review of the entire body of historical evidence on his political evolution.

Some authors who popularize a nationalist-separatist version of Malcolm have mistakenly insisted that his ideology experienced no fundamental shifts or changes, even after the split with the Nation of Islam in March 1964. This interpretation ignores the fact that black nationalism is not a monolithic political ideology, but a spectrum of cultural, economic and political positions which are grounded with the dynamics of black reaction to racial domination in America and throughout the African diaspora. The basis of black nationalism is the national identity and collective experience of African-Americans, a consciousness of subordinated nationality which is at odds with the mainstream culture, ideology, social and political values of the vast majority of white Americans. The roots of this alternative national consciousness were established during slavery, when under difficult conditions blacks were able to construct their own worldview and culture of resistance. In summary, black nationalism as a political and social tradition includes these characteristics: advocacy of black cultural pride and the integrity of the group, which implicitly rejects racial assimilationism or integration; an identification with the image of Africa, which could include an advocacy of emigration to the continent and/or the politics of Pan-Africanism, which recognizes the political unity of blacks throughout the diaspora; the construction of all-black social institutions, such as self-help agencies, schools and religious organizations; support for group economic development, such as black cooperatives, 'Buy Black' campaigns, and efforts to promote capital formation within the African-American community; political independence from the white-dominated political system, and support for the creation of all-black political formations or parties; and support for territorial or geographical separation between the white majority and African-Americans, which would include black control of the political, economic and social institutions which exist in their neighbourhood, city, state or region.

It is crucial to note that there was always an internal ideological tension within the black nationalist tradition. Conservative nationalists have tended to emphasize certain positions, such as strict racial separatism, distrust of dialogue or alliances with white progressive formations, emphasis on African cultural values, and support for private market mechanisms for the development of an entrepreneurial petty bourgeoisie within the black ghetto. More radical black nationalists have been inclined to support a socialist reorganization of economic institutions, have criticized 'Black Capitalist' strategies as ineffective for group advancement, and have embraced a more radical interpretation of Pan-Africanism, which includes a critique of American and European imperialism in the Third World, and a condemnation of capitalism as a system of world domination. Left-wing black nationalism recognizes that institutional racism has evolved in direct conjunction with the maturation and expansion of capitalism into the western hemisphere over four centuries, and that it provides an ideological and cultural justification for the exploitation of the black masses. Racism therefore is a social construct, not rooted inextricably in European genetic or biological reality, and theoretically could be abolished through the destruction of capitalism and the racist social/cultural apparatuses of Euro-American society.

The Nation of Islam represented the ideological positions which historically have been associated with the more conservative tendency of black nationalism. Established during the Great Depression, and led for more than 40 years by patriarch Elijah Muhammad, the Nation of Islam was organized as an extremely rigid, authoritarian structure. Muslim ministers were appointed by the Chicago headquarters, and could be advanced or demoted at will. In this manner, ministers could not easily develop their own local constituencies, which might threaten the authority of the national hierarchy and Muhammad. The Nation promoted a theology which was an uneven amalgam of conservative black nationalism and Sunni Islam, which included a demonology which projected whites literally as 'devils'. The Nation of Islam did not involve itself in the democratic social protest movements of black people in the struggle against Jim Crow, partially to avoid political surveillance or police repression. Within this conservative and patriarchical structure, however, a number of activists were trained who would eventually advocate a more radical interpretation of black nationalism. Malcolm himself was the best example of this ideological evolution.

The second major political tradition in black America, integrationism, also has its historical roots in the pre-Civil War period. Leaders such as Frederick Douglass, Roy Wilkins, Thurgood Marshall, Whitney Young and James Farmer, and civil rights organizations such as the NAACP and National Urban League, have advocated the complete assimilation of black Americans into the cultural, social, economic and political mainstream of white America. For the integrationist, any form of racially identifiable institutions retarded the realization of a colour-blind social order. The integrationist strategy generally did not question the systemic relationship between institutional racism and capitalism, nor was it ever as popular as a cultural ideology among the black working class and poor as it was within the upper levels of the Negro petty bourgeoisie. Consequently, Negro integrationists were usually opposed to all forms of black nationalism as forms of racial chauvinism, whether conservative or radical, Malcolm X was perceived as a nihilistic black 'racist' whose verbal abilities and charisma threatened the goals of the civil rights movement. They attempted to undermine his popularity among the masses of urban, working-class blacks. For example, only days after Malcolm's assassination, Bayard Rustin offered this smug prediction: 'White America, not the Negro people, will determine Malcolm X's role in history.' NAACP journalist Henry Lee Moon was even more determined to obliterate the 'dangerous' legacy of the black nationalist. 'Malcolm was an anachronism', Moon wrote in *Ebony* magazine in April 1965, 'vivid and articulate but, nevertheless, divorced from the mainstream of Negro American thought.'

George Breitman's *Last Year of Malcolm X* goes too far in the opposite direction, attempting to project the entire political trajectory of Malcolm into the political prism of Trotskyism. Malcolm was certainly sympathetic to socialism, and could be termed a *left* black nationalist by February 1965 – a nationalist who also was a Pan-Africanist, internationalist, and supportive of a class analysis to an extent. But there is certainly no evidence that he was on the verge of becoming a Marxist in either the Trotskyist context, or in international Communist terms. Malcolm was moving rapidly toward what might be termed a 'race/class' analysis, a black nationalist who recognized the centrality of class divisions within American society, and who also understood that the concentration of wealth and power in the hands of the capitalist ruling class helped to perpetuate racial exploitation.

Another problem in reconstructing Malcolm's image was created, ironically, by Alex Haley, the editor of the *Autobiography of Malcolm X*, and the author of the historical novel *Roots*. Most Americans, black and white, who have encountered Malcolm have only read the *Autobiography*, a very moving but also misleading work. Haley insisted that Malcolm agree that any tape-recorded statements given and approved would be used in the final text, and that Malcolm was not to be permitted to revise or edit his words in any manner. Malcolm agreed to these terms in the early 1960s. By 1965, as he was reviewing the final drafts, Malcolm 'winced' repeatedly, in Haley's words, at many of the passages which reflected his earlier ideas. Haley himself was a journalist, not a student of black nationalism; politically, he was profoundly integrationist, and inclined toward supporting Republicans. Consequently the *Autobiography* doesn't convey the actual ideological growth and political maturity of the later Malcolm.

Following Malcolm's death and the publication of the *Autobiography*, the Black Power revolt erupted across the country. Community-based activists rejected the reformist politics of the NAACP and embraced the militancy and uncompromising language and style of Malcolm. Yet here again there was ambiguity, as people engaged in this political mimicry. As Julius Lester noted in late 1966, the renaissance of contemporary black nationalism represented 'the angry children of Malcolm X', activists who had rejected integration, black–white alliances, participation in electoral politics, and the belief in the reformation of the system. But nearly every tendency of the nationalist spectrum selected from Malcolm's rich tapestry only those threads which coincided with their immediate interests.

Many black nationalist separatists tried to 'freeze' Malcolm within the framework of a 'race-first' analysis, reducing their mentor's statements during his final year to irrelevancy. The Black Panther Party also attempted to expropriate the image of Malcolm X, but focused on the seemingly insurrectionist elements of Malcolm's discourse. Panther co-founder Huey Newton frequently described his formation as the genuine 'heirs of Malcolm X'. For Panther minister of information Eldridge Cleaver, Malcolm X symbolized an irreconcilable alternative to King and 'the whole passel of so-called Negro leaders and spokesmen who trifle and compromise with the truth in order to curry favor with the white power structure'. But this version exaggerated the actual differences between the late Malcolm and the more progressive phase of King's political life. Indeed, only three weeks before his death, Andrew Young invited Malcolm to come to Selma, Alabama, during a major desegregation campaign. When Malcolm X arrived on 3 February 1965, King had just been arrested. Over 1300 demonstrators had also been imprisoned protesting Jim Crow. Malcolm X confided to Coretta Scott King that he wanted

> Dr King to know that I really didn't come to Selma to make his job more difficult. I really did come thinking that I could make it easier. If the white people realize what the alternative is, perhaps they will be more willing to hear Dr King.

It was at Selma that Malcolm X gave his 'I'm a Field Negro' speech, which was perhaps the most effective presentation of the class contradictions within the African-American community, and the necessity for the masses of blacks to recognize the necessity for radical struggle. Malcolm X observed critically:

> There were two kinds of Negroes. There was that old house Negro and the field Negro. And the house Negro always looked out for his master. When the field Negroes got too much out of line, he held them back in check. He put them back on the plantation ... If the master got hurt, he'd say: 'What's the matter, boss, we sick?' ... [However] field Negroes, who lived in huts, had nothing to lose. They wore the worst kind of clothes. They ate the worst food. And they caught hell. They felt the sting of the lash. They hated this land.

After this historical analysis of the divisions within the black community, Malcolm observed that progressive politics must be based on the tradition of the 'field Negro', rather than the integrationist-oriented black middle class. 'I'm a field Negro', Malcolm X reaffirmed.

> If I can't live in the house as a human being, I'm praying for a wind to come along. If the master won't treat me right and he's sick, I'll call the doctor to go in the other direction. But if all of us are going to live as human beings, then I'm for a society of human beings that can practice brotherhood.

Significantly, Malcolm's definition of liberation had transcended the narrow racial confines of conservative black nationalism to include all of the oppressed.

Only a few commentators two decades ago actually attempted to examine the real record of Malcolm's political evolution from conservative to radical black nationalism. African scholars Ruby and E.U. Essien-Udom correctly noted in the late 1960s that 'alone, or almost single-handedly, Malcolm sought to link the Afro-American liberation movement with the liberation movement of the Third World'. Writing in the *National Guardian* in February 1967, Robert Allen also observed that Malcolm's greatest political contribution was his attempt to internationalize the perspective of the African-American liberation movement. Allen commented: 'Throughout the country a new generation of militant Black youths are turning to Malcolm X's life and work for inspiration and guidance. Their hope is to bring the revolt of the world's oppressed into the stronghold of the oppressor.'

The political vision of Malcolm remains strikingly relevant to our contemporary struggles. As Malcolm insisted in a Harlem address on 15 February 1965, the American Negro's revolt was only part of a 'worldwide revolution' against the 'international Western power structure'. Malcolm opposed the chauvinism and dogmatic separatism characteristic of an element of the black nationalist movement. Blacks should not resort to the sterile tactics and hateful language of their oppressors. 'We don't need a Black Ku Klux Klan', Malcolm advised. 'All we need is black people who believe in the brotherhood of man and who will fight anyone who threatens the brotherhood of man.'

Malcolm also moved away from the blatant sexism of the Nation of Islam in his later development. He recognized from his experiences in Africa that the most progressive nationalist movements had recognized the fundamental equality of women. In December 1964 Malcolm observed:

> It's noticeable that in the [Third World] societies where they put the woman in the closet and discourage her from getting a sufficient education and don't give her the incentive by allowing her maximum participation in whatever area of the society where she's qualified, they kill her incentive.

Such progressive sentiments unfortunately did not usually retard the sexist policies and patriarchal behaviour of many black nationalist males, who simultaneously claimed allegiance with Malcolm in all respects.

Perhaps Malcolm's most lasting legacy is his attractiveness as a loving, warm individual who committed his entire being to the cause of black liberation and social justice. Historian Vincent Harding captures this central characteristic which Malcolm also shared with such dedicated activists from the African diaspora as Walter Rodney and Amilcar Cabral: 'The love [Malcolm X] bore to his people, the overwhelming power of his black consciousness, and the force and integrity of his spirit offered a powerful testimony to the possibilities of human transformation.' Through the real figure of Malcolm X, we can reinforce our own determination to achieve liberation and social justice in the 1990s and beyond.

Bibliography

David L. Lewis, *King: A Critical Biography* (Baltimore, Maryland: Penguin, 1970).

Michele N.K. Collison, '"Fight the Power": Rap Music Pounds Out a New Anthem for Many Black Students', *Chronicle of Higher Education*, Vol. 36, No. 22 (14 February 1990), pp. A1, A29–A30.

Ron Daniels, '1990: The Year of Malcolm X', *Buffalo Challenger* (17 May 1989).

——, 'We Remember Malcolm Day to Launch The Year of Malcolm X', *West Virginia Beacon Digest* (9 February 1990).

George Breitman (ed.), *By Any Means Necessary: Speeches, Interviews and a Letter by Malcolm X* (New York: Pathfinder, 1970).

Bruce Perry (ed.), *Malcolm X: The Last Speeches* (New York: Pathfinder, 1989).

Malcolm X, *The Autobiography of Malcolm X* (with the assistance of Alex Haley) (New York: Grove Press, 1965).

George Breitman, *The Last Year of Malcolm X: The Evolution of a Revolutionary* (New York: Merit Publishers, 1965).

Tom Kahn and Bayard Rustin, 'The Ambiguous Legacy of Malcolm X', *Dissent*, Vol. 12, No. 2 (spring 1965), pp. 188–92.

Henry Lee Moon, 'The Enigma of Malcolm X', *Ebony*, Vol. 72, No. 4 (April 1965), pp. 226–7.

Bayard Rustin, 'On Malcolm X', *New America*, 28 February 1965), pp. 1, 8.

Eldridge Cleaver, 'Letters from Prison: On Malcolm X', *Ramparts* (August 1966), pp. 15–26.

Robert Allen, 'Malcolm X's Fatal Challenge to White Capitalism', *National Guardian* (18 February 1967), p. 5.

Ruby M. Essien-Udom and E.U. Essien-Udom, 'Malcolm X: An International Man', in John Henrik Clarke (ed.), *Malcolm X: The Man and His Times* (New York: Macmillan, 1969), pp. 235–67.

Editorial, 'Malcolm X and Martin Luther King, Jr.: Violence Versus Nonviolence', *Ebony* (April 1965), pp. 168–9.

Huey P. Newton, 'On Malcolm X', *The Black Panther* (7 March 1970), p. 6.

12. Beyond the American Dream: Film and the Experience of Defeat

Michael Klein

A Sense of History

> The Lord had blasted them and spit in their faces.
>   Charles Fleetwood

> If you fail you will plunge into
> A fathomless abyss
> Your body will shatter.
> Your bones will break.
>   Mao

> We stand defeated America.
>   John Dos Passos

> Nothing is absolutely dead: Every meaning
> will have its homecoming festival.
>   Mikhail Bakhtin

The first quote is a cry of anguish by Charles Fleetwood just prior to the defeat of the radical forces in England in the seventeenth century and the apparent disintegration of an opposition movement and a culture that had secured a certain degree of hegemony in the ferment of the time.[1] The others are a more recent response to the experience of defeat. Christopher Hill, in *The World Turned Upside Down* (1972) and *The Experience of Defeat* (1984), has called our attention to that revolutionary moment in seventeenth-century English history, a decade and a half of ferment that went through two stages. First there was a period of visionary intellectual excitement in which the values of the old ruling class and the dominant culture were called in question and anything and everything seemed possible – when, as Gerrard Winstanley announced, it seemed as if 'the old world ... is running up like parchment in the fire.'[2] This was followed by a period of defeat, when the radical forces were routed and a form of the old world restored. Writing in 1972, at the close of the 1960s era, Hill, in describing the radical forces of the seventeenth century as a 'counterculture',[3] and then, a decade later, in writing a book about their experience of defeat, suggested that there are common experiences that radicals share in revolutionary moments, and also in times of reaction when the causes and hopes of the oppositional forces are shattered or restructured by a dialectic that has operated in the interests of the old guard.[4] Thus in Hill's work there is a sustained, implied analogy with the radical renaissance of the 1960s in the US (and perhaps the UK and France) and with the period of reaction and defeat that followed, the Reagan era (and the reigns of Pompidou, d'Estaing and Thatcher). From the perspective of 1992 the onslaught of capital seems even more intense.

In the appropriately named book – *The Experience of Defeat* – Christopher Hill focused on a range of texts – memoirs, court records, pamphlets, poems – in which radicals of the time attempted to understand and to come to terms with their failure to realize their aims, in spite of their initial apparent success, and to sustain themselves and to survive in times of harsh reaction. The range of responses that Hill highlights includes: (a) reaffirmation of the radical cause but projection of its success into the long-term future; (b) despair and disillusion with social, political or cultural action and retreat into the private life; (c) realization of goals and interests that seemed achievable only through radical restructuring of the society and culture, however, which proved attainable – in a fashion – through accommodation (with a certain amount of contradiction) on the margins of the restoration.[5]

Many of the texts that are at the core of Hill's study focus on heroic and problematic elements of the radical experience. The foremost examples are Milton's epic gestural fables *Paradise Lost* and *Samson Agonistes*, fantasies or melodramas that defamiliarize, heighten and clarify familiar situations. Often these texts are attempts not only to record or explain what has happened but also to salvage something for the future, to contribute to the historical memory of a subculture of resistance. These texts are mythic and in a sense genre-based but are not escapist; 'they are the hard realities in projection, their symbolic recognition, [and] coordination'; they are signs whose function is the immediate and 'vivid presentation of values'.[6] Taken as a whole they are meditations on the theme of the possibilities for radical economic, political and cultural transformation and upon the problematic aspects of that process.

Blowing in the Wind: The 1960s

> The times they are a-changin' ...
> Bob Dylan

A sense of freedom is a key ideological component of the American Dream. The dream was rooted in Jefferson's manifesto proclamation of the human right to 'life, liberty and the pursuit of happiness', backed up by the right to undertake revolutionary political action when necessary, and by the assertion that all human beings were created equal. There were, of course, contradictions. Individual pursuit of happiness? Or, as the *philosophes* would have argued, was happiness *le bonheur*, that is the endowment of a community?

In the New World contradictions with other ideological postulates of the dominant culture (the promise of class mobility, the gospel of success–'failure' being somehow un-American), may have been less immediately apparent for most of the population. Moreover, insofar as the dream was significantly based upon subsistence or small-scale economy it could coexist with developing capitalism. However, contradictions were intensified when the basis of the dream became monopoly capitalism, and then imperialism, empire and global hegemony. Thus radical dissent in the US in the early 1960s proceeded from a profound contradiction – alienation from the basis of the dream; rededication to the promise of the dream, to the content, to the ideal of America becoming an equalitarian and communitarian homeland and a beacon to the world.

In the 1960s the US invasions of Cuba and of Vietnam, and the rediscovery of poverty, racism and apartheid at home, drove an irreconcilable wedge between the ideal and reality. Initially the response of the new radical generation was one of rage against the hypocrisy of the system. As the decade progressed enlightenment and romantic ideals merged with Marxism to develop a critique of US imperialism at home and abroad. The 'new' left took a giant step forward: *they* were the apostates; we were the keepers of the flame of the dream. However, after an exhausting decade of struggles, the new radical movement became a victim, not only of repression and cooptation and of the limits of objective conditions, but of modern manifestations of the dream, of the ideology of spontaneous growth and therefore of rising expectations of the New Deal and Kennedy eras. Situated in an economy and society in decline, as limited and decadent as the *ancien régimes* and military empires of France, Spain or Tsarist Russia in the past, dissent has become increasingly marginalized even as it has influenced the general consensus, increasingly ghettoized, self-regarding and limited.

When the grand narrative of one's time has been revealed as the experience of societies elect, coming to terms with the process of decline can be traumatic and painful. A stage on a long march to somewhere. Witness this example of an attempt to come to terms with the experience of defeat: writing on a wall in Berkeley after the Gulf War:

> There was thunder in the streets
> Today we can only speak in codes
> Like spies during the resistance
> Or prophets.
>
> Somehow our generation thought things would
> get better and better.
> Not good enough, but still better.
> And we would takeover and transform the
> garden.
>
> We didn't figure on an ice age
> Hell packaged as heaven, war as peace
> Deceit as enterprise, chaos as order.
>
> Freedom is the person that would turn the
> world upside down.

The 1960s Vietnam era was a period when alternative structures were imagined and collective actions were undertaken on domestic and international issues. There is a discourse that has permeated evaluations of the significance of the radical thrust of the 1960s and of the experience of defeat of the movement. For example, Tom Hayden, in attempting to come to terms with the radical movement's post-1960s experience of defeat sounds a characteristic note: 'We ended a war, toppled two Presidents, desegregated the South, broke other barriers of discrimination. How could we accomplish so much and have so little in the end?' [7]

The achievements of 1960s' insurgency were significant. First and foremost, the anti-war movement brought an end to US involvement in the war in Vietnam. Neither the anti-war movement in the US or Europe nor the protest movement in France against their war in Algeria could claim equal success as a result of their efforts, although they had strong ties with existing left-wing political parties and trade unions. There is, perhaps, no other comparable example in the history of the modern West of an anti-war/anti-imperialist movement so seizing the conscience of a nation and turning the tide against a significant national military commitment. Equally important, the civil rights and Black Power movements succeeded in destroying the foundations of Jim Crow or US-style apartheid. In response to protests in the streets that were an integral part of the radical thrust of the 1960s, the government conceded a series of reforms: voting rights legislation; medicare; better provision of welfare and social services to the poor, etc. In the early 1970s significant gains were also made in the areas of women's and consumer rights, and in the protection of the environment.

This is a considerable catalogue of accomplishment. Yet it falls short of the quest for liberation and radical transformation of the structure and ethos of US society that inspired the readers of newspapers and magazines with emblematic titles such as *Ramparts*, *Second Coming* (a Black Panther Party publication), *Progressive Labor* and *Good Times*. Moreover, as the movement disintegrated many of the reforms of the 1960s were eroded and, lacking a social base, freedoms achieved were corrupted or compromised.

As a result movement discourse in the early 1970s tended to shift from historical analyses of the crisis of the system to attempts to explain or account for its own crisis in historical terms. The reasons for the disintegration of the movement – not only as a source of political protest but also as a value-changing force in society – were complex and varied:

- There was intense repression, especially to the black community and in a more subtle form to white middle strata, as well as cooptation when the economy at home entered a prolonged downward cycle.

- Most of the movement's reform demands *vis-à-vis* the war, civil rights, education, etc., had either been achieved in some form or placed on the nation's political agenda, albeit by the establishment on its own terms, for its own class interests, and within the existing political and economic structures.

- As its symbiotic relationship with liberation struggles in Vietnam and resistance in the ghettos came to an end the movement's ability to sustain mass action decreased – movement political clout, in the final sense, having been a reflection of its objective links with more fundamental sources of power.

- There was a shift to the right within the nation as a consequence of the failure of capital and social democracy to sustain a social and economic consensus, of military defeat abroad and of the failure of radical initiatives at home.

- There was a global shift to the right following the waning of radical initiatives in the Far East, Latin America and some sectors of Europe.

- The movement could not address the concerns, needs and anxieties of the nation in a new crisis (in this case decline and de-industrialization), offer a way out or focus for protest in the language of the new times.

- The movement failed to sustain itself or to coalesce into a national party or broad-based coalition.

- There was exhaustion after more than a decade of intense struggle, and consequently deconstruction into utopianism, terrorism and options that ranged from survival to working from within, to cooptation.

Some of these factors are quite specific. But on the whole restoration of the hegemony of the old order, after the defeat of radical political insurgency, far from being a unique American cultural-political phenomenon seems part of an all too recognizable paradigm. Examples of periods of reaction/restoration following left-wing initiatives that come to mind include mid-seventeenth-century England, Europe in the 1930s (a period that Brecht called the 'dark times'), and Cold War America. Most often the experience of defeat proved transitory. However, this can only be said in hindsight. In the midst of the crisis artists and writers attempted to come to terms with their generation's apparent political failure, and with what it means to survive in a time marked by defeat and marginalization.

Given the ideological hegemony of the forces of restoration, oppositional analyses of contemporary historical experience often have to be conveyed through a form of discourse that is both accessible and covert. Thus conventional genres may be appropriated into serving as vehicles of contemporary comment. The type of art produced may be at once distanced *and* relevant. For example Milton's epic poems and drama based upon biblical myth; or Brecht's *Mother Courage and her Children* (1938) and *The Life of Galileo* (1939); or Caryl Churchill's *Light Shining in Buckinghamshire* (1976) and Edward Bond's *Restoration* (1980) which are historical dramas set in the seventeenth and eighteenth centuries. These are works whose real subjects are the crisis of the author, of his/her generation's experience of defeat, and of the meaning of survival in dark times, although on the surface they may seem to be exotic or far removed from the contradictions of the present. They are also works that trace connections between the past and the present and hence the future, or interrogate a stylized present with an eye to the future.

Images of the Movement in the Fast Lane

Film is truth at twenty-four frames per second.
Jean Luc Godard

At the conclusion of a retrospective on his work in film, Jean Luc Godard asked me what my ten-point plan for happiness was. This was in October of 1972, a crucial time during the Vietnam War. 'Ten-point plan' was a reference to the conditions for peace and neutrality that had been presented by the National Liberation Front in Paris in May of 1969, and were found acceptable by a significant sector of the anti-war movement, in the US and throughout the world. Godard's figure of speech is one example of the way that social and personal concerns were closely interrelated and thus a source of intense commitment.

In the 1960s, oppositional films about the war and related issues were consequently often both passionate and analytic. For the most part production of images of movement insurgency in the 1960s took the form of highly charged documentary films, short campaign films, most notably by the Newsreel Collective, and feature-length productions such as *Don't Bank on Amerika* (1970), *Angela Davis: Portrait of a Revolutionary* (1971), *Fuck the Army/FTA* (1971), and the Jean Luc Godard/Pennebaker production *One American Move/1 AM* (1968), an impressive attempt to problematize the 1960s/Vietnam era. In *Letter to Jane* (1972) Godard and co-director Gorin depart from the campaign film and related investigative documentary genres. Instead they analyse an image of Jane Fonda in Vietnam – that had been circulated worldwide by the press – in order to highlight contradictions in the way that the dominant conventions of the media structure certain roles for intellectuals in relation to oppressed people and their struggles: 'The film asks the question what part should intellectuals play in the revolution, and many others ... the film is a kind of detour that leads us back to ourselves ... the spectator must be able to really think and ask questions.' [8] Taken as a whole, independently produced, radical non-fiction films in the 1960s record not only events but also the concerns and ideological stances of civil rights protests and anti-war resistance, both within the US as a whole and within the army, as well as discussions about the relation of intellectuals and artists (including film makers) to people's struggles in the US and throughout the world.[9]

There are fewer examples of feature-length fiction film production in this period that focus on the political struggles of the 1960s/Vietnam era. *Strawberry Statement* (1970) was a somewhat superficial look at campus rebellion, although it was praised at the time in *Film Quarterly* as having projected some of the spirit of 1960s youth culture. *Medium*

Cool (1969) inserted a conventional narrative within documentary footage of police and National Guard repression of anti-war protest in Chicago at the time of the Democratic Party Convention in 1968. Through a combination of reportage, neo-realism and a romance narrative it attempted to dramatize the August 1968 events, and to explore issues that were being raised by the feminist, student anti-war and black liberation movements. Robert Kramer, in contrast, in his fiction film *Ice* (1969), focuses on urban-guerrilla activities of a revolutionary vanguard. *Ice* is set in a near future that looks very much like the time in which the film was made, and projects a wish-fulfilment fantasy of violent revolution that collapses into a vision of having to survive in isolation and defeat.[10] *The Spook Who Sat by the Door* (1972), another interesting feature-length American fiction film of the period, proceeds through a narrative that suggests parallels between black oppression in the US and Third World armed struggle. Here too, given the conventions of classic Hollywood narrative cinema, 'political analysis is presented dramatically, rather than being argued discursively'.[11] A similar strategy was adopted in *Brothers* (1975), a biopic based upon the life and death of George Jackson, in which the story of his imprisonment and development to the stature of a revolutionary leader is interwoven with the drama of his relationship with Angela Davis.

Edward Bond has commented that 'Brecht was against undue empathy; but there is a proper empathy in the love of truth.' [12] At the end of the 1960s a series of feature films appeared, often the work of European Marxist directors but filmed in English, that were distributed through mainstream US movie theatre circuits, as well as in art cinema houses and on campuses in 16mm. While not eschewing audience involvement, they adopted strategies to distance their material, seeking not to arouse empathy in the audience as an end in itself but in the service of truth and of historical memory. They took as their subject a revolutionary political moment, focused upon one or two key characters, and attempted to analyse a process of struggle that encompassed both achievements and defeats. Examples are Bo Widerberg's *Joe Hill* (1970), and Giuliano Montaldo's *Sacco and Vanzetti* (1970). These films focus upon key moments in early twentieth-century political struggle in the US: the organization of the IWW (who are portrayed very like the New Left of the 1960s) and the linkage of militant indigenous US labour struggle with an international Marxist revolutionary movement (*Joe Hill*); opposition to an imperialist war and victimization by the US ruling class by means of the internal security apparatus of the US government (*Sacco and Vanzetti*). Insofar as both films have key trial scenes they incorporate a certain amount of structured debate and political discussion within their narratives. While the films are not overly analytic there are certain lessons we learn from the mistakes of the protagonists and their lawyers. The theme of *Joe Hill* is his famous testament: 'Don't mourn, organize!' which is sung as a ballad at the end of the film by Joan Baez. The theme of Montaldo's film is conveyed by the Baez/Morricone song 'Here's To You Sacco and Vanzetti', a salute to the two martyrs in their moment of defeat which redeems it as a source of inspiration for future generations. Baez's participation in the films links the past events with the 1960s movement with which she was closely associated. A typology is thus established: the radical politics of the 1960s are situated as a part of a heritage of victories and defeats, a process that is likely to continue until the good society is established.

Consciousness and the Experience of Defeat: *Zabriskie Point*

> Philosophers have only interpreted the world, in various ways; the point, however, is to change it.
>
> Karl Marx

Set against the backdrop of student demonstrations, the music and the ideological and natural landscape of America in the 1960s, Michelangelo Antonioni's film *Zabriskie Point* (1969) presents two young people attempting to come to an understanding of themselves and their situation. While it is a narrative fiction film, Antonioni subordinates plot to theme, constructing an extended meditation on the 1960s, on the problematic aspects of – on the one hand – attempts to overthrow capitalism, given an insufficient basis of working-class support; on the other, of strategies of survival that are dependent upon a certain degree of symbiotic accommodation with the structures or institutions of consumer capitalism.

Like Brechtian drama, Antonioni's film consists of a number of distinct episodes. The film opens with what at first appears to be a naturalist documentary of a planning meeting for a campus demonstration and strike against the war in Vietnam, a series of actions that will include the burning of the campus ROTC building and nearby army recruitment centre. We see faces that would have been familiar in the 1960s: Kathleen Cleaver of the Black Panther Party, Barbara Garson, UC Berkeley activist and author of *MacBird*, etc. We are presented with fragments of debates on issues and tactics which focus upon certain key concerns and questions: what is necessary to make white people as a whole come over to the revolution; what tactics should a vanguard employ in the struggle against the war and racism? Insofar as we are shown fragments of the debate and soon leave the room to follow Mark – clearly a character in a fictional film – we become aware that what seemed to be a documentary is in fact a reconstruction, and that what we are watching is neither real nor simply a story but an analytic parable of the times.

The pseudo-documentary of the planning meeting and the subsequent violent police repression of the campus strike (tear gas, clubs, the shooting of several black students as they leave a building) are contextualized, for as Mark flees from the scene of the confrontation, Antonioni foregrounds signs in the industrial landscape. One property of film is that narratives are performed, are spatialized, are seen. They are situated in a tangible world which in itself possesses certain signifying properties, and which establishes context and representative significance. Landscape, cityscape and a host of artefacts that have signifying properties may thus overdetermine the dramatic action. Antonioni constructs the next segment of *Zabriskie Point* in this way. Instead of concentrating upon the dramatic aspect of Mark's flight he turns his camera on signs in the cityscape that signify capitalist domination, that are indicative of where the sources of power in society lie, and thus not only encircle the campus but in a cultural and political sense contain and are in contradiction to the demonstration and to the student's revolutionary activism. We see signs that define the institutional basis of US society as industrial and finance capitalism (a steel factory, a machine tool company, California Federal Bank, the Bank of America, etc.), and which create illusions of freedom (the face of the Statue of Liberty) and physical and social mobility (happy, prosperous passengers pictured on an American Airlines advertising billboard; people eating Best Foods sandwiches) that are a source of false consciousness and serve as a prop of ruling class hegemonic power.

In the following scene (accompanying Daria, we visit the Sunnydunes Development Company) we witness the production of a TV commercial that cynically constructs/exploits certain aspects of the American Dream, transforming frontier myths into consumer capitalist desires for the greater profit of the company, structuring alienation and providing alienated consumerist solutions to needs and desires that have been engendered by discontent with work relations in urban industrial society. The figures on the TV screen are puppets. Barbie doll-like women. Women in kitchens filled with labour-saving gadgets. Men watering suburban lawns. A child/son in a cowboy outfit. A girl wearing sunglasses standing by a swimming pool. Puppets. Smiling. While looking at these artefacts we listen to the voice-over:

> Enjoy the full relaxation of outdoor living. Bask in the desert sun by your own private pool ... Why be caught up in the rat race? ... Get out into the sun and water your own private garden. Become an independent man. Forge a life of your own like the pioneers who molded the west. Start your life over.

The minimalist plot which occupies the middle portion of the film is concerned with an encounter between Mark, who is on the run, suspected of shooting a cop after the riot police have opened fire on a radical student campus demonstration, and Daria, a somewhat apolitical counterculture hippie, who is driving a funky old Buick on her way to meet a wealthy entrepreneur at a hideaway in the desert at which Sunnydunes is attempting to raise venture capital. The narrative is elliptical, interrupted by detours and subjective visions. The characters come to exert a certain influence upon each other, but more from what the audience comes to understand in responding to the visual metaphors of the film than through what they say to each other. By the end of the film Mark, who was willing to kill for the revolution but has not yet attained a sense of what he was fighting for (in distinction to what he was fighting against), sacrifices himself in a countercultural gesture that conveys a cluster of alternative values. Daria's consciousness is also transformed in an epiphany that is a wish-fulfilment vision of the destruction of consumer capitalism. Unable to change the world in a time of imperialist hegemony and decadence, the characters can only interpret it, transform their own consciousness and that of the audience.

Mark returns to California in the small executive airplane he has stolen. He and Daria paint the plane with psychedelic designs, transforming it into 'a prehistoric bird with genitals', a yippie icon in the sky. Mark decorates the plane with oppositional slogans: 'Freedom'; 'Suck Bucks'; 'No Wars'; 'He/She'. There is also a visual pun on the side of the plane: 'No Wars/No Words', that may simply be a critique of hypocrisy and duplicity associated with US government diplomacy; however it seems more antinomian, a grim and stoical rejection of public discourse as tainted with bad faith. Mark's return to the airport to give himself up is at once an acceptance of defeat and an act of cultural revolution, as he has defiled a leisure toy of capitalism, transforming it into a countercultural advertisement against the war and certain aspects of the dominant ideological consensus. His statement has minimal effect on the world. The police simply gun him down at the airport. But news of Mark's death has a profound effect on Daria's consciousness.

The final sequence of the film takes place at a luxurious penthouse retreat in the desert where Daria has journeyed to meet her employer and perhaps become his mistress. A business meeting is taking place at which the speculator entrepreneurs of Sunnydunes Company are attempting to raise venture capital to finance the development of the western resort that was hyped in the TV commercial in the early part of the film. Daria arrives distraught by the news that she has heard on the radio, is welcomed by her boss, walks past a swimming pool where several decorative women are passing the time and prepares to wait until the business negotiations are completed. While waiting she is met by a Native-American young woman who may be a domestic but also most likely supplies sexual services to the businessmen. It is the expression in the girl's eyes – of willing and somewhat resigned subservience and of welcome, and the implication that she understands what Daria is doing – that sparks Daria's epiphany. Nothing is said. It is all communicated to us and Daria by several brief looks. The girl in the hall has accepted her place in the establishment scale of things, has bartered her talents and her oppression in the US empire for a certain amount of security and material benefit, as did a group of workers we saw earlier in the film accommodating to life in Los Angeles. Daria cannot continue on this course, even in the midst of defeat. She turns and walks away, and with a withering glance destroys the temple of the Philistines.

As the capitalist palace in the desert explodes in flames we realize that we are sharing Daria's fantasy. It is as much a vision of enlightenment as a Samson-like apocalyptic act of retribution and vindication. Antonioni presents us with multiple shots of the building in disintegration, focusing in slow motion on a series of grotesque objects exploding and floating in space: a television set, the contents of a refrigerator, tin cans, sausages and lobsters and bits of meat, a loaf of wonderbread, racks of clothes. It is a vision not only of the destruction of a pleasure palace, of a locus of power where businessmen meet to reconstruct society and nature for their profit, but also an anatomy and a defilement of representative symbols of consumer capitalism, of object-images that in the conventional media are manipulated to engender needs and illusions and symbiotic accommodation to the existing cultural, political and economic system. In the midst of the desert Daria has achieved a consciousness that will sustain her. She and Mark have not changed the world but have been able to interpret it.

Queimada!/Burn!: The Dialectics of the Experience of Defeat

> Freedom is the recognition of necessity.
> Engels

> Freedom in not something that is given to you. It is something that you must take.
> José Dolores

Queimada! both presents and interprets a world of historical struggle. At times it engages our emotions and involvement: history is thus personalized – it is seen in the process of being 'made by people'. While *Queimada!* is an extremely ideological film it is also very human. Indeed its most profound message is that within the framework of historical conditions, history is made by people becoming conscious of their oppression in concrete situations.

Gillo Pontecorvo has described *Queimada!* (1970) as the joining of 'the film of romantic adventure and the film of ideas'.[13] The film was scripted with Franco Solinas with whom Pontecorvo also collaborated on *The Battle of Algiers* (1966). Unlike *Zabriskie Point*, *Queimada!* is set in the historical past. It traces the history of an unsuccessful liberation struggle that took place in the Caribbean in the mid-nineteenth century, against the Portuguese and then the English. At one level it is historical spectacle, a well-produced costume drama with a recognizable Hollywood star, Marlon Brando, impersonating the British adventurer Sir William Walker. But it is also a film of ideas, a meditation about national liberation struggles in general *and* about the dynamics of revolutions that are not able fully to realize their objectives in the historical moment that is allotted to them.

Queimada! is thus an adventure film as well as a discourse on dialectical and historical materialism and the dynamics of the experience of defeat. At various points it speaks to issues that were of concern to radicals in the late 1960s: the war in Vietnam and other national liberation struggles; the dynamics of the relationship of neocolonialism with Third World and aspiring Communist societies that have yet to develop technologically advanced infrastructures; the dilemma of revolutionaries who can achieve certain reforms but whose ultimate radical objectives are in advance of their time. These and related issues are addressed by means of a Brechtian rhetorical strategy: at key moments in the film the flow of the action is interrupted; the principal protagonists deliver a lecture, or a speech, or a formal statement. These interventions are a source of interpretation of the spectacle that the audience is watching.

These ideological interludes are visual – as in the case of *Zabriskie Point* – as well as verbal. For example, the scenes in which British troops and their allies hunt down José Dolores' guerrillas in the mountain villages, burning the houses and terrorizing the old and the women and children who remain in them, are overt reproductions of television and press images of US troops in Vietnam laying waste to peasant hamlets and rounding up the population. The close relation that exists between José and the masses is also visually rendered. There are a number of key scenes in which José is surrounded by and merges with crowds of exaltant supporters. For example, when at the conclusion of the first stage of the revolution the rebel troops advance on the city, José only gradually emerges in a distant panorama of the line of marching soldiers. It is only when we view the scene through Sir William's telescope (that is, see it inscribed in metropolitan bourgeois perspective) that José stands out isolated from the people. That scene concludes with an image that could have been composed by a painter in heroic neoclassical style at the time of the French revolution. Walker and José gallop toward each other from opposite sides of the beach, pass each other, then rein in their horses and turn, so that they now face each other. It is the moment in which their alliance (of landowners of Portuguese background, England – both the government and British sugar companies – and black slaves versus Portugal) has come to fruition and simultaneously begins to disintegrate under the pressure of a new set of contradictions, as the revolution enters a new phase and the former slaves become exploited sugarcane workers.

Analyses of what is occurring are soon communicated to us by several interventions in the flow of the narrative. These ideological interludes, like songs and related interventions in Brecht's plays, interrupt the action, which in *Queimada!* is a graphic and compelling spectacle of intrigue and struggle. First, there is an abrupt shift forward in time (ten years from 1838 to 1848) and place (from the island of Queimada to the Stock Exchange in London). We are unexpectedly alienated or distanced from the flow of the action of the film as a voice that we have not previously heard (and will not hear again) offers an authoritative gloss on the scene:

> Business continued to prosper for the world's leading sugar companies. This is the London Stock Exchange. Ten years have passed. The quotations of shares on the sugar companies continue to rise. Companies are merging, and with the increase in their economic strength grow even more powerful. As a logical consequence they are now able to take personal charge of law and order on their overseas plantations.

The analysis is further developed when Walker delivers a lecture to a seminar-like meeting that is attended by Mr Shelton, a representative of the Royal Sugar Company (which has received the right to own, govern and exploit the sugar plantations for 99 years and in practice now controls the entire economy in Queimada), representatives of the military and government of Queimada, and of Britain who have directly intervened in the island's affairs, taking command of the armed forces and police, initially as advisers, and then bringing in their own troops. This is a clear analogy to the US in Vietnam. However the discourse of the film is concerned with a more comprehensive analysis. As Walker points out in his lecture: 'I want to explain that very often between one historical period and another, ten years certainly might be enough to reveal the contradictions of a whole century.'

The implications of this are further explored in several exchanges between Walker and Mr Shelton, as well as in a flashback sequence narrated by Walker, which locates Dolores' second rebellion in 1848, a year of global radical revolutionary insurgency, somewhat analogous to events in 1968 in the US, Europe and the Third World.

In these and other rhetorical interludes the film offers a Marxist interpretation of the action, highlighting the development that has taken place in Queimada from a bourgeois-democratic revolution with anticolonial aspects to the beginning of a national liberation struggle against capitalism and imperialism. History proceeds dialectically in stages, sometimes in cycles, new contradictions engendering new goals and new alliances, victory becoming defeat and defeats setting the stage for victories. There is a partial analogy to Vietnam (to the French and US aspects of the war) but also a suggestion of something more. When *Queimada!* was first released in 1970, the response of most of its reviewers – myself among them -- was to focus on those aspects of the film that evoked parallels with the US war in Vietnam, although a sustained literal reading of the analogy breaks down in the latter part of the work, when José's second rebellion is militarily defeated, unlike the efforts of the Vietnamese.[14] In retrospect it is clear that the allegory is more complex, that the latter part of the film is also a meditation on more general aspects of the 1960s: the global radical insurgency of the decade (in the US, Europe and the Third World) in which the contradictions of the century were again suddenly revealed and expectations of social transformation aroused; and the experience of defeat of certain radical movements that enjoyed considerable but not sufficient support to achieve their ultimate goals. José's situation, while at onlelevel of the fable analogous to that of the Vietnamese revolution, at another level refers to an aspect of the dilemma of insurgent radical movements at the end of the 1960s, in the US, France and in the developing world.

When José is with his troops and people in their base areas it appears as if hegemony and self-determination are possibilities. In 1838 when the insurgents are part of a broad alliance, reforms are granted and they achieve many of their proclaimed goals, most notably the end to slavery and related racist structures in society, and a just end to the war against Portugal, but cannot proceed further. Walker and Shelton are willing to offer participation in the structures of power but on certain conditions. The price for 'civilization' (certain material benefits) is accommodation to the market economy and to the international power of capitalism, as represented by the Royal Sugar Company and Britain. José Dolores' first taste of the experience of defeat lies not so much in his refusal to work within and accommodate to the institutions of the ruling classes, but in his recognition that there is insufficient basis for his people and their movement to achieve their ultimate goals on their own immediately. A degree of freedom can be preserved, however. In defining it José transforms the radical dilemma of vanguard movements (whether in 1838/48 or 1968) into the beginning of an alternative political creed. The creed is framed, objectified, abstracted from the spectacle of the events of the film, as it is not spoken by José in the midst of the dramatic action, but instead in the third person, by a supporter presenting it as the philosophy and programme of the liberation movement:

> José Dolores says if what we have in our country is 'civilization' ... it is better that we are 'uncivilized', *for it is better to know where to go and not know how than to know how to go and not know where.*

Again, it is a matter of preserving consciousness and historical memory, not so much – as in the case of the radical documentary films of the 1960s or *Zabriskie Point* – of specific historical events or of what one is against, but of understanding the processes of history and preserving a vision of what one is fighting for. In this way the experience of defeat is transformed into an aspect of victory – provided the lessons become generally understood. Thus after his defeat in their second attempt at insurgency (1848) José has again to confront the implications of his vanguard movement's insufficient basis of support. He delivers a speech to his captors, all of whom share his national and class interests but who have supported the government: 'How come they win in the end? ... Others will begin to understand. And you will begin to understand ... Well you will some day because you have already begun to think about it.' We focus on a face in the crowd who is beginning to think about it.

Survival and the Experience of Defeat:
Peckinpah's Testament

> You don't need a weatherman
> To know which way the wind blows
>   Bob Dylan

Hollywood films seldom foreground their ideology – more often it is encoded within the conventions of a popular genre: science-fiction, westerns, thrillers, gangster films, historical adventure. These films are often fantasies, in some cases fantasies of a special kind in that in restructuring the past, heightening/stylizing the present, or projecting a future, they may defamiliarize and thus clarify aspects of their audience's present situation, or provide a forum for the expression of contradictions, concerns and feelings that the dominant culture represses.

Two genre films released in the early 1970s – Sam Peckinpah's *The Getaway* (1972) and his *Pat Garrett and Billy the Kid* (1973) – echo and speak to the concerns and the confusion of a movement on the wane, a movement wasted by internal and external contradictions, subject to repression and experiencing defeat. They bear witness to their times in an indirect but highly significant way. Peckinpah's movies are genre films, and the genres are highly conventional, one a gangster/adventure film set in present time in the southwest, the other a classic western set in the mid-nineteenth century and based upon a mythic American tale. The gangster film *The Getaway* is on the surface simply a story about a bank robber and his wife on the run, both from the gang that set up the robbery and the police. However as the police, conventionally the protectors of the established order, and the gang are in common pursuit of our hero and heroine, and as the gang is run by 'a man with political influence', the film soon acquires political overtones.

In *The Getaway* our hero and heroine (Steve McQueen and Ali McGraw) are thus attempting to survive in an alien and dangerous world. Moreover, in the background of the action we see quite a number of soldiers on leave or on their way to Vietnam. We are viewing America from the perspective of the movement in defeat, from a position of weakness, of being determined by the prevailing forces, of being on the run.

The Getaway is a genre-sanctioned nightmare vision of an attempt to survive in post-movement end of Vietnam-era America, a society characterized by anomie, repression, apathy, and individualistic pursuit of the dollar. America is allegorized in the film as a trash heap of a civilization within which our hero and heroine are nearly smothered. The setting is reminiscent of the valley of ashes in F. Scott Fitzgerald's *The Great Gatsby*, except that the protagonists, instead of being witnesses, are victims. On the run from the police and the establishment politicians' hired guns, McQueen and McGraw take refuge in a garbage dump, only to find themselves absorbed into the rubbish, impacted and then spewed out on to a wasteland-like dump site.

At the end of the film the couple escape across the border to Mexico, a surrogate Third World country. 'Mexico' represents a human, pre-imperialist alternative to the American way of life in the dark times of the 1970s. Perhaps it may also represent yet another new frontier where the endemic American Dream may be retrieved. The film also suggests that, through their immolation in and flight from the belly of the beast, our characters (especially McQueen) have begun to overcome the materialism, wariness of love and of human contact, arrogance, and propensity to violence that were a by-product of their contradiction with an alienating society.

Prior to their escape there is a key scene. Peckinpah is communicating with his intended audience on the level that has far more to do with the *geist* of the times than the plot of the film. The scene is an anti-establishment revenge fantasy. Steve McQueen disarms the police, forces them to lie flat in the gutter and coolly proceeds to destroy their police car, blowing it to bits with a double barrel shotgun: first the headlights, then the side of the car where the emblem 'Police' is emblazoned, then the red flashing light on the side of the truck. The ritualistic defilement of an icon of establishment power and authority is further allegorized in that it is presented in slow motion, like the conclusion of *Zabriskie Point*. It is a scene of pure rage.

The Getaway is a cry of outrage and despair at being in post-movement America, resolved momentarily by terrorist fantasy and transcended by utopian withdrawal. *Pat Garrett and Billy the Kid* is a meditation on the future of post-movement America, an elegy for the past and an attempt to figure out what went wrong. Peckinpah encodes his meditation in an established genre (the western), and a received legend (the tale of Billy the Kid and Pat Garrett). Historically Billy was an ambiguous figure in a minor episode in the transition of New Mexico from agrarian community to investment focus for eastern capitalism. The populist legend of Billy was developed in Walter Burns's book *The Saga of Billy the Kid* (1926), in Aaron Copeland's ballet (1938) and in films that range from Vidor's *Billy the Kid* (1930) to *Young Guns* (1988).

Westerns as mythologized representatives of nineteenth-century historical events often comment indirectly upon life in modern society, as texts in interaction with the *geist* of their intended audience. Read dialectically they often tell us far more about the period in which they were produced than about life in nineteenth-century America. Oppositional texts tend to romanticize outlaws and avengers as rebels against representations of social evil; conservative films tend to praise lawmen and to portray outlaws as sociopaths; works that are cynical or disillusioned tend to cast a cold eye on all the protagonists, offering psychological explanations or deconstructing prevailing myths.[15] In locating and affirming certain patterns in history these works organize experience for the present.

Pat Garrett and Billy the Kid is concerned with an aspect of the experience of defeat, with cooptation and betrayal from within. The film focuses upon a representative of a sector of the oppositional forces who went over to the side of the establishment, perhaps only to achieve goals for which he entered the struggle but which, once certain radical demands had been assimilated, could be more comfortably realized by a change in allegiance. Pat Garrett's name appears first in the title of the film. In a sense he is a counterpart of the Harringtonians whom Christopher Hill described making their peace with the Restoration, or of former progressives in Hollywood who advanced their careers by cooperating with HUAC in the wake of the defeat of the left at the start of the Cold War, or of former 1960s radicals who accommodated to the defeat of their expectations. In the discourse of the film he is a representative of former movement people who, when times change, in order to survive or maintain their interests, take up positions within the establishment, ultimately betraying their former ideals and implementing the policies of the powers that be.[16]

The theme is announced by an exchange of dialogue at the start of the film:

> *Pat Garrett*: It feels like times have changed.
> *Billy the Kid*: Times maybe. Not me.

Indeed the times are a-changing. The 'times' are the 1970s as much as the 1870s. This is not an abstract statement about life in general or an evocation of a moment of transition from the distant historical past. The subtext of Peckinpah's allegorical film is the reversal of history as viewed from 1960s youth culture and New Left perspectives, and as imagined or experienced by the audience.

In Peckinpah's fable Pat Garrett, former friend and comrade of Billy the Kid, who has lived outside the law of the dominant interests of society, goes over to the other side, becomes a bounty hunter in the pay of the big ranchers, and hunts his former comrade down. Garrett is the new man of the times, a professional and me-generation careerist. He is hired by the establishment to corrupt ('make advances on their spirits and their souls') or destroy his former comrades. As the ring that hires Garrett to neutralize or destroy Billy includes not only ranchers and big businessmen but also the Governor of New Mexico and the future US Secretary of the Interior, he is typed as an agent of an unholy trinity of capital, the government and the law.

Billy, in Peckinpah's film, is a figure virtually devoid of introspection or self-consciousness, and thus is an allegorical blank upon which the resonances of the film can cohere. He is defined for us by context, by his environment, by his situation, by allusions to certain archetypes. He is also defined by his style and manner, by a certain set of 1960s movement male gestures and attitudes. He is linked by association, and by the way his image in the film is framed, with national minority or Third World characters and with poor people. He is often situated in communal and fraternal settings. In this way he becomes representative of a style of cultural politics.

At one level of the allegory Billy is a romanticized 1960s radical. As impersonated by actor Kris Kristofferson (who walks through the part, laid back and amiable) he is an anachronism, playing a part in a western set in the nineteenth century. We are thus distanced or alienated from the historical spectacle and respond to Billy as an archetypal representative of certain ideals and attitudes, not simply as a replay of Billy the

Kid. In Peckinpah's parable he is also a type of natural man, of Samson in the temple of the Philistines, of Christ in Jerusalem. He is simultaneously out of date and ahead of his time.

The film's statement does not emerge from the allegorical spectacle alone, but through the interrelation of visual images and choral commentary on the soundtrack. In *Pat Garrett and Billy the Kid* the chorus/commentary takes the form of songs and ballads that are sung by Bob Dylan. As Bob Dylan also appeared in the film as a minor character and observer of much of the action, his presence (Dylan being commonly regarded as the poet-bard of the 1960s) together with the song/image linkage ensured that the film addressed its intended audience as a parable of modern times.

Dylan witnesses Billy's experience of defeat. Peckinpah shrewdly casts him as a character named Alias, who in the early part of the film is often uncommitted in relation to the action he observes and reports. This is more than an in-group joke (Zimmerman alias Dylan), for in portraying Dylan as a man without a clear sense of identity, and as a man of limited commitment, Peckinpah is not only critiquing the role that Dylan played *vis-à-vis* the movement, he is also commenting on Dylan's own record as a survivor, like many in or of the movement, having the ability to adjust to new times while maintaining a certain connection to what came before. Thus it is significant that Alias/Dylan finally allies himself with Billy and his commune.

It is the songs that are heard throughout the film that make manifest the concerns of a movement that had spun out of the fast lane. Dylan's voice expresses the sense of isolation and despair of a movement in defeat ('don't it make you feel so low down'/'Billy you're goin' all alone'), the sense of betrayal ('To be hunted by the man who was your friend'), and of vulnerability to the forces of restoration and reaction ('The businessmen from Taos want you to go down'/'bounty hunters a-dancin' all around you').

There is, however, a counter-movement in the images of the final scene of the film that qualifies and extends the meaning of Dylan's ballad. Part of the counter-movement derives from Billy's acquiescence in his own death (martyrdom) in the scene in which he is ambushed by Garrett. By the end of the film we have the sense that he is a vanguardist saviour figure out of sync with the times. Here Peckinpah's film touches upon issues that Milton wrestled with in *Paradise Regained* and Brecht critiqued in *The Life of Galileo*. The film indicates that renewal will not come from powerful external agents, the two most potent figures in the film being corrupt (Garrett) or marginalized (Billy). Exemplary figures (or movements) may provide the sparks but in the final sense it is up to the people themselves.

By the time Billy is killed Alias (the Dylan figure) and some of the drifters on the fringe of Billy's band are no longer uncommitted. Those who have survived have acquired a sense of identity and have decided to stand by what Billy represents. Whether or not their generation will be capable of taking action remains somewhat ambiguous. It seems unlikely. The film, however, borrows an image from the television screens of the late 1960s and early 1970s to mark hope for the future. As Pat Garrett rides out of town he is attacked by a young boy throwing stones. The memory and meaning of the recent past (Dylan's 'Ballad of Billy the Kid'), the new consciousness of Alias and of Billy's contemporaries who manage to survive, and the resistance of a new generation may lead to renewal. The Pat Garrett who rides out victorious at the end of the film is already a dead man, dead spiritually and soon physically as well, assassinated by the businessmen and politicians once his usefulness is over. The future belongs to later generations with a sense of their own agenda, the outrage of innocence, and the inspiration of historical memory.

Epilogue: *Violent Streets/Thief*

> Not having a correct political point of view
> is like having no soul.
>
> Mao

Films concerned with the defeat of aspirations of 1960s-type oppositional characters continued into the 1980s. *Violent Streets/Thief* (1980) focuses upon the experience of defeat of a post-1960s outsider. Like *Pat Garrett and Billy the Kid* it is cast in a recognizable genre. *Violent Streets* is a thriller, constructed in the style of urban film noir. As in *Queimada!* the melodramatic action is disrupted at key moments by rhetorical statements, by exchanges of heightened dialogue or the presentation of visual symbols. The main characters – Frank, Jessie, Leo and his henchmen – function iconically rather than as rounded characters. Their dialogue and their actions are emblematic, and exist primarily for exposition of the film's larger concerns.[17] The world of the present is thus defamiliarized, explained in Marxist terms, in epic confrontations and ideological set pieces that stand out from the action.

The protagonist of *Violent Streets* Frank (James Caan) has recently been released from prison. He has decided to make it, to operate within the margins of the system to achieve the American Dream. The American Dream is allegorized on a small card that Frank constructed while in prison and keeps with him in his wallet next to his credit cards. It consists of pictures of a substantial home, a wife/mother, a child, expensive cars and other material possessions. He shows it to Jessie

(Tuesday Weld) when he asks her to be his wife, to take on the role of one of the images. 'This is my life', he explains. 'Did you cut it out of magazines?' Jessie asks. Frank nods – 'newspapers, whatever'. The card contains his aspirations and his identity. We are aware that they are social constructions, that his spirit and his soul have been shaped by the dominant media. Frank does not at this point understand that the Dream is synthetic, generated by the same system as his credit cards.

Back in society Frank concentrates on achieving the post-1960s' American Dream of the pursuit of individual happiness and prosperity. He becomes an enterprising owner of a car lot by day and a professional high-tech thief by night. As an owner of the automobile agency he is the epitome of the self-made man. He wears expensive suits, watches and rings. His significant income however comes from his work as a thief. He is employed by Leo to break into safes and steal diamonds and securities. (In this he uses tools with skill like an industrial worker.) The proceeds from the thefts are invested by Leo in his shopping centres and other businesses.

There is a tradition in thrillers and related genre films for gangsters to be identified with corporate capitalism. For example: *Force of Evil* (1948); *Point Blank* (1967); *The Godfather* (1971/1974/1990); *Cutter's Way* (1980); *Once Upon a Time in America* (1984). *Violent Streets*, however, is unusually explicit in its presentation of capitalist work relations. Leo's descriptions of the operation signify that Frank, in opting into the values of the system, has merely become an employee of a capitalist conglomerate, whatever his aspirations or his illusions of freedom and independence.

> *Leo*: I'm the banker ... You're gonna work for me ... Everything's business like ... I thought we'd talk a little business ... You'll get paid what I said. You'll do what I say. I run you. There is no discussion. I want you to work until you are burnt out.

Frank's response to Leo is in terms that are equally ideological.

> *Frank*: I can see my money is still in your pocket, which is from the yield of my labour. What gratitude? You're making big profits from my work, my risk, my sweat.

Leo's response, several scenes later, is a graphic statement about a worker's essential dependency upon his employer, about the powerlessness that lies beneath the trappings of security and the masculine American Dream for workers (no matter how high paid or professional) who have a mortgage and a family. The camera is placed so that we – the audience – are looking up at Leo from a position of subordination:

> *Leo*: You got a home, a car, family and I own the paper on your whole fucking life. I'll put your cunt wife out on the streets to be

fucked in the ass ... I'll wack out your whole family ... You got responsibilities. Back to work Frank.

Paternalistic capitalism and the ideology of the American consumerist Dream seek to control the characters' lives in all respects in *Violent Streets* – control of their hearts and minds (representations of the dream of 'life, liberty and the pursuit of happiness'); control of the work process; control of the surplus yield of their labour; control of their security.

Like Daria in *Zabriskie Point*, Frank reaches the limit of accommodation. The Harringtonian option of realization of one's individual interests within the system does not work. The cost in freedom and self-respect is too much. There is no viable social option. However, his experience of defeat yields a gesture of liberation. In a Samson-like scene reminiscent of the conclusion of *Zabriskie Point*, Frank destroys his American Dream identity card, blows up his house, his office, and sets fire to the hundreds of shining automobiles that are displayed in his vast car lot. These scenes of destruction are stylized, rendered almost abstract by new age music on the soundtrack. Frank then emerges from a final confrontation, in which he blows away Leo, and then, wounded, goes towards the police (also his enemies as they want a share of the take) who are waiting for him on the edges of Leo's estate. It is the climax of *Samson Agonistes*, modified by an ambiguous Hollywood ending. The dynamics of accommodation and of the contradictions in Frank's situation have been made manifest to the audience. As in tragedy we respond with pity and fear and a certain recognition or consciousness. The consolation of defeat is enlightenment without the comfort of illusions. As Hegel commented, 'The owl of Minerva spreads her wings at twilight.'

Marx said that 'the demand that people give up illusions about their conditions is the demand that they give up the conditions which require illusions'. The conditions have not changed. The shadow of the US war in Vietnam, and of the deconstruction of the movement after the war, impacted on cultural production that attempted to come to terms with defeat in the 1970s and early 1980s. In the 1990s the spectre of Vietnam has risen again. Not only did President Bush rewrite the history of that war, as if the US fought and 'lost' because it had one hand tied behind its back, but in doing so he rededicated the US government to a neo-imperialist and interventionalist foreign policy. Thus we return full circle to the Truman doctrine of 1947 that 'in American foreign policy', wherever 'freedom' is threatened, America's security is also involved,[18] but in a situation where there is no 'enemy' and few friends, only territory and spheres of 'free markets' and other powers, as at the start of the century.

BEYOND THE AMERICAN DREAM

However in the early 1990s an alternative American tradition was also being reaffirmed. In the words of one young protester: 'I know we can defeat this war because we stopped the war in Vietnam.' A sense of radical heritage and of the need for unity was not enough. Still this sort of historical memory has seldom existed in modern times in the US. It is, perhaps, significant that radical consciousness, however minority, is developing within the US empire at a time it is becoming an *ancien régime*, militarily powerful but economically spent by the outflow of domestic capital. This is a new factor.

Seeds have to be sown for there to be a harvest. From a dialectical perspective defeat and victory may be a part of the same process. This means going through and beyond the confines of the frontier of the American Dream. The experience of defeat – recognition of defeat in the context of a sense of history and of an oppositional radical heritage – is one way that radicals in the US may come to share and better understand the experiences of oppressed peoples, classes and nations. It is, perhaps, a stage on a long march from the rage of *Samson Agonistes* and the clarity of *Paradise Lost* and *Paradise Regained*. Marx has written that 'language is practical consciousness'. If so the art of the near future will be instructive. As long as we can imagine the world the way it *is* and the way it should be there may be hope.

Notes

1. Charles Fleetwood, quoted in Christopher Hill, *God's Englishmen* (New York: Harpers, 1970), p. 248; also in Christopher Hill, *The Experience Of Defeat* (London: Faber, 1984), p. 307.

2. Gerrard Winstanley, quoted in Christopher Hill, *The World Turned Upside Down: Radical Ideas During the English Revolution* (New York: Viking, 1972).

3. *The World Turned Upside Down*, pp. 273–7.

4. Edward Bond and Caryl Churchill have utilized the English Revolution and the Restoration to comment upon the experience of defeat (resistance and adaptation) in Thatcher's Britain after the radical thrust of the 1960s and 1970s. Caryl Churchill, *Light Shining in Buckinghamshire* (London: Pluto, 1976); Edward Bond, *Restoration* (London: Methuen, 1982).

5. For example Hill cites: (a) Milton; (b) Fox and the Society of Friends; (c) the Harringtonians (somewhat analogous to modern yuppies, and insofar as this group included a number of metaphysical poets, to postmodern intellectuals who theorize the world into a self-referential ivory tower of language).

6. I.A. Richards, quoted by Richard Godden in 'Iconic Narratives', *Fictions of Capital* (Cambridge: Cambridge University Press, 1990), p. 150. Allen Tate cited by Godden in his discussion of verbal icons, pp. 149–50; also Allen Tate, 'Literature as Knowledge', in *Collected Essays* (Denver: Allen Swallow, 1959), p. 27. The rhetoric of twentieth-century moving visual icons (motion pictures) is even more immediate.

7. Tom Hayden, quoted in James Miller, *Democracy is in the Streets* (New York: Simon & Schuster, 1987), p. 16.

8. Michael Klein, 'Letter to Jane', *Film Quarterly*, Vol. XXVI, No. 5 (fall 1973), pp. 62–4. The article was written following discussions with Godard, after I had the good fortune to be able to arrange the US première of the film at Rutgers University in 1972.

9. Michael Klein, 'Filmography: Discourse of the Movement in the Vietnam Era', *Historical Journal of Film, Radio and Television* (October 1990). Also see discussions of oppositional cinema in: *Cineaste* ('Special Issue: Radical American Film'), Vol. V., No. 4 (1972); *Jump Cut* ('Special Section Film and Ideology'), No. 17 (1978).

10. James Roy McBean, 'The *Ice*-man Cometh No More', *Film Quarterly*, Vol. XXIV, No. 4 (summer 1971), pp. 26–33.

11. Michael Ryan and Douglas Kellner, *Camera Politica: The Politics and Ideology of Contemporary Hollywood Film* (Bloomington: Indiana University Press, 1988), p. 33.

12. Edward Bond, 'Introduction', *Bond: Plays Two* (London: Methuen, 1978), p. xv.

13. Gillo Pontecorvo, interviewed by Roger Ebert, *New York Times* (Sunday, 13 April 1969), pp. D 10–11.

14. Michael Klein, 'Burn!', *Film Quarterly*, Vol. XXV, No. 2 (winter 1971–2), pp. 55–6. Also in *Take One* (1972).

15. Billy the Kid, Pat Garrett, Wyatt Earp, Doc Halliday and Jessie James (amongst others) are encoded to play out roles in films that at one level are allegories of modern times. For example: *Billy the Kid* (1930, 1941); *The Lefthanded Gun* (1958); *My Darling Clementine* (1946); *Gunfight at the OK Corral* (1957); *Doc* (1970); *I Shot Jessie James* (1949); *The Great Northfield Minnesota Raid* (1977). See Will Wright, *Sixguns and Society: A Structural Study of the Western* (Berkeley: University of California Press, 1975); Philip French, *Westerns: Aspects of a Movie Genre* (London: Secker & Warburg, 1973); Kim Kitses, *Horizons West* (London: Thames and Hudson, 1969).

16. Terence Butler, *Crucified Heroes: The Films of Sam Peckinpah* (London: Fraser, 1979). Butler notes that Garrett 'betrays his friend ...

BEYOND THE AMERICAN DREAM 231

because of the disorientating impact of social forces', and observes that after the first ambush 'Billy stands before Garrett, his arms outstretched in a Christ-like gesture' (pp. 85, 90).

17. *Thief* was reviewed in the *New York Times* (Friday, 27 March 1981), p. C 12. There was no mention of the ideological significance of the dialogue of the film. Instead it was dismissed as 'excessive', 'abstract', and 'pretentious'. The ideology of the film is simply erased by the critic.

18. David Caute, *The Great Fear* (London: Secker & Warburg, 1978), pp. 30–1. Bernard Baruch described Truman's 12 March 1947 speech as 'tantamount to a declaration of ideological or religious war' (p. 30).

13. The Making of a Consensual Majority: Political Discourse and Electoral Politics in the 1980s

Michael X. Delli Carpini

The economic and political reforms begun in the United States during the 1930s and expanded during the 1960s and early 1970s represented a significant change in the relationship between government and citizens, shifting the boundary between public and private spheres of influence. Much of this expanded government was harnessed to benefit previously powerless groups, often in ways that violated the tenets of classical liberal democracy and free market capitalism. To some degree, this expansion of the state was accompanied by a parallel shift in the terms of public discourse (consider, for example, the imagery contained in a phrase like 'The Great Society'). In general, however, essentially socialist policies were justified using the rhetoric of liberalism: political reforms were defended in terms of individual rights, and economic reforms in terms of equal opportunity.[1] Indeed, some have argued that the reforms of the 1930s and the 1960s were designed to prevent a more conscious and comprehensive embrace of democratic socialism.[2]

The creation of a limited welfare state led to tangible gains for America's politically and economically disadvantaged classes. However, the failure openly to address the relationship among the often competing values of democracy, capitalism and socialism, coupled with the incremental, piecemeal nature of the reforms themselves, resulted in a double bind. Grafted on to essentially unchanged political and economic institutions, processes and values, the reforms were incapable of producing the 'Great Society' that was promised. By the late 1970s these limits were clear. Against the backdrop of 'stagflation', political and economic justice could no longer be sold as costless. No longer assured of the expanding economic pie that helped mask both the limits and the costs of many federal programmes, America needed to confront its half century *ménage à trois* with democratic capitalism and democratic socialism. However, the failure to develop a coherent justification for the socialist reforms of the past 50 years meant there was no 'public language' with which directly to defend them, let alone to advocate for more comprehensive change.

It was in this context that the elections of 1980, 1984 and 1988 took place. While political observers rightly lament the lack of substance in the American campaign process, an examination of these three presidential elections reveals a wealth of information that is, ironically, more useful today than it was during the campaigns themselves. Contained within the rhetoric and polispots are arguments and images that address, even if as parable, the major issues of the last half of the twentieth century. In essence these elections served as a series of referenda on the 'Old Left' politics of the 1930s and the 'New Left' politics of the 1960s and early 1970s.

For the reasons noted above, however, these referenda took place within a narrow ideological space that greatly handicapped attempts to defend the legacy of America's domesticated version of democratic socialism. For both the truly disadvantaged and the truly advantaged, these elections were firmly tied to material interests, a fact that is generally reflected in their voting behaviour during the 1980s. However, for working- and lower-middle-class citizens, teetering between the haves and the have nots, 'self interest properly understood' [3] is arrived at less easily. It is in appealing to this segment of the US electorate that the absence of a language with which adequately to present and defend a progressive agenda was most sorely felt.

Thus, when America addressed issues of race, class, gender, militarism and, ultimately, ideology in the 1980s, it was the right that set the terms of political discourse. Rather than presenting a coherent alternative to the vision of the past, present, and future conjured up by the Republicans, Democrats, for the most part, accepted these terms. And given that the political right and left in America are defined by the rhetoric of these two parties, the impact of this concession was to shrink 'the sphere of legitimate controversy',[4] while at the same time shifting the political centre to the right. That this should happen at an historical moment when the American left needed to expand public discourse on these issues has consequences that go well beyond which party controlled the presidency during the 1980s.

The Democratic victory in 1992 would seem to mark a shift of momentum back to a more progressive political agenda. In some important ways this is true. However, this shift in fortunes took place within a public sphere that had been dramatically altered by twelve years of conservative rhetoric. Viewed relative to the elections of 1980, 1984 and 1988, the election of 1992 represents a victory for the left in America. Viewed from a broader perspective, however, the victory rings more hollow. The late 1980s and early 1990s offered a unique opportunity to redefine the terms of political discourse in the United States. While it would be overly pessimistic to say that this opportunity has been lost, the

1992 election is at best a small step forward after three very large steps back.

In this chapter I explore the ways race, class, gender, foreign policy and ideology were defined during the 1980s. In doing so I try to connect that rhetoric to the voting behaviour of the American public and to the tangible gains and losses made by different segments of that public. My argument is that by controlling the terms of discourse, Republicans were able to construct a consensual majority, and thus to turn back many – though not all – of the gains made over the prior several decades. This conservative victory resulted in part from conditions specific to the 1980s, but ultimately represent the limits to political reforms that do not consciously address the underlying tension between the ideologies of liberal capitalism and economic democracy.

Jesse Jackson, Willie Horton and Race in America

Racial inequality has been an issue in American politics since a Dutch merchant sold a Virginia tobacco farmer 'twenty negars' in 1619.[5] Despite this constancy, issues of race have only periodically affixed themselves to the national political agenda. The late 1950s and early 1960s constituted such a period. The combination of an organized civil rights movement and a spontaneous revolt in the nation's inner cities led the courts, Congress and the Executive Branch to address issues of segregation, as well as of political and economic inequities between whites and blacks.

While the government's response might legitimately be described as too little too late, real gains were made. Between 1965 and 1975 the black infant mortality rate declined from 40.3 to 24.2 deaths per 1000 births.[6] Declines in the percentage of blacks living in substandard or overcrowded housing, begun in the 1940s, accelerated through the 1960s. The percentage of blacks living below the poverty line declined from 55 per cent in 1959 to 33 per cent in 1970. The median family income of blacks, 55 per cent that of white families in 1955, rose slightly to 60 per cent by 1971. In 1960, the average black 25 to 29 year old had completed 2.4 years less education than his or her white counterpart; by 1970 the difference had shrunk to 0.5 years. By 1970, 1977 of the 2702 school districts in the South had been desegregated. The percentage of Southern blacks registered to vote nearly tripled from 1955 to 1968, with black turnout following a similar if less dramatic increase. Largely as a result of these changes (and other federally mandated changes in state electoral laws), the number of blacks elected to government more than tripled during the 1960s and 1970s.

None of the statistics presented above suggests that America had successfully dealt with its *de jure* or *de facto* racial problems in the 1960s and 1970s. Blacks remained significantly less well off economically and politically, and were discriminated against in a variety of ways. As the beginning of a national effort to address racial inequality, this period held great promise. In retrospect, however, these improvements represent not a still-rising tide, but a highwater mark. For all the measures presented above, blacks are either no better off today, or are worse off, than they were 15 years ago. An 18-year-old black male in 1993 is more likely to be in jail than in college.

What accounts for this backslide? The declining economy of the late 1970s and early 1980s certainly led to a more fiscally conservative mind-set, yet this does not explain the exclusion of most blacks from the economic recovery of the last three-quarters of the 1980s.[7] An alternative explanation is found in the attitude among much of white middle America that enough had been done to 'level the playing field'. In its most extreme form, this view often devolved into a belief that blacks had become politically and economically advantaged *vis-à-vis* whites. This is not an inevitable conclusion for whites to have drawn, however. Public opinion data suggests that whites hold mixed, often contradictory views concerning race and civil rights in America. The dominance of conservative, even racist beliefs in the 1980s resulted in part from the ability of the Republican Party to exploit these beliefs, especially among whites most directly threatened by the economic and political gains made by blacks. This, coupled with the failure of mainstream proponents of civil rights to defend past reforms, led to a gradual shifting of public discourse on race during the 1980s. And with it came a shift in electoral support.

White electoral support for the Democratic Party's social agenda has always been tenuous: since Franklin Roosevelt, only one president has received a majority of the white vote in presidential elections. Significantly, however, this one president was Lyndon Johnson, a relatively vocal proponent of civil rights reforms in the 1960s. In the political environment of the 1960s, the Democratic Party's stand on race was in the mainstream. By the 1980s, however, this was no longer the case. In the 1980 and 1984 presidential elections, only slightly more than one in three whites voted Democratic.[8] This 'white flight' meant that blacks, once a pivotal group in the Democratic Party's presidential coalition, were no longer able to swing elections. In turn, issues of race were even less likely than usual to become part of the national agenda. Indeed, one of the legacies of Ronald Reagan was to make issues of race a political liability.

In one of the most effective examples of 1980s 'newspeak' Reagan and his campaign strategists succeeded in defining groups that argued or organized on the basis of race (as well as of class, gender and sexual preference) as 'special interests'. As a result, in the 1980 and 1984 presidential campaigns, race was very much a non-issue. The few attempts made by Democrats to challenge this (for example, when President Carter questioned the motives behind Reagan's launching his 1980 campaign in the deep South) backfired under charges of 'reverse discrimination'. Significantly, the most widely covered racial issue in the 1980 presidential campaign was an anti-semitic remark made by Jesse Jackson during the primaries.

This return of race to the realm of invisible politics characterized the Reagan years. Of course, when prominent elites (for example, Secretary of Agriculture Earl Butz) were caught making racial slurs, they were publicly punished. But rather than demonstrating the depth of racial stereotypes, these incidents (and public reaction to them) were interpreted as evidence that the United States was beyond the era of racial politics. The term 'discrimination' itself lost its unstated prepositional phrase 'of blacks by whites', and instead came to mean *any* discrimination. This, in turn, often meant the 'discrimination' of racial quotas, special hiring practices and other attempts to redress over 350 years of racial inequity. Of course, racial issues continued to be addressed periodically, most often in response to particularly brutal examples of racism, which, not coincidentally, were on the rise in the 1980s. As often as not, however, when racial issues emerged, they were presented by political elites and in the mainstream media as aberrations, or as the last vestiges of an outmoded attitude. The only open discussion of structural racism to occur during the Reagan years focused not on domestic politics, but on South African apartheid.

By the late 1980s, the combination of black economic distress and increasing racial conflict forced race back on to the national agenda. The context of this renewed attention was very different than in the 1950s and 1960s, however. As Carey McWilliams notes, by the 1980s 'legal segregation [was] a hazy memory, and ... in the media ... and hence in the view of most Americans – race [was] visible largely in relation to crime and the sleazier forms of interest group politics.' 9

Even news stories about white racism subtly devolved into stories about black racism. For example, in the late 1980s racial inequality, racially motivated attacks on blacks, and allegations of police brutality led local grassroots groups to organize several visible, often confrontational demonstrations in New York City. In ways reminiscent of media coverage of the anti-war movement of the 1960s,[10] the central story soon shifted from racial inequality to the more flamboyant, inflammatory behaviour of some black grassroots leaders. In the end, the motives and tactics of a few black leaders were used to discredit what was a very diverse black movement with a host of legitimate grievances.

It was in this context that the 1988 presidential campaign took place. Race was no longer invisible, but neither was it a major component of either party's political rhetoric. Instead, it served as a thinly veiled subtext to other political and social issues. The Democratic Party's (and so liberal America's) constrained discourse on race is best exemplified by the rise and fall of Jesse Jackson's primary campaign. Jackson finished second in the primaries, garnering 29 per cent of the vote to Michael Dukakis's 43 per cent. Nonetheless, the only group that supported Jackson over Dukakis were blacks, who cast 92 per cent of their votes for him. In contrast, only 12 per cent of white primary voters cast their ballots for Jackson. This racial split was not lost on the media, who continually covered Jackson as a candidate who could not win the Democratic nomination; a candidate who at best 'spoke' for blacks and at worst might be a liability for whomever did get the nomination. This split was also not lost on Dukakis, who subtly played up the racial issue by calling himself 'the inevitable' Democratic nominee. Both the decision *not* to choose Jackson as Dukakis's running mate, and to keep Jackson relatively invisible during the general election, further illustrates how race had become a liability for Democrats in the 1980s.

While race was a liability for the Democrats, it was an issue to be exploited by the Republicans. And exploit it they did. Bush spoke in the code words of racial discrimination, as had Republican candidates since Barry Goldwater, railing against crime, drugs and the liberal agenda. The skilful use of television images left no doubt about what the real issue was, however. In the infamous 'Willie Horton' campaign spot, viewers were shown a picture of a glaring black man who, while on prison furlough, had raped a white woman. Playing on the same racist stereotypes that fuelled groups like the Ku Klux Klan and the John Birch society, this campaign ad served as the lens through which campaign spots about crime and drugs were viewed, and with which seemingly neutral statements about these issues were decoded. It is not that the racist (as well as the factually misleading) elements of this ad were missed by the Democrats or the news media, both of whom cried foul. Nor was it that the public was inundated with the ad -- it was only shown regionally and for a few weeks of the campaign. To the contrary, the effectiveness of the ad came from its notoriety. By campaign's end, 60 per cent of the American public knew about the Willy Horton ad and the controversy surrounding it. The ad's power was in its ability to raise and define the issue of race (and so elicit racist sentiments) without Bush having to do so. And on election day white America voted for Bush 60 per cent to 40 per cent, while black America voted for Dukakis 86 per cent to 12 per cent.

The primary and general elections of 1988 proved to be accurate signposts for the direction racial politics would take in the late 1980s and early 1990s. Blacks continued to make some largely symbolic inroads in electoral politics, with Jesse Jackson winning the new House seat representing the District of Columbia, David Dinkins winning the mayoral race in New York City, and Douglas Wilder winning the governorship in Virginia. All three won by taking a majority of the black vote while losing a majority of the white vote, however. And all three, along with other black leaders of mainly urban areas, were given the helms of sinking ships, as the financial neglect of the 1980s took its toll. This, in turn, added to the perception that blacks, once elected, were unable to govern effectively. The vigour with which federal officials and the media publicly tried Marion Barry for his abuse of the public trust in the District of Columbia, especially in comparison to the relatively low profile given the corrupt behaviour of white Congressmen and Senators in the much more significant savings and loan scandal, exemplified the extent to which race continued to colour the way in which seemingly non-racial issues were interpreted.

The state of non-white America outside the electoral arena has been even less ambiguous. At this writing, poverty continues to plague people of colour at three to four times the rate it affects whites. Approximately half the black and Mexican-American female-headed households in the United States live in poverty, as do almost three-quarters of female-headed Puerto Rican families. Unemployment among blacks is four times that of whites, and as many as half of young black males are unable to find work. Poverty, unemployment and the resultant violent crime are especially concentrated in the inner cities of the United States, and so disproportionately fall on the shoulders of blacks and Hispanics. Deteriorating social services, especially in urban areas, has meant a rise in a variety of health problems: AIDS is significantly more common among blacks than whites, and in some inner cities nineteenth-century diseases like tuberculosis have approached epidemic proportions. The abuse of drugs like alcohol, heroin and crack, common if deadly means of escape for the poor and destitute, also disproportionately afflict blacks.

While the economic plight of blacks has reached crisis proportions, federal, state and local aid that indirectly benefits blacks continued to shrink during the Bush administration. Large, older cities were especially hard hit by this decline, lacking the resources to make up this lost revenue through increases in personal taxes, and being held hostage by companies that threatened to move if corporate taxes increased. Any attempt to address problems of racial inequality directly came under increasing attack from the White House. Under the rallying cries of 'reverse discrimination' and 'quotas', George Bush vetoed a 1990 civil rights bill designed to assure nondiscriminatory hiring practices. And the Education Department's Assistant Secretary for Human Rights, in a classic example of the new meaning of discrimination, ruled that scholarships designed to recruit minorities to college violated the Civil Rights Act prohibition of discrimination on the basis of race.

Lacking the language to defend government policy that *is* designed to give preferential treatment to blacks, and unwilling to pay the political price necessary to create this language, the Democratic Party contributed to the shrinking public discourse on race. For example, when reintroducing the civil rights legislation vetoed by Bush, Democrats downplayed its racial significance, calling it a 'women's rights bill'.[11] And, in an effort to distance themselves from the bogey of 'quotas', Democrats added language to the bill that explicitly banned the use of quotas, and took to calling the legislation an 'anti-quota bill'. As a result, rather than stimulating an open dialogue on race in the United States, the debate over this legislation devolved into a public shouting match over which party was *more* opposed to quotas.

Of course the great irony is that 'quotas' – in the worst sense of the word – continued to be used, though in increasingly cynical ways. This was dramatically illustrated by the nomination and eventual confirmation of Clarence Thomas to the Supreme Court seat vacated by the great champion of civil rights, Thurgood Marshall. Simply by nominating a black to replace Marshall, President Bush paralysed many Democrats into supporting Thomas, despite his less than stellar judicial record and his public stands against affirmative action, abortion and a number of other policies that had been part of the Democratic agenda during the 1960s and 1970s. While Thomas's nomination was in doubt, and while it drew tremendous public attention, it was revelations of improper personal behaviour, not larger issues of constitutional law, that fuelled this debate. Again we see the price paid by Democrats for not having fully established the logic and ethic of these civil – and economic – rights policies.

As government rhetoric closed off discussion of race in America, street-level race relations have continued to deteriorate. Cities are characterized by both *de facto* segregation and racial confrontation, and bias-related incidents continue to rise. Similar patterns in race relations are found on college and university campuses. With structural racism effectively defined out of the white political agenda, issues such as drug abuse and violent crime have become laden with racial subtexts. The increasingly hardline approach to these social problems, in which treatment and rehabilitation have given way to harsher penalties and more prisons, is at least partially motivated by white backlash. From the prosecution of teenage blacks, charged with raping a white, female investment banker in New York City, to the prosecution of the black rap group, Two Live Crew, for sexually explicit lyrics, punishment of young black males has become a symbolic spectator sport in contemporary America.

Many blacks, in an attempt to force their grievances on to the political agenda, have turned to more provocative leaders, rhetoric and action. Others, seeing little hope for consistent help from white dominated institutions, have opted for an increasingly separatist strategy.[12] However, seen through the lenses of the mainstream media, and couched in the language of liberal democracy, these approaches simply confirm white America's suspicions that blacks in America are misguided.

One final example illustrates the economic and political plight of blacks during the early 1990s, and the extent to which, more than two decades after the publication of the Kerner Report, the United States remains 'two societies, one black, one white – separate and unequal'.[13] In the midst of historic bailouts of the savings and loan and banking industries, the black-owned 'Freedom Bank' of Harlem was allowed to go out of business in 1990 without any federal assistance to the bank or its depositors beyond what was stipulated by the Federal Depositors Insurance Corporation. The federal government's decision was a financial one. If savings and loans in (white) Texas, or banks in (white) Connecticut fail, it could cause a panic that would spread throughout (white) America. The failure of the (black) Freedom Bank would cause no such run on money. In short, black America in 1990 was sufficiently separate and unequal that its financial problems would have no affect on white America.

Bluebloods, Bluecollars, and the Construction of Class

America's 'war on poverty', declared by Lyndon Johnson in 1964, was never very hard fought – by 1968 Johnson had turned his back on the recommendations of the Kerner commission, feeling they were too critical of his efforts to date. By 1968 he was also very much preoccupied by a war of different sorts in Vietnam. Nonetheless, the 1960s and 1970s did show a tangible effort to address problems of poverty in the USA. Between 1960 and 1979, the percentage of Americans living below the poverty line declined from over 18 per cent to under 7 per cent.[14] Programmes such as Aid of Families with Dependent Children (AFDC), Food Stamps, Medicare and Medicaid also improved the condition of America's poorest citizens. The percentage of poor people who had *never* visited a doctor declined from 19 per cent in 1963 to 8 per cent in

1970. The infant mortality rate among the poor fell by 33 per cent (the rate of decline was even greater for poor blacks). The percentage of Americans living in substandard housing fell from 35 per cent in 1950 to 8 per cent in 1976. Participants in programmes such as the Manpower Development and Training Act (MDTA) and the Comprehensive Employment and Training Act (CETA) had lower levels of unemployment and earned higher wages than their untrained brothers and sisters. Poor children who participated in project Head Start were 60 per cent less likely to be assigned to special education classes, 45 per cent less likely to be held back a grade, and scored several points higher on standardized IQ tests than their classmates who did not participate in the programme.

These modest inroads among the truly disadvantaged do not, of course, indicate anything like economic equality in the United States. Income distribution remained largely unaltered during this period, with the richest 20 per cent of America's wage-earners controlling between 41 per cent and 44 per cent of the nation's yearly income, while the poorest 20 per cent consistently brought home only 5 per cent of that gross income. Nonetheless, some indications of a changing distribution of wealth existed. Perhaps most significantly, the percentage of wealth controlled by America's richest half per cent declined from 25 per cent in 1965 to 14 per cent in 1976 – the lowest per cent recorded in the twentieth century.

The election of Ronald Reagan marked a decided turn in America's approach to the rich and poor. Running unabashedly against the 'welfare state', Reagan couched his class arguments in the language of populism, the work ethic and the trickle-down theory of the distribution of wealth. Throughout the Reagan era critics charged that national economic and social policy was a thinly veiled effort to aid the rich at the expense of the less well off. However, in the rhetorical environment of the 1980s these arguments were unconvincing and fell, for the most part, on deaf ears. Nonetheless, the evidence bears them out with unrelenting consistency.

In 1980, the average salary for CEOs in the United States was 25 times what an average blue-collar worker earned – hardly evidence of economic equality. By 1990, however, this ratio had jumped to almost 100 to 1. Between 1980 and 1988 the number of millionaires, decamillionaires and centimillionaires in the United States tripled, while the number of billionaires went from under ten to over 50. Between 1977 and 1988 only the richest 20 per cent of American families had incomes that increased in constant dollar terms. Over this period the average income of 80 per cent of American families declined in real terms by over US$1,000, while the income of the wealthiest 10 per cent increased by US$16,913 (the *increase* for the richest 1 per cent was a staggering

US$134,513 a year). By the mid-1980s the richest half per cent of America saw their share of the national wealth jump back up to 27 per cent – the greatest percentage since 1939. And while the rich got richer, the poor got poorer. During the 1980s the overall poverty rate in the United States returned to where it was prior to the War on Poverty, while record numbers of the elderly, women and children entered the ranks of the poor.

'Where a person's treasure is', said Congressman William Gray, quoting from scripture, 'there you'll find his heart.' [15] The 1988 campaign, pitting the blueblood lines of George Herbert Walker Bush against Michael Dukakis's immigrant, blue-collar past, served both symbolically and in real terms as a referendum on the Reagan philosophy, unmasked from the disarming, bumbling style of 'the great communicator'. It was also another referendum on the now modified New Deal/ Great Society politics of the Democratic Party. The class element in this campaign went beyond bloodlines. Bush's embrace of Reaganomics, his emphasis on voluntarism (characterized by his theme of 'a thousand points of light'), his pledge of no new taxes, and his support for a cut in the capital gains tax, all clearly presented his vision of America to America. And Dukakis's platform and rhetoric, while interspersed with the language of managerial efficiency, and while toned down in response to Bush's successful attacks on 'liberalism' (discussed below), was still very much in line with the New Deal/Great Society rhetoric that defined the Democratic coalition.

Significantly, in this referendum the Republican Party did less well than it had in the 1984 presidential race, with Bush drawing 54 per cent of the two party vote (compared to 59 per cent for Reagan in 1984) and Dukakis drawing 46 per cent (compared to Mondale's 41 per cent). Nonetheless, this election, even more than the 1980 or 1984 elections, clearly demonstrated the split between rich and poor in the United States. A list of the only demographic groups to give a majority of its support to Dukakis reads like a litany of America's politically, socially, and/or economically disadvantaged: blacks (86 per cent), Hispanics (69 per cent), those earning under US$10,000 a year (64 per cent), Jews (64 per cent), the unemployed (62 per cent), residents of large cities (58 per cent), unmarried women (57 per cent), union households (57 per cent), those without a high school diploma (56 per cent), those earning between US$10,000 and US$19,999 a year (53 per cent), teachers and students (52 per cent), and blue-collar workers (51 per cent). At the same time, Bush's strongest support came from white fundamentalists (81 per cent) or white protestants more generally (66 per cent), Southern whites (67 per cent), those earning over US$40,000 a year (62 per cent), married men (60 per cent), professionals and managers (59 per cent), those between 45 and 59 years old (57 per cent), and those with some college or a college degree (57 per cent).

These statistics suggest that those with easily identified class interests – those groups who most clearly won or lost economically during the Reagan years – voted those interests in the 1988 presidential election. But what about the not insignificant proportion of the voting public whose interests were more ambiguous? As noted above, the real income of fully 80 per cent of American families declined during the ten years prior to 1988. For many of these voters, who they voted for depended in large part on how they defined themselves and how they defined the clientele of the Democratic and the Republican parties. And here again the limited terms of political discourse advantaged the Republicans. The penchant for all but the poorest and richest Americans to consider themselves 'middle class' is not new, but the perception of this middle-class existence changed significantly in the 1980s. The norm was no longer defined by the blue-collar row houses of the 1930s and 1940s, nor even by the modest suburban tracts of the 1950s and 1960s. The 'imperial middle', as defined since the late 1970s, has had a decidedly upper-middle-class character.[16] It is not that most Americans *actually* live this upper-middle-class existence, nor even that most of them *believe* that they do. Instead it is that the vast majority of Americans identify with this lifestyle, aspire to it, and believe (perhaps fantasize is the more appropriate word) that it is within their reach or the reach of their children.

This distorted self-identification has implications for political rhetoric, and for how this rhetoric is received. Again the range of discourse is constrained as appeals not aimed at the imperial middle are viewed with suspicion. However, the misidentification of most people with the upper middle class means that the objective interests of most Americans are not addressed. Policies that most directly advantage the wealthiest 10 or 20 per cent of the population are successfully packaged as benefiting the 'average' American. At the same time, policies that are far more likely to improve the lot of *real* middle Americans (let alone those on the lower rungs of the economic ladder) are rejected out of hand. Nowhere is this clearer than in the 1980s debate over taxation. The evidence clearly establishes that income tax cuts have disproportionately benefited the wealthiest segments of America, while increases in 'flat' taxes (gasoline, alcohol and tobacco taxes, sales taxes and lotteries) disproportionately fall on the shoulders of the lower middle class and below. Nonetheless, the rhetoric of 'no new taxes' won the day for both Ronald Reagan and George Bush throughout the 1980s. Indeed, Walter Mondale's acknowledgement that he would raise taxes if elected president in 1984 was viewed as political suicide within the limited confines of political discourse in the 1980s.

The implications of the 'upscaling' of middle America's self-image were especially apparent in the 1988 presidential campaign. In many ways the election was similar to most that have occurred since the New Deal. The election hinged on which party could most successfully appeal to middle America. On the one hand, Michael Dukakis had to convince the American public that George Bush and the Republicans were representatives of the rich, and so not in touch with the needs of middle America. Bush, on the other hand, had to convince them that Dukakis and the Democrats were the party of the 'deserving poor' and other marginal groups, and so out of touch with the needs of middle America. Where a majority of Americans would align themselves if they 'properly understood' their self-interest is an open question, but the illusion of the imperial middle made this issue moot: in a choice between Michael Dukakis's and George Bush's images of middle America, the latter rung more true in the discourse of the 1980s.

The four years of the Bush administration clearly demonstrated which class interests were served by his election. Significant in both symbolic and real terms, his Secretaries of State, Treasury, and Commerce were 'graduates of the best private schools, second- or third-generation multimillionaires with a collective net worth of about $250 million'.[17] While agreeing to a modestly regressive tax increase, President Bush continued to hold the line against progressive income tax reform. Unable – for political and economic reasons – to raise corporate or income taxes, state governments continued to shift the tax burden to those least able to bear it through regressive measures like sales tax, gas tax, lotteries, and so forth.[18] While unable to convince Congress, Bush continued to lobby for a cut in the capital gains tax. Federal aid to social programmes, the cities, education and so forth continued to decline relative to inflation, while almost inconceivable amounts of money were allocated to bail out the savings and loan and banking industries. And while a deep recession hit all sectors of the US economy, those who never recovered from the recession of 1982 were driven even deeper into poverty and despair. As Kevin Phillips notes,

> ... the America Bush truly represented was that of old multigenerational wealth – of trust funds, third-generation summer cottages on Fischer's Island and grandfathers with Dillon Read or Brown Brothers Harriman – which accepted the economic policy of the Reagan era despite its distaste for its arriviste values ... The Republicans had evolved from 'cloth coat' Middle Americanism under Richard Nixon to aggressive new-money capitalism under Ronald Reagan and finally to the old-money, Episcopal establishment under George Herbert Walker Bush.[19]

In the midst of this continued dismantling of the welfare state and the steady rise in poverty, attitudes continued to harden regarding crime and drug use. Entering the 1990s, the United States led the industrial world in the percentage of its population that was in jail. Punishment rather than rehabilitation has become the goal of criminal justice. Talk of root causes for poverty and crime are more likely to mean genetic than social, and references to the 'deserving' poor hearken back to the social darwinism and draconian policies of the nineteenth century. In this constrained ideological space, liberal defences of the welfare state take on a hollow, unrealistic ring.

Gender Politics, Gender Economics, and the New Traditionalism

As with blacks and the poor, the struggles for women's political, economic, and social liberation are closely intertwined. In the colonial era, the right to participate in politics was tied to the ownership of property.[20] Since few women legally controlled the wealth they helped produce, formal political participation – either through voting or holding public office – was rare. Nonetheless, since women did occasionally hold title to land (most often through inheritance or through the death of husbands) political participation by women was not unheard of prior to the formation of the United States. Ironically, the revolution for independence in 1776 set in motion the loss of even those limited political rights. The constitution of the United States left it to the states to determine who was eligible to vote. Property restrictions were maintained in most states, but these restrictions were at first reduced, and by the 1830s, essentially eliminated. With the loss of this *de facto* barrier to the vast majority of women, the states faced the issue of women's suffrage directly. Their response was *explicitly* to limit the franchise to males. Despite an active role by women in the abolitionist movement and a vocal suffragette movement in the late nineteenth century, not until 1920 were women granted the right to vote throughout the United States.

Of course the winning of this formal right was only one step in the larger emancipation of women. Key to this emancipation was the ability to gain control of their labour. While women had always worked, their work was tied to the household – working the family farm, giving birth and raising children, doing domestic chores, and so forth. As such, women's experience with and authority in the 'public' realm was limited. In addition, the equating of public with political, a central tenet of liberal democracy, further discounted the civic worth of women. Initially, the ability of women to escape the confines of home resulted from larger social forces – most often war. Just prior to the Second World War, about 25 per cent of women worked outside the home. During the war, 6 million women took jobs for the first time. And, despite successful efforts to force women out of the workplace after the war, in 1950 34 per cent of women were still working outside the home.[21]

The 1960s and 1970s were critical, if only partially successful, decades for the women's movement. Between 1960 and 1980 the per cent of women working outside the home rose from 38 per cent to 52 per cent, the largest increase in any 20-year period in US history. During this period, female voter turnout (relative to men) continued to rise, with women accounting for over half the votes cast in a presidential election for the first time in 1980. Only 35 per cent of those graduating from college in 1960 were women, but by 1971 this had increased to 42 per cent, and by the early 1980s more women than men were graduating from college. The number of single women increased in the 1960s and 1970s. Birth rates, which had risen dramatically after the Second World War, began to decline in the late 1950s, and remained low throughout the 1960s and 1970s. This latter trend was aided when, in 1960, the Food and Drug Administration approved the birth control pill.

Increasingly freed from the home, women took active leadership roles in a number of the civil rights and New Left organizations that formed in the 1960s. In addition, the number of grassroots and government organizations devoted exclusively to women increased. In 1964, aware that women needed to be organized *as women* if they were going to have their agenda addressed by the political system, the National Organization for Women (NOW) was formed. And while the Presidential Commission on the Status of Women, established by President Kennedy, ultimately concluded that an equal rights amendment was not necessary, it did draw national attention to 'problems of discrimination in employment, unequal pay, lack of social services such as childcare, and continuing legal inequality'.[22] In 1963 Kennedy issued a presidential order requiring that civil service hires be made 'without regard to sex'. In that same year Congress passed the Equal Pay Act, which required private employers to provide equal pay for the same work.[23]

By the 1970s, the women's movement was the dominant social movement in the United States. Having had their agenda and their participation marginalized in many of the male-dominated New Left organizations, the feminist movement struck off on its own. As the movement grew, its agenda expanded. While entrance of women into the public world remained a goal, feminists also came to argue that the personal was political. Increasingly, the women's movement saw and developed the links between feminism and issues such as class, race, sexual preference and militarism. The result was a much more heterogeneous, less middle-class movement.

As in the 1960s, the movement could point to tangible, if limited, results. In 1972 Congress passed Title IX of the Higher Education Act, which prohibited sexual discrimination in any education programme receiving federal aid. The enforcement capacity and jurisdiction of the Equal Employment Opportunity Commission was expanded. And the tax codes were changed to allow working parents to deduct childcare costs. In 1973 the women's movement won what is arguably its greatest victory when the Supreme Court handed down its abortion decision in Roe vs. Wade.

As with both race and class, these victories constituted only the beginnings of a move towards a just society. Throughout this period, women continued to earn only 60 per cent of what men did, largely because women remained disproportionately in less valued and less well-paid jobs. The Equal Rights Amendment, passed by Congress in 1972, fell several states short of ratification. While the number of women elected to local office increased, their representation in Congress remained a paltry 4 per cent. The ability to work outside the home often came in addition to maintaining primary responsibilities for raising the family, doing the housework, and so forth. The vast majority of single-parent households were headed by women, adding to the financial and psychological burdens of working women. In a workplace and society unprepared to address these issues, women in general and women heads of households in particular made up a disproportionate segment of the poor.

At best, the 1980s represented a holding period for the feminist movement. While women continued to vote, attend college and work outside the home at relatively high rates, few tangible gains were achieved in the workplace or the political arena. The election of Ronald Reagan, supported as he was by the fundamentalist New Right, signalled a shift away from the feminist agenda of the 1960s and 1970s. The new conservative social agenda, claiming to be pro-family, pro-life and pro-traditional values, was a thinly veiled attempt to turn back the clock on gains made by women. Women continued to win symbolic victories such as the appointment of Sandra Day O'Connor to the Supreme Court and the vice presidential nomination of Geraldine Ferraro, but the substantive battles in the workplace, the voting booths, the courts and in Congress were being lost with greater frequency. Court decisions regarding Title IX, and Congressional limitations on federal funding for abortion, limited the scope of gains made in the 1970s. Legitimate concern over issues of child abuse, drop-out rates, teenage pregnancy and juvenile crime were twisted in subtle and not so subtle ways so as to be blamed on the changes wrought by the women's movement. The term feminism itself began to take on a negative connotation, even among those who supported its goals. Women's organizations were put increasingly on the defensive, having to devote time and resources to the maintenance of gains already made rather than to the pursuit of new ones. The few new initiatives developed during the 1980s, such as comparable worth, were met with great scepticism and resulted in only marginal, local success.

Women themselves, never as homogeneous a political block as other disadvantaged groups, were torn by the Reagan counter-revolution. Nonetheless, in general women were less likely to support the conservative agenda or to vote for Ronald Reagan. In 1980, for example, 47 per cent of women voted for Reagan, compared to 55 per cent of men. In 1984 the percentage of women supporting Reagan had increased to 57 per cent, though this was still less than the 61 per cent of men who did. Unmarried and/or working women were a good deal less likely to vote for Reagan than married women and/or women who worked at home. Women were also less supportive than men of many of the conservative social and economic programmes of the Reagan administration. To the extent that any group supported the New Left agenda during the 1980s, it was women.

George Bush's personal attitudes about women were on record as early as 1984, when he announced, prior to his debate with Geraldine Ferraro, that he was going to 'kick a little ass'. In the 1988 campaign, while distancing himself somewhat from the populist far right, he opposed abortion and favoured the overturning of Roe vs. Wade. As much as through policy stands and campaign rhetoric, however, the 'new traditionalism' evident in the late 1980s could be seen through the popularity of Barbara Bush. In many ways she was the consummate pre-1960s woman: a housewife who devoted herself to her children and to her husband's career. There was little need for George Bush to articulate his view of women or of their roles in society. His view and his party's view (which had removed support for an equal rights amendment from its national platform in the 1980s) was expressed best and most accurately through the image of his wife. Indeed, in a campaign process lacking the language or means openly to discuss core issues such as the role of women, public comparisons between the 'liberated' Kitty Dukakis and the 'old-fashioned' Barbara Bush served as surrogates for public debate.

Michael Dukakis, fearing a conservative backlash, downplayed his pro-choice, pro-women stands. In this muted public discourse, in which the logic and ethic of women's liberation went largely undefended, the American public chose George (and Barbara) Bush, 53 per cent to 47 per cent. More significantly, of the 20 per cent of the electorate (as measured in exit polls) who considered abortion one of the most important issues of the election, 63 per cent voted for Bush. As a group, women were less supportive of Bush (50 per cent) than were men (57 per cent). Unmarried women, especially likely to be adversely affected by the new traditionalism, supported Dukakis by a 57 per cent to 42 per cent margin. It is difficult to know what difference a more forceful defence of women's liberation might have made to the Dukakis campaign – a case could be made that the differences between the two candidates and parties were clear by election day. Nonetheless, evidence of the potential of the gender gap can be seen by looking at early support for the two candidates. In May of 1988, when Dukakis was more aggressively advocating women's issues, males were split evenly between Bush and Dukakis in public opinion polls. Women, however, supported Dukakis 53 per cent to 35.

Once again the 1988 campaign proved an accurate marker of what was to come. Executive orders banned the use of US foreign aid (both directly to individual countries and through contributions to UN organizations) for information about, or the performance of, abortions. In the Webster case, the Supreme Court chipped away significantly at the foundations of Roe vs. Wade. Throughout the 1980s Congress had prohibited the use of federal funds for abortions, but in the 1991 Rust case, the Supreme Court upheld the executive order preventing counsellors at federally funded family planning clinics from even mentioning abortion as an option for dealing with a pregnancy. Significantly, George Bush's appointee to the Supreme Court, David Souter, was the critical vote in that decision. Bolstered by these decisions and by the president's vocal support, anti-abortion groups increased their activities, and numerous state legislators introduced increasingly conservative abortion legislation. Despite the mobilization of numerous pro-choice groups against this reactionary movement, such limiting legislation has passed in several states. The ruling in 'Planned Parenthood vs. Casey' (1992) suggests that this Republican-appointed Court is willing to stop short of overturning Roe vs. Wade, but it also reinforced the right of states to legislate restrictions that did not impose 'undue burdens' on the women seeking abortions. In addition, the timing of this decision – during a presidential election year – and the slim majority on which the decision rests, make it difficult to know what the long-term plans of this Court actually are. Regardless of the ultimate outcome, however, the mere fact of this debate demonstrates the extent to which the gains of the 1960s and 1970s were under attack in the 1980s and early 1990s.

Though in a different way, the nomination of Clarence Thomas to the Supreme Court was as significant for women as for blacks. His stands on abortion and affirmative action were serious threats to a number of gains made by women during the 1970s. And the televised, often torturous hearings regarding Anita Hill's accusations of sexual harassment drew unprecedented public attention to this usually ignored problem. The public discourse generated by those hearings, and the visible evidence of the price paid by women (and blacks) for their underrepresentation in government, played a major role in mobilizing women in the 1992 elections. As such it serves as a hopeful reminder of the public's ability to respond politically and communally to perceived injustices. Nonetheless, it is important to remember that immediately following the hearings, majorities of men and women, blacks and whites, supported Thomas over Hill. And, in the end, Clarence Thomas was confirmed to the Supreme Court.

Setbacks for women have come in other arenas as well. The continued rise in poverty, the cutbacks in already limited social spending, the general downturn in the economy -- all disproportionately affected women. The domestic violence and crime that inevitably increases in hard economic times also fell most heavily on women. And, as US and international industry attempts to subvert and sidestep union contracts and government regulation, the most tedious, dangerous and low-paying work continues to be shipped out to the Third World, where, again, women are most likely to be exploited.

Flags, Tanks and a Kinder, Gentler Nation

US public opinion concerning foreign affairs generally and military intervention more specifically has always been a curious mix of isolationism and jingoism. In general, Americans oppose the use of troops abroad, but this tendency, with few exceptions, is easily overwhelmed by appeals to patriotism, self-interest and the horrific nature of the enemy. Whether that enemy is 'godless communism', 'a tin-pot dictator' or 'Hitler incarnate', this villainization allows the strategic, ideological and economic reasons for intervention to be viewed as moral ones. This mentality is especially easy to evoke when the enemy is culturally, religiously and ethnically different from the white, European, Christian, middle-class elite that still defines America's increasingly inaccurate self-image.

As the only conflict in US history to be opposed by a majority of Americans *while* troops were engaged in combat, the Vietnam War stands out as a notable, if only partial, exception to this pattern.[24] That public opinion turned against the war in 1968 is clear. Between November 1967 and February 1968 those believing the US was making progress in the war dropped from 51 per cent to 32. By late March 1968 President Johnson's approval rating had fallen to 26 per cent, a 13 point drop in less than five months. By April 1968, a majority of Americans opposed the war for the first time. Public agreement that the United States had made a mistake in sending troops into Vietnam went from 39 per cent in late 1967 to 52 per cent in early 1969.[25] This unprecedented loss of support resulted from a variety of factors: genuine concern about the war's morality; growing horror at the human cost of war as portrayed on television; a sense that the war was either unwinnable or would be too costly in American lives and money to win; and a desire to end the increasing tension at home.

The Vietnam era profoundly influenced the ways in which the general public, political leaders and military people think about war. As with many of the changes that occurred as a result of the 1960s, however, little open, constructive dialogue took place. Indeed, so complex, intense and ambiguous were the feelings resulting from America's defeat, that immediate public reaction was to repress, rather than reflect on, the experiences and lessons of Vietnam.[26] The result was a political vacuum, interspersed with disconnected, often contradictory beliefs, attitudes and opinions, concerning the role of force in foreign relations.

The first serious attempt to fill this vacuum was made during the Carter administration. Building more off the public's weariness than its active support, Carter implemented many of the foreign policies advocated by the New Left. Covert action and limited warfare were no longer the central tools for achieving US goals abroad. The US developed a relatively coherent human rights policy, which was integrated into its larger foreign policy. Defence spending declined, as did the sale of armaments to foreign nations. The US also allowed nations and regions greater autonomy in settling their own internal disputes, and attempted to integrate its foreign policies into a global, international framework.

The Vietnam era provided the left with a rare opportunity to shift public discourse on foreign policy. Even this modest shift was short-lived, however. The 'stagflation' of the late 1970s (created in part by OPEC's oil embargo), the Iranian hostage crisis, and the Soviet invasion of Afghanistan, were quickly interpreted by both Democratic and Republican leaders as the failure of Carter's well-intentioned but naive approach to foreign affairs.

The failure of the left fully to exploit the opportunity provided by the

Vietnam era allowed the right to regain control of the political agenda. This shifting discourse could be seen in the cultural politics of the 1980s. The brief reign of the 'anti-hero' – the 1960s' and early 1970s' somewhat nihilistic response to the Vietnam era – ended, replaced by a growing machismo. The Vietnam 'revenge' film, exemplified by the series of *Rambo* movies, became popular. [27] Movies like *Top Gun*, little more than multi-million-dollar advertisements for the armed services, fuelled a growing infatuation with the military. The victory of the US hockey team over the Soviets in the 1980 winter Olympics was covered like a surrogate military victory over this arch-enemy, while the 1984 Olympics, set appropriately in Los Angeles, became one long, colourful commercial for America. The increasingly reactionary approach to domestic politics (discussed above) dovetailed nicely with this new 'macho' mentality.

Ronald Reagan, his image crafted more by his movies than his political past, was a key to translating this cultural and social conservatism into public policy. His patriotic 'get tough' attitude proved the perfect panacea for a nation unable to accept a changing world order. During Reagan's tenure, military spending increased dramatically, as did the willingness to use it. Indeed, the eight years between America's final withdrawal from Vietnam and Reagan's stationing of Marines in Beirut increasingly seem a mere respite from 40 years of US military intervention in Third World nations.

The deployment of US troops in Lebanon proved a misguided flexing of muscle that resulted in the largest loss of US troops since Vietnam. Such a disaster could easily have been interpreted as evidence of the limits of military solutions to international problems. However, within days of the attack on the Marine barracks in Beirut, US troops invaded Grenada, silencing critics as Democrats and Republicans 'rallied round the flag'. Presented with photographs and news copy orchestrated by the military, and given little reason to question the necessity, legality or morality of the invasion, Americans applauded this long-sought military victory.

Reagan next set his sights on Nicaragua. Unlike Grenada, however, the administration faced substantial Congressional and public opposition to direct military intervention. This opposition provides an important example of both the ambiguous, malleable nature of the public's new-found militarism, and the difficulty in translating specific points of resistance into a more general critique of military intervention with a more coherent oppositional ideology. Numerous grassroots organizations in the United States opposed intervention in Central America, and were able, within limits, to get this message to the general public and to members of Congress. While many of these groups had fairly sophisticated critiques of the situation, and saw the struggles in Nicaragua (and

El Salvador) as part of a larger set of issues, it was seldom on these ideological grounds that the case was made to the American public. For strategic reasons, it was assumed that neither the general public nor a majority of Congresspeople would oppose the administration's Nicaraguan policy on broad, philosophic grounds. In essence, the lack of a language with which to debate such issues (as well as the lack of public arenas in which to debate them in any serious way) meant that the argument would have to be made on a more visceral, case-specific basis. In the case of Nicaragua, this symbolic 'hook' was Vietnam.

By and large this strategy was successful. Despite concerted efforts by the Reagan administration to convince them otherwise, the American public saw this fight as too similar to Vietnam: the vague, ideological justifications for intervention; the domestic nature of the dispute between the Sandinistas and the Contras; the gradual escalation of US involvement; the jungle terrain; the likelihood of a protracted engagement.

Given an environment in which 'legitimate' spokespersons provided alternatives to intervention in ways that struck a responsive chord, the public was capable of opposing the use of military force abroad. Absent a more comprehensive, informed and reasoned logic, however, there was little likelihood that the public's specific opposition to the use of US force in Nicaragua would lead to a rethinking of other aspects of foreign policy. The Reagan administration quickly (and correctly) concluded that, while the public would support quick, decisive military excursions, it still suffered from 'the Vietnam syndrome'. In the short run, US military objectives in Nicaragua (and elsewhere) would require the use of surrogate troops and, ultimately, covert actions. The United States could arm the Contras, the Afghanistan rebels, the El Salvadoran death squads and the like, and could provide military advisers and technical assistance to them, but the US public, much to the dismay of political and military leaders, was still gun shy. Direct military action would have to be limited to relatively defenceless opponents and/or to quick strikes (e.g. the bombing of Libya).

The Irancontra affair resulted, in part, from the administration's failure to mobilize public support for US military intervention in Nicaragua.[28] The resulting scandal did some damage to the Reagan presidency. It also provided an opportunity for rethinking the rightward lurch of US foreign policy. However, the absence of investigative reporting in the mainstream press, the relative lack of public outrage, the momentary hero-status of Oliver North, the aborted criminal cases, and the lack of direct fallout for either Ronald Reagan or George Bush, instead signalled a general resignation as to the inevitability of such actions, setting the stage for an even more aggressive foreign policy.

As with the other policy areas discussed in this essay, the 1988 election provides ample evidence for this atavism. George Bush, while only a few years older than Michael Dukakis, was, unlike Dukakis, old enough to have served in the Second World War. His worldview was very much shaped by that experience, and by the Cold War mentality that dominated the following four decades. He was a former director of the CIA. He was clearly involved at some level in the covert operations surrounding the Irancontra dealings. During his campaign he appealed to the lowest forms of blind patriotism with his visits to flag factories and his attack on Dukakis's veto of a 'pledge of allegiance' bill in Massachusetts. He also played up his military past, using film footage of his rescue-at-sea during the Second World War in his television campaign.

Dukakis, though running on a much less militarist platform, quickly tried to out-macho Bush. In the process, he not only lost credibility with the voters, but he unwittingly helped shrink the already narrow range of discourse on foreign policy. His visit to a military base, where he rode about in a tank, backfired so badly that film footage of his joy ride was used in *Bush* commercials. Dukakis also fed the growing jingoism by playing on American fears of foreign (especially Arab and Asian) ownership of US businesses and property, and by constantly alluding to Bush's cosy relationship with Manuel Noriega. Even the media's fascination with Bush's 'wimpiness' and Dukakis's diminutive physical stature fuelled the growing machismo in America.

Particularly revealing was the controversy surrounding Dan Quayle's avoidance of combat in Vietnam by enlisting in the Indiana National Guard. Quayle was the first 'Vietnam generation' politician to be nominated for so visible an office. As such, it marked an important stage in America's public reconsideration of that era. That the central controversy raised by his nomination was his *failure* to fight, strongly indicates the extent to which public discourse over the war in Vietnam had been captured by the right. This shift is also seen in the negative publicity generated by the 'allegations' that Kitty Dukakis participated in anti-war protests during the early 1970s.

In the end, the campaigns of *both* Michael Dukakis and George Bush addressed foreign policy and defence issues in a way that legitimized the hardline approach of the 1980s. I am not, of course, arguing that the 1988 campaign presented the American public with an open, informative debate on foreign policy and defence issues. It did, however, symbolically address these issues in ways that established George Bush's hardline credentials. And this message was not missed by the public. Within this constrained dialogue, George Bush and the Republicans were at a decided advantage. 'National defence' was the second most frequent issue mentioned by voters in the 1988 election, when asked in exit polls to explain their vote. And of those that mentioned this issue, an astounding 84 per cent voted for Bush.

A Second World War fighter pilot who once headed the CIA, and who was fighting to live down the reputation of being a wimp, is a dangerous combination for a commander-in-chief. Not surprisingly, it wasn't long before US soldiers were back fighting in the Third World. The invasion of Panama represented a new phase in the return to limited warfare that had begun during the Reagan administration. The enemy was slightly more formidable and the legitimacy of the action less clear (there was, for example, no 'invitation' from neighbouring countries, as there had been in the Grenada invasion). Again, however, the invasion was met with strong support from the American public. Unlike Reagan's failure to mobilize support against Nicaragua, Bush successfully built a consensus for the use of American troops. Throughout the 1988 campaign, and, even more so during the first months of 1989, the Bush administration painted Manuel Noriega as a drug-selling, mad, ruthless dictator. Using the combination of tight media controls and relatively quick military action that had been so successful in Grenada, popular opinion was rallied around the new president's use of force. The invasion of Panama was less 'clean' than Grenada's had been – the fighting lasted longer, there were more civilian casualties, Noriega proved somewhat more difficult to capture than had been expected, and almost four years after the invasion, thousands of US troops remain in Panama. Nonetheless, the invasion was an unqualified political success.

Despite the use of force in Panama, events in Eastern Europe and the Soviet Union raised hopes that the major source of international tension over the last 40 years was waning. The way in which these events were interpreted is instructive. The rapid collapse of 'hardline' Communist regimes could have generated several public dialogues: Was the Soviet Union the military and economic threat the American public was led to believe over the past 35 years? What were the successes and failures of this particular variant of Communism, and might there be lessons that would be instructive not only for the East, but for the West as well?

Of course, the world events of 1989 and 1990 were *actually* interpreted in the United States through the myopic lenses fashioned during the 1980s. The 'collapse of Communism' simply reinforced the 'triumph of capitalism'. Complex events in Eastern Europe and the Soviet Union were treated as simple and homogeneous, while at the same time no connections were drawn between events there and those in Africa, South and Central America, or the United States. Strikes in Soviet coal mines were covered widely in the US press, put forth as evidence of their struggle for 'freedom', while striking coal miners in Kentucky and West

Virginia went largely unnoticed and, when covered, were presented as emblematic of the failed strategy of unions in the United States. The defeats of Communists in elections in Eastern Europe were extensively covered, while the successes of socialists in South American elections were ignored.[29] The opportunity for the United States to participate constructively in both an international and domestic dialogue was lost.

In the end, rather than diminishing the probability of US military action, the breakup of the Eastern bloc actually increased it. The use of military force was becoming the only way in which the administration could assert its will overseas and divert public attention from the increasing number of seemingly intractable problems at home. The political and economic upheaval in the Soviet Union, Eastern Europe and China led to great uncertainty concerning the future balance of world power, adding to the administration's sense of urgency in controlling those events. However, economic pressure, once America's alternative to military force, was increasingly ineffective as Japan, a united Germany and a restructured European Community presented formidable economic and political rivals. In addition, despite the Soviet Union's own problems, Mikhail Gorbachev had become the dominant political leader on the international scene, shaping world opinion in ways usually reserved for US presidents. Finally, the 'end of the Cold War' also meant that a very large American military (and the sizeable weapons industry that had built up around it) was looking for new ways to earn its keep. For a short while the administration continued to focus on Latin America, this time using the military to take the war on drugs overseas. This policy failed to garner the kind of public support generated by the invasions of Grenada and Panama, however, and also lacked the international visibility necessary to thrust the United States back into the centre of international politics. The Panama invasion had demonstrated the value of creating an identifiable villain so as to build and maintain public support for the use of military force.[30] In August of 1990, Saddam Hussein, the 'new Hitler', provided George Bush with just such a villain.

While it is clear that Hussein's invasion of Kuwait was a serious violation of international law, it is also clear that, from the start, George Bush's strategy was aimed at the use of military force. The US made little effort to find a diplomatic solution to the rising tensions between Iraq and Kuwait in the first half of 1990.[31] Once Iraq invaded Kuwait, however, the administration set off on an intransigent policy seemingly designed to prevent negotiation from working. International efforts on the part of the US were all focused exclusively on putting together, through economic and political incentives and threats, a coalition to legitimize the use of force. Efforts by others to reach a negotiated solution were ignored or sabotaged by the US, though the appearance of negotiation was kept up. The day after Congressional elections took place in November, Bush escalated the commitment of troops, shifting the US military from a defensive posture to an offensive one. At the same time, rhetoric shifted from the defence of Saudi Arabia to the liberation of Kuwait. Additional references were made to protecting American interests and 'the American way of life'. After giving sanctions less than half the six months it was originally estimated it would take for them to have a serious impact on Iraq, the administration began to push aggressively for a military solution. Iraq, at several points, appeared willing to pull out of all but a few disputed areas of Kuwait, if it could be done in a way that would 'save face' for Hussein and the Iraqi people. But George Bush, in true John Wayne (or Ronald Reagan?) style, responded that Hussein 'doesn't need any face – he needs to get out of Kuwait'. Efforts on the part of the Iraqis, Jordanians, Palestinians and Soviets to tie a retreat from Kuwait to a conference addressing larger issues of stability, national boundaries and militarism in the Middle East were rebuffed by the US. In late November the US, again using its economic and political influence, was able to orchestrate a UN resolution authorizing the use of 'any means necessary' to force Iraq out of Kuwait after 15 January 1991. On Saturday, 12 January, after only two days of debate, both Houses of Congress narrowly passed resolutions concurring with the UN resolution. One day after the 15 January deadline, the US, along with its allies, began the aerial bombardment of Iraq and Kuwait. After six weeks of unimaginably intense bombing, and several days of 'mopping up' with ground troops, the Iraqis were forced out of Kuwait.

The march from the rhetoric of the 1980 presidential campaign, to the military buildup of the early 1980s, to the invasions of progressively larger and more distant nations (Grenada, Panama and Iraq) seems to have provided the American public with ample information about the Republican Party's vision of 'the new world order'. And the nearly unanimous support given to each of these invasions, coupled with the Republican presidential victories in 1980, 1984 and 1988, suggests that a substantial majority of the public approved of this vision. Nonetheless, the limited nature of public discourse during the 1980s and early 1990s begs the question of how citizens would have reacted if given the opportunity to consider a range of alternatives.[32] The ability of the administration to manage public opinion successfully was especially clear during the Gulf War. The military, led by soldiers who were field commanders, fighter pilots and the like in Vietnam, were aware that a gradual buildup of troops and a slow escalation in fighting would erode public support for the war. The massive initial concentration of troops in Saudi Arabia and the unparalleled use of force against the Iraqis was the direct result of this 'reading' of Vietnam. Decisions as to what targets to bomb, when and how to deploy ground troops, how best to limit US and civilian casualties, whether or not to institute a draft, and so forth, were based as much on how it would play on the evening news as on its military value. Similarly, the careful censorship of media reports, the use of a pool arrangement in which journalists were escorted to designated sites, the barrage of carefully edited film footage of (supposedly) successful airstrikes, the regular briefings by military and administration spokespersons, and the constant reprimands to the media about any reports that did not tow the administration line, were all aimed at winning the battle for the hearts and minds of the American public by limiting the possibility of alternative interpretations of events.33

The administration was also remarkably effective at shaping the public's collective memory of the Vietnam War and the anti-war protests, thereby helping to assure support for the Gulf War. A key component of this manufactured consensus was establishing the myth that the war in Vietnam was lost because the military was forced to fight 'with one arm tied behind its back'. Of course, while Vietnam *was* a limited war, this simplification flies in the face of a ten-year war in which 50,000 Americans and countless more North and South Vietnamese died, hundreds of thousands of people were maimed, North Vietnamese cities were carpet bombed, entire villages in both North and South Vietnam were destroyed, acres of forest defoliated, and billions of dollars spent. Absent a forceful articulation of these facts, however, and given a decade of subtle and not so subtle recreations of the Vietnam era, the administration's revisionist interpretation became accepted history.

Similarly, the administration was able to caricature the Vietnam War protests as the acts of a few marginal and unpatriotic individuals whose influence was blown out of proportion by the media. In addition, the target of these protests, according to this revisionist history, was the GI himself. Again, absent a strong refutation, half truths become whole ones. While the anti-war movement of the early 1960s did represent a minority of the population, it was consistently portrayed in a negative light by the mainstream press. Not until middle America turned against the war in large numbers were protestors presented as legitimate.34 In addition, while some returning GIs were mistreated by some anti-war protestors, these incidents were exceptions. Protestors opposed the policy, the administration and (for the most sophisticated protestors) the system that produced the war. The soldiers fighting the war were viewed as victims, not villains. Indeed, many protestors were vets and/or the parents, siblings, friends and lovers of those serving in the war. Nonetheless, the successful portrayal of those who opposed the Vietnam War as unpatriotic was one of the great strategic victories of the right. In doing so, it robbed those who were potential opponents to the Gulf War of their strongest role model, and intimidated both protestors and the media into a much narrower range of discourse.

The success of the Gulf War, like the wisdom of the decision to go to war itself, is as much a matter of interpretation as of fact. Certainly the relative ease with which the Iraqis were defeated and their apparent inability to use either chemical or nuclear weapons should raise doubts about the need for such a massive use of force. And the staggering financial cost of the war, the loss of as many as 200,000 Iraqi lives, the incredible destruction in Kuwait and Iraq, the further dislocation of the Kurds, the environmental disaster in the Gulf, the repression of the pro-democracy movements in Kuwait and Saudi Arabia, and finally, the continued rule of Saddam Hussein, provide credible reasons for questioning the logic and ethic of the Gulf War. For these critical interpretations to take hold, however, they must be articulated by spokespeople with access to the mainstream media, and as with so many of the issues discussed here, the Democrats have been unwilling to play this role.

Card-carrying ACLU Members and the L-word

The 1930s and 1960s, for all their reformist tendencies, did modestly expand political discourse in the United States by rethinking the role of government, and by putting issues of class, race, sex and militarism on the political agenda. Perhaps the most significant, lasting achievement of the Reagan–Bush era has been to force many aspects of these issues out of the mainstream by redefining what Daniel Hallin calls the spheres of consensus, legitimate controversy and deviance.[35] While the shrinking of acceptable political discourse is evident in each of the specific examples discussed above, first Reagan and then Bush made more general attacks on liberalism, and on the role of government in American society.

For Reagan, the rhetorical enemy was Washington. Under the rubric of new federalism, he attacked national government as too big, too distant and too inefficient to address people's needs. State and local governments, he argued, were much better suited to this job. Part of this argument required establishing (falsely) that the federal programmes of the 1960s and 1970s were unmitigated failures, that the federal government was attempting to do too much and trying to solve problems simply by 'throwing money' at them. Of course, there is another interpretation of these programmes. Even programmes that worked were underfunded, and declines in their success paralleled cuts in funding relative to the size of the problem.[36] In addition, the vast majority of the federal bureaucracy was not located in Washington, but instead was located in local, state and regional offices around the country. Finally, most of the growth in bureaucracy that occurred in the 1960s and 1970s was not federal, but state and local.[37] Nonetheless, absent a vocal defence of past policies, and a reasoned debate on the strengths and weaknesses of national, state and local government, Reagan was able to convince much of America that the problems of race, poverty and so forth could only be solved through a combination of trickle-down economics and state and local action.[38]

While he attacked the role of national government, Reagan also successfully shifted the ideological spectrum significantly to the right. The New Left agenda was never firmly entrenched in the mainstream, and so was a relatively easy target for Reagan's not inconsiderable rhetorical skills. This agenda was blamed for many of the political, economic and moral problems facing the United States. In its stead Reagan offered a New Right social agenda, advocating the preservation of the traditional family, prayer in schools, banning abortion, etc. This is not to suggest that these New Right issues were accepted by a large portion of the public, but rather that they became issues of serious debate against which the centre and left were defined.

This redefinition of the political arena continued in the 1988 campaign. By labelling Michael Dukakis a 'card-carrying member of the ACLU', Bush was doing more than stating fact – he was defining the ACLU as outside the realm of legitimate debate. Even the phrase 'card-carrying' was designed to evoke the spectre of 'card-carrying communists' first raised during the McCarthy witchhunts of the 1950s. But now the *articulated* bogey was not communists but members of an established, mainstream civil rights group. Of course groups like the ACLU were targets in the 1950s as well, but only under the guise of a search for communists. Now the ACLU itself was being painted as illegitimate.

A similar dynamic is found in the phrase 'a George McGovern Liberal', commonly used by Bush to describe Dukakis during the 1988 campaign. In 1972 McGovern had represented the mainstream wing of the New Left – the part that was willing to work within the electoral system and the liberal democratic rules of the game. Despite his crushing defeat, much of his agenda was taken up by the Democratic Party throughout the 1970s. Now his image was being used to evoke the radicalism of the 1960s. In the use of this phrase, Bush not only redefined the New Left, painting its moderate representative as deviantly radical, but also redefined Dukakis by presenting his quite mainstream views as far more liberal than they actually were. In short, by shrinking the range of liberal, let alone leftist ideas deemed appropriate for public discourse, Bush further shifted the political consensus to the right, while also constraining the sphere of legitimate controversy. The extent to which discourse had become constrained in the United States is perhaps best exemplified by Bush's frequent and derogatory reference to the 'L-word' during the 1988 campaign. Not only was the label 'liberal' now enough to connote deviance, but the word itself had become, somewhat mockingly, literally unspeakable.

It was this confined public space that made Bush's stands on race, class, taxes, sex, foreign affairs and the like so effective. Reagan's rhetoric shifted the domain of domestic politics from national to state government, while Bush's rhetoric shifted it from government itself to the voluntary action of citizens. By narrowly defining the political agenda and the range of acceptable political solutions, Bush forced Dukakis, and so the Democratic Party more generally, either to out-conservative Bush, to admit to views that were perceived as radically deviant, or to remain silent. Of course Dukakis could have challenged Bush's re-creation of the past, but for a variety of reasons (a concern that Bush was correct in his assessment of the public mindset; the fact that neither he nor the Democratic Party was strongly progressive; the fact that the left had little choice but to support him) he did not opt for this strategy until very late in the campaign.

The ability of Reagan and Bush to redefine the terms of political discourse did more than simply win elections. By agreeing to these terms, the Democrats essentially closed off serious debate on a host of economic and social problems for what constituted a 12-year moratorium. A generation of young Americans now perceive Jimmy Carter as a softhearted liberal who failed precisely because he was liberal, and George McGovern as a radical leftist. Questions of how government should act have given way to debates over whether government should act at all.

None of this is to suggest that concerns over race, gender roles, the environment, education, poverty and the like have disappeared. Few mainstream politicians on the left or the right would publicly deny the right to equal political and economic opportunity. Few would deny the importance of education, or of preserving the environment. Few would deny the need to help the poor and destitute. But it is precisely the casual consensus on these issues that neutralizes their political relevance. What is increasingly excised from public discourse is the connection between these values and concrete, collective political action. What is lost is the sense that government has anything but the most tangential role in assuring they are achieved.[39] The result is often a bizarre mix of rhetoric and action, in which candidates from both parties run as Democrats and govern as Republicans. George Bush was able to declare himself both the 'environmental' and the 'education' president, while advocating policies that further limited the ability of government to address either issue. David Dinkins won the mayoral race in New York by running on a progressive agenda, yet, for reasons largely beyond his control, slashed social programmes while increasing the size of the police force. When, as a result, blacks, women, the poor and other disadvantaged segments of American society fail to achieve the levels of success now deemed their right, the implicit conclusion drawn is that they must lack the 'right stuff'.

The Election of 1992: One Step Forward?

In November of 1992, for the first time in 16 years, the American public elected a Democrat to be President of the United States. This election marks an undeniable shift in the trends discussed above. While there is much one can point to in the 1992 campaign as evidence of a return to the progressive politics of the 1960s and 1970s, it would be a mistake to draw such parallels without carefully considering the context in which this election took place. Did Bill Clinton and the Democrats win by accepting the terms of discourse as set by the Republicans over the past twelve years, or by changing those terms? Will the Democrats govern by honouring the limits of liberal democracy or by redefining them? The evidence from the campaign, the election, and the early days of the new administration is mixed.

For the first time in US history, a black woman was elected to the Senate in 1992. The number of blacks in the House increased from 25 to a record 38, including the first blacks since Reconstruction to be elected from five southern states (significantly, all but one of these black officeholders were Democrats). And the election of Bill Clinton to the presidency should mark a decided improvement in the style and substance of the politics of race in the United States. Certainly in much of his rhetoric, Clinton has shown a great sensitivity to the plight of black America. Nonetheless, a closer examination oF the 1992 campaign and election points out the extent to which the politics of the last twelve years has constrained public discourse and thus lowered the expectations of the left.

Much as in the campaigns of the 1980s, race was essentially a non-issue in 1992. Jesse Jackson, the only national Democrat to address issues of race in 1984 and 1988, did not run for the presidential nomination in 1992, and was effectively muted during the general election for fear that he would alienate the moderate white voters that

Democrats were hoping to lure back to the party. Indeed, the fact that Jackson played only a marginal role during the Democratic convention was viewed by political pundits as evidence of Clinton's strength. The most visible black Democrat during 1992 was Ron Brown, the party's national chairperson, and a person with more corporate than civil rights connections. While Clinton occasionally wooed black voters, he was equally likely to use such opportunities to alleviate white fears about his views. This tactic was clearly behind his public lambasting of the little known rap singer Sister Souljah while speaking before the NAACP.

The low visibility of race as a campaign issue is especially troubling given the context in which the campaign took place. Recall that during the primary season the city of Los Angeles erupted in the most violent and sustained racial uprising since the mid-1960s. Though triggered by a 'not-guilty' verdict for the policemen accused of − and videotaped while − beating a black motorist, the root causes were clearly broader grievances concerning racial injustices. While the beating, the verdict and the subsequent turmoil received a great deal of media coverage, its impact on campaign discourse was minimal and short-lived. Tellingly, most candidates and officeholders downplayed the issue out of fear of 'politicizing' the event! Overall, Clinton's comments about Sister Souljah, Ross Perot's reference to blacks as 'you people', and the controversy over black singer Ice-T's song 'Cop Killer' received greater attention in the campaign than the LA uprising and its social, economic and political roots.

Thus, while the 1992 election may be evidence of a repudiation of the more extreme elements of racial backlash, it does not appear to be much more than this. Continuing recent trends, Clinton received only 39 per cent of the white vote, while garnering 82 per cent of the black vote. In this context, it seems likely that he will be able (or willing) to mobilize the kind of sustained public support necessary to redress the grievances of the last twelve years, let alone the last 350.

Similarly mixed signals were sent by the Democrats regarding issues of class. As the sign in his campaign headquarters − which read, 'the economy, stupid' − made clear, Clinton won the 1992 presidential election by focusing on the longest and deepest recession in a decade. When asked for the one or two issues that most influenced their choice for president, 43 per cent of voters said the state of the economy, while another 21 per cent said the deficit and 20 per cent said the high cost of health care. No other issue was mentioned by over 15 per cent of the voting public. And more than twice as many voters who mentioned the economy and jobs voted for Clinton (53 per cent) as for Bush (24 per cent) or Perot (23 per cent). The advantage for Clinton among those who mentioned health care (67 per cent, versus 19 per cent for Bush and 14 per cent for Perot) was even more dramatic. Perhaps most significantly, Clinton won pluralities among most of those middle- and working-class groups who, in recent years, had voted Republican.

But it would be a mistake to see this vote as a reconstruction of the New Deal or Great Society coalitions. American voters have always 'voted their pocketbooks', and a faltering economy can make the most popular president look bad. To be sure George Bush suffered from what appeared to be a lack of compassion and from the sense that he lacked a domestic agenda. His inability to respond convincingly to a citizen's question regarding how he had personally suffered from the recent economic decline – asked during the second presidential debate – came to symbolize these tragic flaws. Nonetheless, the 1992 Democrats were no vanguard for the oppressed. While playing up his humble roots, Clinton ran campaign ads that called welfare 'a second chance – not a way of life'. While promising to tax the rich, he also promised to cut the taxes of the 'middle class'. And the substance behind his call for 'structural change' was a plan to revitalize the nation's economic infrastructure and to develop a corporate-government partnership modelled on Japan. It is little wonder that a Fortune 500 executive remarked shortly after the Democratic convention that 'big business has no trouble with the idea of a Clinton presidency'. And as one participant in Clinton's post-election 'economic summit' concluded, 'Liberals are going to get projects. Conservatives are going to get the economy.' A look at Clinton's key cabinet appointments seems to bare this observation out: the chairman of a large Wall Street brokerage house as his White House economic adviser; a moderate Senator and business advocate as Treasury Secretary; a congressional budget-cutter as head of OMB; and a Fortune 500 CEO as his chief of staff. Vice President Al Gore's dissolution of his predecessor's 'Council on Economic Competitiveness' (a government-business partnership aimed at further deregulating industry) is an encouraging sign. Yet early indications are that cutting the federal deficit will take precedence over stimulating jobs. And while the appointment of Hillary Clinton to head the task force looking into health care is promising, most other indications are that reforms in health care will be modest at best. George Bush may be remembered as the Herbert Hoover of the 1990s, but there is, as of yet, little indication that Bill Clinton will be the next FDR.

The elections of 1992 provide many reasons for optimism regarding gender issues in the United States. The Republicans' attempts to shift attention away from the economy by focusing on the decay of the traditional family backfired badly – Dan Quayle proved no match for Murphy Brown regarding the issue of single parenthood. Mobilized by the Clarence Thomas–Anita Hill controversy, more women ran for public office in 1992 than ever before in US history. None of the three women running for governorships won, but 21 of the 34 female candidates for other state-wide executive offices did, including all 4 who ran for state attorney general, 4 of the 7 who ran for lieutenant governor, 3 of the 5 who ran for state treasurer, and 2 of the 5 who ran for secretary of state. In addition, a record number of state legislative seats were won by women. While these victories add only incrementally to women's totals, a little more than 20 per cent of all state-wide elected offices and a little less than 20 per cent of all state legislative seats are now held by women. When the 147-member Washington State Legislature convened in 1993, nearly 40 per cent of the legislators were women – the highest percentage in the country and the closest to the elusive 50 per cent mark ever achieved by a state congress.

Women candidates fared well for national office as well. In the Senate four of the eleven women candidates were elected, with Lynn Yeakel losing a very close race to incumbent Arlen Specter, one of the principal 'villains' in the Anita Hill–Clarence Thomas controversy. In the process, several firsts were achieved. There will now be a record six women in the Senate. As noted above, Carol Moseley Braun will be the first African-American woman elected to the Senate. And California will be the first state in which *both* US Senators are women – Barbara Boxer and Dianne Feinstein. Of the record 106 women running for the House, 47 of them won, including 24 non-incumbents. This brings the percentage of women in the new House to nearly 11 per cent – also a record. Not surprisingly, 5 of 6 women Senators and 35 of the 47 Congresswomen are Democrats. All of the newly elected female members of Congress also support abortion rights. Significantly, the new Senate Judiciary Committee now includes two women.

The presidential race also provided glimmers of hope regarding the status of women. The election of Bill Clinton seems to assure that new nominees to the Supreme Court will be supportive of the right to an abortion. The executive 'gag' order preventing federally funded counsellors from giving information regarding abortions has already been rescinded, and President Clinton has signed additional executive orders decoupling foreign aid from the issue of abortion and allowing the use of fetal tissue in medical research. At this writing Clinton also seems committed to making the 'abortion pill' RU486 available in the United States, to ending the kind of sexual harassment in the military exemplified by the infamous 'Tailhook' incident, and, in a different kind of gender issue, to ending the ban on homosexuals in the military. And Hillary Clinton – now Hillary Rodham Clinton – promises to be a very different role model than Barbara Bush, and will undoubtedly play a significant role in a variety of substantive policy decisions.

Again, however, it would be a mistake to read too much into these encouraging signs. With 6 per cent of the Senate, with 11 per cent of the House, even with 20 per cent of state legislatures and executive offices, it is still underrepresentation. Electoral success also varies dramatically by state – for example, only 4 per cent of Kentucky's 1993 state legislature will be women. And only 3 of the 24 women who won a seat in the House actually defeated incumbents. More significantly, the national campaign was remarkably devoid of gender issues. Issues of abortion, sexual harassment, pay equity, childcare, while raised at meetings with individual groups and leaders, were avoided in both the debates and in the media campaigns of both parties. Only 13 per cent of voters selected abortion as one of the most important reasons they voted as they did, and of these, 54 per cent voted for George Bush. And despite the inability of the Republicans to make 'family values' a campaign issue, 68 per cent of voters said they thought government should promote traditional values rather than promote tolerance for non-traditional views. Finally, consider the generally negative reaction to Hillary Clinton's remark that she was 'no Tammy Wynette standing by her man', and her tongue-in-cheek suggestion that she could have 'stayed home and baked cookies' rather than become a lawyer and political activist. More to the point, consider the Democratic Party's reaction to this flack – Ms Clinton was given a new, more feminine hair style, given a less visible role, and entered a contest for the best cookie recipe. Ironically, but significantly, at the 1992 conventions it was Barbara Bush, not Hillary Clinton, who gave a primetime address.

The new administration's approach to foreign policy is especially unclear. Bill Clinton initially opposed the use of military force in the Gulf. In addition, as a student he was opposed to the Vietnam War and avoided the draft. Admittedly, the details in both cases were complicated, and were not unambiguous examples of taking the moral high ground. Nonetheless, they offered the Democrats, in the context of the 1992 campaign, the opportunity to rebut the Republican worldview which had dominated foreign policy for the prior twelve years. To be sure, the fact that Americans rejected George Bush's efforts to use Clinton's past against him is encouraging. But the Democrats' defence of the past was that these issues didn't matter any more: the Cold War is over, the turmoil of the 1960s and early 1970s caused us all to do things that might not be justifiable, and so on. In essence they conceded the historical record to the Republicans, and thus the way in which Vietnam War, the Cold War, the Gulf War, and so on are used rhetorically and strategically in the future.

Certainly a Clinton administration promises to be less militaristic than the past three have been, and the nature of the times helps assure that defence spending will consume a smaller part of the national budget. However, the Democrats failure to articulate a strong, new vision of the post-Cold War world during the campaign appears to have hurt them already. By sending US troops to Somalia and ordering several bombing raids of Iraq, George Bush may have done more to shape the new administration's foreign policy during the two and a half months between the election and the inauguration than Clinton himself had. Having spent the campaign either avoiding foreign policy issues or assuring the public that he, too, can be tough, the new president seems destined to use foreign policy as the test of his manhood.

In the end, the attempt by Republicans to paint Bill Clinton as just another liberal Democrat failed in 1992, but it failed in part because Bill Clinton is not a liberal. As one of the leading spokespersons for moving the Democratic Party to a more centrist position, Clinton's nomination and victory is testimony as much to the strength of the Republican Party over the past twelve years as to the resurgence of the Democrats. True, the extreme right-wing rhetoric of the Republican convention was a miscalculation. But it, too, serves to show how the range of discourse in America has shifted rightward. Clearly the ideological gap between Patrick Buchanan and Bill Clinton is a large one, but what of the gap between George Bush and Bill Clinton? Between Bill Clinton and Jesse Jackson? The measure of these ideological distances remains unclear.

This is not to that suggest all is lost for the left in America. A significant portion of Clinton's braintrust has roots in the New Left politics of the 1960s, and both Clinton and Al Gore have articulated several issue stands that are consistent with that agenda. In addition, Clinton's constant calls for change and his populist, occasionally communalist rhetoric is open to interpretations that are more radical than intended. But in the end, Clinton won by exploiting people's desires for something different rather than by informing those desires. He is the first president to emerge out of the 'sixties generation', but like many from that generation, he was more an observer than a participant – he held the culture and politics of the day to his lips, but did not inhale them. How this clearly curious observer of that era will react to his new found power is unclear. Perhaps it will be his chance to represent the ideals he skirted but never embraced. Or perhaps what we have seen is what we will get – a politician skilled at the art of compromise, but who, in theend, knows which way the wind blows.

One Step Forward, One Step Back?
The Limits of American Political Discourse

In his 1992 State of the Union address, as he had in his prior two, and in his inaugural address in 1989, George Bush pressed his theme of voluntarism, arguing that government is limited in what it can do to solve America's domestic problems. In a sense, it was the very act of saying this that made it so. Twelve years of essentially unanswered attacks on progressive government have firmly established the notion that, as Ronald Reagan proclaimed in *his* 1980 inaugural address, 'Government is not the solution to America's problems -- Government *is* the problem.'

The notion that 'government is the problem' is deeply rooted in America's political tradition. 'At the heart of American politics', writes James Marone, 'lies a dread and yearning. The dread is notorious. Americans fear public power as a threat to liberty.' 'The yearning' to which Marone alludes 'is an alternative faith in direct, communal democracy'. However, even this 'democratic wish' is not an endorsement of government. To the contrary, it is based on the notion that 'the people would, somehow, put aside their government and rule themselves directly'.[40]

The gains made by blacks, the working class, the poor and women during the 1930s and the 1960s were achieved by coupling America's yearning for democracy with the notion that government could be an instrument of the people rather than an enemy of them. This is an inherently unstable marriage in the context of America's liberal democratic traditions. Ronald Reagan -- and to a lesser extent George Bush -- were able to exploit this instability by making populist appeals that resonated with the public's 'yearning' for self-rule, while also reawakening their 'dread' of government. But conservative populism is no more comfortable with liberal democracy than progressive populism, and thus no more firm a foundation upon which to build.

After nearly a decade of watching the world change in dramatic ways, America's yearning for community re-emerged in 1992. Of course, without an appropriate public language or a public sphere designed to accommodate it, this yearning was expressed in odd, unsatisfactory ways. Nonetheless, it could be seen in the remarkable appeal of the multibillionaire populist Ross Perot. It could be seen in the popularity of new media formats that were more substantive than usual (for example, Perot's half hour 'info-mercials') and that allowed for more direct input from the public itself (for example, the 'talk show' format used in the second presidential debate). It could be seen in both Clinton's and Perot's constant calls for greater civic involvement. And it could be seen in all three candidate's -- including twelve-year incumbent George Bush's -- claims to being the 'candidate of change'. To be sure the proximate cause of this restlessness was the poor state of the economy, but to end the discussion there is to miss the point.

And yet in some crucial ways that is exactly where the Democrats did end the discussion in the 1992 campaign. By making vague references to 'change', they raised the expectations of the American public. But by failing to engage in an open dialogue about the direction of that change – about both its costs and its promise – they have made it less likely that these expectations will be fulfilled. At times Clinton came tantalizingly close to seeing this: his use of the 'town meeting' format during the campaign and his post-election 'economic summit' demonstrate his desire to create a public sphere. And in his 1993 inaugural address, he attempted to re-establish the connection between popular democracy and progressive government with his promise to 'give this capitol back to the people to whom it belongs' and to restore 'government [as] a place for what Franklin Roosevelt called bold, persistent experimentation'. But for government to be the instrument of bold, persistent, democratic and progressive change, we must first broaden public discourse not only beyond the ideological parameters set during the past twelve years, but beyond those set by the logic of liberal democracy.

Notes and References

1. These reforms were also tied into the language and traditions of democratic action and community that exist at the margins of American culture and politics. Such appeals have always been tenuous, however, and have seldom been able to sustain mainstream social movements. In addition, they often become blurred, blending in with the more firmly established values of classical liberalism. See Russell Hanson, *The Democratic Imagination* (Princeton: Princeton University Press, 1986); M.X. Delli Carpini, 'Vietnam, Ideology, and Domestic Politics', in M. Shafer (ed.), *The Legacy* (Boston: Beacon Press, 1990); and James A. Marone, *The Democratic Wish* (New York: Basic Books, 1990).

2. See Frances Fox Piven and Richard Cloward, *Poor People's Movements* (New York: Pantheon, 1977); *Regulating The Poor* (New York: Random House, 1971); Benjamin Ginsburg, *The Consequences of Consent* (Reading, MA: Addison-Wesley, 1982); Thomas Ferguson, *Fall of the House of Morgan* (forthcoming).

3. Alexis de Tocqueville, *Democracy in America* (New York: Anchor books, 1969), p. 525.

4. Daniel Hallin, *The Uncensored War* (New York: Oxford University Press, 1986).

5. C. Whalen and B. Whalen, *The Longest Debate* (Washington DC: Seven Locks Books, 1989).

6. The statistics on race in America are drawn from J. Schwartz, *America's Hidden Success* (New York: Norton and Co., 1988); F. Harris and R. Wilkins, *Quite Riots* (New York: Pantheon, 1988); and Whalen and Whalen, *The Longest Debate*.

7. This 'economic' argument also points out the extent to which these reforms were perceived as tangential: they were legitimate pursuits only to the extent that they were relatively costless to the rest of the population.

8. Voting statistics presented throughout this essay are drawn from G. Pomper (ed.), *The Election of 1984* (Chatham, NJ: Chatham House Press, 1985); G. Pomper (ed.), *The Election of 1988* (Chatham, NJ: Chatham House Press, 1989); and M. Nelson (ed.), *The Election of 1988* (Washington DC: Congressional Quarterly Press, 1989).

9. C. McWilliams, 'The Meaning of the Election', in G. Pomper, *The Election of 1988*, p. 199.

10. See T. Gitlin, *The Whole World is Watching* (Berkeley: University of California Press, 1980).

11. Their logic was that women's rights were less controversial, and that, as a majority of the population, an appeal to women's self-interest (as opposed to blacks) could be politically beneficial. At the same time, however, afraid that even this would appear too much like bowing to 'special interests', the bill's sponsors limited the legislation's effectiveness by severely restricting the amount of money women could collect for damages.

12. For example, attendance at all-black colleges and universities is on the rise, as are all-black dorms, fraternities, etc. on predominantly white campuses. More recently, blacks at several predominantly white high schools and colleges have opted for separate proms and graduation ceremonies. And public speakers advocating black separatism, such as Professor Leonard Jeffries and the Nation of Islam's Mohammed Khalid, have become common at events sponsored by black campus organizations.

13. The US National Advisory Commission on Civil Disorders, *The Kerner Report* (New York: Bantam Books, 1968).

14. Statistics are drawn from J. Schwartz, *American's Hidden Success*; and K. Phillips, *The Politics of Rich and Poor* (New York: Random House, 1990).

15. As quoted in 'Gray: Bush Shortchanges the Nation's Poor', *The Philadelphia Inquirer*, 23 April 1989.

16. For an interesting if anecdotal analysis of the role of popular culture in creating and maintaining this upper-middle-class self image, see Benjamin DeMott, *The Imperial Middle* (New York: Morrow Press, 1991).

17. K. Phillips, *The Politics of Rich and Poor*, p. 212.

18. Efforts to confront these issues through increased taxation at the state level, such as those attempted by Governor James Florio in New Jersey or Governor Lowell Weicker in Connecticut, were met with intense opposition, often by those who would, ironically, be most likely to benefit from them.

19. K. Phillips, *The Politics of Rich and Poor*, p. 212.

20. Historical facts about women and politics and the women's movement are drawn from R. Darcy, S. Welch and J. Clark, *Women, Elections, and Representation* (New York: Longman, 1987); and S. Evans, *Born for Liberty* (New York: The Free Press, 1989).

21. Statistical data concerning women in the workforce is drawn from S. Evans, *Born for Liberty*; and US Census Bureau, *The Statistical Abstract of the United States* (Washington DC: Government Printing Office, 1989).

22. S. Evans, *Born for Liberty*, p. 275.

23. Information concerning women and public policy is drawn from S. Evans, *Born for Liberty*, 1989; and J. Gelb and M. Lief Palley, *Women and Public Policies* (Princeton: Princeton University Press, 1987).

24. Prior to the 1930s there were, of course, no systematic public opinion polls, but there is no historical record to suggest that a majority of citizens opposed any of the major uses of US troops from the War for Independence to the First World War. While support for the Civil War certainly waned in the North, Lincoln's electoral victory in 1864, over challengers such as McClelland, who advocated a peaceful solution to the conflict, suggests that this opposition, even at its peak, did not constitute a majority.

25. Based on Roper polls as reported in P. Braestrup, *The Big Story* (New Haven: Yale University Press, 1978); D. Hallin, *The Uncensored War*; and Gallup polls as reported in B. Wattenberg, *The Real America* (New York: G.P. Putnam and Sons, 1976).

26. M. X. Delli Carpini, 'Vietnam, Ideology, and Domestic Politics', in M. Shafer, *The Legacy* (Boston: Beacon Press, 1990).

27. B. Taylor, 'The Vietnam War Movie', in *The Legacy*; M. Novelli, 'Hollywood and Vietnam: Images of Vietnam in Popular Film', in M. Klein (ed.), *The Vietnam Era* (London: Pluto Press, 1990).

28. There is growing if circumstantial evidence that the arms for hostages deal may have been cut during the 1980 presidential campaign. A growing number of former members of the Iranian government and the Carter administration have suggested that Reagan's campaign staff, led by William Casey and aided by George Bush,

agreed to provide arms to the Iranians if they agreed *not* to release the hostages being held in the US embassy until *after* the election.

29. For an excellent exploration of the inequitable coverage of political events in South America as compared to Eastern Europe, see L. Weschler, 'The Media's One and Only Freedom Story', *Columbia Journalism Review* (April 1990), pp. 26–31.

30. M. Edelman, *Constructing the Political Spectacle* (Chicago: University of Chicago Press, 1989).

31. Indeed, only days before Iraq's invasion of Kuwait, American diplomats made clear to the Iraqis that the US had no treaties with Kuwait and felt no obligation to respond should Iraq use force.

32. The fact that women were less supportive of the war than men, that a majority of blacks opposed the war, and that support generally declined when Congressional Democrats raised doubts about the use of force, all provide some evidence that the aggregate support for the Gulf War masked some ambivalence. Further evidence for this is found in a series of focus groups I conducted with Scott Keeter. In these discussions, conducted just after the hostilities ended, people initially expressed overwhelming support for the war. But when asked to talk about their views in greater depth, most acknowledged they were unconvinced the war was necessary, and they remained cynical as to the real motives for the war. Most also acknowledged that they would have preferred a peaceful solution to the conflict and suspect that such a solution might have been possible.

33. M. Hertsgaard, *On Bended Knee* (New York: Farrar Straus Giroux, 1988); J. MacArthur, *Second Front* (New York: Hill and Wang, 1992).

34. T. Gitlin, *The Whole World is Watching*.

35. D. Hallin, *The Uncensored War*.

36. J. Schwartz, *America's Hidden Success*.

37. W.D. Burnham, *Democracy in the Making* (Englewood Cliffs: Prentice-Hall, 1986), Chapter 12.

38. Reagan's success benefited from the fact that suspicion of 'big government' runs through populist rhetoric of both the left and the right in America. Throughout the 1960s, 1970s and 1980s, New Left proponents and their progeny advocated for greater decentralization of government decision-making. Jimmy Carter won office in 1970 in part by running as an outsider who would make government more accessible and who would shrink the federal bureaucracy. The left's vision of a decentralized government is, of course, very different to the right's in many ways. Not the least of these differences would be a continued role for the federal government in redistributive and regulatory policies.

39. A similar tension can be seen on college and university campuses, where vague commitments to racial, cultural and sexual diversity dominate, but where those attempting to integrate such diversity into the curriculum are increasingly accused of 'brainwashing' students into 'politically correct' (i.e. nonracist, nonsexist, nonethnocentric and critical) thought.
40. J. Marone, *The Democratic Wish*, p. 1.

14. US Television and the Gulf Conflict

Gene Michaud

What follows is an exploratory examination of some of the events surrounding the conflict in the Gulf and the representations of those events as they were constructed by American television. Even a cursory look at the ways in which commercial television news presented the various issues which arose from the US government's response to Iraq's annexation of Kuwait illuminates some significant trends in the mainstream media's ability to promote the views of a politically powerful conservative bloc while marginalizing oppositional voices. This chapter cannot probe every facet of American television's handling of the crisis in the Middle East; however, I believe the material gathered here offers some insights into the relations of power as they currently find expression in the US media.

It is a significant fact of life in capitalist countries that systemic competition to accumulate and control material, cultural and technological resources guarantees continuing conflict between and among dominant and subordinate groups who occupy the social space at any given historical moment. Furthermore, some elements of these conflicts spill over into the realm of mass media representation: images of the civil rights and anti-Vietnam War movements were widely circulated on American television in the 1950s, 1960s and 1970s.[1] In most cases, however, television has only presented such material when the level of resistance begins to cause conflicts among members of dominant social groups. Even in these situations, television often works to contain discursive elements which would seriously challenge elite power. In fact, with a few notable exceptions, television coverage of significant events seldom *totally* censors the oppositional views of social actors involved in contesting the interpretation of those events. Rather, by allocating a considerably larger amount of their resources, in terms of broadcast time, technology and reporters, to cover spokespeople who hold dominant positions within the social order, and by generally accepting the interpretative framework which they articulate, network television practices usually work to undermine anti-establishment opinion. Emphasis on 'official sources' generally devalues all other social actors, and continued reiteration of dominant frames of discourse (by officials and reporters) results in the construction of discursive parameters which marginalize oppositional views.

Political theorist Antonio Gramsci applied the term hegemony to characterize these processes, in which groups at the top of hierarchical social structures use their power to control various forms of organized communicative activity.[2] Daniel Sallach has noted three operational motifs which constitute the hegemonic processes: firstly, the inculcation of the dominant social group's values; secondly, the censorship or suppression of oppositional views; thirdly, the construction of parameters which define the limits of legitimate discussion and debate over alternative beliefs, values and worldviews.[3] The very terms 'beliefs', 'values' and 'worldviews' signal a theoretical construction of hegemony as an ideational phenomenon – more precisely, as the production of ideology, which is rooted in and sustains the favourable material conditions of dominant social groups. Though some critics, scholars and theorists have adopted a reified version of hegemony in which the views of social elites become the central and often sole concern of their analysis, it must be remembered that the social arena over which specific groups have dominion is nonetheless *always* contested space; inculcation, censorship and exclusionary discursive tactics would otherwise be unnecessary.[4]

The representations of the Middle East War in the American media, and especially those furnished by television for public consumption, provide examples *par excellence* of the dominant media's role in the processes of legitimating the views and values of the country's most powerful social groups. At every turn in the evolving story of the conflict, the mainstream mass media adopted, supported and reinforced the discourse proffered by the conservative political leadership of the United States and its military spokespeople, while ignoring or marginalizing the voices in opposition to government policies. In so doing, the US media has provided a textbook demonstration of the ways in which power can be deployed to dominate the content and signifying practices of the channels of mass communication.

It is important to understand that the organizational structure and goals of the US television industry have continued to follow the patterns established by industrial production in the United States. With the single exception of Public Broadcasting System (PBS) programming, which is financed in part (though decreasingly) by the federal government and in part by corporate grants and individual viewer contributions, the television content available to most Americans is the product of the commercial broadcasting industry. Since the beginning of large-scale television broadcasting in the US, three commercial networks, the American Broadcasting Company (ABC), the Columbia Broadcasting System (CBS), and the National Broadcasting Company (NBC), have dominated American television production.[5] As with other major US corporate institutions, these organizations are structured hierarchically and are driven by the same economic goal: the increase in privatized capital accumulation. Though the growth of cable television services and the advent of videotape player/recorders for home use have decreased the numbers of Americans who rely exclusively on the three commercial networks for their entertainment, television network news still dominates the American public's informational sphere. Not only are the organizational structures and economic interests of the major television networks similar to other large US commercial enterprises, but the networks rely on corporations for profits through the sale of advertising time. Additionally, they are subject (again decreasingly) to federal government regulation in their overall operations and depend upon key government spokespeople as sources of news information. As a result, the commercial networks are structurally inclined to provide their audiences with images and information which are consonant with the values and views of those with whom they share power at the top of America's social hierarchy.

To understand American television's role in reporting the Middle East War, it is important to realize the extent to which television dominates all public arenas of discourse in the United States. Over 98 per cent of the population has access to at least one television set in their homes, and the average American adult watches more than 32 hours of televised programming each week. Moreover, studies of American viewers over the last decade found that 60 per cent chose television as their preferred source of national and international news, and that a majority of viewers find television the 'most believable' of all news sources.[6] In other words, with the possible exceptions of time spent at work (for those who have full-time employment) or asleep, television viewing occupies a larger portion of the daily lives of a majority of American adults than any other activity. One result of this extensive engagement is that Americans generally tend to trust televised reportage of news events.

In relation to the events of the Gulf War, the American public's tendency to rely heavily on television for information often took on obsessive characteristics. From the moment when President Bush ordered the bombing of Iraq and Iraqi positions in Kuwait, the three major US commercial networks and the Cable News Network (CNN) began broadcasting 24-hour coverage of the war.[7] As the war continued, there were reports in several major newspapers that thousands of US citizens were developing what became known as 'CNN Syndrome', in which viewing television coverage of the war became virtually their only daily activity. As might be expected, a large number of these compulsive viewers were eventually identified as family members or close friends either of US soldiers stationed in the Gulf or of people who live in the regions where the war was being fought. CNN's particular response to this problem was, predictably, more television: by the war's second week, their daily coverage of the conflict included a one-hour programme in which trained psychiatrists took phone calls from distraught viewers.

The significant amount of public interest in the Gulf from the earliest stages of the Iraq/Kuwait crisis placed demands on US television network news departments to seek out and present a broad spectrum of related information about national and international events. As a consequence, the major networks did provide their viewers with news about the growing anti-war movements both in the US and internationally, though these activities always received considerably less media attention and emphasis than the daily pronouncements from various US government officials. Opposition to the prospect of war in the Middle East developed quickly and included groups from different strata of American society; however, the speed at which the Bush administration pursued its war policies and brought the military operations in the region to a resolution was in part tactically calculated to render anti-war opposition irrelevant.

The willingness of the networks to present some aspects of the anti-war movement was especially evident before the onset of armed conflict, when a number of US political elites (especially US Congressmen and Senators) appeared on television urging the Bush administration to allow the UN-sponsored economic boycott of Iraq, coupled with a restraining force of 250,000 American troops amassed along the Saudi Arabian border, to compel the Iraqis to withdraw from Kuwait rather than resort to potentially costly and possibly risky military action. However, because most of the televised information about the anti-war movement was presented as a continuation of this governmental policy debate, the deeper criticisms articulated by anti-war spokespeople were generally not available to the American public through television news programming. For example, an aggressive attempt by some anti-war spokespeople to link the US administration's policy on Kuwait with its military invasion of Panama one year earlier, and to suggest that its real policy was one of adopting any rationale available to it in order to justify the repeated use of military force to control significant areas of the globe, never received serious attention. US television's 'anti-war' discourse was thus defined by and contained within the debate among the politically powerful about the merits of an economic boycott relative to the use of military options.

An example of a CBS evening news broadcast in October is instructive in regard to the ways in which network television simultaneously reported and contained information about groups engaged in the effort to challenge the views of President Bush and other official spokespeople. The broadcast began with several stories relating to the Gulf crisis: it included the reiteration of statements by the president and other members of his administration condemning Saddam Hussein, a story about Western hostages being held by the Iraqis, and information about the buildup of US forces in Saudi Arabia. These items were then followed by a series of stories about daily national events in the US according to a format which has dominated the network presentation of news for more than a decade: a story on the economy, one on urban crime, one on new medical procedures, etc.

The final piece in this evening's broadcast, which is generally understood in terms of the format as the 'human interest' story, was about the American anti-war movement. The report began by evoking, through narration and imagery, the Vietnam anti-war movement, then moved to current images of student anti-war activists meeting, discussing strategy and preparing signs for a demonstration. The short synchronous sound and image 'bites' featured a young woman student expressing her opinion that the economic sanctions against Iraq could work and might save the lives of American troops, and a group of activists chanting 'No blood for oil!' during an anti-war march. The narration constantly depicted the efforts of these anti-war college students as a kind of ritual activity, to be understood in much the same way as college fraternity parties or springtime excursions to Florida, a rhetorical stance which also reinterprets the story's initial images of student protests during the Vietnam War. The piece offers no detailed explication and analysis of anti-war views, but rather presents oppositional activity as a time-honoured aspect of American student life during wartime. Significantly, this journalistic position was later made explicit in an ABC news programme, 'The Gulf War: Answering Questions for Kids', in which anchorman Peter Jennings explains to a group of American children at his feet that anti-war activities are a long and honourable American tradition.

By avoiding any serious and concrete discussion of the political ideas which motivate anti-war activists in favour of an emphasis on ritual and tradition, the CBS news story empties the anti-Gulf War movement of its specific political and historical content. Further, by formally framing the information about the movement as a 'human interest' story, the activities of anti-war groups are also seen as quaint and innocuous phenomena which are somewhat related but largely incidental to the 'hard news' coming from official sources. Finally, the placement of the story at the *end* of a broadcast which *begins* with official versions of the Middle East situation guarantees that government views will receive extensive airing and emphasis which remains uncontaminated by oppositional voices and information. In the most general terms, the networks can thus claim to be covering 'both sides of the story' while casting oppositional views, and those who hold them, into the margins of political discourse.

In fact, the formal methods cited above are typical of those employed by the commercial networks in presenting information about anti-establishment movements. Citing the work of sociologist Dorothy Smith, Gaye Tuchman characterizes the institutional patterns of gathering and presenting news as '..."interested procedures," methods of not knowing that are embedded in the legitimated institutions they reproduce.' [8] Using principles of 'frame analysis' developed by Goffman to probe the ways in which news is constructed, Tuchman elaborates on the specific methods by which news gathering and presentation in the United States contribute to hegemony. Noting that the process of 'framing' involves organizing discrete and arbitrary slices of ongoing human activity into recognizable events, she points out that a key aspect of this process necessarily entails limiting information about the possible ways in which events in the real world are interconnected. 'We create ... the relevance of our collective past to our present and future actions by invoking *elements* of the past to justify present actions' (emphasis added).[9] Consequently, one key practice in the framing of current events is the application of highly selective historical information which provides a context for understanding new information.

In its coverage of the Gulf War, the television news agencies allowed government spokespeople to make the choice as to which elements – which aspects of history – to employ for justification of its actions. As noted above, the US military incursion into Panama was carefully avoided, as it clearly represented a contradictory case for the rationale that government agencies were promoting to justify the Gulf War. The United Nations had passed a resolution condemning American military action in Panama, thereby branding the US as an 'outlaw nation' that had 'violated international law'. Since the Bush administration now had a great deal at stake in characterizing Iraq in exactly this light, any mention of its earlier invasion of Panama (or of the previous conservative government's various operations in Nicaragua, El Salvador and Grenada) could prove damaging to its newly constructed image as the upholder of international law. Compliant television reporting never pursued the rather obvious contradictions to this pose which recent US history provides, choosing instead to allow the administration's framework for its current policies to stand unquestioned.

But perhaps the most glaring case of television's tendency to allow government spokespeople to manipulate elements of history to frame and thereby justify its actions in the Gulf came at the very onset of the war. It is hardly surprising, given the hold that American television has on the United States public and the interest created by five months of US military buildup in the Gulf, that President George Bush's televised speech on the evening the war began was the single most watched event in American television history. In the course of presenting an explication about the necessity of using military force to drive the Iraqis from Kuwait, Bush addressed the largest foreign policy issue in recent American history: the Vietnam War. As indicated by the images of anti-Vietnam War demonstrations included in the CBS news story about the 'new' anti-war movement, the spectre of America's involvement in Vietnam has hung over every US foreign policy debate since the mid-1970s. It has become the constant reference point for more recent US military operations, deployed discursively by all US political factions (with considerably different inflections and intents) when debates about the use of American military force to resolve international conflicts have surfaced. It is not surprising, consequently, that Bush felt compelled to confront the potential implications of 'another Vietnam War' when justifying his present actions. What is surprising was television's willingness to accept his construction of that war.

Stating that the Gulf War would 'not be another Vietnam', Bush provided the following interpretation of the earlier conflict: 'In that war, we had to fight with one hand tied behind our back.' He then went on to point out that, in the case of the Gulf, not only the people of the United States but a broad coalition of international governments supported the use of force against Iraq. His second reference to Vietnam, related to this point, had to do with a guarantee that the war against Iraq would not be a lengthy conflict. Though this view of the Vietnam conflict adumbrates the issues which the war years raised in the US, in the many hours of continuous television coverage of events in the Middle East which followed Bush's speech, and during which these statements were repeated on numerous occasions, not one television reporter or anchorperson advanced a serious challenge to this interpretation of the Vietnam War.

Television's relative silence on Bush's statements about the Vietnam War must be understood within the context of the ongoing historical debate about that war and especially the role which the American news media played in reporting the conflict. The media, and television in particular, have been castigated by both the left and the right for their reporting of the war. The left has maintained that mainstream news agencies failed to investigate the deeper moral, political and economic issues on which the US government's policies during the Vietnam War era were based. Conservatives have advanced the view that most television reportorial activity during the war betrayed the media's 'liberal bias' by promoting anti-war sentiment which in turn led to an erosion of public support for the war. Though the leftist critique has largely been ignored, two extensive studies of media coverage during the war (including one financed by the US Department of Defense) have both concluded that careful review of mainstream print and television reports about the Vietnam conflict reveals no 'liberal bias'.[10] However, since the conservative attacks on the media's coverage of the war have often been delivered by powerful and prominent spokespeople (most recently Ronald Reagan during his eight-year presidency), mainstream news agencies have been constantly on the defensive regarding their coverage of the Vietnam War. Indeed, the case can be made that one key factor in American television's significant shift in the 1980s toward a more conservative, pro-administration stance regarding its coverage of the US government is its sensitivity to right-wing criticisms of its role during the Vietnam War era.[11]

By allowing the Bush interpretation of the Vietnam War to stand, television news agencies may have handed the conservative bloc a decisive victory in its 16-year-long battle to rewrite the history of that period.[12] First, the 'one hand tied behind our back' construction is based exclusively on a military assessment of the conflict: it reduces the wide range of political views which produced serious challenges to elite authority during the Vietnam era to a simple pro-war/anti-war dichotomy. It further places the responsibility for both the length of the war and its ultimate loss on those *Americans* who held anti-war views during the conflict; significantly, the contribution of the Vietnamese to the struggle for control of their country disappears altogether. It also masks the significant amount of destruction that US military forces visited upon Vietnam and its people. Additionally, by scapegoating the American anti-war movement, this view of history also lays the groundwork for a conservative defence of the Gulf policies in the event that the speedy victory promised by Bush did not materialize.

In fact, the American television networks' complicity in accepting this specific interpretation of the Vietnam War was signalled in the early stages of the developing Middle East conflict by the media's willingness to accept and promote the government's pro-military stance regarding the crisis. Each network hired a series of retired military personnel as 'special consultant', and each step of the buildup of US forces in the

Gulf region was subject to their 'expert' analysis. These analyses were coupled with state-of-the-art computer graphics designed to simulate the ability of military technology to 'target' specific areas of the Gulf region. A handful of liberal media critics worried that this mode of presentation made the military activities in the Gulf look like computer games instead of the deadly serious operations that they clearly were. Few took note of the fact that the confluence of these graphics with the analysis of recently retired military personnel produced an almost exclusively pro-military vision of the crisis, a fact underlined by ABC anchorman Peter Jennings' assertion at the beginning of the American ground offensive that this step was 'inevitable'. Fewer still pointed to the reason why network news producers were forced to rely so heavily on computer generated graphics to cover the events in the Middle East once armed conflict was initiated: from the beginning of 'Operation Desert Shield' to the end of 'Operation Desert Storm', the military carefully controlled all aspects of news gathering and reporting, which in turn made simultaneous network broadcasts of the actual events as they occurred in the Middle East virtually impossible.

The specifics of the procedures developed by the Bush administration and enforced by the US military concerning media coverage in the Gulf are worth noting in some detail; they were generated in part as a response to the role the media had played during the Vietnam War and in part by the largely successful attempts to eliminate or significantly curtail media access to subsequent US military operations in Grenada and Panama. Reporters were organized into groups, or 'pools', each of which was placed under the supervision of a military public relations officer. This officer would determine where each reportorial pool would be allowed to go and who they would be allowed to interview. Further, each reporter had to turn his or her final report over to military authorities for clearance before the information could be printed or broadcast. Because the networks were not allowed on-site to generate live television coverage of the unfolding events, they often had to depend on graphics to represent visually the action as it took place. Thus, while the views of anti-war spokespeople, as noted earlier, were never totally censored, the actual images and sounds of the conflict were severely constrained by military control over news gathering and reporting procedures.

In the end, American television's dependence on official spokespeople and military experts for explanations and contextualization of the Gulf conflict paid a large dividend to these sources at network television's own expense. Several reporters and television anchorpeople were sharply critical of the military's control over reportorial procedures, claiming that such control seriously infringed the public's need to have access to important information as it developed. Military spokespeople countered that the pools were the best way to deal with the logistical problems which the large number of reporters in the Gulf area had created, and that all reports had to be screened in order to guarantee the security of military operations was not breached and the safety of American troops in the area was not compromised. To the extent that the public's actual concern over these issues was addressed, polls taken during the conflict suggested that many Americans were inclined to accept the military's arguments regarding the need substantially to limit media coverage of ongoing operations. Thus, in a conflict among the powerful, the media elite found that their tendency to serve as a largely uncritical conduit for pro-military perspectives on the Gulf crisis had led to the widespread acceptance of a conservative political framework within which they, too, could be seriously constrained. Though the American public's willingness to support military censorship must be viewed as a matter of grave concern in respect to the potential threat to any semblance of democracy which such a view embodies, it cannot be seen as surprising given television's adoption and promotion of a militarist vision of events in the Gulf.

Notes

1. See, for example, Michael J. Arlen, *The Living Room War* (New York: Penguin Books, 1982).

2. Antonio Gramsci, *Prison Notebooks* (New York: International Publishers, 1971).

3. David Sallach, 'Class Domination and Ideological Hegemony', in Gaye Tuchman (ed.), *The TV Establishment* (New Jersey: Prentice-Hall, 1974), pp. 165–6.

4. For an excellent discussion of these issues, see Douglas Kellner, *Television and the Crisis of Democracy* (Boulder, Colorado: Westview Press, 1990).

5. For an in-depth history of the rise of the American television networks, see Erik Barnouw, *Tube of Plenty* (New York: Oxford University Press, 1975).

6. Cited in Kellner, *Television and the Crisis of Democracy*, pp. 22–3.

7. ABC, CBS and NBC began phasing out their 24-hour-a-day coverage of the war within 72 hours. CNN continued broadcasting round-the-clock coverage of the war for several weeks.

8. Gaye Tuchman, *Making News* (New York: The Free Press, 1978), p. 196.

9. *Ibid.*, p. 195.
10. Daniel Hallin, *The Uncensored War* (New York: Oxford University Press, 1986).
11. See Michael Hertsgaard, *On Bended Knee: The Press and the Reagan Presidency* (New York: Farrar Straus Giroux, 1988).
12. See, for example, Julian Smith, *Looking Away: Hollywood and Vietnam* (New York: Scribner, 1975).

15. The 1990s and Beyond: After the Gulf

Noam Chomsky Interviewed by Michael Klein

KLEIN: You have written characterizing the US as an ageing Empire in economic decline that is taking on global militaristic functions. Can you expand upon this, and what you see as the main contradictions in 'the new emerging world order'?

CHOMSKY: One critical feature of the emerging new world order is the virtual withdrawal of the USSR from the world scene, signs of which were already visible in the 1980s with the levelling off of military spending, and stagnation of the economy. This has several important consequences. First, it removes a deterrent that has somewhat impeded the US in its assaults against Third World independence. Second, it means that large parts of Soviet areas of influence may revert to their quasi-colonial relation to the West, in effect rejoining the Third World. Third, it eliminates the dominant ideological framework for intervention.

What was unclear until recently was the form the new phase of the traditional assault would take, how it would interact with the growing rivalries among the three major First World power centres who manage the 'tripolar' global economic system that began to coalesce 15–20 years ago, and in what ways the domestic populations in the dominant power centres might be marginalized and controlled.

Since 1917, the alleged Soviet threat has often provided a convenient framework for various forms of intervention, but now new pretexts are needed. An important aspect of the new situation, internal to the US, is the growing resistance to intervention that has developed since the late 1960s. It is in this context that the US has to find new ways to carry out the global enforcer role it took over from the traditional imperial powers.

The Gulf War has its lessons in this regard. Bush administration internal documents stress that a 'much weaker enemy' must not merely be defeated but pulverized. This has to occur 'decisively and rapidly', so as not to 'undercut political support', recognized to be weak. The central lesson of the new world order, as of the old, is simple enough but has to be re-enforced: 'What we say goes', as George Bush recently put it. In brief: we are the masters and you shine our shoes.

The police functions if you like – the functions of establishing and maintaining a certain kind of order, especially in the Third World – were a key aspect of a role the US took on after the Second World War, the Truman Doctrine being one expression. It had of course undertaken that function regionally throughout its history. However, after the Second World War there was a qualitative change, as now the US effectively organized and managed a global economic, political and military system.

By the 1970s, after Vietnam, that role was essentially unsustainable. The US no longer had the economic base for it. At this time – it was called the Nixon Doctrine – the US tried to farm out its enforcer function, to arrange for regional surrogates to be 'cops on the beat', as the administration put it. With the changes of the subsequent years, the US is now more free to use force itself with impunity, the Soviet deterrent having disappeared, but in new ways because of the relative decline of the US national economy. Accordingly, the conception has been evolving of the US as a mercenary state. The financial editor of the *Chicago Tribune*, for example, in a recent article says that the US ought to sell 'protection', in effect to run a global protection racket mafia-style. The comparative advantage of the US at this point in history resides primarily in the capacity to organize violence, for itself, or for the common interests of the industrial powers. So we move from the Nixon Doctrine, of local 'cops on the beat', to the US as world enforcer again, at times financed by its rivals (and enjoying a huge capital flow from the family dictatorships that manage Gulf oil production). But as before there are limitations. A problem will be to ensure that the economic rivals do their part in the alliance, and to keep the domestic population deluded and frightened, so that there will be public support for intervention.

K: How can the mobilization of domestic public opinion be sustained for policies that are a substitute for development of the national economy?

C: The problem is what has been called the Vietnam Syndrome. It is interesting that it is described by the establishment as a disease that has to be overcome. But the malady is real, and stubborn. The options for intervention – given changes in the American culture in the last 20 years – have been pretty much limited to two. One is clandestine terror and subversion. (For example from 1980 to 1988 over 1.5 million black people were killed in the regions surrounding South Africa as the result of terror operations backed by the US and

Britain. One could also talk about Latin America.) The second is the kind that has occurred on a regular basis in the 1980s. Pick a weak and relatively defenceless target; organize a huge media propaganda campaign to convert the intended victim into a demon that has to be exorcized; terrify or enrage the domestic population; and then win a rapid, miraculous, decisive and overwhelming victory over the monster, so that everybody sighs with relief and praises the courage of the leaders who had the strength to save us in the nick of time from the threat. This is the model that was used in Grenada, in Libya (with respect to 'international terrorism'), in Panama (Noriega and 'drug trafficking'), in a sense in Nicaragua, and just recently again in the Gulf (Saddam Hussein as 'Hitler'; Iraq as 'a nuclear threat'.) There was an interesting article in the *Boston Globe* by Fred Kaplan in which he quotes General Powell as saying there are only two more demons left in the world – North Korea, and Fidel Castro; but of course it will always be possible to employ the media to invent another, if necessary.

The internal constraint is US public opinion, especially since the 1960s. In some cases it is simply the belief that we should tend to needs at home, that the world is not our responsibility. But there is also a growing moral opposition to the US using force in the world for its own interest, or the interest of privileged sectors. The external constraints are now primarily economic. For example, who is going to pay for the action and for maintaining US military capacity? There are also political constraints: as current world manager the US has to try to maintain decent relations with other industrial powers, despite their differences. It is also significant that the US is heavily dependent upon Japan, not only for capital but for its advanced technological military equipment. These are among the reasons why the US wants to maintain control over the Gulf. The Gulf is of course a rich source of capital; in addition control over Gulf oil is an indirect tax on Japan and German-based Europe, as well as a possible source of influence over them.

K: Two cultures often co-exist in the United States. Given the Orwellian political discourse of the dominant media, especially with respect to events in the Gulf, do you think there is a possibility of a mass movement in the US sustaining significant resistance to military adventures and on the domestic front as it did in the 1960s?

C: We have to look at events in perspective. There have been great changes in the last 30 years. It's a much more civilized society than it was then, something that causes much concern among the commissions. As the public changes, the institutions of domination have to adapt to a certain extent. For example, the media are somewhat better than they used to be. They are a bit more responsive to a range of opinions and there is some diversity inside that you wouldn't have found 20 years ago.

K: Would that be part of the legacy of the 1960s?

C: Yes. The 1960s were a time of awakening in many respects. The main thing that was happening was a breakdown of apathy, a willingness to challenge and question authority. The effect on American culture was very substantial. You can see it all over the place. Even scholarship became capable for perhaps the first time of facing the traditional scandals that had been swept under the rug, for example the fate of minorities and of the indigenous population in the US. Many other orthodoxies were also subject to question, and quickly crumbled upon further enquiry. The legacy of the 1960s has by now extended into much of the society. I think that is a permanent legacy. It even affected war policy in the Gulf.

K: One of the most frightening things about the Gulf War of 1991 is the way that it was portrayed as something else. It didn't exist in the media, especially television: instead there was something called 'Operation Desert Storm', and a lot of high-tech images (often computer simulations) and pre-censored news presenters' reports. Do you think that if the conflict had developed into a protracted war that American public opinion would have challenged and resisted the course of events?

C: That is certainly what the war managers believed. They believed that 'a war' had to be avoided. And it was. There was no war, in the sense of a combat in which two sides shoot at each other for a sustained period. It was a slaughter. American combat casualties were scarcely beyond the level of Grenada. The killing was all at a safe distance. The US command knew they couldn't risk a war but that they could get away with a slaughter, an operation with the virtue that it teaches the right lessons to Third World upstarts who don't follow orders. It is a warning, a sign of what the US can and will do to maintain its power and dominance.

K: Are you optimistic or pessimistic as you look further into the future?

C: I think there are slow changes going on; they are slow but are deep and genuine and have had a positive effect upon people's consciousness. On the other hand there are things that are very frightening: there is a general social collapse; the country is moving toward a kind of Third World society, with a very privileged sector and a huge sector that is moving towards Third World standards. This is a result of a social policy that was consciously developed in the

1970s and 1980s. Along with intervention on a global scale to attempt to maintain the US manager role, it is a kind of rational response of the system to its economic decline. In this situation the welfare state for the corporations and the very rich has to be strengthened even further while the much more limited welfare state for the poor is no longer viable and has to be cut back. This has been a conscious social policy, and has been pursued with devastating social consequences.

The mass culture as a system of domination has succeeded in its major goal, which is to atomize people and marginalize dissent. The operative ideal of democracy is that each person should be isolated, sitting alone in front of the tube. The passive worker takes orders. Work is a kind of a black hole that you enter into every morning and come out of every evening, but has no meaning, and the rest of life consists of being an individual consumer. That is the ideal – it has had a significant effect on popular consciousness. This is a big victory for the corporate system in general, a triumph of the media and the public relations industry.

The destruction of the unions was a part of the process. The destruction of the working class culture was another part. These were big victories for established power. The destruction of most forms of association has been another victory, for them, and a defeat for meaningful democracy.

K: At various times in the recent past there has been a popular movement of dissent and resistance in the US – a radical opposition; the emergence and re-emergence of 'new subjects' of history. What do you see as the prospects for the 1990s?

C: There was a substantial popular 'movement' that was radical, that challenged authority and sought alternatives in the 1960s, but it was limited to certain social sectors. In the 1970s it got significantly larger, more diffused possibly, but it had a much greater outreach, more cultural and social impact, and by the 1980s it expanded even more, with a much broader social base. It is a particular kind of 'movement'. A lot of these people would not call themselves 'left', but share assumptions that are egalitarian and libertarian. Many important changes have taken place in the Churches in the US (although this can be double-edged). Many of the people involved are deeply committed and very courageous people of great sincerity with a real and abiding concern for those who suffer and are oppressed.

There are both advantages and disadvantages to this kind of 'movement', which is often local and issue-oriented. The advantage is that it is extremely hard to crush. It is always there, and it is always coming out somewhere else. It endures. The disadvantage is that its impact is only kind of glacial. It is difficult to have an immediate, sharp impact. It is often only possible to have an indirect or a partial impact upon things. So that is where we are today.

Index

A Soldier's Story (film), 22
ABC (American Broadcasting Company), 276, 278
abortion, books on, 167; campaign for right to, 169–70; medicaid withdrawn, 165, 249; Roe vs. Wade, 247–9; under Clinton administration, 265–6
ACLU civil rights group, 260
Action in the North Atlantic (film), 14
Afghanistan, Soviet invasion of, 251
African Diaspora, 199, 204
Agnew, Spiro, 61
Aid for Families with Dependent Children (AFDC), 240
AIDS, among blacks, 238
Ali Bey, Omar, 197
allegory, politics of, 30–4
American Association of University Professors, 89, 98–9
American Century (Luce), 6
American Committee for Cultural Freedom (1951), 31
American Dream, 2, 6; freedom and, 208; in Violent Streets (film), 226–8
'American History' (poem, Harper), 123–4
Ammons, A.R., 138
Amnesty International, music tour, 151
Anka, Paul, 144
anti-communism see communism
anti-Semitism, in plays and films, 21–2
anti-war movement see Vietnam War
Antonioni, Michelangelo, Zabriski Point (film), 214–17
Aptheker, Herbert, American Negro Slave Revolts, 14
Ashberry, John, 118
Asphalt Jungle (film), 22
Austin, Regina, 'Sapphire Bound', 180
Autobiography of Malcolm X (Haley), 201–2
Avalon, Frankie, 144

baby boom generation, 160–1, 163
Baby M case (1986–7), 166
Bacall, Lauren, 10
Bad Day at Black Rock (film), 24
Baez, Joan, 20, 151, 214
Balaban, John, war poetry of, 137
Bambara, Toni Cade, The Salt Eaters, 179–80
Banks, Carolyn see Friedman, Morris
Barbary Shore (novel, Mailer), 34–42
Barry, Marion, 238
Bay of Pigs see Cuba
Beat literature and poetry, 24

Beatles, The, 145–6, 149
Beauvoir, Simone de, 128; The Second Sex, 157
Beck, Hubert, The Men Who Control Our Universities, 88
Bending the Bow (poems, Duncan), 135
Benjamin, Walter, Origins of German Tragic Drama, 37–9, 41–2; 'Theses on the Philosophy of History', 30, 43, 52–4, 125
Berkeley Barb, 71, 76
Berkeley, University of California at, 89, 102; campus commune, 77; early protests against HUAC, 71; People's Park, 78–9; Sproul Hall sit-in, 5–6, 90–6; Yellow Dog newspaper, 74
Berlin Story (film), 22
Bernstein, Leonard, 106
Berry, Chuck, 144, 146
Berryman, John (poet), 118, 124–5
Bill of Rights, Economic (New Deal), 16
Billy the Kid, populist legend of, 223
Bishop, Elizabeth, 126
black community, external crisis, 193–4; internal crisis, 193–4; violent crime in, 194–6, 239–40, see also black movement; black women; racial issues; racism
black culture, and poetry, 138
black integrationism, tradition of, 201
black movement, 61, 73; Black Power, 197, 202, 210; nationalism, 198–201, see also black community; black women; racial issues; racism
Black Panther (underground newspaper), 73
Black Panthers, 61, 202; writings in anthologies, 99
black people, and purges at Livingston College, 108
black women, different experiences of, 174–6, 189; and feminism, 182–3, 187–9; and racism, 174, 182–4; radical elders, 179–80, 187–8; radical subjectivity, 178–81, 183, 185–6; and sexism, 174, 176–7, 183–5; writers, 177–81, 188–9, see also black community; black movement; feminism; racial issues; racism; women
Blake, William, 70, 74, 134
Bly, Robert, poetry, 72, 135
Bogart, Humphrey, 10
Bond, Edward, 213; Restoration, 211
Bonnie and Clyde (film), 60, 64–6

Bono, Sonny, 150–1
Book of Daniel (novel, Doctorow), 44–54
books, movement and anti-war, 98; New Left radicalism, 98, *see also* individual authors and titles; magazines; poetry
Bové, Paul A., 120
Boxer, Barbara, Senator, 265
Brando, Marlon, 65
Brant, Beth, *A Gathering of Spirit*, 121
Braun, Carol Moseley, 265
Brecht, Berthold, 211, 213, 225
Breitman, George, *Last Year of Malcolm X*, 201
Bringing It All Back Home (Dylan album), 145–6
Brooks, Gwendolyn, 126
Brothers (film), 213
Browder, Earl, and CPUSA, 17
Brown, Andrea, 197
Brown, Ron, black Democrat, 263
Buchanan, Patrick, 267
Burn, Walter, *The Saga of Billy the Kid*, 223
Bush, Barbara, 248, 266
Bush, George, and 1988 presidential campaign, 237–8, 242–5; and 1992 presidential campaign, 263–4; attitude to women, 248; and foreign policy, 253–5; on government, 268; and Gulf War, 6, 256–7, 280–1; interpretation of Vietnam, 280–1; redefinition of liberals, 260–1; and reverse discrimination, 239
business, and control of universities, 86–9

Cable Network News (CNN), coverage of Gulf War, 276–7
cable television, 276
Cabral, Amilcar, 204
California, University of *see* Berkeley, University of California at
Calvino, Italo, 'Right and Wrong Uses of Literature', 119
Candles in Babylon (poems, Levertov), 127
capital, capital formation in black community, 199–200; and domination of education, 87–8, 104
capitalism, in films, 216–17, 219–20; late, 3–4; Mailer's view of, 35–6; monopoly, 36–7; and pop music, 152; and racism, 201; radical opposition to, 76–7; in thrillers, 227
Capra, Frank, films, 15–16
Carson, Clayborne, 199
Carter, Jimmy, US President, 251, 261
Casablanca (film), 10, 14

CBS (Columbia Broadcasting System), 276, 278–9; Network News student survey, 96
censorship, cinema, 17–18; television news, 274–5, 278–9
Cervantes, Lorna Dee, 121
Chesler, Phyllis, *Sacred Bond*, 166
Chicago, *Rising Up Angry* (newspaper), 73; Yippies in, 79
Chicago Democratic Convention (1968), 59–60, 75, 213
Chile, 3
China, 3, 18, 69, 256
Chisholm, Shirley, autobiography, 183–4
Chodorow, Nancy, *The Reproduction of Mothering*, 164
churches, changes in US, 289
Churchill, Caryl, *Light Shining in Buckinghamshire*, 211
CIA counterinsurgency, 75
cinema *see* films
CIO, organization in South, 21; Political Action Committee, 15, 17; purges (1945–50), 19, 22; strikes (1945–46), 17, 35
City University, New York, 97
civil rights movement, 11, 17, 24, 105, 210; and popular culture, 20, 123–4, 133; and reverse discrimination, 239
Civil War, English, 70, 206–8
Cixous, Hélène, 128; *The Laugh of the Medusa*, 164
class, in 1988 campaign, 242–5; in 1992 campaign, 263–4; in American politics, 240–5; aspirations of Americans, 243–4; in Second World War, 14–15; and underground press, 73
Cleaveland, Bradford, 6, 91
Cleaver, Eldridge, novelist, 59, 99, 202
Cleaver, Kathleen, Black Panther, 214
Cliff, Michelle, 'Women Warriors', 177
Clinton, Bill, US President, 262; defence/foreign policy, 266–7; inaugural address, 269; prospects for administration of, 264, 267
Clinton, Hillary Rodham, role of, 264–6
Cold War, beginnings of, 3, 18; end of, 255–6; films, 21–3; and political repression, 11–12, 88–9; student challenges to consensus, 92
Columbia University, 73, 78
communes, 77–8
communism, anti-communism of McCarthy and Nixon, 17; in military, 13–14; Progressive Labor group, 75; repression of, 10–12; suspicion of, 32–3; and university faculties, 89, *see also* Cold War; House Un-American Activities Committee

Communist Party of USA (CPUSA), 12, 17, 42
Communist Political Association, 17
Comprehensive Employment and Training Act, 241
Conant, James, President of Harvard, 89
'Conspiracy of Hope' music tour, 151
Copeland, Aaron, *Billy the Kid* (ballet), 223
Correa, Gina, 159
Counter-Tradition (Delaney), 100
Counterattack (film), 14
criminal justice, and black community, 194–6; punishment as goal of, 245
Crosby, Stills and Nash, 150
Crossfire (film), 22
Cuba, 3, 69, 92
cultural politics, 24; of 1980s, 252, *see also* popular culture; radical culture
Cultural and Scientific Conference for World Peace (1949), 35
Cummings, E.E., 120

Daily Worker, left criticism in, 23
Dances with Wolves (film), 5
Daniels, Ron, 197
Davis, Angela, 106; autobiography, 183–6
Dead Kennedys (punk rock band), 150
Dean, James, 65
DeBerry, Clifton, Socialist Workers' Party candidate, 96
'Degrees of Gray in Philipsburg' (poem, Hugo), 134
Dell, William (1646), 69
Democratic Party, and 1992 election, 233–4, 262–4, 269; class base of, 242–4; conservatism of, 261–2; foreign policy (1992 election), 266–7; and New Deal, 16, 17; and race in 1988 election, 235, 237; and reverse discrimination, 239; revival of, 25, *see also* Clinton, Bill; Jackson, Jesse
Deutscher, Isaac, 93
Dickinson, Emily, 126
Dinkins, David, Mayor of New York, 238, 262
Dinnerstein, Dorothy, *The Mermaid and the Minotaur*, 164–5
direct action politics, in 1960s, 64–5
discrimination, and racial issues, 236; reverse, 239
Dissent (magazine), left criticism in, 23
Doctorow, E.L., *Book of Daniel*, 44–54; 'False Documents', 51; on Rosenbergs as alien, 33–4
Dolan, Paul *see* Quinn, Edward
Dominican Republic, invasion of, 92

Donner, Frank, 99
Donovan, 99
Dos Passos, John, 7; *U.S.A.* trilogy, 4
Douglass, Frederick, 99–101, 201
Dove, Rita (poet), 121, 123, 126; *Parsley*, 125–6
Dr Strangelove (film), 25
draft, resistance to, 71–2, 75, 92
drama, from Berkeley rebellion, 93
Dream Songs (poems, Berryman), 124
drugs, among black and hispanics, 238; and revolt against capitalism, 77; US war on, 256
Dukakis, Kitty, 248, 254
Dukakis, Michael, and 1988 presidential campaign, 237–8; attitude to women, 249; and class in 1988 campaign, 242, 244; foreign policy, 254; presented as radical, 260–1
Duncan, Robert, *Bending the Bow*, 135; 'Seventeenth Century Suite' (poems), 137
DuPlessis, Rachel, on Rich, 165
Dylan, Bob, 20, 25, 99, 150–1; 'My Back Pages', 143; in *Pat Garrett and Billy the Kid*, 225–6; poetry of, 131–4; radical music subculture, 143, 147–8; response to rock'n'roll, 145–6
Dymtryk, Edward, 21

Eagan, Andrea, 159
East Village Other (newspaper), 74
Eastern Europe, collapse of communism, 3, 255–6
Eberhart, Richard, 'Aesthetics After War', 135
economy, 1970s stagflation, 79; as issue in 1992 elections, 263; reforms, 232; Second World War, 16, *see also* capital
education, capital and, 87–8, 104–5; Einstein on, 5–6; and history, 109; HUAC control of, 88–9; Mesthene's theory of, 103–5; origins of public, 87; as training, 90–1, *see also* students; universities
Einstein, Albert, on education, 5–6
El Salvador, US intervention in, 108–9, 253
elections, 1980s, 233; 1988 campaign, 235, 237–8, 242–5, 254–5; 1992 presidential, 233–4, 262–7
Eliot, T.S., 118–20
English, Deirdre, 170
Equal Employment Opportunity Commission, 247
Equal Pay Act, 246
Equal Rights Amendment (ERA) (1972), 157, 246–7
Essien-Udom, Ruby and E.U., 203

Fabian, 144
Fair Employment Practices Commission, 17
family, and women, 166
Farber, Jerry, 'The Student as Nigger', 75-6
Farm Aid concert, 151
Farmer, James, 201
fascism, campaign against, 12-13
Fast, Howard, 14
Faulkner, William, 118
FBI, and deconstruction of Livingston, 106; and destruction of counterculture, 78; and Malcolm X, 199
Feinstein, Dianne, Senator, 265
feminism, attitude to men, 169-70; and backlash (1980s), 166-8; and black women, 182-3, 187-9; French influence, 164; and mother-hating, 162-3; origins of, 157; political aims of, 246-7; and pronatalism, 158-9; under Reagan, 247-8; and women's poetry, 128, 130; and working women, 167-8, *see also* black women; motherhood; women
Ferraro, Geraldine, vice-presidential candidature, 247-8
Fiedler, Leslie, on Rosenbergs, 30, 32, 43
films, and the American Dream, 206-29; censorship, 17-18; and Cold War, 21-3; from Berkeley rebellion, 94; as political touchstones (1968), 65; radical movement, 212-14, *see also* Hollywood; individual film titles; television
Firestone, Shulamith, *The Dialectic of Sex*, 161-2
Fitzgerald, F. Scott, *The Great Gatsby*, 222
Fleetwood, Charles (17th cent), 206
folk songs *see* music; songs
Folkways Records, 24
Food Stamps, 240
Footprints (poems, Levertov), 127
'For Ethel Rosenberg' (poem, Rich), 130
Force of Evil (film), 22
Ford, John, 22
foreign policy (US), 228; and 1988 election, 254-5; Chomsky on, 285-7; economic influence on, 256; and military intervention, 250, 253, 286-7; post-war, 18; public opinion and, 91, 287; under Carter, 251, *see also* Gulf War; Vietnam War
Fort Apache (film), 22
France, 3, 209; student riots (Paris, 1968), 59, 69, 94

Free Speech Movement (FSM), 71, 78; campaign (1964), 92-6
Freed, Alan, 144, 145
Freedom Bank of Harlem, failure of, 240
French Revolution (1793), 69-70
Friday, Nancy, *My Mother/Myself*, 164
Friedan, Betty, *The Feminine Mystique*, 157, 161; *The Second Stage*, 161, 166
Friedman, Morris and Carolyn Banks, *American Mix* (anthology), 99
Friends of Families, 166
Frith, Simon, 143
From the Movement Towards Revolution (Bruce Franklin), 100
Fruchter, Norm, 79

Gans, Herbert, 72
Garson, Barbara, 214
Genesis (band), 149
Gentleman's Agreement (film), 21
Georgia, criminal justice in, 196
Gerson, Kathleen, *Hard Choices*, 167
Ginsberg, Allen, 71, 78; 'Howl' (poem), 131-2; *The Fall of America*, 131
Ginsburg, Faye, *Contested Lives*, 167
Giovanni, Nikki, 'Woman Poem', 172-3
Glass, Marty, *Dock of the Bay*, 72
Godard, Jean Luc, 212
Good Times (magazine), 210
Goodman, Paul, 71, 99; on Berkeley rebellion, 91
Gorbachev, Mikhail, 256
Gordon, Linda, *Woman's Body, Woman's Right*, 164
Gordon, Mary, 168
Gore, Al, US Vice President, 264, 267
government, American view of, 268; and control of universities, 86-9; expansion of state, 232, 268; infiltration, 85; and mass media, 274; Reagan's attacks on federal, 259-60
Gramsci, Antonio, political theorist, 275
Great Britain, 3; punk rock in, 149-50
Greene, Felix, *The Enemy: What Every American Should Know About Imperialism*, 100
Greensboro, North Carolina, sit-in, 82
Greenwich Village, left culture in, 24
Grenada, US invasion of, 252, 255, 287
Griffith, Marlene *see* Muscatine, Charles
Gross, Louise and Phyliss MacEwan, 'On Day Care', 163
Guardian, left criticism in, 23
Guilty by Suspicion (film), 5
Gulf War, 3-4, 256-7, 259; and anti-war movement, 277-8, 280; avoidance of US casualties, 288; Bush's speeches, 6, 256-7, 280-1;

INDEX

Gulf War *continued*, effect on US foreign policy, 285–6; and reference to Vietnam, 280–1; response of Americans to, 4–5, 257–8, 276–7; and US television, 274–83

Haight-Ashbury 'diggers', 79, 132
Haley, Alex, *Autobiography of Malcolm X*, 201–2
Haley, Bill and the Comets, 144
Haraway, Donna, *Manifesto for Cyborgs*, 162, 174, 181
Hard Choices (Gerson), 167
Hardin, Tim, 99
Harding, Vincent, 204
Harper, Michael (poet), 121, 123–5
Harringtonians, English Civil War, 223
Hawks, Howard, 22
Hayden, Robert (poet), 121–3
Hayden, Tom, 209
health care, among blacks and hispanics, 238; as issue in 1992 elections, 263
hegemony, in media presentation, 275
Heidegger, Martin, 120
Hewlett, Sylvia Ann, *Lesser Lives*, 167
Higher Education Act, Title IX, 247
Hill, Anita, against Clarence Thomas, 250
Hill, Christopher, *The Experience of Defeat*, 206–7; *The World Turned Upside Down*, 206–7
Hiroshima, 2
Hiss, Alger, trial, 19
'History as Apple Tree' (poem, Harper), 124
Hochchild, Arlie, *The Second Shift*, 166
Hoffman, Abbie, 63; *Revolution for the Hell of It*, 65
Holly, Buddy, 144–5
Hollywood, and Cold War, 21; cooperation with HUAC, 223; and New Deal social dramas, 20–1
Hollywood Committee to Defend the First Amendment, 10
Hollywood Ten, and HUAC, 10
Home of the Brave (play), 21
Hook, Sidney, anti-Communist, 13
hooks, bell, 169; *From Margin to Center*, 161
Hoover, Herbert, 24
Horton, Willy, and Republican party 1988 campaign, 237
House Un-American Activities Committee (HUAC), 3, 71, 223; and cinema censorship, 17–18; as Communist front organization, 31; and education, 88–9; and Hollywood Ten, 10; student demonstrations against, 92

'Howl' (poem, Ginsberg), 131–2
Hughes, H. Stewart, 82–3
Hughes, Langston, 138
Hugo, Richard, 131; poetry of, 134–5
Humphrey, Hubert, 'politics of joy', 61
Hussein, Saddam, as 'new Hitler', 256–7; survival of, 259
Huston, John, film director, 22
Hyde Amendment, on abortion, 165

Ice (film), 213
'I'm a Field Negro', Malcolm X speech, 202–3
immigrants, and radical culture, 6
income distribution, 241–2
Independent Citizens Committee of the Arts, Sciences and Professions, 17
individualism, as social policy, 288–9
infertility, feminism and, 158–9
integrationism, black political tradition, 201
Iran contra affair, 253–4
Iranian hostage crisis, 251
Iraq, US bombing of, 267, *see also* Gulf War
Ireland, 3
Iron Curtain (film), 22
'It's All Over Now, Baby Blue', 133

Jackson, George, *Brothers* (film about), 213
Jackson, Jesse, 1980 presidential campaign, 236; and 1984 presidential campaign, 192; and 1988 presidential campaign, 192, 237–8; and 1992 presidential campaign, 262–3
Jackson, Louis N., 197
Jackson State University, 106
Jameson, Fredric, 120; *The 60s Without Apology*, 69
Japan, US dependence on, 287
Jarrell, Randall, war poetry, 135–7
Jefferson Airplane, (band) 147–8, 151
Jefferson, Thomas, 84–5, 99
Jennings, Peter, ABC news, 278, 282
Joe Hill (film), 213–14
John Birch Society, 237
John D. Rockefeller Fund, student survey by, 96
Johnson, Lyndon B., 59, 235; administration of, 75; and Vietnam War, 25, 61

Kafka, Franz, 118
Kampf, Louis, *The Politics of Literature*, 100
Kaplan, Cora, on women poets, 126–7
Katz-Rothman, Barbara, 159
Kazan, Elia, 21
Kennedy, John F., US President, 82

Kennedy, Paul, *Rise and Fall of the Great Powers*, 2
Kennedy, Senator Robert, assassination, 59
Kent State University, killings at, 106, 148
Kerner Report, on poverty, 240
Kerr, Clark, 93, 96, 101; *The Uses of the University*, 90–1, 103, 105
Key Largo (film), 10
King, Coretta, 106
King, Martin Luther, 59, 99, 197–8
Kinnell, Galway, 138
Knock on Any Door (film), 22
Korean War (1949–50), 11, 22
Kramer, Jane, *Paterfamilias: Allen Ginsberg in America*, 132
Kramer, Robert, *Ice* (film), 213
Krassner, Paul, yippie, 62
Kristeva, Julia, 164
Ku Klux Klan, 237
Kubrick, Stanley, 20, 25
Kunkin, Art, *Los Angeles Free Press*, 71
Kupferberg, Tuli, 74
Kuwait, invasion of, 256–7, 259

labour movement, CPUSA and, 17; Taft-Hartley law, 18, *see also* CIO
Lang, Fritz, 24
Lardner, Ring, Jr, 22
Last Year of Malcolm X (Breitman), 201
Laurents, Arthur, 21
Lazarre, Jane, *The Mother Knot*, 164
Leary, Timothy, 77
Lebanon, US Marines in, 252
Led Zeppelin, 149
Lee, Spike, films of Malcolm X, 197
left, political, and 1980s elections, 233; view of Vietnam, 281, *see also* civil rights movement; Democratic Party; New Left; popular front; radical movement
Lerner, Michael, Friends of Families, 166
lesbians, as mothers, 166
Lesser Lives (Hewlett), 167
Lester, Julius, 76–7, 202
Levertov, Denise (poet), 126–9, 135
Levine, David, caricaturist, 66
Levine, Philip, 'Animals are Passing from Our Lives', 138; 'On the Murder of Lieutenant José de Castilo', 126
Lewis, Jerry Lee, 144
liberalism/liberals, redefined by New Right, 260–1; rift with radicals, 61–2
Liberation News Service, 73
Liberation Now! (anthology), 163
Libya, 287
Life in the Forest (poems, Levertov), 127

Lipton, Marcus, MP, 150
Little Richard, 144
Live Aid concert, 150–1
Livingston College, deconstruction of, 103–7; experiment, 100–2; faculty purges at, 107–9
Long, Gerald, 66
Lorde, Audre, 126; 'Eye to Eye' (essay), 173–4, 188
Los Angeles Free Press, 71
Los Angeles riots (1992), 263
Lost Boundaries (film), 21
Lowell, Robert (poet), 118, 120
Luce, Henry, 'the American Century', 2
Lukacs, Georg, 118, 120
Luker, Kristen, *Abortion and the Politics of Motherhood*, 167
Lynton, Ernest, Dean of Livingston, 102

McCarran Internal Security Act (1950), 12
McCarthy, Joseph, 33; attack on New Deal, 17
McCarthy, Senator Eugene, presidential campaign, 59
McGovern, George, liberalism of, 260–1
McGrath, J. Howard, 33
McLuhan, Marshall, 99
Madison Kaleidoscope, 76
magazines, left culture in, 23–4; material for university readers, 99; and radical movement, 210
Magdoff, Harry, 93
Mailer, Norman, *Barbary Shore*, 34–42, 44; 'The White Negro', 35
Malcolm X, and black nationalism, 199; books about, 199, 201–2; compared with Martin Luther King, 198; as icon, 197, 201–2; 'I'm a Field Negro' speech, 202–3; and liberation, 203
Maltz, Albert, screenwriter, 21
Mandela, Nelson, at Wembley (1990), 151–2
Manifesto for Cyborgs (Haraway), 162
Manpower Development and Training Act, 241
Manson murders, 148
Marcuse, Herbert, 71, 74
Marshall, Paule, *Praisesong for the Widow*, 179
Marshall Plan, 18
Marshall, Thurgood, 201
Marx, Karl, 228–9
Marx, Leo, 7–8
Marxism, Mailer's enthusiasm for, 35; radical shift towards, 75
Masses and Mainstream, left criticism in, 23
Matthiessen, F.O., 5–6

INDEX

Medicaid, 240; abortion withdrawn, 165, 249
Medicare, 240
Medium Cool (film), 212–13
Meet John Doe (film), 15
Merrill, James, 118
Mersmann, James, *Out of the Vietnam Vortex*, 135
Merwin, W.S., 'For a Coming Extinction', 138
Messianism, 52–3
Mesthene, Emmanual, Dean of Livingston, 102–7
Mexico, Chicano poetry, 121; as metaphor, 222; riots (1968), 59
'Middle Passage' (poem, Hayden), 122–3
Mifflin Street, Madison, party, 78
military, discrimination against Communists in, 13–14; and US coverage of Gulf War, 282–3, *see also* draft
Miller, Sue, *The Good Mother*, 167
Mills, C. Wright, 11, 12, 25
Milton, John, 70, 211, 225, 229; *Paradise Lost*, 207; *Samson Agonistes*, 207, 228
Mine Mill and Smelter Workers, film by, 23
Mintz, Leo, 144
Mission to Moscow (film), 13, 14
Mitchell, Juliet, 128
Montaldo, Giuliano, *Sacco and Vanzetti*, 213–14
Monthly Review, Marxist journal, 5–6
Moon, Henry Lee, 201
Morrison, Jim, 63, 65
Morrison, Toni, *Sula*, 178–9
motherhood, and choice, 158–9, 162–4; demographic changes in, 169–70; and feminism, 160, 163–4; guilt about, 168; and mothering, 165–6
Moynihan report, on black families, 163
Mr Deeds Goes to Town (film), 15
Mr Smith Goes to Washington (film), 15
Muhammad, Elijah, 200
multi-ethnic democracy, Second World War and, 14–15
murder, and black males, 195
Muscatine, Charles and Marlene Griffith, *The Borzoi College Reader*, 99–100
music, political pop (1980s), 150–2; and post-war labour militancy, 17; punk rock, 148–50; as radical subculture, 141–3; rock'n'roll, 143–5; West Coast Rock, 145–8
Musicians United for Safe Energy, 150

NAACP, civil rights organization, 201
Nation of Islam, 199; conservatism of, 200–1; sexism of, 204

National Assembly on the Future of the Family (1979), 166
National Citizens Political Action Committee, popular front and, 16–17
national liberation struggles, 3
National Organization for Women (NOW), 246
National Urban League, 201
NATO, formation of, 22
Naylor, Gloria, *Mama Day*, 179
NBC (National Broadcasting Company), 276
Nelson, Rick, 144
New Deal, in films, 20–1; programmes, 16; and shift of political balance, 15–16
New Left, and Carter's foreign policy, 251; and Clinton administration, 267; political culture, 24; targeted by Reagan, 260; women's support for, 248
New Masses, left criticism in, 23
New Right, and motherhood, 165, 168; social agenda of, 260
New York, 24, 236
New York Times, 73
Newfield, Jack, 72
newspapers, left culture in, 23, *see also* magazines
Newsreel Collective, 212
Newton, Huey, Black Panther leader, 61, 202
Nicaragua, US intervention in, 252–3, 287
Nixon, Richard, 17, 61, 286
No Nukes (film and album), 150
Noriega, Manuel, 254–5
North Star (film), 14
Nothing But a Man (film), 23

Ochs, Phil, 25, 99
O'Connor, Sandra Day, 247
Oglesby, Carl, 99
Olson, Charles, 118, 120
Olympic Games, and US foreign relations, 252
O'Neale, Sondra, 'Inhibiting Midwives, Usurping Creators', 181
Oracle, 77
Orangeburg, S. Carolina, 59
Ortiz, Simon J., 121
Orwell, George, 118
Our Bodies/Ourselves 163–4
Ourselves and Our Children, 163–4

Paine, Thomas, 85, 99
Panama, US invasion of, 255, 277, 279, 287
Paris, student revolt, 59, 69, 94
Parker, Pat, 126

Parsley (poem, Dove), 125-6
Pat Garrett and Billy the Kid (film), 221, 223-6
Paxton, Tom, 99
peace movements, and protest songs, 20
Pearl Harbor, 13
Peckinpah, Sam, *Pat Garrett and Billy the Kid*, 221, 223-6; *The Getaway*, 221-3
Penn, Arthur, film director, 65
Pentagon demonstration, 59-60
People's Songs, 24-5
Perot, Ross, 263, 268
Petchesky, Rosalind, *Abortion and Women's Choice*, 167
Peter, Paul and Mary, (band), 20
Pink Floyd, (band), 149
Pinky (film), 21
'Planetarium' (poem, Rich), 129-30
Plath, Sylvia, 118, 126
Playboy, articles for college readers, 99
poetry, 93, 117-18; by women, 126-31; and US ethnic diversity, 121-6; of Vietnam War, 135-8, *see also* individual poems and poets; songs
Polikoff, Nancy D., 158
political parties, students' choice of, 95-6, *see also* Democratic Party; Republican Party
political reforms, 232
politics, aestheticization of, 64
Politics of the Heart (anthology), 158
Pollard, Vicky, 'Producing Society's Babies', 163
Polonsky, Abraham, 22
Pontecorvo, Gillo, *Queimada* (film), 218
pop music *see* music; radical music subcultures; songs
popular culture, and anti-war movement, 59-63; and civil rights movement, 20, 123-4, 133; divided (1968), 59-61
popular front, 1930s movement, 13; and Cold War, 10-12; culture and censorship, 18; influence in 1960s, 24; origins in US history, 15; and political shift to right, 16-17
Port Huron statement, 6
Portugal, 3
post-modernism, in poetry, 120
Pound, Ezra, 118-20, 138
poverty, among blacks and hispanics, 238; in black community, 195-6; war on, 240-2
Powell, General Colin, 287
Prayers for Private Devotions in War-Time (Harvard University Chapel), 4-5
President's Commission on Campus Unrest, (report), 94
Presley, Elvis, 144-5

Press Syndicate, underground, 73
press, underground, 71-5; destruction of, 78
Pride of the Marines (film), 21
prison population, 196
'Prisoners' (poem, Jarrell), 137
Progressive Labor group, 75
Progressive Labor (magazine), 210
Progressive Party, defeat (1948), 19, 22
protest movements *see* Vietnam War
protest songs, (1960s) in university anthologies, 99; late 1940s, 20
Protonatalism: The Myth of Mom and Apple Pie (essays), 162
Public Broadcasting System (PBS), 275
Puritanism, influence of, 76

Quayle, Dan, 254, 264
Queimada (film), 217-21
Quinn, Edward and Paul Dolan, *The Sense of the Sixties* (anthology), 99

racial inequality, in American politics, 234-40; continuing, 192-3, *see also* segregation
racial issues, in 1988 presidential campaign, 237; in 1992 presidential campaign, 262-3; Los Angeles riots (1992), 263
racism, black, 236-7; black women and, 174, 182-4
Radford-Hill, Sheila, 'Considering Feminism as a Model for Social Change', 182
radical culture, 1960s counterculture, 67-8, 75-9; of left, 23-4; roots of, 6-7; and underground press, 71-2
radical music subcultures, 141-3, 152; Dylan songs and, 146; West Coast Rock, 147-8
radicalism, 17th century, 206-8; decline of, 208-11, 289-90; and magazines, 210; opposition to status quo, 75-6; persistance of, 109, 229; in poetry, 118-19, 131, 138-9; prospects for, 289
radicals, accommodation with establishment, 223-4; allegory of Billy the Kid, 224-5; rift with liberals, 61-2
Radu, Judith, Berkeley student, 95
Rambo (films), 252
Ramparts (magazine), 210
RAND Corporation, 103
rape, of black women, 194-5
Rat (New York underground newspaper), 73

INDEX

Reagan, Ronald, and criminal justice, 196; and feminist movement, 247–8; foreign policy, 252–3; on government, 268; and income distribution, 241; and political issues of race, 235–6
Rebel Without a Cause (film), 65
record industry 143, 148, *see also* music; songs
Red Danube (film), 22
Red River (film), 22
Republican National Convention (1940), 15
Republican Party, class base of, 242–3, 244–5; consensual majority in 1980s, 234; and criminal justice, 196; vision of 'new world order', 257; white support for, 235
rhythm and blues *see* music, rock'n'roll
Rich, Adrienne, 126; *Of Woman Born*, 164–5; poetry of, 129–31
Ricoeur, Paul, 43
Riesman, David, minority groups in music, 141
right, political, New Right, 165, 168, 260; shift to, 15–17, 67, 210–11; view of 1960s, 67, *see also* Bush, George; Reagan, Ronald; Republican Party
Rios, Alberto, 121
Rise and Fall of the Great Powers (Kennedy), 2
Rising Up Angry (newspaper), 73
Robeson, Paul, 11, 20, 106
Robinson, Earl, (songs), 14–15
Rodney, Walter, 199, 204
Rogin, Michael, 32–3
Rolling Stones, The, 61, 145, 148
Roosevelt, F.D., 1944 campaign, 15; and Hiss trial, 19; New Deal, 16; post-war popularity of, 17
Rosenberg, Julius and Ethel, 11, 19–20; as allegory, 30–4, 44–54; Rich's poem about Ethel, 130
Rossman, Michael, 78
Rousseau, Jean-Jacques, 109
Rubin, Jerry, Yippie leader, 61, 63–4, 76–7
Rudd, Mark, anti-war radical, 63, 66
Ruddick, Sara, 'Maternal Thinking', 165–6
Rustin, Bayard, 201
Rutgers University, 89, 101, 106; faculty purges at Livingston, 107–8, *see also* Livingston College
Rydell, Bobby, 144

Sacco and Vanzetti (film), 213, 214
Sainte Marie, Buffy, 99
Salt of the Earth (film), 23

San Francisco Bay demonstrations, 92
SANE organization, 92
Sartre, Jean Paul, 118–19
Savio, Mario, Sproul Hall sit-in, 6, 8, 90–1, 93, 101
Scherr, Max, *Berkeley Barb*, 71
SDS (Students for a 'Democratic Society'), 73–5, 78
Second Coming (magazine), 210
Second World War, and US economy, 16; and US status, 2–3
Seeger, Pete, 11, 20, 99
segregation, CIO and, 21; de facto, 239; in education, 87, 234; legal changes, 234; legal (Jim Crow), 82, 85, 193, 200, 202, 210; political, 12, 234
Sex Pistols, (band), 149–50
sexism, black women and, 174, 176–7; in Nation of Islam, 204
Sexton, Anne, 126
sexual revolution, 77–8
Shahn, Ben, campaign poster, 15
'She and the Muse' (poem, Levertov), 128
Silber, John, 'Poisoning the Wells of Academe', 103
Sinatra, Frank, *The House I Live in* (film 1945), 15
Sing Out (folk music magazine), 24
Sister Souljah, (rap singer), 263
Sisterhood is Powerful (anthology), 163
slave trade, 6; in poetry, 122–3
Slick, Grace, 99, 147
Smith Act (1940), 12
Snapshots of a Daughter in Law (poems, Rich), 129
Snyder, Gary, (Zen poet), 79
'social Heracliteanism' (Mesthene), 104
social support, for women, 166–8
socialist realism, as Soviet infiltration, 18
Solinas, Franco, *Queimada* (film), 218
Somalia, US troops in, 267
Song, Cathy, 121
Song of Russia (film), 14
songs, from Berkeley rebellion, 93; protest, 20, 99; 'Anarchy in the UK' (Sex Pistols), 149–50; 'Ballad for Americans', 15; 'Blowin' in the Wind', 134; 'Come on Baby, Light My Fire', 61; 'Draft Dodger Rag', 25; 'Hound Dog' (Presley), 144; 'My Back Pages' (Dylan), 143; 'Subterranean Homesick Blues' (Dylan), 146; 'The House I Live in', 14; 'The Times They are A-Changin', 131, 134; 'We Shall Overcome' ('We Will Overcome'), 25; 'With God on Our Side', 134, *see also* music; poetry

Soul on Ice (bestseller), 59
Souter, David, 249
South Africa, 150
South America, 254–5
Southwell, Robert, 'The Burning Babe', 137
Soviet Union, American view of, 13–14, 18; and collapse of communism, 255–6, 285; nuclear capacity, 3, 35
Specter, Arlen, Senator, 265
Springsteen, Bruce, 150–2
Stalin, Joseph, 13
Stanworth, Barbara, 159
Steiner, George, 'The Hollow Miracle', 126
Stevens, Wallace, 118, 120
Stevenson, Adlai, 10
Stockholm Peace Petitions, 11
Stone, I.F., 93
Stop the Draft Week (Oakland 1967), 59–60
Strawberry Statement (film), 212
Student Nonviolent Coordinating Committee, 199
Student Peace Union, 92
students, 1960s demonstrations, 92; demographic changes, 97; disaffection of (1968), 63; failure of political power, 79; fear of draft, 75–6; opinion surveys, 95–7; success at Berkeley, 93–4; and underground press, 71, *see also* Berkeley; education; universities
Sula (Morrison), 178–9
Sun City project, 150
surrealism, in underground press, 74

Taft-Hartley law, 18
Taking State Power (John Leggett), 100
taxation, 1980s debate, 243–4
television, 1968 programmes, 59–60; domination of in US, 276
television industry (US), structure of, 275–6
television news, bias towards establishment, 274–5, 278–9; and Gulf War coverage, 274–83; and interpretation of Vietnam, 281; and military constraint in Gulf War, 282–3; and radical popular demonstrators (1968), 62–4
'The Acolyte' (poem, Levertov), 127–8
The American Moment (Thurley), 135
The Battle of Algiers (film), 60, 65–6
The Best Years of Our Lives (film), 20–1
The Big Heat (film), 24
The Boy with Green Hair (film), 22
The Color Purple (Walker), 177–8
The Day the Earth Stood Still (film), 23
The Devil's Party, college reader, 100
The Dialectic of Sex (Firestone), 161–2

The Diamond Cutter (poems, Rich), 129
'The Dragonfly-Mother' (poem, Levertov), 128
The Feminine Mystique (Friedan), 157, 161–2
The Getaway (film), 221–3
The Graduate (film), 59
The House I Live in (film 1945), 15
The Long Walk Home (film), 5
The Salt Eaters (Bambara), 179–80
The Second Sex (de Beauvoir), 157
The Second Shift (Hochchild), 166
The Second Stage (Friedan), 161, 166
'The Sick Nought' (poem, Jarrell), 136–7
The Sorrow Dance (poems, Levertov), 127, 135
The Spook Who Sat by the Door (film), 213
The Teeth Mother Naked at Last (poems, Bly), 135
The Vietnam Era (Klein), 1
The Will to Change (poems, Rich), 129
Thomas, Clarence, and Anita Hill controversy, 250, 264–5; appointment to Supreme Court, 239
Thoreau, Henry, 8, 99
Thurley, Geoffrey, *The American Moment*, 135
'Tongue-Tied in Black and White' (poem, Harper), 124
Top Gun (film), 252
'Transcendental Etude' (poem, Rich), 130–1
Truman, Harry S., 10, 16–18, 42
Tuchman, Gaye, 279
Turn Toward Peace movement, 92
Turner, James, 197

United Front against Fascism, 12, 15
United Nations, 17; and Gulf War, 257, 279
United States, economic decline of, 7–8, 285; as 'enforcer state', 7, 286; ethnic diversity and poetry, 121–6; history and poetry of, 120–1; legacy of 1960s, 287–8; political shift to right, 15–17, 67, 260, 267; pre-eminence of, 2–3, 67; social policy of individualism, 288–9, *see also* foreign policy (US)
universities, British courses on American studies, 120; changes in text 'readers', 98–100; and concept of academic freedom, 91, 98; control of, 86–9; cultural changes within, 98–100; new generation of teachers, 97–8, 107; Open Admissions policies, 97, 105–6; utopian communes at, 77–8, *see also* Berkeley, University of California at; education; Livingston College; students

Uphaus, Robert, *American Protest in Perspective* (anthology), 99
US–Soviet alliance, 2–3, 13
utopian communes, 77–8

Valenska, Lucia, in *Quest*, 162
Veblen, Thorstein, *The Higher Learning in America* (1918), 86
Vidor, King, *Billy the Kid*, 223
Vietnam Day Committee, 92–3
Vietnam War, analogy of *Queimada*, 219–20; anti-war movement and popular culture, 20, 59–63; Gulf of Tonkin, 72; and Gulf War, 280–1; parallels with Central America, 108–9, 253; poetry of, 135–8; protest movements against, 3, 5–6, 92, 209; and public opinion, 61, 250–1, 258–9; radical music subculture against, 147–8; radical view of, 6, 75, 281; RAND Corporation and, 103; 'revenge' films, 252; revisionist memory of, 258, 281; shadow of, 228; Tet offensive, 59–61; veterans as students, 97
Vincent, Gene, 144
violence, in black community, 194–6; black women and, 172–3
'Violence in Intimate Relationships' (essay), 172
Violent Streets (film), 226–8

Walker, Alice, *Meridian*, 181; *The Color Purple*, 177–8; *The Third Life of Grange Copeland*, 180–1
Walker, Margaret, *Prophets for a New Day* (poems), 138
Wallace, Henry, US Vice President, 3, 5–6, 10, 16
Wallace, Michelle, *Black Macho...*, 164–5, 187
Waltz, Jon, 99

Wanger, Walter, 20
Warhol, Andy, 64
Warshow, Robert, 30, 43
Watts, Alan, 99
Weavers, blacklisted, 20
Weinberg, Jack, 72
welfare state, Clinton's attitude to, 264; dismantling of, 245; limited, 232
White Heat (film), 22
Why Children? (essays), 158
Wilbur, Richard, 118
Wilcox, Preston, 197
Wild One (film), 65
Wilder, Douglas, Governor of Virginia, 192, 238
Wilkins, Roy, 201
Williams, William Carlos, 118, 120
Winstanley, Gerrard, 207
women, in 1992 elections, 264–6; control of labour, 245–6; demographic changes, 169–70; Malcolm X and equality of, 204; poetry by, 126–31; and political changes, 245–50, *see also* black women; feminism; motherhood
women's movement, 210; 1960–80, 246–7
Woodstock rock concert, 77
Wordsworth, William, 70–1
Wright, James, 118–20, 131, 138

Yankelovich, Daniel, 96
Yeakel, Lynn, 265
Yes (band), 149
yippies, 62, 79
Young, Andrew, 202
Young Guns (film), 223
Young, Whitney, 201
youth, power of, 82–4; and radical music, 142–3

Zabriski Point (film), 214–17, 228

www.ingramcontent.com/pod-product-compliance
Lightning Source LLC
Chambersburg PA
CBHW031408290426
44110CB00011B/307